Resonare Christum

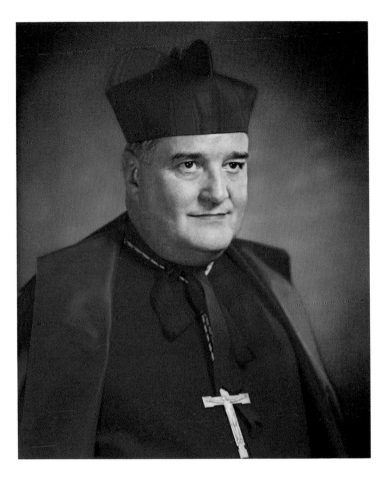

Portrait by Jonas

Resonare Christum

Volume III
1969–1979

A Selection from the Sermons
Addresses, Inverviews, and Papers
of

Cardinal John J. Wright

Prepared and Edited by
R. Stephen Almagno, O.F.M.

Ignatius Press   San Francisco

Imprimi Potest: Roderick Crispo, O.F.M.
Minister Provincial
Provincial Curia
New York City

Imprimatur: + John R. Quinn
Archbishop of San Francisco

Cover by Victoria Hoke Lane

All monies accruing to the editor from the publication of this book will
be paid to the Catholic Institute of Pittsburgh, Inc., for works of
religion, charity, and education.

Memoriae et Laudi

Iohannis I. Wright
Cardinalis

Sanctae Romanae Ecclesiae

Summis Honoribus Functi

De Humanis Pariter et Christianis Litteris

Optime Meriti

Contents

Preface

The task of preparing for publication this selection from the sermons, addresses, interviews, and papers of Cardinal John Wright (1909–1979) has been an entirely pleasant affair. Pleasant, because of the trust placed in me by the Wright Family and by the Cardinal's executors. Pleasant, because I was able to work in the congenial atmosphere of the University of Pittsburgh, which was an object of Wright's love and concern. Pleasant, because of the encouragement and cooperation from so many of his friends and admirers. And, finally, pleasant, because "to be reminded" of Cardinal Wright "is always the greatest delight to me, whether I speak myself or hear another speak of him" (Plato, *Phaedo*).

The Cardinal's words are presented with as little intrusion as possible. This is his book. Each text speaks for itself. The notes endeavor, simply, to put a background to the text.

I know that this text will be welcomed by Cardinal Wright's friends, and I hope that this book may possibly be of interest and give insight to someone who had not the privilege of knowing him.

It remains only for me to thank, especially, the Most Reverend Donald W. Wuerl, S.T.D., (Wright's secretary and successor as Bishop of Pittsburgh) for his *Introduction;* and Marylynne Pitz for researching Wright materials in *The Pittsburgh Post-Gazette* and assisting me with the preparation of the *Index*.

I also wish to thank my family, Dean Toni Carbo Bearman, Ph.D., the Most Reverend Norbert F. Gaughan, the Reverend Roderick Crispo, O.F.M. (my Minister Provincial), Professors Roy B. Stokes and Sally Buchanan, Fathers Alessandro Falcini, O.F.M., Simeon Distefano, O.F.M., Robert Simpson, O.F.M., Michael-Dominic Ledoux, O.F.M., and Doctors Jeffrey Huber, Ph.D., and Patricia Carroll, M.D., for their cooperation and encouragement.

With this final volume—started at the University of Pitts-
burgh and completed, while on sabbatical, in San Francisco—I
now conclude my work on the Wright papers. The Ignatius
Press—with money provided by Cardinal Wright's Family, friends,
and the Franciscan Province of the Immaculate Conception
(New York)—has published six volumes: *Mary Our Hope* (1984),
The Saints Always Belong to the Present (1985), *Resonare Christum
I (1939–1959): The Boston and Worcester Years* (1985), *Words in
Pain* (1986), *Resonare Christum II (1959–1969): The Pittsburgh
Years* (1988), and *Resonare Christum III (1969–1979): The Rome
Years* (1995). A seventh volume, *Cardinal John Wright: the Biblio-
phile,* was published—as an elegant monograph—in 1980 by the
Pittsburgh Bibliophiles. And, as specified in the Cardinal's *Last
Will and Testament,* all royalty proceeds accruing to the editor
from the sales of these books were paid to the Catholic Institute
of Pittsburgh, Inc., for the works of religion, charity, and
education.

In 1246–1247, when Friar Thomas of Celano—Saint Francis'
biographer—came to the end of his *Vita Secunda,* he wrote these
words: "We have written these things out of happiness over your
memory, about which, while we live, we will try to tell others,
if only in a stammering way" (Celano, *Vita Secunda,* CLXVII:221).
Celano's words are precisely my own sentiments as I complete
this seventh volume and my task—a holy privilege indeed!—as
Cardinal Wright's Literary Executor.

R. Stephen Almagno, O.F.M.

The University of Pittsburgh
School of Library and Information Science

The Franciscan Friary
San Francisco, California
January 27, 1994

Acknowledgments

Publication of this book was made possible by the generous donations of:

Robert L. Bertolli
Fr. Charles T. Carey
Alice Fennessey
Mr. and Mrs. John R.
  Fitzpatrick
Harriet Wright Gibbons
Mrs. Vincent de P. Goubeau
Mary A. C. Healy
Helen M. Horrigan
Dr. and Mrs. Edward M.
  Mahoney
Kay McAvoy
J. Frank McKenna
Mr. and Mrs. John McSorley,
  Jr.
Frances O'Hara
Florence C. Pollock
Alfred Wright

Anna Brady
Mr. and Mrs. Norbert
  Dougherty
Nancy Fennessey
Dr. and Mrs. Henry Gailliot
Jane Q. Gomperts
Mr. and Mrs. Richard G.
  Haltmaier
Mr. and Mrs. George A.
  Hinton
Ellen Madden
John J. McAuliffe, Jr.
William V. McCarthy
Philip J. McNiff
Dr. John Mc Sorley
Virginia Paine
John A. Volpe
Robert Wright

13

The editor gratefully acknowledges permission to reprint already published material from the following:

Columbia for "The Church of Promise" and "Witness of the Laity".

Homiletic and Pastoral Review for "The New Catechetical Directory and Initiation to the Sacraments of Penance and Eucharist" and "What was the Real Mind of Pope John?".

Osservatore Romano for "Pope John and His Secret", "The Sacred Heart of Jesus: Persuasive Symbol for Our Times", "Crisis in Vocations: Causes and Solutions", "Saint Elizabeth Ann Seton", "Pope Pius XII: A Personal Reminiscence", "The Hunger for the Spirit and the Sense of Vocation" and "Confirmation: The Layperson's Ordination".

Our Sunday Visitor for "A Conversation with Desmond O'Grady".

U.S. News and World Report for "Interview with Alex Kucherov".

Worcester Telegram for "Doing the Wright Biography Will Require Some Subtlety".

The Rome Years
1969–1979

Introduction

In 1969, Bishop John Wright was named a cardinal of the holy Roman Church with the title of the Church of Jesus the Divine Teacher. At the same time, he was transferred to head the Vatican office for priests, the Congregation for the Clergy. In June of that year, he took up his permanent residence in Rome. I went with him as his secretary and began an adventure that lasted ten years—until his death in August 1979.

One of the aspects of Cardinal Wright's life in Rome was once described in a syndicated news column as "his refusal to be stuck behind a desk". This description referred to his preference for pastoral work over clerical duties in an office. This side of the Cardinal's priestly life was expressed in the great deal of traveling that characterized his stay in Rome. These trips, which usually come under one of three headings: official business, visits to gatherings of priests, and pastoral or speaking engagements, all related to his love for and service of the priesthood.

This apostolate of carrying words of joy, consolation, hope, and faith to others had on more than one occasion received the personal encouragement of the Pope. Once in private audience with our Holy Father, the Cardinal asked if he had any particular solution for the many problems facing the Church. The Holy Father replied that he knew no other solution than to preach the Faith and then repeat it and repeat again. From the time the Cardinal arrived in Rome until his final incapacitating illness, he took very seriously the injunction to preach the word, "both in season and out of season, when convenient and inconvenient". The list of cities he visited in Italy alone read like a highway map from an Italian tourist office. His travels also brought him to most of the major cities of Europe, many times to the United States, and to a multitude of nations on every continent.

This present collection contains some of the talks delivered on those apostolic journeys. As I leaf through them, waves of memories come flooding back. The memory of the Cardinal's goodness, joy, and ministry still lives on in his words and in the hearts of many people long after God called him to his eternal reward.

Cardinal Wright's funeral Mass and burial took place in his native city of Boston. He had been away from Boston for thirty years, ten as Bishop of Worcester, Massachusetts, ten as Bishop of Pittsburgh, Pennsylvania, and ten at the service of the Holy See. Yet for four days, there was a constant stream of visitors to the church where the Cardinal's body awaited burial. Men and women, young and old, many of whom could have known the Cardinal only through the stories of their parents, came to pay their respects. In Pittsburgh, where I have the privilege of serving as bishop, it has been a full twenty years since Bishop Wright served as the eighth bishop of this See. And yet his name is heard almost as regularly as if he were continuing his episcopal ministry among us today.

Perhaps the secret to understanding the unique human and spiritual qualities of Cardinal Wright rests in our analysis of why he is so remembered—everywhere he served.

John Wright, as priest, bishop, and cardinal, had a vision of the Church that saw her—the Body of Christ—as a unity of believers: laity and clergy, women and men, young and old, working together to carry out in a visible manner their personal faith in Jesus Christ. This vision of a working unity of faithful followers of Christ united with their bishop was essential to all that Cardinal Wright said and did. The uniqueness of his ministry was his ability to get others to share that same vision of the Church. All believers were called, empowered, encouraged, and asked to work together, utilizing their individual, God-given talents and gifts to build up the one reality that made them one in Christ—the Church.

Following in the footsteps of Bishop Wright in Pittsburgh, it is easy to see how well he accomplished his mission. On his lips, the teaching of the Church seemed to be what it has been called since the days of the apostles, "the Good News". Cardinal Wright had an infectious smile that cheered all he met. His wit and humor dominated any remarks he made, whether they were solemn pronouncements from a cathedral pulpit or talks to each and every group that ever invited him to speak.

Yet it is also clear that the secret of Cardinal Wright's communicability lay, not in his ability to tell funny stories or make witty remarks, but in the underlying reason for so spontaneous and contagious a joy. John Wright was most of all a man of unshakable faith. He was not ashamed of that faith in all its ramifications. He was, therefore, able confidently to speak the truth of the Gospels in plain and clear terms, neither hesitant to preach to those who did not accept such doctrine nor unsure himself what the message was. It was this strong and undisguised faith in the Lord and in His Church that was the foundation for what was much more obvious to the casual visitor, listener, or photographer—his joy.

Pope John Paul II, who for many years as Cardinal Wojtyla was a dear friend of Cardinal Wright, spoke of the Cardinal on August 15, 1979, at Castelgandolfo. He called him "a good man who preached our Lord's message with faith and straightforwardness". The Holy Father continued, "Cardinal Wright crowned with a holy death a life totally spent for Christ and His Church, as a priest, as a bishop in the United States, as a Cardinal in charge of an important Congregation." The Pope added, "He was always beloved of those who knew him because he hid beneath his good-humored nature a singular clarity of ideas and a unique goodness and sweetness."

Cardinal John Wright was a profoundly happy man. This was apparent to all who heard him preach, to all whom he blessed and confirmed in scores of dioceses in America and Europe, to all who visited him in his office either in the States or

Rome, to all in the wider community who knew him as a good neighbor.

Such joy and happiness in the life of a person charged with great responsibilities is not at all inconsistent with the full recognition of the suffering or privation that are the tragic aspects of the human condition. It did not render the Cardinal insensitive or unwilling to do more than his part in remedying them, but it did preserve him from that air of personal offense which sometimes characterizes individual reaction to evil in the universe or to the inadequacies of its inhabitants. The John Wright I knew never hurt the people around him while trying to remove the causes of so much hurt in the world.

Even a brief glance at the history of this churchman reveals a constant commitment to and personal involvement in human efforts to meet human needs. The themes on which he frequently spoke were social justice, racial tolerance, brotherly love, community solidarity, peace, justice, fair housing, proper education, care of the elderly, inspiration of youth, and protection of the underprivileged—not just faith, hope, and charity. He was one of the co-founders of the International Commission for Religion and Peace long before it was fashionable in the '60s to protest against war. The talks of Cardinal Wright read like a book of prophecy to subsequent social legislation. His joy was always a reflection of his inner light, and that inner light always directed him toward people and human problems.

Anyone who knew Cardinal Wright knew of his love for children. He saw so much possibility in them. Once in Rome, a young couple, working for B'nai B'rith, visited the Cardinal and brought with them their nine-month-old child. During the chat, the baby snuggled comfortably in the arms of this red-clad prince of the Church. As they all got up to end the visit, the Cardinal handed the baby back to his mother and warned her, "Take good care of him. He could grow up to be another Isaiah or Samuel for your people—or another St. Paul for us."

Cardinal Wright's greatest love was the Catholic Church. He

once told the Knights of Columbus at their New Haven Convention (1969), "The Church is the single, living, unified Body of Christ at work in the world; as a body it has parts but they are not dismembered—if your local Church is in communion with Rome, it is so intrinsically, so essentially, so vitally united to the center that it is all one, even as there is no divided Jesus Christ the source and center of the Church of Hope." On another occasion, the Cardinal wrote: "The Church—the One, Catholic, Holy, and Apostolic Church—is ultimately without meaning except as the living Body of Christ at work in the world." John Wright was Catholic—but he was never sectarian. Once when asked by a fellow bishop how large his diocese was, Bishop Wright replied, "Oh, about two and a half million people." "That's impossible", retorted his episcopal friend. Bishop Wright had counted in his mind everyone in western Pennsylvania, not just the Catholics.

Cardinal Wright's years in Rome were turbulent ones for the whole Church. The late '60s and early '70s were marked by some confusion, agitation, and stress within the Mystical Body of Christ. They were not the best times to hold a position of authority or responsibility at any level of the Church, let alone one very close to the top. But Cardinal Wright faced this task with the same dedication and vigor that so characterized all his pastoral ministry. He used his office to speak to an even wider audience—and to speak to them of God. Like an Old Testament prophet, John Wright did not always say things that everyone liked. But he never stopped telling us of God. This collection reflects, thanks to the skill of its editor, Father R. Stephen Almagno, O.F.M., this aspect of Cardinal Wright's prodigious effort. His regard for papal teaching was completely in keeping with his lifelong respect for the unique place the voice of the Vicar of Christ within the community of believers—within the Church.

Zeal for the word of God and love for Christ's Church motivated this priest, bishop, and cardinal. He conceived his task to be that of telling all men and women of God's love for them, that Jesus who died is now alive, and that the Church is the way to Christ and His Father. This zeal accounts not only for his travels to all parts of the world—travels that consumed his energies—but also for the voluminous pages of talks, sermons, homilies, and articles that poured from his pen, even into his last declining months. This explains the rigorous schedule he insisted on, even as it became increasingly clear that his body was wearing out.

When Cardinal Wright was first named to the Congregation for the Clergy in Rome, His Holiness Pope Paul VI asked him what he would miss most in giving up his Diocese of Pittsburgh. He replied that more than anything else it would be the opportunities he had as a bishop to teach the Faith.

Probably more than any other characteristic that dominated his life, Cardinal Wright was a teacher of the Faith. He was not lacking in gifts that made him a natural orator and exponent of the word of God. Nor did he lack the zeal that permitted him to dedicate these gifts full time to the service of God's Church. It was fitting that the titular church assigned to Cardinal Wright by the Pope was the Church of Jesus, the Divine Teacher.

From the point of view of the historian, the life of John Wright is a remarkable one. His involvement in peace movements, social justice, and human rights causes, his theological expertise in the preparatory work and his active role in the sessions of Vatican Council II, his advocacy of a wider place for the laity in the life and mission of the Church, the force of his personality on the pastoral scene of three dioceses, the captivating quality of his oratory, the prodigious quality of his written talks, homilies, retreat conferences, articles, and spiritual writings, as well as his ten years as the first American to take a place in the Roman Curia as head of one of its offices, with worldwide responsibilities, and his services as a counselor to three popes demand the serious attention of those whose vocation it is—as historians—to study, sort, and codify such accomplishments.

This brief effort of mine is not to tell the history of John Cardinal Wright. But as one who served him as secretary for many years—all of the years he served in Rome—and as one who follows him as bishop of a large and vigorous see, the Diocese of Pittsburgh, I still stand in great awe of the gifted man whom God chose to serve His Church in so many ways. Cardinal Wright was a living witness to the maxim that more will be asked of those to whom much is given. Great were his talents and he freely shared them with all he touched . . . whether in Boston, Worcester, Pittsburgh, or his beloved city of Rome!

+ Donald W. Wuerl
Bishop of Pittsburgh

I

Teachers of the Faith

To those of you to whom the commission to teach the Faith has been entrusted—and that means every believer—I might address the encouragement of Saint Paul to the Romans while offering these thoughts that they "might impart some spiritual grace to you, to strengthen you, that is, that among you I may be comforted together with you by that faith which is common to us, both yours and mine."[1]

You have a lofty mission; you have a sublime task: to communicate the divine doctrine to men and teach them the certain road to everlasting happiness . . . in other words, to convey not just *theology* in the more technical sense of that word, not even more refined *theologies,* but the Faith. Your mission is not to convey some professional theologian's point of view—however good it may be—or to indulge—as he may indulge—in speculations about the Faith, but to communicate it as witnesses, as prophets, to convey the simple, clear, and direct word of God Himself, to give evidence of the Way, of the Life, of the Truth. The Lord Jesus was never a professional theologian. He was—He is—and always shall be a witness, a prophet of certain truths, which are largely inexplicable. Believe me, you are not so much theologians as witnesses, teachers of the Faith who are continuing His mission of testimony in the world of today.

It is quite true that even after his secession (apostasy) from God through Adam's sin, man kept and still keeps his capacity and the possibility to recognize the Lord through reason and turn to Him as to his beginning and his end through natural will.[2] But it is likewise true that in the divine plan for redemption,

This address was delivered, in Italian, at Passo della Mendola, Trent, Italy, on August 9, 1969, during a Seminar on Catechetics.

the ordinary and necessary means for saving mankind consists in evangelization, preaching, catechesis, that is, communication of the divine revelation.

Human philosophy could be the suitable and capable means for promoting research and knowledge of God.[3] It could be; but in fact, as Saint Paul said, men *"evanuerunt in cogitationibus suis"* —men became foolish in their thoughts—they changed the very truth of God into lying.[4]

It is not man's philosophy or science which reaches true knowledge of God. Consequently, "it pleased God to save men through the foolishness of preaching."[5] And it will not be man's efforts and works that will open the gates of everlasting happiness to him: "Not by reason of good works which we did ourselves, but according to His mercy, He saved us through the waters of regeneration and renewal by the Holy Spirit; whom He has abundantly poured out in us through Jesus Christ our Saviour, in order that, justified by His grace, we may be heirs in the hope of life everlasting."[6]

The necessity for evangelization and catechesis derives from these two facts: on the one hand, man's practical impossibility of knowing the truth concerning his eternal destinies; on the other hand, free and merciful divine giving, which has called and raised up man to cause him to participate in his inward life: *"divinae consortes naturae"* and his happiness: "We shall be like him, because we shall see Him as he is."[7]

It is clear that it is not possible to know and believe the truths manifested by the Lord and admit and receive Christ's divine mysteries unless we have proper understanding of them, consequently, unless we have the necessary corresponding evangelization.

The Apostle Paul plainly said so: "How then are they to call upon Him in whom they have not believed? But how are they to believe Him whom they have not heard? And how are they to hear, if no one preaches?"[8]

God's sincere will that all men shall be saved was affirmed by the apostle and is clearly and securely founded in Jesus' command to preach the gospel to all people.[9] All, from the apostles down to the last catechist in the most obscure village in the world, who devote themselves to this evangelization are carrying out Jesus' command, cooperating in the salvation of all. You are amongst those, and I greet you as teachers of the Faith. You are teachers of the Faith because you tell people of something which they cannot acquire on their own; you are teachers of faith, because you set men upon the way to "the substance of things to be hoped for" and accompany them on the road toward the mastery of that truth by faith.[10]

It is said that people, especially young people, are looking for concreteness and authenticity. This is true. But we must remember that man has always wished to try to touch and experiment with whatever he sees and whatever comes into his mind, whether such *concrete experience* be for the better or for worse.

Adam recklessly put out his hand to the forbidden fruit; unbelieving Thomas put his finger in the Divine Redeemer's wounds; man has always desired and always tried to find out for himself, not only in theory, but by making a practical test of concrete reality.

This perennial need had increased or has at least been accentuated, and man, especially young mankind, will not admit anything unless he can try and see for himself. Hence contestation, even insensate and violent contestation, protest against everything which is not clear, which cannot be proved by experience to be concrete, consistent, real, and authentic.

Indeed ground is being gained by the tendency to derive the truths of being from the subject itself (subjectivism) and to derive norms for action and conduct from existence itself (existentialism). No more instruction and indoctrination from the exterior, no more imposition from outside, but development and assertion of the individual, with more unforeseeable and anarchical results than ever.

That much-applauded development of one's own capacities, one's own aspiration, one's own rights, which is so widespread

27

at all levels and in all sectors, more or less derives from the supposition that man is himself the principle of his being and his doing. As you well know, the true, authentic reality is very different, because man is dependent in his being, just as he is dependent in his doing.

Others do not go so far as to derive and borrow everything from man as subject, but try, and make industrious efforts, to measure God by their own yardsticks and cut Him down to their size. Their intention, or rather their excuse, is to adapt presentation and formulation of the truths to the modern mind; they end by forging a God to their own and others' liking. So we are faced with troubling silences and grave mutilations concerning fundamental truths of the Faith and the Church's traditional testimony.

A God with no angels and no miracles, a man called Jesus, in whom the Godhead was at work; a Virgin with no divine supernatural motherhood. All these and many other concepts destroy God; at least the *new God* is not the God of Abraham, of Isaac, and of Jacob; of Peter, of Paul, of the Christian saints; of the Faith of our Fathers.

The tendency to wish to be like God is very ancient, and so is the wish to mold a God to our own taste. Pagan mythology proves it; Christian heresy confirms it. Saint Hilary of Poitiers stood up against this temptation and this tendency: *"Quorum impietas est, Deum non ex Dei ipsius professione, sed ex arbitrii sui voluntate metiri: ignorantes non minoris impietantis esse Deum fingere quam negare."* [11] Their impiety consists in measuring God not by what He has said of Himself, but by their own preferences, forgetting that describing God mendaciously is just as bad as denying Him.

Those who put God aside in order to put man in His place — even though they may still speak of Jesus — those who forge a god to please themselves, are certainly not authentic teachers of the Faith. A god who is the result of pseudo-mathematical speculations — the god of the philosophers — even though he be a cosmic god, or a poetic god, the *Alpha and Omega* of other created things—is not that God who shines in every page of Holy Scripture and who transcends not only me and my country, and my culture, but also all history and all creation, of which I am only the slightest part.

Authentic is equivalent to genuine. Water is genuine and pure when it gushes from a spring and without being altered or polluted arrives at our lips to quench our thirst and refresh us. Authentic and genuine doctrine is that which gushes from the spring and reaches our minds without being altered, without being mixed, without being polluted, and enlightens it; it reaches our heart and liberates it. Saint Paul had to speak of the very many who already in his time were adulterating God's word; he contrasts his own sincere manner of speaking with theirs. He spoke from God, before God, in Jesus: *"Non sumus sicut plurimi, adulterantes verbum Dei sed ex sinceritate, sed sicut ex Deo, coram Deo, in Christo loquimur"*. We are not as many others, adulterating the word of God; but with sincerity, as coming from God, we preach in Christ, in God's presence.[12]

Fidelity to doctrine can and often ought to reach the point of fidelity to the formulation consecrated by the Church and by usage, even to the point of fidelity to single words. This not only because of what is contained in Scripture, of which not a jot or title shall pass away, but also because of the formulation of fundamental truths, which have been set forth and consecrated by the Magisterium and the Church's tradition.[13]

To take an example, *consubstantial* is not simply of the same substance, and transubstantiation cannot be replaced by *transfinalization* or *transignification*. Of course, formulations, expressions, and words are not the truths and the realities in themselves, yet they are authoritative statements of them and the means of reaching them, in such a way that our minds may safely grasp the truths and realities themselves, insofar as it is given to the limited human intellect to do so.

The much-applauded theological exposition can sometimes

29

be dangerous and have harmful effects, because a new presentation, different formulation, or replacement of a consecrated and defined term can misrepresent the essential truth.

Besides this authenticity, which I would describe as objective, teachers of the Faith must have an authenticity that I would call personal and interior. I was not educated in a Catholic elementary school, but I thank the Lord for having in my youth come under the formative influence of educators who were *persons* not *personages* — of deep Christian faith.

One episode in particular has remained stamped in my inmost soul and I still feel the impression of the moment when it occurred. One of the boys in our class died, aged about eleven. Our religion teacher took us to visit and pray around his body. While we all were standing there in dismay and silence looking at our classmate and friend's immobile face, she, the teacher, said, with unforgettable power, warmth, and love, but above all, faith: "Stephen is not dead. It doesn't matter what things seem; he is alive. He is alive in God!"

She went on speaking with such inward, profound conviction, about Holy Scripture, the evidence given by the saints, and, with such persuasive force, of life in God—not the permanence of our little contribution to history, not of our immortality in our descendants and in our achievements—poor Stephen had none of those things—but of our life in Jesus, thanks to baptism, our life in God, thanks to Jesus, who having died and risen again, will die no more. The way she spoke and what she said left an indelible impression on us. She was an authentic teacher of religion: she had, she lived, she sensed the Faith; she conveyed Christian belief by means of a kind of healthy, creative, and evangelical contagion of faith, which not even the most boring kind of *theology* has been able to kill, at least in me.

This is what I mean when I speak of authenticity, of inward genuineness. The Church's truths and realities are not only the object of abstract knowledge but are lived, are tasted in the depths of the soul. Saint Gregory the Great said: *"Quilibet praedicator verba dare auribus potest, corda vero aperire non potest."* [14] But if the preacher can only speak words to the ear and not open the heart, experience shows that the effect is very different according to who says the words. The effect is not bound to the words, but to the person who utters them. A master of pedagogy of other days said: "It is easier to instruct than to educate. In order to instruct, it is enough to know something and know how to convey it; to educate you must be someone" (Adalbert Stifter). If this is true for natural, social, and civil education, it is even truer of spiritual, supernatural training for the life of faith.

To be someone spiritually, interiorly, is not easy, and not a light, short-term matter. The Divine Master points to one way only, one means only of being someone in him and bringing forth much fruit for him: of being living roots. *"Ego sum vitis, vos palmites; qui manet in me, et ego in eo, hic fert fructum multum; quia sine me nihil potestis facere."* I am the vine, you are the branches; who remains in Me and I in him, he brings forth much fruit; for without me you can do nothing.[15]

In action, it is of the greatest importance to know the nature and the purpose of catechesis in teaching religion. You know more about these things than I do, because you have been studying them deeply for a long time and in the light of the new science. I will just make a few brief observations, in order to give you a fuller idea of what I think.

As you know, there are various differing ideas about the nature of catechesis. Some understand it—perhaps we may say, used to understand it—as teaching and training, most often solely by rote, in the first fundamental elements of the truths of the Faith. Others consider it as an authoritative and official statement of salvation (such as is made by a herald), and that this has to receive assent, faith from man. Others again regard it as a cordial family conversation which ought to be engaging and convincing. Finally, some think of it as initiation and guidance to practice of Christian life.

There is some truth and something useful in all these concepts, so long as we bear the true and proper purpose of catechesis well in mind. It is not simply a matter of teaching something, of imparting new concepts, catechism formulas, passages from Holy Scripture and the liturgy. All these things are serviceable and necessary, but they are not the substance. The substance is to lead to the Faith, to lead to life, to lead to love of God. The great Augustine put it this way: *"Hac ergo dilectione tibi tamquam fine proposito, quo referas omnia quae dicis, quidquid narras ita narra, ut ille cui loqueris audiendo credat, credendo speret, sperando amet."* Make love of God your aim and to it refer everything you say; everything you relate, relate in such a way that he who hears you may believe, believing may hope, and hoping may love.[16]

True catechesis is therefore not simply a matter of teaching and believing some truths; it is an introduction and an encounter, a demonstration and a reception, a gift and an act of loving God. Augustine himself explained the distinction between believing in God and believing God: "This is God's work, that we may believe in Him whom He had sent."[17] He says, that you may believe in Him, not that you may believe Him. It is true that if you believe Him you will also believe in Him. But it is true that the devils believe Him, but do not believe in Him. With reference to the apostles, we can say in the same way. We believe Paul, but not in Paul: we believe Peter, but not in Peter.

Whoever believes in Him who makes the impious man just, his faith is imputed to him for justice.[18] So what does believing in Him mean? It means: by believing, loving; by believing, being devout; by believing, turning to Him and incorporating ourselves among His members. This is the Faith that God requires from us.[19]

I said before that people—especially young people—desire and need concreteness and authenticity. Well, what is more concrete, more authentic than God? You have the great mission of giving God, in catechesis, in teaching religion, God as He is, as He has been revealed, as He has manifested Himself, as His beloved Son made Him known to us. This is why I spoke at some length about authenticity in teachers of the Faith, because they have to communicate God just as He is, and have to communicate Him frankly (with *parrhesia*) and forcefully (with *energia*), for these are characteristics of God's word. In other terms, you have to teach in such a way that those who are listening to you will not merely feel the bare and simple word of man in you, but the word of God. Saint Paul thanked the Lord and praised the Thessalonians because they received his word as God's word: "For this we give thanks ceaselessly to the Lord because you received the word of God, which you heard from us, you received it not as the word of men, but (which it truly is) as the word of God, which works in you, which you have believed."[20]

The question of the content of catechesis is a topical one. People used to argue about how to teach, now they are arguing about what to teach and are drawing up catechisms for different ages, sectors, and milieux. I will not go into this matter now, for it needs to be examined thoroughly. Before I end, I will only indicate a number of fundamental themes, which all teachers of the Faith should keep in mind. When I say all I mean all—from the Supreme Pontiff down to the last Bantu catechist, from the bishop to the priests in charge of the most remote parishes.

There is much talk of the Spirit nowadays, but some of that talk is misleading rather than helpful. Indeed, I have seen the question "Who is the Holy Spirit?" answered in a little Italian catechism with the words "He is my big mate"! I really don't know how a child can be led to worship the Holy Spirit when He is described to him in such terms. It escapes me how a child can take such a God seriously, presented to him like that.

Then there is more and more talk, and it is not without deep interest, of what is called Catholic Pentecostalism, and several like spiritualist movements—not to call them movements of the Spirit.

But what I want to point out, and indeed, with force, is that the principal and fundamental subject of every catechesis is

Jesus, His divine person, His preaching, His expiatory death, His Resurrection, His Ascension, His presence amongst us—in people who need us—in His people, acquired with His Blood, in His organized and organic Church, in the *Paraclete* diffused in *cordibus nostris* whom He promised and sent, in the Eucharist, as described so beautifully in the old Italian folk hymn, *Gesù Sacramentato.* In every case, always the center: Jesus!

Apostolic preaching, the early Church's catechesis converted the pagan world. What was it but presenting Jesus and reporting His life and words? Who or what will ever be able to give a renewed Christian spirit to this age of ours, if not Jesus, if not the presentation, the gift of Jesus? Not only the Jesus of the Gospel according to Saint Matthew, but also the Jesus of the experiences and meditations of Saint John; of Saint Paul, of mystics, of poets, saints, and of us sinners, right down to today.

Before he begins anything else, in his Prologue, Saint John answers the question *Who is Jesus?* He is the Word of God; the Incarnate Word, the Word full of grace and truth.

It is fundamental and essential in every catechism to teach and cause people to feel who Jesus is: God—Man, and Redeemer of all, especially now that some have reached the point of rejecting (that is not too strong a word) the Incarnation and all theology based on this unutterable mystery. These are much worse than the old iconoclasts, for they are trying to destroy not so much the figure and the image as the person and the very reality of Jesus.

It is indispensable to present the Church's nature, her constitution, her work, and her purpose. I do not mean the Church in her outward and (in the legitimate sense) historical form, but her spiritual, supernatural activity, her essence as the Mystical Body, of which Christ is the Head, which He left here upon the earth, organized in history, visible in human society.

Much of the doctrinal and practical confusion concerning the Church and the Church's Faith comes from the fact that people do not remember that being Christian above all means spiritual sharing in the Body of Jesus, through which all become one in Him: "There is neither Jew nor Greek, slave or freeman, male or female, for you are all one in Christ Jesus."[21] The Second Vatican Council affirmed that the Church is *"in Christo veluti Sacramentum seu signum et instrumentum intimae cum Deo unionis"* — in Christ as a sacrament or sign and instrument of inward union with God.[22] Therefore, just as we cannot do without Jesus, so we cannot do without the Church, the sole ark of salvation for all.

Let me recall, in connection with the profundity of the reality of how being a Christian differs from every other level of being, an extreme but somehow significant incident. I had gone to Assisi, and went up from there to the Carceri, together with an old English lady, with whom and with whose descendants both my family and I have kept up a long and cordial correspondence.[23]

We came upon a peasant with his donkey, which was struggling to drag along a cart certainly bigger and heavier than it could manage. The donkey halted; it would not budge. The peasant whipped and beat it brutally. The English lady, a true animal-lover, sprang to defend it and scolded the peasant. His only reply was: *"Ma, perchè non posso batterlo col bastone? Non è Cristiano!"* —Why can't I hit him? He's not a Christian!

He was a big, rough, ignorant man. I am sure that in these more ecumenical times he would have had more respect not only for the old English woman, but also for the donkey—at least I hope so! But in those wild days—I'm referring, you know, to twenty-eight years before the Council!—perhaps that man felt—*modo vago*—what being Christian means, what the difference is between a Christian and everything else that God has created. Say what you will, this is something that some people do not know and no longer acknowledge. I hasten to add that while agreeing with the peasant's dogma, I deplore his moral theology. Donkeys may have no Christian rights, but Christians have duties toward all that God has made!

Being Christian, that is, belonging to Christ, the Son of God, having God in our souls, having the well-founded hope of being able to be happy forever in His sight, is a wonderful thing, a unique thing, which the Christian ought to know, ought to feel, ought to taste. In this time of general syncretism, of often ill-understood ecumenism, it is absolutely necessary to remember and to teach what the Christian is and what his profession of being a Christian entails. A Christian is a child of God, a brother of Christ, his neighbor's servant, a voluntary slave in mankind's service.

There is a fashion, a vogue, these days for the anthropological dimension in catechesis also. This anthropology is often not only a proper regard for the psychological, sociological, and environmental facts about those being catechized but is also an effort to adapt the immutable divine doctrine to contingent states and data. It seems to me that the first thing to do is to know man, particularly since there is so much divergence among present tendencies in thought about and evaluation of man.

Some think he's some kind of angel, and pass into angelism, by trying to eliminate all sense of guilt and sin, of moral misery and spiritual infirmity from man, especially from the child.

Others think of him in purely horizontal terms, with purely temporal ends; they orientate and urge him to evaluate and accomplish himself in time and enjoy life as it goes by. This is not truth or reality. Man is a poor little being shaped from mud and subject to sin. But his nature turns him to God; by the Lord's benign gift, he is destined to enjoy God forever. His religious life, his Christianity consequently may not be restricted to more or less philanthropical social living, but ought to be decisively and generously aimed at gaining an eternity of happiness and enjoying it.

But for the Church, man is the steward of all creation, God's image, therefore a person. Man is master of the machine and technology, not just a part of the works. Man is a pilgrim, and not only on the face of the earth; today he is a pilgrim to the moon; tomorrow he will be a pilgrim in the depths of space, then in the entire universe, illuminated by millions of suns, but illuminated even more by that love which moves the moon, the sun, and the other stars.[24] Man is a pilgrim in all this creation: but he is a pilgrim to eternity.

Allow me to make a brief concluding remark. The indispensable and characteristic dimension of Christian life and therefore of catechesis, is the dimension of joy. I am not sure, but this dimension of joy sometimes seems to me almost to have vanished from the Church. Joy is a victim of theological aggiornamento; it has been smothered, even buried under research, opinion polls, statistics, bibliographies, the six hundred and eighty pages of the new Dutch catechism—not to mention—its eighty-nine pages of corrigenda.[25]

It would be disastrous if joy disappeared from catechesis. Saint Augustine tells us that it is a fundamental of catechesis to teach joyfully: *"Cum gaudio quis catechizet";* and he gives the reason: *"Multo gratius audimur cum et nos de eodem opere delectamur"* —we are listened to more willingly when we take delight in what we are saying. We ought not only give but also taste and delight in what we are communicating. Here is the whole secret and power of teaching religion; it is loving what we want to say so deeply and vitally in ourselves that we can exult and delight in it and so, by the Lord's grace, teach and convey it to others.[26]

II

The Church of Promise

I think it fair to say that the mood within the Church today is one of apprehension. I suppose a more accurate, certainly more spiritual, word to use in describing that mood, would be to call it a mood of solicitude. This puts us in the tradition of Saint Paul who, confronted with the problems which vexed or threatened the early apostolic Church, confessed that he felt profoundly moved by a solicitude for the Church as a whole in her every part.

Such is our mood today. We meet, all of us, in small groups for conversation, in large groups for policy-making conventions dominated by a solicitude sometimes too anxious to articulate. Sometimes we are so tormented that we articulate, either in our speeches or our resolutions, with exaggeration or with excessive passion, the kind of defeatism and emotional discouragement which is the caricature of solicitude, indeed not solicitude at all, but anxiety run ragged.

I sense this mood in Catholics who love the Church and are concerned with her relation to the world, including the image she projects and the influence she exercises within the world. It is healthy insofar as it reveals a love for the Church and a proper preoccupation with the problems of the times. It is unhealthy in that it can undermine the Faith, diminish joy in that Faith, and increase the sense of frustration which is the father of confusion and renders you impotent to help the Church you love so much. That mood is undoubtedly intensified by some of the sad, not to say scandalous, events reported in the papers you read every day, hear whispered about by your children, carry in your minds as

This address was delivered at the Knights of Columbus Center, New Haven, Connecticut, on August 20, 1969.

you go about your work, and inevitably find creeping into your conversations, particularly those about the state of the Church.

Accordingly, I think it wise to meet this mood head on. First of all, let me underscore that the present mood of solicitude, not to say downright worry, in the hearts of those who love the Faith is nothing new. I already have mentioned that I take the very word from the vocabulary of Saint Paul over one thousand and nine hundred years ago. I might suggest that within the lifetimes of most living men, the Church has been faced with crises, scandals, betrayals, compromises which differ in no way, except perhaps by degree, from those which account for this solicitude. Some of these occasions for solicitude have been regional, but the region covered two-thirds of the world, as for example where established atheism has threatened to snuff out the light of faith in the years since 1920. Some have been local, as for example in the dreadful threat to the Church and her life in France during the first decade of this century, in Italy a generation before, in Germany at about the same time when Kulturkampf so gravely threatened the survival of Catholicism. Some of the threats have been worldwide and remarkably like certain of the worst aspects of the present crises, since the threat came not so much from without (attacks from without sometimes strengthen the Faith) but from within, as it does now, and on the level of ideas and values profoundly challenged and, by attempt at least, discredited. Such was the modernism which swept through the Catholic world like a contagion in the days of Saint Pius X.

Obviously, the mood of a somewhat morbid solicitude which grips hearts at the moment is best dispelled by faith, by greater faith if you already believe strongly, by better faith if you still retain any elements of that divine gift. "I believe, O Lord, help Thou my unbelief!" is a prayer which from the time it was written in the Sacred Scriptures has served to strengthen faith where it was under attack and dispelled anxiety concerning the Faith where it seemed warranted by disturbing events.[1]

However, not only faith but also the reading of a bit of history helps to put back into perspective the view of things which is so upset by the confusions of the moment and unsettled by the solicitude of those who must keep the Faith through these hours of anxiety. I have special reasons, which speedily will become obvious, for choosing but one of several moments in history which have paralleled our own, both in their discouragement lest the Faith be dying and in their tendency to fear that the end of all that we cherish must be close at hand. In the last two thousand years, there have been a score of such periods. I recall but one, and I recall it because it so remarkably resembles in its mood and its elements our own moment of history.

Samuel Eliot Morison, one of the best-read professors of history at Harvard, is the source of the recollection that the year 1492 was one of the most discouraged years in the history of Europe.[2]

At the end of the year 1492 most men in Western Europe felt exceedingly gloomy about the future. They had ample reason to feel so. The princes and monarchs were in amazing degree mental cases and in any case were divided deeply from one another on the temporal and political level. Alexander VI was Pope that year, and all of us who were taught our history by certain Protestants or a special kind of Catholics, who are not *afraid to face the truth,* know what a disaster that was—although, truth to tell, despite the morals of his early days and the manners of his family, I always have had a secret suspicion that he did a better job than he is generally attributed—but here I confess to prejudices which will come out later. In any case, in 1492, long-established institutions, ecclesiastical, academic, and political, were decaying. Frustration was in the air. Well-meaning people were growing cynical or desperate. The limited in intellect were giving themselves up to vice and aimlessness. The sensitive and intelligent, appalled by the threats of the future and the problems of the present, tried to escape the solicitudes of 1492 by studying the classical pagan past.

This particular *flight from reality* turned out to be the source of a blessing in disguise, for that is how the great Western Renaissance began. From the study of a pagan past, they acquired a new enthusiasm for beauty on the level of art, architecture, and poetry. They began to create new music, new styles of life, and above all, they began to look for new frontiers, new worlds to conquer.

Permit me to dwell on this for a moment, because it provides a parallel well worth our meditation. The *Nuremberg Chronicle*, in a folio dated July 12, 1492, forecast that the end of the world in fire and flood could not possibly be far off.

I never look out the window of my office in Rome without thinking of that particular period of solicitude. It is an extraordinary antidote to any morbid solicitude which might overcome me as a result of the mail and the newspapers on my desk, reporting the solicitudes of the present. The first thing I see as I look out my window is the dome of Saint Peter's, one of the great monuments to the Renaissance that was the result, in the way I have indicated, of the discouragement of intelligent people over the seeming fate of the institutions—religious, cultural, and other—which they cherished but considered to be doomed, so doomed that they turned from them to the study of classic antiquity.

Nearer to my window, a mere matter of a few feet from the window ledge, is one of the ends of Bernini's colonnade, another monument to the new beauty that grew out of the refuge from the old despair. It bears an inscription proclaiming its completion under Pope Alexander VII, who, a few years before, had served as papal nuncio in Westphalia, Germany, trying to bring to an end (in the pattern of papal nuncios then and now) the conflicts between the nations which added up to the Thirty Years' War. His very name is a reminder to me that even wars come to an end, so long as there are men working for peace somewhere loose in the world, and the things of art and science, such as account for Bernini's colonnade, are brought back into the service of a religion that was thought to be dying only a few years before.

The symptoms of that oncoming death in 1492 were again remarkably like the symptoms which many interpret as marking the end of institutional and revealed religion in our own day. It was a year of weird religious developments. All over Europe, there were breaking out forms of witchcraft, black magic, abberrations of the religious instinct, underground movements and like religious abnormalities which, then as now, increased the solicitude in the hearts of believers. While the intelligent and sophisticated—always a minority, now as then—were taking refuge in the study of the ancient classics, the more simple-minded citizens of more primitive taste or instinct went in for astrology, contestation, and general dissent.

I need not labor the parallel, need I, between 1492 and the present? The universal mood of dissent on the one hand and of the anxiety on the other reveals its presence everywhere. You now see the first in the Piazza Navona and on the Spanish Steps in Rome; you see the second at the Vatican. You see the first on the edges of Boston Common, on the corners of selected streets in San Francisco, or in any of the other places where either the hippies or the rebellious gather. You see the evidence of the solicitude on the faces of university presidents, wondering whether to send for the police, and you hear the echoes of it in the speeches of the more intelligent of our political leaders. The rumor went around recently that the whole state of California was going to slide into the Pacific on April 15 that year—do you remember? As a devout New Englander, I was deeply disillusioned by the newspapers dated April 16!

I need not speak of the resurgence of witchcraft. The newspapers have carried accounts of this nonsense in terms of a priest in England, an ex-priest and his wife in Switzerland, a series of soothsayers in Holland, orgies of a liturgical and even more debased kind hither, thither, and yon, none of them new to the 1960s and 1970s, but somehow characteristic of our times. There

42

has been a dramatic resurgence of interest in astrology. Even newspapers which no longer carry essential information, like ship arrivals, and of course suppress any references to births or heartbreaking news, carry columns providing astrological guides for each day.

If the political conflicts, religious confusion, and intellectual decay did not lead you to the temptation to despair, the conversations with our teenage children would, and so rather than abandoning yourselves to the dark arts, to witchcraft, to drugs, or to hippiedom, you are looking for new interests, not so much in classical antiquity as in the new technology and the promise of the age of space. And although filled with solicitude, you are sustained by faith, by faith and a bit of history.

For suddenly in 1492 explorers began to open up not merely a new world but an entirely new perspective. In a couple of generations after the extraordinary exploit of Christopher Columbus, the mood of the whole world had changed. Missionaries were setting out for the ends of the earth, and the foundations were being laid for a new type of civilization, of commerce, of exploration and discovery, which would not merely revolutionize but energize religion, politics, and culture generally. The English produced fewer witches and gave us a run of poets, headed by Shakespeare. The French grew weary of their dissolute sorcery and gave us new art, new music, new poetry, new theater, new interests for all the world. The Spaniards and the Portuguese were hard at work, in a matter of years, building a future in the New World which would surpass even the best periods of their history in the Old World, at least in certain basic ways of service to all mankind, and there were born unbounding ambitions and inspired enthusiasms, producing a new period of exploration, discovery, and civilization, as a result of a change of mood from defeatism and discouragement to hope and the desire for accomplishment. All this may be said, without undue simplification, to have been the result of the exploit of Christopher Columbus, sponsored by a believing queen.

43

At a given moment in 1492, in the midst of all the moaning and groaning, the Niña sailed slowly into the harbor of Lisbon with the news of the discovery of a New World. Historian Morison notes the "complete and astounding change that then took place". Sir Charles Oman declared: "A new envisagement of the world has begun, and men are no longer sighing after the imaginary golden age that lies in the distant past but speculating as to the golden age that might possibly lie in the oncoming future."[3]

It is a little too early to say whether, as a result of the recent exploits of the astronauts and the opening up of the new world of space, "a complete and astounding change" will take place and we suddenly will turn from the dissensions of the present and the hankering after the past to "the golden age that might possibly lie in the oncoming future". For my own part, however, optimist that I am, I think that such will prove to be the case and that something like that which followed on the exploits of Columbus, perhaps something even greater, will follow on the journeys to the moon and the ventures into the depths of space beyond the moon. As a matter of fact, I became certain of this while I was listening to the astronauts, symbols of the greatest potentials of our present-day scientific technology, reading from the first pages of Sacred Scripture, for all the world to hear, during their orbiting of the moon at Christmas time, on the Apollo flight.

One night in Rome, I was present when Jim Lovell showed us the films of the landing on the moon, the first bus stop on the journey to the ends of creation. While he talked and we watched the first tentative steps on the dust of the moon's surface, I remembered a magnificent talk that Pope Pius XII gave a few months before he died, a talk in which he said that he could not understand the universal pessimism about the prospects for life and for all created things, in the hearts of people who are standing, as is our generation, on the shores of space, no longer with a little globe to conquer, occupy, and exploit—but with the whole cosmos to make our own and, thanks to our new technology and, please God, reborn confidence in ourselves and in God, to bend to our purposes. Well, I cannot understand such pessimism either—and it is not because I follow the Pope (though I tend to do so for excellent reasons) in his evaluation of the times, but because I have read the story of humanity's past, including 1492, and have sensed the direction of humanity's future, beginning with elements, wise and foolish, which are revealing themselves today.

Now let us bring these reflections a little closer to that which chiefly explains our solicitude, namely, the Holy Catholic Church. Many share your anxiety over many things which are happening in the Church. You are deeply moved by a spirit of solicitude for your Holy Mother, the Church. If you did not have such a mood, one might think that there was something the matter with your common sense, not to say your faith and your love. But if that mood were to overwhelm you, one would know for certain that there was something the matter with your hope as well as with your faith. One might also fear that you had lost your perspective and had so forgotten the history of your religious community, even in this area of the world, as to have become the victims of a *collective amnesia.*

I suppose that everyone thinks that his diocese is having a rough time at the moment. I do not happen to know what is the nature of the particular problems of most American dioceses, but I do know that, in the old phrase, there is no clause in Father Adam's will which exempts any of them from the troubles of this life, including the denial by some of our brethren of Father Adam himself!

Let us take a look at the history of one typical American diocese, choosing that of Hartford because it is the home of your Knights of Columbus. The Diocese of Hartford was established on November 28, 1843, and the situation in the city of Rome, from which I have come in order to be with you, could not possibly have been less promising than it was in November

1843, when Pope Gregory XVI sat down to sign the document that brought this diocese into being. As a matter of fact, one almost asks why he bothered to sign it; the future was so bleak. There was little chance, humanly speaking, that the venture would work out as it has done. There were revolutions all over the place, and most of the people who were coming here were coming as voluntary or involuntary emigrants from lands where they were starving to death and subject to persecution, largely because of their religion. As for Rome, on the very day of Pope Gregory's coronation, the ceremonies were interrupted by a group of what now would be called in Italy *manifestatori*. The movement they represented was determined at all costs to get rid of the Pope, the papacy, and all the *structures* leading to or from both. They were not fooling, and as a matter of fact, they were not entirely mistaken in some of the charges which added passion to their demonstrations, noisy protests, and highly organized dissent.

In Hartford, as throughout New England, there are many descendants of those angry young men who gave Pope Gregory XVI and later Pope Pius IX a bad time. Some of those descendants are Knights of Malta. Most of them are Knights of Columbus. The overwhelming majority of them not only have long since settled for the institutional Church but are worried sick by the attitude toward her of those whom they regard as *new breeders* — not without reason for grave concern and sincere solicitude.

The other day, there came to my office in Rome a very respectable Italo-American who, after a presentation of the woes and worries of the moment in his parish and diocese, ventured the suggestion that the bishop be removed, the auxiliary bishop transferred, the pastor fired, and the parish committee dissolved. He also had a remark to make, to which I was by temperament more open, that the organist be deprived entirely of access to the choir loft. Despite the passion of his criticisms, there was no mistaking his love for the parish. I asked him how long he had lived in it, and he replied that he had arrived in America from

Italy only a very few years before and had taken up residence immediately in the parish to which he had become so devoted. I asked him from what town in Italy he came, and when he told me I could not keep from thinking that it would have been absolutely impossible for his great-grandfather not to have belonged to one or another of the anticlerical organizations of the nineteenth century, particularly the *carbonari*. Here he was fighting to reform and preserve his parish out of sheer love for it, while his every ancestor in all probability would have devoted equal energy to destroying the parish where the family then lived and certainly to outlawing if not exiling the Pope.

I mentioned this to him, and he made an extremely interesting remark: "I have no interest in what my ancestors tried to do, to tear down the parish church, but I will not permit the closing of the parish school in my parish at home or any change in the liturgy which makes my wife, my children, and myself no longer feel at home in the parish church we love!"

Well, give him a thought or two when you are about to throw in the sponge because of seeming rejection of religion by your eighteen-year-old son immediately after his first introduction to what the professor is pleased to call the history of Europe or, even more sad, his theology professor has offered him as the secret of the universe!

The Archdiocese of Hartford used to be part of the Archdiocese of Boston in days which I found, generally speaking, abundantly satisfactory. Sometimes I hear rumors that the Archdiocese of Boston is having troubles of one kind or another, and, because I love it dearly for a thousand reasons, this causes me great solicitude. But then, fortified by faith, I pick up the history book, and there I read the Archdiocese of Boston was established by Pope Pius VII. I'm afraid he had to delay the establishment of that ecclesiastical jurisdiction because he was having hell's own time with a man named Napoleon. As a matter of fact, Napoleon had arrested him and held him captive, now in one place, now in another, usually in the snowy, inaccessible towns along the passes in the maritime Alps between Italy and France. In any case, on April 8, 1808, Pius VII was on his way into exile again under the political pressures of the times. One of the last things he did before he left was to authorize the establishment of the Diocese of Boston, for which a large number of those present here in the hall, including myself, are deeply grateful to him. But the first bishop of Boston, Bishop Cheverus, who was a victim of the same revolutions in which Pius VII had been caught up, could not be consecrated for two years after his nomination because the exile of the Pope made it impossible for them to get the proper documents.

Do not misunderstand me. I am not denying the reality of the present troubles in the Church, nor am I minimizing them by a single degree. Most assuredly I am not mocking your worries or underestimating the ground for your solicitude. I simply am pleading for the strengthening of your faith, the heightening of your hope, the maturing of your charity. Moreover, I am suggesting that these desirable ends will be served by the remembrance of history, beginning with the histories of your own families. I hardly need tell you why the fathers and mothers, the grandfathers and grandmothers, the great-grandfathers and great-grandmothers of most of your families came here in the first place. They did not come here because they had no worries or solicitude at home and thought they would like a change in the places of their rejoicing, their affluence, and their absence of cares. Neither did they come here gladly — or, more exactly, they did not leave their own countries gladly, not a bit of it. They came here in tears and in flight from *Trouble,* with a capital T, as the Irish always have given the word *trouble,* and with a small *t* in the case of most other more ebullient nationalities. But it was *trouble,* no matter how you spelled it, and in every case. Many of them thought the end of the world had come, and their journey to America was made with heavy hearts. They went to work in the New World without much support from those who already were here and with very little with which to do the magnificent job that they did.

Let me now move to a discussion of what is my present work and why I ask you to pray for it, not because it is all that difficult, but because it is extremely important to you and to the renewal of the Church that is the object of your well-founded solicitude.

Contrary to a general impression, the Congregation (or *ministry*) of which I am president is not concerned exclusively nor even primarily with the problems of priests. Our Congregation is concerned rather with what would be the solution of most of the problems of all of the priests who have problems, if that solution were promptly worked out and promptly accepted. As a matter of fact, our Congregation is concerned with what would be the solution of most of the problems of most of the people I know, priests or laymen. It is concerned with work—in this case, the pastoral work of the clergy and, more particularly, that work of catechetics, the teaching of the Faith, which is increasingly not only a concern, but also a responsibility of the laity.

Our Congregation has for its competence the pastoral work of the Church, the everyday task of instruction in the Faith (as distinct from debates concerning theology, which are the responsibility of two other congregations), the high privilege and tough job of making Jesus Christ better known and loved. If that work were being done and can be done by all the priests in the world, we would have fewer problems. If we were all working at that full-time—with our whole mind, our whole heart, and all our soul—we would have no problems of the kind usually publicized. We would have problems of health perhaps, occasionally economics, budgeting of time, and personality conflict, because of the desire of each of us to do the job better than anyone else.

Accordingly, while there is a section in our Congregation devoted to the life and ministry of priests as there is a section devoted to airport chapels and to pilgrimages for the increase of piety among the devout, the principal section, I would venture to say, is that given to the work of teaching and preaching the *unfootnoted Faith* of our Fathers. When I once spoke of this *unfootnoted Faith*, which is the primary object of our concern, I was taken to task by an American magazine, which implied that this meant I was a hidebound conservative whose mind was utterly closed to the new theology and any of the new directions of things. The criticism was profoundly unfair—as I think the author knew—because nothing could be further from the truth. My point was that, whatever my personal recollections or prejudices, it is the Congregation for the Doctrine of the Faith that is responsible for the *footnoted theologies,* as is also the Congregation for Seminaries in no small degree. But our Congregation is concerned with the preaching of the Catholic Faith, the methods of teaching that Faith, as it was transmitted from the Fathers.

If this work—the right word for which is evangelism—were being done day in and day out, every year, all over the world, priests would go to bed each night extremely tired, but they would wake to face a new day extremely exhilarated. This of course is true of all those, priests and laity, who take the Christian life seriously and seek to spread the Faith. Busy priests may be tired priests; they may even occasionally be bewildered priests, bewildered by the sheer magnitude and the eternal implications of their work. But they are never problem priests.

In every corner of America, Canada, and Mexico, there are scores of these priests, and you know them well. They are too busy with the problems of others, for such is their life and ministry, to be bothered about the problems of themselves. They suffer from no identity crisis. They know exactly why they asked for ordination and received it so gladly and so unselfishly. They are too preoccupied with bringing men to God and God to men to become the victims of purely personal, individual fits of self-pity or any other form of preoccupation with self. They are totally given to the total service of the total community and the total Christ. That means, to me at least, that they are saints, and there are far more of them alive and at work in our dioceses and our parishes, despite all our problems, than we are inclined to think.

The part of the Knights of Columbus in building the climate which produces such priests has been enormous.

When I was a boy, the Knights of Columbus in my home parish gave me, by word and example, encouragement which has shaped my life; encouragement in the practice of the Faith, encouragement in solicitude for the interests of the Church which teaches the Faith, example in the attitudes which should flow from the possession of the Faith. For this I am thankful!

Throughout the years of my priesthood, I have been inspired by the works of the Knights of Columbus, works of piety, works of instruction, works of mercy. I merely note such programs as the instruction in the Faith provided by the Knights of Columbus by mail to all those who apply for such instruction; the inevitable presence of the Knights of Columbus to recite prayers for the dead at wakes; the special honors paid by the Knights of Columbus to the bishop of the diocese when he is present for a ceremonial occasion; the vigils in honor of the Real Presence of Christ in the Blessed Sacrament maintained on certain feast days by the Knights of Columbus as a group and individually. I mention merely in passing the fact that the local council of the Knights in my own home parish was the first council known to me to have among its officers the only black man who happened to be a member of our parish back in the 1920s and 1930s, when, it is commonly asserted, we were living in a period of singular lack of sensitivity and fraternal instincts in our intergroup relations! For all these things I am thankful!

The ring on my finger is a gift from some Knights of Columbus in the council [No. 121, Brighton, MA] of which, as a priest of my native city, I am a member. That ring has of course intense overtones of personal sentiment, but as my episcopal ring, it is also a symbol to me of an essential attribute of the Knights of

Columbus: the desire to be identified with the hierarchy in all that the hierarchy is or exists to do for everyone within the Church and the general community.

As the bishop who founded the Diocese of Worcester, I have a special debt to the Knights of Columbus. The order there took the lead in helping me to build the new diocese committed to my care. They particularly identified themselves with the service of the cathedral as the center of the life of the diocese, with the works of our hospital and especially with the program for unwed mothers, which we started in a remodeled and much-beloved old New England house within the city limits of Worcester. I well remember how one Halloween night there had been rumors of disorders scheduled by the unruly for the area around that house. The young girls had heard the rumors and naturally were terrified. I did not call the police or any other special guards. I called the Knights of Columbus, and they stood in the pouring rain all around the property on which the house stood until there no longer was danger of trouble.

In Pittsburgh, among the first to call on me when I was transferred to that diocese were the leaders of the Knights of Columbus. The purpose of their visit was not merely to welcome me as the bishop, but above all it was summed up in the only question that they put to me: "What special burden of yours do you wish us to help share? Where and how can we help?"

I had not been in Pittsburgh long enough to know all the needs of the diocese, and so my answer was largely instinctive as indeed was their response. I said that I hoped to strengthen the existing program for retarded children, for children born with grievous handicaps and, as a result, *exceptional* in their educational needs, and the development of their faculties and their personalities. I confessed that it would be difficult for me, a Catholic bishop, to get from the average foundation the kind of money to do the extra building, extra research, extra work of every kind to open up new frontiers of service to such children, service performed of course chiefly and best by the Catholic sisters who have pioneered in this field of special education.

The meeting with the Knights did not last thirty minutes, but it would have taken thirty years for me to raise the kind of money that their subsequent hard work made available during the last ten years—while they were at the same time taking care of their existing local commitments, national commitments, international commitments, and other internal commitments, mostly religious, of the order.

As episcopal chairman of the Department of Social Justice in the United States Catholic Conference, it became my responsibility to launch a task force to help meet, in the name of the bishops, the problem of the inner city, with its overtones of group relations, color, poverty, juvenile delinquency, and social decay which are now so familiar and so embarrassing to us all. It did not cross my mind to turn to a government agency, a philanthropic foundation or indeed the Bishops' Conference alone for the needed money. I put myself immediately in touch with your Supreme Knight, John McDevitt, and I asked him for a major part of the dough. He pointed out that he could not act independently, especially where money is concerned, but in no time, the word came back that the Knights of Columbus had made a three-year pledge, which in fact made the task force a possibility.

I had and have no illusion that this money was forthcoming because John McDevitt and I happen to be lifelong friends. It was forthcoming because it is the way the Knights of Columbus respond when the American bishops seek out their help.

The Knights of Columbus already had made possible for the service of the bishops and the Church the growing organization that is CARA—a coordinated effort to study scientifically exactly what are our technical problems, to get them down in black and white so that we can proceed in an orderly fashion to their intelligent as well as prayerful solution.

I have some idea of what the Knights of Columbus have

accomplished in the way of social work in Canada, in Mexico, and therefore throughout all of North America. I came here to say *thank you* for all this.

When I was a young priest who knew no one and whom no one knew, I was eager to help promote a climate for peace as soon as possible after World War II. The first meeting for such a project I ever attended was under the auspices of the Knights of Columbus. It was in New York City and had been convoked by Judge John Swift. Dr. George Herman Derry was chairman of the Knights of Columbus peace program, and that program, immediately following World War II, was my introduction to a series of peace projects, Catholic, civic, and ecumenical with which I have been identified ever since. I owe the Knights of Columbus a word of thanks for their part in that chapter of my life.

As an American bishop, I am grateful for the belltower that the Knights of Columbus erected in our national capital and on the grounds of our Shrine to the Immaculate Conception, patroness of our nation. That tower is not a symbol of any kind of triumphalism (as is sometimes alleged), and it is in no sense a waste of money. It is a symbol of all the values of which belltowers in every corner of the world and from the earliest beginnings have been the effective symbols: the need that men and nations be called constantly to the worship of God, the need for reminders of God's presence among us, and of God's Providence over us, most especially in those places otherwise given up to the sounds of voices which speak for purely personal, partisan, temporal, or otherwise less than fully human hopes.

Coming from Rome, I must thank you for what the Knights of Columbus have done there: for what they did in making possible the so-modern shortwave transmitter for the Vatican Radio, so necessary to bring the message of the Holy See beyond the various curtains which have fallen between some nations and their brethren elsewhere; for what they provided in the way of playgrounds and programs for underprivileged children in the

54

crowded, problem-ridden center of Catholic Christendom. Coming from Rome, I owe you thanks no less fervent for all that you have done in the name of the Catholic Church in other parts of the world, where war always has occasioned the solace to afflicted which has characterized the Knights of Columbus wartime and postwar programs, the latest example of which is their generosity through the Holy Father to the people of Biafra.

May I say a particular word of thanks for the editorial policies of your publication, *Columbia,* and particularly for your recent support of the Church in her position in defense of human rights, human dignity, and human life itself? One must applaud particularly your defense of life in its very beginnings, where God may wish, against the objective evil that is contraception, as well as your defense of life in its growth to birth against the brutal evil that is abortion.

Is there anyone here present who regrets having been born? The very ultimate in melancholic-depressed insanity would be the expression of the wish that you had never been born. Everybody loves life, at least his own. Such a love is instinctive. The Knights of Columbus have tried to communicate that love for the individual person who happens to have had the good luck to be born to all those whose gift of life is threatened by the planned economies, purely political aid programs, and coldly materialistic programs respecting conception and birth which are abroad at the moment.

Speaking of the defense of life, to the conception and birth of which you have been loyal in such strongly Christian terms, there is one other aspect of its primacy about which I would like to speak very briefly and without any offense. I might wish that the Knights of Columbus, in their local councils and in their solemn assemblies throughout the country, were as alert and articulate about some of the other threats to life, particularly the lives of adults when nations have recourse to war, as they are, and very properly are, in the case of the lives of children. The Knights of Columbus always have been wise to the threats to life in its beginnings—to the contraceptive campaign, to the abortion campaign, and all the little schemes related to both, but I wish you were equally alert and equally articulate in the prodigal manner in which life suddenly becomes dispensable once war becomes an instrument of national policies or the means to settling international disputes.

Recently, I have found it extremely interesting to notice how many of the same names appear on, let us say, the boards of directors of the World Population Control Board, the commissions for aid to Latin America, and other impoverished zones and, with marvelous consistency, in those posts or rooms of the Pentagon where it is decided how many hundreds of thousands of young men's lives are *dispensable* in order to gain a given hilltop in Southeast Asia—to cite an imaginary example—or to make the world safe for democracy in other parts of the world. Is it not strange that those—I name no names—who as men in control of, let us say, the World Bank or the Defense Department or the World Population program, so frequently turn out to be the same men—not to say the same man? Is it not curious how grateful they are—or he is—in various parts of the world and under various political systems, to the parents who had the boys who grew up to be soldiers, while at the same time hoping that the soldiers, in the happy chance that they survive, go home to sterilized wives and to nuptial love productive of no new life?

This is one of the mysteries that I submit for your meditation when you are formulating resolutions about war and peace, about taking a *positive attitude* toward governmental programs for birth control in Latin America, among Negroes, in poor districts, and in the parts of the world which depend upon us for considerably more than powdered milk, abortion pills, contraceptive devices, and study clubs in how to be sterile, though married, and happy, though the victims of an unholy system that is anti-life, anti-human, and, since we are talking within the privacy of a Catholic den and therefore may indulge our little prejudices, anti-God.

The anti-life mood of our civilization includes many militaristic aspects to which we Knights of Columbus have not been as sensitive as we have been to the anti-baby movements. Accordingly I ask you, the representatives of the largest and best organized group supporting the United States bishops, to master and to implement in its totality their pastoral letter of November 1968 on *Human Life in Our Day*.[4] You already have defended the part of it that supports the Holy Father in his plea for peace and for protest against the horror that is war. Contempt for human life has become, in our technocratic civilization, an across-the-board thing. So the defense of human life never must be selective, as it is in the case of many people, not merely liberals but also conservatives. We must be against the slaughter of innocent life in every form, or our case is insincere and illogical concerning the specific threat to life that we choose to be touchy about. You must be against whatever is anti-life in modern military, medical, surgical, political, or family morality. You must be for whatever promotes life—all across the board. Selective liberals, selective conservatives, selective patriots, and selective lovers leave something to be desired.

You must say *Yes* to technology designed to find effective ways of exploiting space, of using science, of probing the ocean, of making the desert flower in order to provide whatever food may be needed for that banquet of life to which all are invited. You must say *No* to whatever technology prevents life, destroys life, or maims life—whether in the act of love, or in the womb of a mother, or in the building of peace, and the correcting of international injustices. You must say *Yes* to any diplomatic means, judicial means, medical means, or other means by which life is fortified. You must say *No* to things like napalm, concentration camps, slums, denial of opportunity to love within marriage, if one chooses marriage, and to cooperate with the creative power of God in producing life as well as the providential power of God in preserving it.

Together with your bishops and the Pope, you must take a

consistent, across-the-board, positive position in favor of life—
life in its beginning, life in its growth, life in its education, life in
its prospering, life in its freedom and immunity from external
compulsions or dangers to its integrity, life as long as you can
keep life alive—and you cannot compromise it at any point or
you undermine your position from the very beginning and all
across the board.

Because you say *Yes* to life and *No* to its prevention or
destruction, you must support new ways to produce food, as
through the wonders of the developing oceanography, the untold
treasures of what are now the jungles of India, Africa, and Latin
America, all to the end that those jungles may become orchards,
the lunar landscapes of places like Peru may become gardens, the
deserts may become attractive, the battlefields may become extinct,
and life may become once again no longer a thing of tension and
anxiety, but a thing of joy, beginning with birth—formerly
called, by the way, a *happy event* in decent families.

Above all, we never must allow slogans like *too many mouths to
feed* to justify our prevention of life, or slogans like *my country,
right or wrong* to justify our wars against life. We never must
allow love for self or love for country to silence our deeper
loyalties to life and to God's law. The world could become, you
know, a graveyard by so-called *democratic processes* just as quickly
as it could by Nazi processes—especially if science in its various
forms and personal morality is allowed to become autonomous—
no longer responsive to the common good, to the Providence of
God or to God Himself—let alone our neighbor.

As men unqualifiedly on the side of life, you must oppose
loyally and positively but implacably any policies or any programs which would decide who is to be born or from whom
new life is to come. We must defend our brothers, once they are
born, when the suggestion comes that they may be *expendable*
for policy reasons unexplained and unacceptable. As we defend
our brothers unborn, and while we may react positively to those
elements of government programs which are on the side of life,

we must react negatively and boldly to any parts of government programs or private programs, programs at home or abroad, which threaten life, threaten to crush it out with abortion or threaten its future by controlling the freedom of people to perpetuate their kind, threaten this freedom by pressures or techniques contrary to God's law.

And we must not get fooled by any talk about God's Providence in these matters! Not long ago, the contraceptionists among Catholics used to say that we traditionally left too much to the *Providence of God* and that they were weary of this phrase. Parenthood, they said, should be *responsible* — which means the free result of human and autonomous choice.

Anyone in his right mind will agree — so long as love for life is not smothered in the life of love. But be on guard against a new appeal that is being made forsooth to the *Providence of God,* such an appeal as showed up amazingly in a speech at Notre Dame University when a powerful politician said in effect: Now it is in the Providence of God that we should work with those who are trying to ration life, where once it was the Providence of God that we increase and multiply! Policies have changed, at least on the lips of politicians, clerical and lay. The Providence of God has not — except, again, in the minds of time-servers, clerical or lay.

You have asked that I include a quick view of the personality and work of the contemporary papacy and the Pope.

Jacques Maritain, probably the most intelligent layman of our century, once said of these modern popes that there is no greater evidence of the presence of the Holy Spirit among us than the luminous teachings, examples, and characters of the popes in his own lifetime: Leo XIII, Saint Pius X, Benedict XV, Pius XI, Pius XII, John XXIII, and Paul VI — no two alike in temperament, in background, or in charismatic gifts, but no one repudiating the teachings or policies of another, or disagreeing with another, or breaking faith with the others. And so, I would find it difficult to express differences with the Pope or to speak unfavorably of his leadership and his teaching. Attribute my deep-seated prejudice for the Pope not to lack of intellectual independence or the *American spirit,* but to the kind of confidence which prompted Maritain's remark. Maritain's judgment, I am confident, will also be that of history, once the tumult and the shouting have died, about the alleged *political* inadequacies of Pope Pius XII, let us say; the excessive simplicities, as is sometimes pretended, of Pope John XXIII, or the failure to be *with it* of Pope Paul VI when *mods* are pressing for novel and *more contemporary* approaches to ancient threats to liberty, to love, and to life itself, not to mention to the Faith.

I would take my place by Catholic instinct at Cardinal Newman's side when he argued that the burden of proof—and that proof must be clear, considered, and weighed long and prayerfully—is always on the side of those who presume to take their stand against the Pope, even on a point of policy, let alone faith and morals even as proclaimed by his ordinary teaching authority, even without infallibility. And so by instinct, but also for solid theological reasons, I take my stand on the side of the Pope in any of the present crises, questions, or controversies— whether with respect to morality, to sound doctrine, or to social order. No mere counting of heads, even usually bright heads, would embarrass me in my instinctive response to so much of the dictates of Faith and so many of the lessons of history. Nor is this because I am a member of the Roman Curia, a bishop, or a Knight of Columbus. This instinct, not only associated with a fascination which the papacy merely as an historical phenomenon always has had for me, dates back over most of the years of my life as, I suspect, it does over most of the years of the lives of most Catholics.

In my own case, it found expression at every stage of my life as a Catholic. In high school days, I was a one-man vigilance committee in the public school I attended to make sure that, whatever else they said about the Church, they never attacked the Pope without my asking, "When did he say that? On what page of what book do you find it? What were the circumstances of the times?"

In the years of college, I remember the voice of Pope Pius XI coming over the radio for the first time in history that the chief shepherd of all the world was heard by all the world as he spoke. Back in those early days of radio, some of us listened at stores and garages to hear the voice of the Pope. Nothing I have heard since on radio has thrilled me as much.

In seminary days, at audience in Saint Peter's or at the Vatican, I heard Pius XI speak against totalitarianism and the threat of war and Pius XII speak of the dignity of the person and the essential elements of the eventual world peace.

In graduate days, as a priest-student, I did special studies on the resistance of the papacy to modern nationalism, militarism, impersonalism, and the other forces destructive of religious piety, the primacy of the person, and the spiritual elements of the common good.[5]

In youthful days of priesthood, I wrote on the Pope and the war, the necessity for the Vatican as an oasis of sanity in a world chaotic with nationalistic rivalries and conflicting imperialisms.[6]

As a young bishop, I used to love to preach on the Roman spirit and the manner in which it rebuked and refined a certain parochialism, chauvinism, ghetto, and parochial mentality which so often characterized our own and other Christian peoples.[7]

All this again as by instinct, I linked not so much to any pope as a person, nor to the Roman Church as an institution, passionately though I loved and love her, but to Christ of Whom the bishop of Rome is the vicar. Hence, I sometimes think, the instinct which made me choose my motto as a bishop: *"Resonare Christum corde Romano"* — To echo Christ with a Roman heart.[8]

I beg the Knights of Columbus and all believers to bring an American mind and American heart to the problems of the Church and the world, but I beg you no less to bring a Roman heart to the problems of the Church in America. The Church, in a sense that may be discussed and of course must always be defined, can only be Roman and Catholic; you must keep it Catholic by the intensification of the strength, the prestige, and the faith and works of your own diocese and of every other diocese. You must keep it Roman by your loyalty, as individuals, as diocesans, and as an order, to the Holy Father.

The local Church is not the total Church, though the whole Church is at work in the local Church and vice versa. And the Catholic Church is not the antithesis of the Roman center of the Roman Church. The universal and the one, the worldwide and the local, are reconciled and blended in the holy Roman Catholic Church.

And so I accept with joy the invitation to speak a brief word or two about the work of Pope Paul, what he is doing in our day in behalf of the universal Church from his base at the center of its unity.

What he is doing can be summed up under a few headings:

I. *Certain gestures:* 1. Pope Paul is a man who apparently finds it easier to express by *gestures* the hopes that he and millions share for the Church in the world, hopes which elude all mere words and bypass long speeches. For instance, the rings he gave to all the bishops at the end of the Second Vatican Council and the matching ring that he himself wears all the time, an inexpensive and very simple ring, a symbol of that fraternity in the Faith and the work which we really mean by collegiality. He asked all of us to wear it, certainly on certain occasions, as a symbol of fraternity as well as fealty.

2. The ring he gave the Archbishop of Canterbury, on the spur of the moment, as the Archbishop of Canterbury was getting into a car to leave Saint Paul's in Rome. Pope Paul took off his ring spontaneously and handed it to the Anglican prelate as a symbol of ecumenism and of the prayer that we all may be one.

II. *The journeys* he has made, with such fatigue but with such obvious purposefulness, to the roots of our Christian heritage in Jerusalem the first year he was elected, so that he might meet there the ecumenical patriarch of the Orthodox Church; to the United Nations, so that he might demonstrate our desire not to come to terms with the spirit of the world but to play our part in the building of a better world; the trip to Bombay, to show that our sympathies go way beyond the usual geographical limits of traditional Christendom; to Fatima, to remind us that prayer helps too and that there are certain centers where we pray with greater piety; to Istanbul, in order that he might build up the prestige of his Orthodox brother, the ecumenical patriarch, who lives under conditions so perilous to Christianity; to Latin America, to dramatize the problem of poverty and refresh the Faith in a tired continent; to Geneva, the historic center of Protestantism, to bear his honest, brave witness both to his own position in conscience and to his affectionate respect for theirs, but above all, to demonstrate that ecumenism at the moment is best realized in collaboration with one another, Catholic and Protestant, in the support and promotion of sound social movements; to Africa, both to help create a climate of peace in that troubled continent and to pray at the shrines of the saints whose blood will be the seed of the Church in that continent which many believe, and I am one, will be without doubt the continent of the twenty-first century.

The reactions throughout the world have been one of the greatest grounds for our hope for the future of the organized Church—and there is by the way no other known to historic Christianity than the organized Christian community. It is hard to understand why some Catholics fail to see this, while other Christians and even non-Christian believers in God so often perceive this so clearly. And so when Pope Paul walked in before the leaders of the Protestant world and said to them, "My name is Peter!" Eugene Carson Blake, far from taking offense, saw that line as being in the same spirit as that of Pope John when he told a group of Jews who came to see him: "I am Joseph, your brother."

III. *His teachings:* Pope Paul has set forth honestly and exactly the terms on which and on which alone he could talk conscientiously while at the same time teaching with faith, charity, and hope. His teachings, encyclicals, and conferences, all without exception, are geared to this idea we have been talking about: life and life more abundant—life itself in the encyclical *Humanae Vitae;* life abundant in the encyclical *The Progress of Peoples.*

Then almost every Wednesday he talks to the pilgrims who come to Rome about some aspect of the personality and the teachings of Jesus Christ, the life of every Christian person and institution.

IV. *His clear desire to implement Vatican Council II:* His reform, if you like, of the curia (I would be more inclined, using the more usual vocabulary of a Catholic, to say his *renewal* of its original purposes). The patience with which he tries to ride the storms of the hour. The silence in the face of attack and of misunderstanding, a silence reminiscent of the lines of Scripture which recall how, in the face of calumny, "Jesus kept silent."[9]

V. Finally, *his determination* to do these things with courage, without compromising faith, and without yielding to pressures, political or religious, other than those of conscience and the will of God, with which conscience must correspond at all times. This of course has been implicit in his encyclicals and in his pronouncements.

Well, what am I getting at? I am trying to beg you in this time of turbulence, this time of great solicitude as we said in beginning, but also this time of fantastic promise for the Church, for your bishops and, above all, for future golden ages to come, the magnificence of which we cannot even dream: to keep close to the Pope as the living, visible, audible symbol of the whole thing! Don't take too seriously these distinctions between the periphery of the Church and the center of the Church. No one is at the periphery of the Church who is alive with her life of faith and love.

There is no periphery. If you are in her at all, you are at the center. The Church is not a pie with a center, a periphery, and arguable portions—whether in the nonbeliever's sense of a *pie in the sky* or in the sense of some believers that it is a kind of pie measured as other things created or *cooked up.* The Church is the single, living, unified Body of Christ at work in the world; as a *body,* it has parts but they are not dismembered. Christ is all and in all—not perfectly yet but more than the half-hearted think.[10]

I used to love to hear read, during the ceremonies at the end of Masses on great feasts, the papal blessing with its references to the local Church: *this Holy Church of Worcester, this Holy Church of Hartford, this Holy Church of Philadelphia, this Holy Church of San Francisco.* Be proud of the local Church to which you belong, but don't think of it as only a periphery.

If your local Church is in communion with Rome, it is so intrinsically, so essentially, so vitally united to the center that it is all one, even as there is no divided Jesus Christ, the Source and Center of the Church of Hope.[11]

III

Pope John and His Secret

On this visit to Genoa, you have asked me to talk about Pope John XXIII; and I will do so with great joy, because it seems to me that there is a deep relationship between Pope John's thought and work and the question of vocations.

To be sure, I have not come to look for vocations among you. You are married, and I do not want to upset your marriages! Marriage is a holy state, but it is very different from the priesthood! In the Western world, at least, I suspect that only an ill-informed woman would marry a priest. A priest's work goes on for about twenty hours a day, for about fifty-two weeks a year, and for the whole of his life. The priestly vocation demands such a complete giving of self that it would be unreasonable and unjust, if not simply crazy, to bind a woman as a wife to the destinies of a Catholic, apostolic, Roman priest, above all in this twentieth century.

The priest has to be wedded to the Church. He has to be totally dedicated to her. He is a member of every Christian family, the spiritual father of all the children of all families.

If one of you happens to be free to make such a gift of himself . . . good for him!

But I have to talk to you about Pope John.

Everybody has had something to say or has written something about Pope John!

Many have represented him as a sort of revolutionary, especially in the spiritual, and above all in the priestly, life. But he was nothing of the kind. You only have to read his *Journal of a Soul* to see that he was a priest in the most traditional Catholic

This address was delivered, originally in Italian, at Genoa, Italy, on December 21, 1969, on the occasion of a Serra Club meeting.

pattern.[1] That is to say, his personality, his spirituality, and his undertakings—everything he did and everything he was—derive from a theology of the priesthood and a kind of priestly piety that many of those who make use of his name to justify their own ideas of priestly style of life could not but despise. To tell the truth, they do despise it. The warmth of his personality and his amiability apart—both obviously consistent with his idea of priestly *style*—he was straight out of the manuals of priestly perfection so common in an age some of us thought (and perhaps hoped) had died with the popularity of *The Imitation of Christ*.

A few examples will be enough to reveal his spirit: —his attachment to the Spiritual Exercises, every year; —his devotion to the daily Rosary, and—if I may use the expression—the pastoral quality of his speeches, his desire to be among the people as their leader in prayer, to attend popular feasts and processions; —his immense veneration for the Fathers of the Church, especially for Saint Ignatius of Antioch (the Theophorus, God-bearer) and for all those who fostered orthodoxy in doctrine; —his love of pastoral teaching for the reform of the social system. We can take the encyclical *Mater et Magistra* as an example;[2] —his concern for maintaining the integrity of the Faith of the Fathers, his predecessors, back to the Evangelists and to Jesus himself; —his motto *Obedientia et Pax*. This did not mean that he was empty-headed and thought that everything was just fine, like someone who cannot see the end of his nose and has no ideas of his own. No, it was the result of an inner struggle which is summed up in the Gospel's words *"abneget semetipsum"*, and in those of Saint Ignatius of Antioch: "It is better to be a Christian and not say so than to say so and not to be so";[3] —his love for priests, his positive attitude toward ecclesiastical celibacy . . . even to the point of tears! We can say this because we know it from his letters to his family, from one of his Spiritual Testaments, from his encyclicals dealing with other matters, for example, *Pacem in Terris,*[4] and from his defense of life and the family

...not to mention the obligations of his high Magisterium, which he felt profoundly. It may be said, and I am saying it now, that if Pope John had to write an encyclical on married love and human life such as Pope Paul VI has had to write, he would certainly have followed the same line of thought and might have been even stronger—his passionate love for children. In regard to this, I think it interesting that the first evening following the solemn opening of the Second Vatican Council, after speaking to the people who had gathered by torchlight in Saint Peter's Square, he bade them good night with the words:

> I now give you the blessing. Next to me I love to think that there is the Immaculate Virgin, whose lofty prerogative we are celebrating today [it was October 11th, the liturgical Feast of the Divine Motherhood]. I have heard that some of you have been recalling Ephesus and the torches that were lit around the basilica in that city on the occasion of the Third Ecumenical Council in 431. I saw the remains of Ephesus with my own eyes some years ago, which record the proclamation of the dogmas of Mary's Divine Motherhood...Love of God, love of the brethren. All, buoyed up now by the peace of the Lord, go forward together in good works!
>
> When you go home you will find your children. Give them a hug, and say: this is from the Pope. Perhaps you will find some tears needing to be dried. Have a word of comfort for those in pain.[5]

Looking at young people on another occasion, he exclaimed: "So much youthfulness—how can it be concerned only about the things of this earth?"[6]

All this goes to show that if Pope John were a revolutionary, he was one in the way of those who are in the Catholic Church and stay in her, not of those who leave!

In a word, he was no *progressivist.* But he was not a conservative either, nor a reactionary, not even a liberal; he was not a priest of the future, and not even one of the past. He was a priest of that priesthood of Jesus Christ, which is of yesterday, today, and forever!

In short: he was loyal to the past, open to the future, and loving toward both. In one word, he was *catholic,* in time, because he was most devoted to the memories of the past, above all, those of the Faith, but looked forward hopefully to a future more worthy of a human person, of the human family, of the temporal community, and of the Church herself.

This is why some curious characters find it magical that he was so *catholic* in his worldwide appeal, despite the fact that he was catholic in space, he was typically Italian, not to say Bergamese. No! He was *Roman,* in the broadest and noblest meaning of that word, in the sense that "Christ is Roman", because he shared the needs, sufferings, hopes, and yearnings of the whole world: in the Church, from the most aged cardinal to the youngest Bantu priest; in the human world community, from the highest to the lowest.[7] He shared the interests and labors of presidents and prime ministers as well as those of the most humble workers and peasants.

You may remember photographs of Pope John with President Eisenhower, both of them bursting with laughter, and seen by everyone; you may remember him with a child in a hospital on Christmas morning, both he and the child smiling; with the prisoners in the Regina Coeli jail in Rome, both he and they all smiles; with pilgrims from all over the world—always smiling. What was he smiling at? At the Church? No, no, never! At the world's problems? No, never! Behind those smiles was a heart full of anguish but also the patience of God!

That was because he knew that he and others could not solve the Church's problems and the world's problems on their own; but needed help from God, and the merits of the saints, those of the Madonna above all—they needed the wisdom of tradition, especially of the Faith. The real source of his joy was his joy in the Lord!

He it was who wrote on the occasion of Advent in the first year of his pontificate, to Cardinal Micara, Vicar General of Rome, saying: "Let us be brave, Eminence!" Later on, at Christmas, he said in Saint Peter's:

Our heart enters your homes, which are all lit up by the warmth of your expectation of the birth of the Divine Savior; it swells with tenderness, to offer you the greetings of our fatherly prayers and good wishes. We should like to remain by the tables of the poor, in the workshops, in the places of study and science, by the beds of the sick and the old, wherever people pray and suffer and work for themselves or others! Yes, we should like to lay Our hand on the heads of the little ones, look the young in the eyes, encourage mothers and fathers to do their daily duty! To all we should like to repeat the words of the Angel: "I bring you news of great joy; a Savior is born to you."[8]

From all this, we can easily see that Pope John never thought that *God is dead* and that the Church was in fatal crisis. On the contrary, he believed that the Lord is risen, that the Church is young, that the victory of Christ, of the Church, of the Faith, of Hope, and of Charity is all foreordained. He took seriously Christ's words: "I have overcome the world. . . . I will be with you even to the end of the world"; and the words of his namesake, the Apostle John: "The victory that overcomes the world: your faith."[9]

He was not revolutionary, certainly not against the Church and her structures, and still less a revolutionary against the Faith! What then was the secret of this man in whom all saw, if not the figure of a father, then perhaps that of a grandfather? All felt that about him: Catholics, Orthodox, Protestants, Jews, and atheists.

The secret was simple. He did not love that which we call *humanity*, because humanity of that sort does not exist. It is an abstract thing; it has no face, and no address to which we might send a letter of blame or good wishes, or a Christmas card, or a summons to call at the police station. Humanity has not a trade. Pope John loved *the person, all persons, any person.* Humanity, as such, does nothing good to us or bad to us; it is a concept and cannot be loved or hated by normal people.

Let me take an example. During the same week that I paid my first visit to Genoa and the Serra Club, I had gone to the Holy Father, John XXIII, about a problem existing in the United States at that time. I had been asked to talk over with him a problem that some bishops, notably Cardinal Meyer, were pondering. I was received in audience, as we say. I was a simple bishop, certainly unknown to the Pope! While waiting in the anteroom, I felt very worried and kept wondering what form of address I ought to use when speaking to him (you know I don't speak Italian very well!). But I had no chance, as it turned out, of choosing one of the respectful ways of addressing him, for the *Primate* of the Catholic Church began the audience by saying that he, the Pontiff, was happy to make my acquaintance. I was just an ordinary bishop, as I said, and definitely quite unknown to him.

We never got round to the problem about which I had come to Rome. Would you like to know why?

In order to put me at ease, he made a joke. "This name Wright", he said, "is impossible; no one knows how to pronounce it; it only has one vowel, and five consonants! It's like something out of a Russian novel."

He picked up a card from his desk. "Before the Bishop with the strange, almost unpronounceable name arrived, my experts put this here to warn me that, in order to safeguard my dignity, I ought to pronounce your name phonetically, using the sound of the abbreviation for Italian Radio and Television — RAI — and put a T at the end."

"They've given me all kinds of information," he went on, "so that I can know just as much about you as you know about me. That's another way of keeping my dignity. I see you were born in 1909; you were at the Gregorian, and you have been secretary—you poor unfortunate—to two archbishops. You have founded a diocese, the name of which is beyond me [Worcester], and were then transferred to the diocese of Pittsburgh. . . . "

I said, "Holiness, you sent me there!" He looked at the memorandum, saw the date of the transfer, and said, "You're right. So I did. But see what they did to me! I was once Patriarch of Venice! We priests are always being moved about."

He opened a drawer, took another card, and asked, "So you're at Pittsburgh? Is there a college there?"

"There are seven, Holiness", I said.

"Does one of them specialize in technology, a kind of technological institute?"

"Yes, Holiness; it's near where I live. It's called the Carnegie Institute."

"Really? Well, do you know a street called Fair Oaks Avenue?"

"Yes. Two streets from where I live."

"Good," he exclaimed, "there is a certain professor from Venice who is teaching in that Institute. He wants to marry a girl from Venice. She's a teacher too, but in the state of California. This professor saw my Venetian secretary's name with mine in the newspaper when I was elected Pope, and he has written to me to ask for an apostolic blessing for his marriage. My secretary could have gone into any shop around here and had a parchment sent to America, with the Pope's Blessing on it, and it would have been valid and genuine. Yet when he saw that the Bishop of Pittsburgh was down on the list of audiences for today, he asked me to send a medal personally, and a Blessing, some rosary beads, and various little souvenirs. Would you do that for me?"

I answered, "It will be a privilege."

But now came the incredible thing. In his holy simplicity, he asked, "Would you invite this young couple to your episcopal palace to give them these gifts in the Pope's name?"

I replied, "Holiness, I haven't any palace, but a fairly comfortable house—actually it's a bit big. But I'll phone the professor as soon as I get back, if you will tell me his name."

The Pope said, "The young lady lives in the state of California."

"Holiness, California is farther from Pittsburgh than Moscow is from Rome!"

"How on earth did they meet each other, then?" he exclaimed.

"Holiness, I don't know. May I mention again that I don't know their names."

"Ah! Yes! Well, here are their names and the date they are to be married. Invite them along, give them the Holy Father's gifts, and encourage them! Then, at the right moment, *ask them first whether they have been going to Sunday Mass; then suggest a good confession and lots of prayers before the nuptial Mass*"!

This was Pope John! And this was his secret! With all the problems that came to his desk, with all the anguish felt by Christ's Vicar, with all his preoccupations and concern for all the Churches, and . . . as we know now . . . with all his ailments —at that moment he was thinking *personally* how to encourage *two persons* in the *most personal* and pastoral of ways. For him, the center of the world (the whole moral universe) was always the person, starting from the divine person of Jesus the Lord, Son of the Living God, center and supreme object of his faith, Jesus living in the Holy Catholic Church, Jesus reflected in every person, in that of the professor, of his future bride, in *my* person, in *every person*.

The *person,* the teacher in the Carnegie Institute, his bride, the bishop, the priest, in the presence of Jesus Himself, they are never isolated from the Church. They not only belong to the Church, but in a very deep Catholic sense, they form part of it and through it are linked with Jesus Himself. The Church founded by Christ—and we must add, the institutional Church!

He joked, laughed, smiled, but never forgot that he was the Supreme Pontiff, Head of the Church, Christ's Vicar. Inevitably, like all the Roman pontiffs—not less than Pope Paul VI—he felt himself to be the guardian of the *institutional* Church, even though he saw himself, as does every Pope, as the Church's servant—*Servus Servorum Dei.* The *person* was not in the least abstract for him, and neither was the Church purely mystical, disincarnated, or abstract. It was also a Person whom one knows and loves, the Church instituted by the Lord Jesus, with the Holy Spirit as her soul, giving her the power to survive the crises of the centuries, even—if you will—those periods of triumphalism, which is nowadays described as a symptom of decline, or those periods of iconoclasm, which are not less sick. For him, the two basic things were the *human person* and *the Church,* including the institutional Church, as Christ willed and human nature demands.

For Pope John, for Pope Paul, for you—and truth to tell—for Jesus Himself, the link between the person and the institutional Church always includes the priest.

Pope John said, "Once this transcendence of religion above everything else has been guaranteed ['Christ did not take part in sports or politics', the Pope once remarked cryptically and in passing], the Pastor, whether he be Pope or country priest, will find that the people will come to him with ever less diffidence and with growing enthusiasm."[10]

The need of the hour is the rekindled hope that we shall always have priests like Father Serra, like Pope John, like Pope Paul, like Peter and Paul the apostles, like the best of your own parish priests and their associates. This is why Pope John respected the person and loved the Church. Now we can understand the words of a journalist describing Pope John's return from Ostia on March 24, 1963. He reported his exclamation: "So much youthfulness—how can they be worried only about the things of this earth?" and went on: "The Pope encouraged them to set their sights high, to the highest aim of all: *the priesthood.*"[11]

But, like the collegiality of bishops and the Church's whole life, this priesthood goes back to Peter, the Vicar of Christ. Peter's Successor has been there in every part of the Church's history, not as a juridical entity only but as the theological foundation of all the faith, hope, love, and unity which make the Church a community. It is so today—it will always be so. Now we can see how Pope John loved the person, the Church—and Jesus above all—from his earliest youth, and, though never dreaming that he should be Pope, loved the papacy too, passionately, with peace and obedience.

His former secretary, Monsignor Loris Capovilla, tells us in his book *The Heart and Mind of John XXIII* that the Pope's ideas about the papacy were extremely clear. Here are a few of them:

The history of the world in the millennium that preceded Christ and in the two millennia that have succeeded Him is contained in the two Testaments, which describe the relations between God and mankind.

In the Old Testament the Lord speaks to His beloved people, to whom He gave the task of preparing the world for the coming of His Universal Kingdom, the Church.

The confidant, the recipient, and the interpreter of the divine words was a man, the greatest man of ancient history: Moses.

God's light always shone in him. Everything takes its inspiration from him: the Patriarchs who went before him, the Judges, the Kings, and the Prophets who followed him. *Moses is the center of the Old Testament.*

In the New Testament, God resumes His relationship with man, but not with one race only: with all the peoples of the earth. This shows that the mystery of the Chosen People had been entirely revealed. The Lord, Who often and in various ways spoke to the Fathers in the Old Testament through the Prophets, now sent *His own Son,* Jesus Christ, God made man, in order to speak more clearly and with more majesty.

God sent Him to warn, to prepare the law that would be universal, to proclaim Himself the light of the world—the Way, the Truth, and the Life—and to seal with His own Blood the supreme sacrament of the inward union of the divine with the human. Christ's law is the holy rule of regenerated humanity, the everlasting Good News to be announced to all nations, both present and future.

Jesus, Son of God and Son of Mary, needed only thirty-three years to complete His mission. But at the time when His life was drawing to its close, He willed that His Presence should be extended into the centuries to come—through the two mysteries of the Eucharist and the Papacy.

Among His followers was one whom Jesus chose with great care: Simon, son of John. Jesus chose to call him Peter, as if through that one name and the image it suggests He wished to give greater prominence to the mission He would entrust to him. "And I say to thee, thou art Peter, and upon this rock I will build my Church, and the powers of hell shall not prevail against it. And I will give to thee the keys of the kingdom of heaven, and whatever thou shalt bind on earth shall be bound also in heaven, and whatever thou shalt loose upon earth shall be loosed also in heaven" (Mt 16: 18–19). And again: "Feed my lambs. . . . Feed my sheep" (Jn 21:15–17).

Just as in the Old Testament, Moses—Aaron's brother—was God's great confidant, lawgiver, and prophet, so also in the New Testament Peter is Prince of the Apostles, teacher, pontiff, and universal pastor. The world looked on with confidence when the Lord chose Peter. The choice raised Peter above his lowly origins.

The world received him with love; it admired him and wished to follow him.[12]

Was there, perhaps, some divine secret in Pope John's pontificate? Yes, there certainly was! But it is also Pope Paul's secret, for it belongs to the papacy itself. It is a special identity with the person of Christ.

But, you may well ask, what was the problem I had gone to him to discuss? The fact is that it had to do—and he knew it—with the staggering problem of vocations, the finding of new aides to the Pope and images of Christ. I had with me a bundle of sociological surveys, psychological studies, impressive statistics. The truly holy man never got around to them! After ardent promises and requests for prayer, he eased me on my way, sending pledges of prayer and pleas for yet more pastoral work to the worried bishops at home.

"What did the Pope say about our problem?" Cardinal Meyer asked when I phoned him that I was home. I could only reply that he had personally asked me to do a bit of pastoral work with a couple about to marry—and that he said my name was impossible to pronounce!

"Well, what about our problem and all those reports?" the scholarly American prelate persisted. I would only reply that the Pope clearly thought there was need for much prayer and lots more love of persons.

"Is that supposed to be the solution of this complex problem?" he asked wistfully. "I doubt it," I replied, "but the Pope seemed to think it was the unavoidable beginning."[13]

IV

Priesthood, Humanism, and the Cross

I am asked to speak this evening on the priesthood—which is a
vast subject, and humanism which is also a big subject, and the
Cross, the radiant shadow of which is across all history and
across all creation.

The first topical thing to be said about the priest in our day is
that he lives in a *secularized society.* This is certainly true of the
priests of the Western world, of whom I am one and therefore
whose life I know best. We might debate all day what we mean
by a *secularized society,* but I am assuming that when we speak of
a *secularized society* we mean a de-sacralized society. I am not
sure there was, in fact, a completely sacral society; certainly in
the last twenty centuries there has not been such a sacral society
in the Western world, although recently, it became fashionable
among some authors to pretend that there had been in order to
explain what they meant by more pluriform societies or regimes
of separation of Church and state. But one questions how *sacral,*
in reality, were the societies which were not actually theocratic.

Secularized implies that our society was formerly otherwise.
The idea that once there was a *sacral* society implies that there
was a society somehow gathered around the Church, priesthood,
the hierarchy, and the concept of the sacred as the core of the
society. But at all times, even the most religious, there were
certain phrases—as, for example, the secular arm and the *secular
power*—which argued the simultaneous presence of strong secular elements in the almost allegedly *sacral* periods. They were
part of a *secular* society surrounding, competing with, interacting
on a *sacral* culture.

This address was delivered, in Italian, at the Residenza Universitaria
Internazionale, Rome, Italy, on May 8, 1970.

78

Then, there is a suggestion that the work of the priest must be somehow different in our society than it was in earlier societies. Assuredly there are differences of approach to society and its problems. There are differences of emphasis in teaching or in service relationships to society; there are differences in techniques in different cultures and civilizations. But if the word *essential* may still be used in our age of phenomenology and existentialism, as, please God, it may, then the work of the priest, the work that is essential to the priesthood because the work of Jesus Christ, "yesterday, today, forever the same", is not a changing work.[1] It is not essentially different in America from what it is in Italy; it is not different in the twentieth century from what it was in the thirteenth century, or the fourth or the first century, so far as the essential work of the priesthood is concerned. Priests may look different to different generations of people, but they look the same to God at all times in all the essential aspects of their work.

The things that challenge the priesthood, the problems which especially confront the priest in one period of time, in one place or another, from one country to another, even from one city to another, even from one floor of the presbytery to the other, are all pretty much the same. There is nothing new about them. If you read the contemporary press, you find nothing especially different in the problems of the priesthood from what you read in the Acts of the Apostles written twenty centuries ago, but you find described the same essential priesthood and the same essential work. There are differences of what we might call the *problematic* of this same unchanging priesthood and therefore the members of the unchanging priesthood — the priests. The challenges that confronted Saint Paul, for example, who was not only a priest, but also a fairly respectable *theologian* even by our advanced standards, are those which confront us all. He talked about them all, celibacy, structures, moral lapses, indifferentism, and just about the whole bit.

He talked about conflicts of authority; another ecclesiastical preoccupation in every century and every place. He talked about avarice—some priests are tempted by avarice, some by the flesh, some by power, some by politics. And one way or another, Saint Paul finds all of them in his day pretty much as any routine review published by priests might do in our own times.

Essentially, the problem which confronted him was the problem of talking to a society that lacked the Catholic Christian Faith. Saint Paul talked to a generation that had never heard of the Christian or Catholic Faith and yet that, in a sense, was hyper-religious. When he talked to Athens, he said: I see you are very *religious* people; you have a host of gods! He said that he had come to talk to them about only one God, a God unknown to them. That was the problem of the priest in Paul's day: to establish the claims of the One God as against scores of gods in whom people devoutly believed.

Cardinal Newman tells us that in our generation we face almost precisely the reverse problem. We talk to people who *have been* Christians, who *have been* Catholics, and for whom—or for some of whom, and they influence the others to a great degree—the only God they know is dead; He has disappeared from their lives, so that they are religious, unreligious, or antireligious. The problematic that confronts the priest (and above all the bishop) is the problem that faced Augustine, namely, a changing culture, sometimes a crisis in culture, which he is unhappy to see go. This was the problem of Saint Augustine and Saint Jerome. It involves not a multiplicity of gods to challenge us, but a *Götterdämmerung* calling into question *all* religion and a multiplicity of other than religious interests.

So in our own day, many of us feel sad about the passing of the liberal arts culture, and classical culture, and we feel bewildered by certain aspects of the technological culture which appears to be replacing these. So do many priests; so do many laity, so much so that many have said that the problem of our day is not a crisis of faith, or a crisis of authority, or a crisis of hope, but a crisis of culture. This change has made some of our vocabulary and structures a little difficult to understand, to interpret, and to live with. It has also made the preaching of the Faith of our Fathers unclear to their grandchildren.

What does the priest bring to all this confusion? Everything he has in the way of personal gifts; but—let's be honest—these are relatively superficial. There are some *charismatic* personalities on the scene, but Cardinal Cushing, who has many and great charisms, used to observe that the charismatics, when they were tired, were like everybody else! They looked like everybody else, talked like everybody else, complained like everybody else. They were like the rest of us, made out of the slime of the earth. When they were consecrated priests, they held special posts, some high, some low, some extremely important, some unimportant, some obscure, some on the front page of the paper; but they had two eyes, one nose, two nostrils, one mouth, two ears, two hands, so much strength and so much grace, and by and large that constituted the most they brought to the service of the Church and God's people, except for an occasional insight of some special sort the charismatic importance of which it was for the Church to decide.

What, then, does the priest bring—I mean, the priest like you, like me, who may not be particularly charismatic, but plain priests, doing the best we can to straighten out the mess, beginning with ourselves. What does such a priest bring to the Church?

He brings a *witness,* a very special witness. Every baptized Christian brings that witness in a sense. As a matter of fact, there are a number of philosophers and poets that we call pagan who brought part, at least, of that witness. That is why Dante was accompanied by Virgil through much of the *Divine Comedy* back in the days of truly Catholic thought when it was recognized (not in the sense of Descartes, who made faith and reason so distinct, but in the sense of the Catholic "isms" which made them allies) that Virgil, too, was a witness to certain divine truths, certain human values, not, to be sure, the total truth brought into the world by the Incarnate Son of God, but put into the nature of things by the Creator. He was a witness, for example, to the natural law. Virgil bore witness to God; so did Homer; so did Aristotle, a witness so fascinating that we can easily be so fascinated by their philosophy as to be diverted from the greater witness brought into the world by the Son of God through revelation, as Pope Pius XI remarked. But in any case, in the Catholic view of things, these became friends: Reason and Faith. The God of Creation and the God of Redemption were seen as the same God. Father Karl Rahner has said that the great heresy of our day is due to the fact that many people think that the God of the Redemption is different from the God of the Creation, almost contradictory to Him, as, according to them, are Love and Law. Father Rahner points out that there are theologians who think not only that the God of Redemption is different from the God of the Creation, but that they are almost enemies of one another. The God of Creation was the God of the Old Testament, juridical, legalistic, speaking in negative terms, as *Thou shalt not steal, Thou shalt not commit adultery.* Whereas the God of Redemption doesn't talk in terms of duty and of obligation (so they say), nor does he insist on laws. He talks only in terms of love, of mercy, of identification with the sinner, rather, perhaps, even than of healing him, lest feelings be hurt by telling a man he's out of order, that he has violated the natural law, and that you love him so much you're going to tell him what the law is in the hope that, having chosen to obey it, he may love you in return, and others as well, and also God.

But the priest is sent specifically to bring us a special, unique relationship to God, the knowledge of the *Sacred* — sacred truth, sacred love, sacred beauty. Jesus Christ stood in the midst of men as the *sacred* made living, and put at the service of all those whom He could reach. The ordained priesthood, as distinct from the general priesthood of the laity, has the same function; and — like Jesus Christ — and this is worth meditation in the light of certain current controversies: he is expected to bear witness unto the crucifixion of his flesh, twenty-four hours a day, seven days a week, fifty-two weeks a year. *He must not divide his heart.* His life must be as nearly as possible the imitation of Jesus Christ, totally. Living under a law that is motivated by love, and that results in service — service of many, many different kinds — beginning sometimes with sitting by the bedsides of the sick when no one else would go near them, because it is a time of epidemic. But also the service of preaching the Truth, unashamed, unqualified and no matter how unpopular it may prove. This service made Jesus Christ extremely unpopular; it cost John the Baptist his head, and the first apostles, save one, were put to death for their imitation of the uncompromising witness of Christ.

Moreover, the priest has an ontological connection with this personification of the sacred in Christ Jesus. As a result, he lives in every culture — liberal arts, philosophical, developed, on the way to development, technological — as a man who is *distinct* but not *separate* from all the people around him.

That distinction requires that the priest have certain characteristics. We have chosen — I think wisely — to state those characteristics in terms of a type of *humanism* because every age, every culture sooner or later develops a species of humanism — which means a scale of values, a priority of loves, an order among the things that one thinks important. At the basis of every serious humanism, there is the idea that these choices are not necessarily mutually exclusive, but are synthesized or integrated in a way of life which, if it is truly humane, we call *humanistic.*

There have been types of humanism which have been somewhat less than humanistic, but which bore the name of *humanist.* For example, there is a certain natural humanism. One of the great pagan poets summed that humanism up in a single line, a line that is still valid if it be fully understood: *I am a man, a human, and nothing human is foreign to me.*[2] Pursued far enough in its implications, it would lead to an authentically Christian humanism, because if it took into consideration all the needs of a man, it would take into consideration his eternal longings, his spiritual capacity, his need for God, his destiny for eternity. These would not be *alien* to the pagan humanist, but a part of him. This natural humanism, however, all too often has not taken into consideration the supernatural, the spiritual, the need for grace. This would obviously be an inadequate humanism for the priest, who has to reflect the sacred to us, stand in the midst of men, distinct but not separate, even as Jesus was distinct but not separate from mankind. Sometimes this natural humanism has taken on an artistic form, and so we had some great periods of art, even in the Christian centuries, when the art was the creation of men who were of relatively little faith, relatively little morality, weak in their commitment to Christianity and appreciation of the sacred that integrates the truly human and super-adds the divine.

This became true even of some priests. Indeed, it became true of some bishops. I shall mention bishops only at a safe distance of space and time. It was certainly true of Talleyrand; only at the last minute did he remember that his hands had been anointed with sacred oil, that he was a *sacred* thing. You remember, in the description of his deathbed, how he turned his hands over and said: I should be anointed *here;* I am a priest!

There is also a humanism that is technological, and, in proper relation to the sacred, it may yet become our salvation. During the synod, this thought was powerful in my mind when the astronauts, who had just walked on the moon, gave a talk to the cardinals and other prelates present in the synod.[3] When one of the members of the College of Cardinals asked if walking on the moon and seeing the world in the perspective of all space, seeing the depth of space and the planets as no man had ever seen them before, had had any effect on their spiritual lives, one astronaut said: "I will answer for all three." He implied that in answering for all three, he was answering for all astronauts, even those who cannot talk about spiritual things in public and are obliged to tell the press that during their journey they didn't meet any angels and didn't see God!

He spoke of the kindness of the Pope in providing special

guides through the Vatican Museum, the Sistine Chapel, Saint Peter's—and added that all the beauty of the work of human hands in the Vatican Museums, all the ecstasy of the work of Michelangelo in the Sistine Chapel, and all the wonder of the dome and the splendor of Saint Peter's—all these together are as nothing to the beauties that God has prepared for those who love Him. Virtually the words of Saint Paul, but on the lips of an astronaut! One felt that a synthesis is underway whereby technological humanism will become a complete humanism, scientific in its premises, spiritual, even Christian, in its conclusions.

There is, of course, a literary humanism that has paralleled this scientific humanism: the humanism of Petrarch, of Dante, of Shakespeare, the humanism of I know not what authors in the Eastern civilizations. These have been humane but inadequate humanisms when they left out values never alien to the complete man. They emphasized many things that are essential to the *happy* men here below, but some literary humanists leave out many things that are not alien to man, in terms of Terence's phrase: *I am a human, therefore nothing is alien to me.* [4] The need of God is human; the knowledge of God is human; faith makes its contribution to a human exigency, a human demand.

Then there have been certain mystical humanisms; there have been some types of *angelistic* attitudes which are excessively unworldly; they leave out some of the things which shouldn't be alien to a man. Some *supernatural* humanisms have consisted in a species of *fuga mundi,* a flight from the world, even a contempt of the world in a false sense, since it is possible to *renounce* but never to *despise* the beauty, truth, and valid goodness that God has created. We are told, in the first pages of Sacred Scripture—as the astronauts reminded us when they looked at the globe from the moon, that when God looked upon the work of His hands, He found it *good.* There have been some *mystics* who didn't quite agree with Him!

And so, a complete humanism finds place for whatever things are noble, true or beautiful; that place may be subordinate, even incidental, but it is a true place in the total reality, the total object of our love, the total truth, the total validity that we welcome as the work of God the Creator, a created good and sometimes made by us an occasion of sin, but made holy by the Creator, hallowed yet more by God the Redeemer.

Thus humanism is the humanism of Saint Paul, who, just as Terence for the pagans, summed up in one line the essence of humanism for the Christian when he said: "All things are yours, but you are Christ's and Christ is God's", which is to say: All things are yours, if you use them in accordance with the will of Christ and, thus, unto the glory of God.[5]

Such, in substance, is the humanism you and I shall be talking about when we speak about the humanism of the good priest, and, nowadays, of the *stable* priest. Wherever you find an insecure priest, suffering from an identity crisis, some one of those things is missing: and he has forgotten that he belongs to Christ, and that Christ is of God, so that all these things may safely be his, to use for God's purposes and in accordance with the sacrality which is his as a man distinct but not separate from the people of God whom he serves.

So, what is the function of Christian humanism? Why are we attaching such importance to the Faith lived in a humanistic way of life: music, books, arts, things which our generation tends to downgrade a bit? Have you noticed the tendency to make churches as bare as possible? Have you been disturbed by the apparent pleasure in music as unmelodious as possible? Has it occurred to you that sometimes there seems a conscious effort to make the proposition which should be crystal-clear in its truth, as mystifying as possible?

What is the function of the Christian humanist? It is, in part, to synthesize experiences into a humane pattern, a sane formula for living. The function of the priestly humanist is obviously to reconcile heaven and earth, nature and grace—if I may evoke a neglected distinction, grace and nature—God and man, time and eternity, all in the pattern of the one High Priest, Jesus

86

Christ. In whatever sense, let us recognize that these are distinct from one another and that there is a necessity to reconcile them; that they are not all one thing; that everything is not material, nor is everything spiritual; everything isn't sacred in the same sense, and no work of God is entirely *profane;* but that all things, visible and invisible, encompassed by the Incarnation, can be reconciled in a divine humanism which makes provision for the beauty, the goodness, the validity of each creature and yet for the harmony of all. A function of the priest is to achieve this harmony by pointing out how all things are ours, but may not be ours forever. But that we are Christ's so long as we adhere to His Faith and values, taught by nature but not by nature alone; delightful to reason but transcending reason even on the level of *nature,* since the heart has its reasons that the head does not understand.[6] Moreover, the total person, the total soul, has its requirements and reasons that the body must find difficult to meet unaided by grace and one's higher self.

So, again, the function of the truly humanistic priest (and he need not be a *professional intellectual*) is to show how all things are ours, if we use them according to the will of Christ and for the glory of God and service of His people, to reconcile those things which are disparate, even apparently opposed. He does this in a thousand ways. He may do it by the sheer example of his holy patience. The best confessor I knew in years gone by had not left his wheelchair for twenty-three years; but he reconciled countless people to God and to one another; and the things that they had found evil, in the sense of occasions of sin, obstacles in the way of their perfection, he turned into means of frequently heroic sanctity. He never travelled from nation to nation nor gave startling lectures on how to solve the theological or political crises of the moment, but he bore his witness, that of Jesus Christ, and built whole lives in the pattern of Christ.

I know one priest who is deaf and dumb; but he bears a fantastic witness. He lost his voice under the influence of gas in the Second World War, and he bears his witness by his writings and his actions, by writing of beauty, truth and goodness, of Christ and God and all the people of God he has met in his life, and he visits prisons and the poor with heroism, holiness, and humanism obviously elevated by God's grace.

So, the function of the priest is preaching, above all at the moment, proclaiming God's message, with the liturgy and the sacrifice of the Mass as the core and crown of his preaching and his own good works as its proof—not necessarily highly structured works since these, in the absence of sheer kindness, easily become a burden if highly programmed. The poor are often weary of being the object of our *benevolent* programs, and above all our *researches* into their personal problems. But by personal kindness and good works done in the spirit of Jesus Who—to the best of my knowledge—sponsored no research projects, took no courses in sociology, and did not work for the government welfare department. He went to the ordinary synagogue of any town in which he found himself and preached to the people in any marketplace, and he went through the cities and towns simply *doing good.* By ordinary works, the humanistic priest, perpetuating that example, achieves the synthesis of things human and things divine, as did Christ.

By His incarnation, Christ came into the world to unite all of heaven and all of earth. We hear that sung again and again at Christmas Mass: the reconciliation of man with God, of faith with reason, of man with man, and of all in Christ.[7]

Before the priest can be Christ in our midst, there are certain characteristics he must possess; the rest of our reflections will be concerned with these, though not with all of them—that would take a four-year course in theology, a several-year stay in the seminary. A Jewish doctor giving a conference on this point said wisely that it all boils down to the *job* the priest has to do; that it is this *job* which unifies all his other interests and puts them all to work; it is this job that makes him like to Christ, not in the sense that the priest is a *functionary,* a spiritual civil servant, but that he has a work to do, a mission to accomplish.

Christ came with a *mandatum* — but I hesitate to use the word *mandatum* in speaking of priests in these days of frenzied freedom and suspicion of authority. So one simply says he has a task, whether it is a task given him by God, as in a vocation — a *vocation* as opposed to a mere *job* — a task that doesn't require much *job analysis* to know what it is. It is a task that arises out of the nature of things, the very needs of the people, the human instincts and contradictions of the decent man. It is a *humanistic* task, hallowed by ordination, through which he brings the divine to earth. Before he can do this, the first and fundamental fact — and I am almost embarrassed in mentioning it — is that he must be a man, a mature person.

I am not here entering into the debate on the ordination of women. Even if only historically the priest happens to be a man. He wears a man's clothes — and he wears such male clothes even when he wears a soutane that identifies him as distinct but not separate from other men. The soutane says merely: I am a priest, as others are not. It also says: I am a man apart, not as a *professional*, but as Aaron was.

Most rectories do not yet have answering services on the telephone, as offices of *professionals* tend to do. One always grows anxious when priests talk about being a *professional* group and having a *professional* standing. One begins to hope this doesn't mean people will have to talk to a stenographer or middleman before they can talk to the priest. Will he have an answering service during the night, so that someone else will give him the message that I need him *here and now,* because I am about to face God? Will he have trade union regulations saying that he is available from nine to five, but if I fall into serious need at eight o'clock I must die in it rather than interfere with him, because he has *professional* standards to observe. The priest must be available twenty-four hours a day, seven days a week, fifty-two weeks a year, even if for wise reasons, willed by God, and according to the heart of Christ, he is on vacation, even if he withdraws into the desert for prayers and, I suspect, such rest as even Jesus did. Remember, the Scriptures tell us He was tired. If He was tired, then He withdrew to the mountain for rest, without offending His sacred vocation. But He remained *available;* and, even on the mountainside, His preoccupation was with the people.

The priest begins by being a *man.* If he is less than a man, he will never be wholly worthwhile; he may be ordained but he won't be a complete priest. Cardinal O'Connell once said: "You can pour holy oil and holy water on a thug until you have emptied buckets of both; but at the end he will be a consecrated thug, but a thug all the same unless interior intentions and a disciplined man are present." So, one begins with the *man,* a complete *man.*

Here one intrudes an anecdote, guardedly and with great discretion. Not long ago there came to see me an unhappy priest who had gone through a civil marriage. I give no clue which would make it possible to identify the nation from which he came. I exclude Italy and the United States. Pick China, if you will; the population is the largest there, and it will take the longest time to find the case. The unhappy priest had abandoned the priesthood to go through with his civil marriage. At the end of our conversation, he said: "Would you be willing to see my wife? She is in the next room, waiting." This was in the Congregation for the Clergy, and I suppose she was the first woman who had come to discuss the priesthood in that Congregation. He said: "She would like to talk to you, but she has made one condition upon which she insists, and that is that she talk to you alone." I said I would be happy to see her.

He opened the door of the waiting room, and his wife came in. She walked by him as if he did not exist; as a brother priest, one felt badly about it. She closed the door, and then did a significant thing, also heartbreaking: she quickly opened the door to see if he were listening and, when she found that he was not, but in fact was at the opposite end of the room, she said to him: "Go and wait for me at the end of the corridor!"

She then pointed to me, after she was sure no one could hear her, and she used the title of the letter by Emile Zola: *J'accuse.* I asked what I had done, since I had never met her or the priest before. She said: "I don't accuse you *personally.* But I accuse you as the representative of an institution, the *institutionalized* church. In God's name, why did you ordain *that?*"

I said I had not ordained him. She replied: *"Somebody did!"* Then she added: "Two weeks after we were married, I discovered that I had not married a *man;* I had adopted a *small boy.* I had an adolescent on my hands, a mixed-up kid".

With mounting fury, she said: "The other day, while going through his possessions, I found a letter addressed to the Pope, asking if he could be laicized with permission to marry me, because *I* wish to return to the sacraments. I don't know whether *he* wishes to do so or not, but I do wish to return to the sacraments, and he knows it. So, he wrote a letter to the Pope." Then she added: "I have come to urge that the Pope *not* grant the dispensation, because if the dispensation is granted, I might have to marry him in the Church. *And then I am stuck, I am finished.* As it is now, my plan is this: I think I love him, although it would be more exact to say I pity him. I am willing to take two years to make a man out of him. Then I am going to put him out, and I am going back to the sacraments and back to my work of teaching. I am going to try to make him enough of a man so that he will understand that I am kicking him out for his own good. As it is now, if I kicked him out, he'd cry on the street; he'd dissolve, and that would be unjust. I, too, have a grave fault to atone for—but it is you, the Church, that *j'accuse* for ordaining an *immature man!*"

Was she just in her *J'accuse?* I wish I could say she was not. But everyone knows too many cases of clergy who have traveled on a kind of treadmill through the seminary, with no one really knowing them, no one asking them their most intimate desires;

no one ever talking with them about the things that make a man (and they are not all sexual, please God). A man is a sexual animal, but he also is a rational animal. He is a mystical animal; uniquely, he is a laughing animal. There are scores of aspects of manhood that have nothing to do with sexual desires, but which have a lot to do with the mature exchange of funny stories, with mature conversations about history, politics, philosophy, all the things that interest a man. I suppose that even interest in sports is a constitut element of a man. But this was not a complete man, and no one knew that better than the woman who married him. She said: "We have nothing to talk about; we sit and look at the television until my eyes are blind. He isn't stupid; it's just that he hasn't ever been awakened intellectually. He is not mature."

So, the first point about the humanistic priest is that he is a *man*. Second, the humanistic priest is a *man of love,* love to the point of self-annihilation, not individualistic self-fulfillment alone. The test of love is not whether you feel fulfilled; more often it is whether you are prepared to annihilate yourself. For all the people who are fulfilled by their marriage, there are others who are sorrowed or feel frustrated in their marriage, as the man who is married to a cancer patient or whose children may have brought him disillusion, but they are at ease because at one with God's will.

But we are speaking now of the Christian order of things, Christian humanism, Christian love, the love that finds in the glory of the Cross the key to its riddles and the point of its pain, when these inevitably reveal their presence in a life of self-giving. The priest who dies at his post, exhausted by his work, or the priest who deliberately seeks out those who are likely to be contagious in their sickness or thankless in their irremediable frustration or folly—is this not love? It is self-fulfillment, very much so, but only in a Christian sense, a mystical sense; otherwise, it involves self-annihilation, in the pattern of Christ Jesus. The love in such a priest puts him always, again like Christ Jesus, on the side of life. Jesus described Himself as having *"come that they may have life and have it more abundantly".* [8] He came to hallow life, to make every form of life more beautiful, but, above all, more holy.

Hence the reason why no mere external *imitation* but an ontological relationship to Christ must be the basis of the identity between the priest and Christ. It is also the reason why the humanism of the priest, as of all believers but for even greater reason, must be *Christocentric* or *incarnational.* It is bound up with the joy of the Paschal Mystery and yet the suffering of the crucifixion. The humanism of the priest involves a paradox: the greatest joy imaginable and the greatest renunciation possible: the joy of the Risen Jesus and the Church around the Risen Jesus, and yet the suffering of the Crucified Christ. Precisely as Saint Paul proclaimed: *I shall glory, but only in the Cross of Christ. I must crucify my flesh;* and yet: *All things are mine, for I am Christ's and Christ is God's.* [9]

Robert Hugh Benson, though perhaps not so much a great theologian as a theological preacher, describes the ontological connection between the ordained priest and Christ about as well as it can be described, saying that when the priest, preaching from the pulpit says, "I say to you", that must never be understood as: "I *personally* say to you", "I *individually* say to you", but must mean "*Christ* says to you." [10] Is it unfair to suggest that many of us priests have forgotten that truth and are preaching ourselves, rather than Christ? The ontological nature of the priesthood is such that when one says: "*I* say to you", he is really saying, or should be saying, "*Christ* says to you". So when the priest says in the sacrament of penance: "*I* absolve you", what arrogance it would be to pretend that *he* absolves you. What he means is: "*Christ* absolves you: *I* act for *Christ,* ontologically united to Him. It is not merely a *function* that I have to go about absolving or reconciling people: It is a *power,* a living *energy* I have by reason of my oneness with Jesus in the form of being called priesthood." This is why one cautions in the face of talk about the priest as a *professional* and the priesthood as *self-fulfillment* or a function. When we hear the priest at the altar say:

"This is *my* body, this is *my* blood", we do not for a moment think that these are *his*. It is not *his* body, not *his* blood. *He is talking as one with Christ.*

This ontological union with Christ is so intimate, so profound, so indissoluble, that one finds it difficult to use the word *laicize.* One understands *dispensed from obligation,* but when someone says: I'd like to be *laicized,* it is hard to know what the word means. It is like resigning from the human race: Where should the letter be sent by one who wishes to forfeit life or no longer be a human. How is one debaptized? One may forgo his priestly exercise or functions, but the initial union with Christ is ontological and therefore forever.

The humanistic priest is *incarnational* in the sense that he is identified with Jesus in all that Jesus took upon Himself. Father Battista Mondin, in his book *L'Uomo e il Mondo; il Cristo e la Chiesa,* discusses briefly but admirably the three possible types of humanism, namely, the efforts to reconcile the sacred and the profane, the things of this world and the things of heaven, things human and those divine. He points out that in history there have been certain distinct approaches to the *reconciliation* of these. There has been a *secularist* tendency, a *sacralist* tendency, and an *incarnationalist* tendency in working out a humanism.

The most common tendency in our days is the *secularist* tendency, secular humanism. Father Mondin notes that among theologians, at any rate, certainly those of good faith—and good faith, like innocence, must always be presumed until the contrary is proved—even the secularist tendency has, in fact, an evangelical purpose. One reason which has brought the concept into such prominence in our days, even among priests, is the wish, even if not always fully conscious, to use a secular service, even work for secular agencies, to render the message of the gospel more intelligible and more accessible. Words are used like *intelligible* and *interesting* because they are *significant* to a society so exclusively secular in its premises, spirit, and purposes. So the *secularist* who remains a believer says his desire is to make the

94

gospel message somehow meaningful to a generation which, like ours, has lost contact with the dimension of faith and recognizes only values which are empirical and *of this world, scientific.*

Faith too, however, is a form of knowledge. It invites research and involves adventure and experience. But it is also bound up with literally infinitely more than any possible secular approach; it involves revelation, listening to Jesus Christ and to the Holy Spirit. It is never merely *doing.* The Scriptures tell us: *Jesus began to do and to teach.* [11] Both words are essential to the task and the witness which Jesus came to begin and which the priest uniquely perpetuates. If either be missing, the experience of our priesthood is incomplete. So is our humanism.

Then there is a *sacralist* tendency. Father Mondin contends this is a reaction—and perhaps it is—to the secularist, activist temperament of the times. The present writer regrets that Father Mondin lists here Maritain, who in the days of my youth was my great hero in what pertains to humanism and the dignity of the person. [12] But Mondin feels that Maritain has reacted so strongly against the embracing of the profane that he had become *sacralist.*

Incarnationalist humanism avoids both *integralism* and *mere activism* and—we have tried to say—in the words of the ancient Mass, calls upon us to use the goods of this world so that we may enjoy the goods which are eternal. [13] This is the very heart of Christian humanism and is made possible by the Incarnation's hallowing of all things, of which the priest is the witness and the agent for Christ, as Christ is the agent for God.

What, in such a humanism, are the other qualities of the priest? We can mention them briefly. The problem of Christian humanism—and it does have a terrible problem—is present in the life of every believer, but, above all, that of priests. The front pages, especially of the sensational publications, are filled with the *tensions* of some priests. It is only the journalists who have so recently discovered them; the rest of us have known them all our lives. Our spiritual forefathers knew them well; some broke under them, though many returned to their priesthood, having

95

retained their ontological union with Christ. The basic problem of Christian humanism is real; it is easy to flee from the world; to hide in the mountains and forget it all, *letting them fight it out among themselves.* But the contemporary priest, who must be in the midst of it all, in the midst of the fight, distinct but not separate, suffers from the problem of Christian humanism expressed unforgettably by Gertrude Von le Fort. She spoke of the *terrible tensions of the devout,* the devout layman like Thomas More and millions of others, priests included. *The terrible tension of the devout puts the Incarnation, the Cross, and the Resurrection at the heart of incarnational humanism.*

We priests may have become so self-conscious as to think that we are the only ones who suffer from it. What about the women who devote their lives—outside the convent—to careers in the world in which they remain virgins? What about the men who, as artists or scientists, or ordinary layfolk, live and love the law of God? What about *their* tension? Saint Paul acknowledged it, speaking of two laws constantly working inside him. Saint Augustine felt it, saying: *I have only one heart, but it is drawn in diverse directions.* But he kept it all subordinate to Christ and the will of God.

How often Christians have forgotten how our loves must be subordinated and reconciled to one another. In one of the galleries of the Borghese Palace, there is a painting called *Sacred and Profane Love.* It shows Sacred Love at one end of a bench and Profane Love at the other, both facing in opposite directions. Assuming that the distinction between the two Loves is not one of morals, it is the function of the priest to reconcile these. We have only one heart, not two. We do not have a heart with which we love the world, and another with which we love God. We have one heart, and within that one heart we have to work out our priorities. That, again, is the essence of Christian *humanism.*

In one of the galleries of the Vatican Museum, there are two great paintings that never fail to bewilder me, at least from the point of view of our present subject. One is called *The School of*

Athens. Separated from it by a door there is another painting of a group called: *The Dispute about the Sacrament.* In one painting, there are the philosophers, all those who live by *reason.* In the other painting, there are the saints, the mystics, those who live by *faith.* I often wish one could mix them a bit, get some of the saints into the *School of Athens,* and some of the philosophers into the *Dispute about the Sacrament.* This is the task of the humanistic priest: to bring together sacred and profane love; the work of the God of Creation, and the work of the God who is the Redeemer, Reason and Faith together.

Next, the humanistic priest is a man of *compassion* — not only a man of charity in the sense of *bountiful* which that holy word has come to have. Compassion is very different from both charity and sympathy.

Bruno Scott James, an English priest who identified himself for years with all poor students in Naples, describes the humanistic priest in terms of *compassion.* He says: *Charity has a child like unto itself, and this child we call Compassion. It is not Charity, but it is a child of Charity, the Effect of Charity on a man when confronted with the human condition.*

It is, then, the virtue whereby a person is inspired to give himself to others, to share in their sufferings while doing his utmost to alleviate them. It is a virtue of the strong, because the weak are too fearful of themselves to have *compassion,* though they may have charity: they dare to give away things, but they do not dare to *identify,* as the compassionate must.

It was compassion that brought Christ down from heaven to earth. From the materialistic point of view — and, I might add, from the governmental or political point of view — compassion may well seem useless; it is a waste of energy more often than not. It is true that the compassion of Saint Francis, when he kissed the leper, did not heal the leper's body, but it may well have healed his soul. By compassion, we strengthen ourselves; no one gives himself in compassion without receiving; and when we empty ourselves for others, in the example of Christ, we receive in measureless abundance from the Father. As reported in the translations of Scripture cherished by our Fathers, Jesus did not say: "I have *charity* for the multitude", but "I have *compassion* on the multitude."[14]

Finally, the humanistic priest is a man of learning. Saint Francis de Sales speaks of the learning appropriate to their times which must characterize every generation of priests. In an age of philosophy, the priest must be a philosopher; in an age of technicians, he must have not only an interest in but a sympathetic knowledge of what technology is attempting. He must have this not merely to temper the inevitable tendency to *scientism* and technocracy, but, above all, to be able to relate it to his task, which is reconciliation, the reconciliation of all extremes.

The humanistic priest is a man of faith, and therefore he subordinates his knowledge, however great, to the Faith. When this is stated in concrete terms of subordinating one's theology to the Magisterium, some necks begin to stiffen. And yet when this is stated in the terms of Saint Francis de Sales, the subordination of one's personal theological speculations to the authentic teaching of the Church on faith and order takes on a different aspect.

In this connection, one places great hope in the new document published by the Sacred Congregation of the Seminaries and in the documents on the continuing education of priests published by the Congregation for the Clergy, as well as the document of the Council on the priesthood. If we are faithful to these, we will be what the old *minor orders* proclaimed that we must be, for example, men who can *read.* The old Order of Lector told us that we must not merely read to the people, but read *intelligibly,* so that they will understand what we are saying. It told us we must study the Sacred Writings, above all the Bible. But it did not confine our readings to this; we must read the lives of the saints, we must read the theologians, and the wise men of all times and cultures.

One thinks here of the beautiful line in Dante, where the

chorus of angels sing as they see Dante approaching: Here is one who will increase our love. How? By the things he will tell them about the earth; by the things he will tell them of life of a totally different order, but still God's work and the expression of His majestic power and creative love.

Every man who seeks to be a humanistic priest, without falling victim to the terrible tensions of the devout life, must build within himself what I shall call *an island within*. Probably most of us have dreamed of owning an island where he can retire when the battle is too fierce, the tensions too great. The favorite island of my dreams was on a lake. I have never even visited it, but I have thought a lot about it, and I have often been tempted to think that I would like to withdraw there, particularly when the debate becomes futile and the attack unfair or even battle-fatiguing. For such crises, a wise author of years ago speaks of the necessity for an *island within* on which, from the first moment we begin our education, we store up all the poetry and music we can hear, all the books we can read, all the art we can see, all the friendship we can cherish, all the lively conversations we can hold, against the day when the tension is so unbearable and the temptation so overwhelming that we need, briefly at least, to withdraw to the *island within* and enjoy the goodness, truth, and beauty stored up there through all the years of our formation.

We have already noted that the humanistic priest is a man of joy, joy in the Faith, which means in Christ. Again I appeal to Saint Paul as a theologian: humanism without Christ is joyless. If you doubt it, look at the faces of the grim *dissenters* who have become fashionable. If only they would smile! After all, this is not the first time there have been crises in the priesthood. A dear friend of mine, a man to whom I owe much in my own formation, broke with the Church under the tension of *Modernism* in its 1911 form. He tried to form a religion of *humanism without Christ, humanism without the Faith.* But in his old age, he wrote an article, a carbon copy of which he gave me and for which

99

during the Council I sent home. His article was entitled: *Is Humanism a Religion?* After all these years of trying to make it one, he summed up his experience in this sentence: *The first curse of the Almighty on those who deny Him is to deprive them of their sense of humor.* He went on in later articles to tell how grim, earnest, purposeful, reforming, and unhappy is the life that leaves out Christ and Him crucified. Of course, there is a paradox in all this; but it is the paradox, again, of the joy of Easter and the suffering of Good Friday.

One is deeply convinced that the lack of maturity, revealing itself in the so-called crisis of identity, of which some priests have said that they are the victims, is due to the fact that we have forgotten these simple things: that the priest must be a *man;* he must reconcile *loves;* he must establish *priorities;* he must not annihilate anything except himself when priestly *love* demands it; he must not despise anything that God has made, and must not fail to reverence all that God the Redeemer has hallowed. From these things he acquires that quality which is the special characteristic of the humanistic priest, the total priest. I refer to the virtue of stability.

We live in an unstable world. Because of our attachment to the Church, we like to reflect on the stability of the Church. *Stat crux dum volvitur orbis!* [15] We therefore become disturbed at signs of instability in the household of the Faith. But there is instability in every family; there is instability in every business house, in every profession. There is instability in the universities. Is it unfair to say that there is a certain instability in every government on the face of the earth?

In such a moment of history, the priest is a model — or should be — of *stability* in an unstable world. Let me offer one anecdote, and with it conclude these considerations. It comes from a neutral source. Miss Dorothy Thompson, a noted American writer, journalist, and critic, wrote an article on the results of a painstaking investigation she made in the concentration camps after the overthrow of Nazism. [16] Many of the lessons that she learned in this study of the concentration camps are very relevant for us. For example, she discovered the superficial nature of the culture of the people who built these places. She tells about visiting the comfortable villa of a total savage, which was decorated in exquisite taste. On the bedside table, there was a book by Thomas Mann and a book by Jack London—God knows how those two were brought together, but they were both there. There was a hi-fi set. Less than one hundred yards away, was one of the principal crematories for the destruction of Jews, gypsies, Polish people, and priests! How superficial the culture! How close to the surface the savagery!

But the most dramatic lesson that the journalist carried away was this. She asked one question of the people who had survived the horrors of the concentration camp: many Jews, some intellectuals, many political personalities—from Italy, France, Germany, Hungary, Poland. She asked all this question: In the midst of all the hell that was the concentration camp; surrounded by all the horror rife in these prisons, horrors that depersonalized, destroyed personality and sanity, as well as health, what group remained sane the longest? What group of people remained useful the longest? What group of people—note carefully this—retained their sense of *identity* the longest? What people were the last to suffer from a crisis about *why* they were alive, or *who* they were, or *what* was their task? What group, what nationality, what profession, what race, forgot themselves and their problems so that they could serve the others who had the same problems? She said the answer was almost invariably: *the Catholic priests.*

Now, who were those priests? Well, one was Father Ricquet, the Notre Dame preacher. Many were Polish country pastors. Others were German and Austrian priests, some were Italians. How did they keep their sanity? How did they keep their *sense of identity?* How did they keep their *stability?* How did they remain *civilized* when everyone else was going mad? They did it because they knew what their *vocation* was, what their *task, their part in the total scheme of things, their relationship to Jesus Christ* who, once dead, dies now no more; they had some intuition into their relationship to the plan and the Providence of God. They had their priority of values and loves. Their commitment was total— and single. They knew who they were and why. In a word: they were *priests*.

V

Interview with Alex Kucherov

Kucherov: Your Eminence, you once said that Christianity is
            in for difficult times ahead. Is that still your feeling
            on the basis of what you have seen since coming
            into the Vatican?

Wright: It is. In fact, when I was in Pittsburgh, I described
            the coming crisis in terms of a *winter* that was
            approaching—winter for Christianity, winter for
            belief—a much longer period than a decade or
            two.[1] I could well imagine its lasting the rest of
            this century, or until something cataclysmic hap-
            pens that would cause a whole new direction.

Kucherov: What about the Vatican Council? Wasn't that sup-
            posed to bring renewal to Roman Catholicism?

Wright: I don't think Pope John XXIII called his Council
            in the spirit of lighthearted optimism that is super-
            ficially attributed to him. He called the Council—
            and deliberately invited to it the Protestant leader-
            ship and the Orthodox leadership—so that he could
            line up some seed ideas that could be planted under
            the hard ground of the winter that lies ahead and
            that could mature in common Christian dialogue
            for blossoming in the eventual and inevitable spring
            of a renewed faith, when the ancient values of the
            gospel would make their synthesis with the new
            technology—and more particularly with the atti-
            tudes induced by the new technology.

            You see, for a long time we lived in a liberal-

This interview was published in the August 31, 1970, issue of *U.S. News and World Report*.

	arts civilization. The great universities of England, the United States, Germany, France were liberal-arts universities. They've been replaced in the main by technological institutes, by technology—which is to say that the sense of *know why* has yielded to the sense of *know how*. Now, this brings with it inevitable changes of attitude.
Kucherov:	What kinds of changes?
Wright:	Once people know how to do things they develop the idea that since they can do them maybe they shall. And when they've decided they shall there develops a funny feeling that it's permitted to them.

So it is with the discovery of new machines of warfare. Look how quickly we in America decided we *could* drop the atomic bomb once we knew how to, and the only people consulted were the *know how* people—not the *know why* people. So it is with abortion. We developed new techniques of abortion. We say, "Well, now, this works. We know how—so why not?"

It's a quick solution to a problem which otherwise would take a lot of education and a lot of thought. And, to tell the honest truth, we're not a people who like to think, or to meditate, or to speculate. *Know why* is no longer all that popular among us. *Know how,* oddly enough, is called *Yankee know how,* isn't it?

And we've succeeded in exporting our *know how* to the ends of the earth—thus bringing our products to various countries, but with them too often a considerable amount of ill will against us on the purely political side and on the cultural side.

I think Pope John anticipated all this. I think he realized, as sensitive souls have from the beginning—

John Wesley, for example, and Vladimir Soloviev, the Russian philosopher, among the Orthodox—that when the *springtime* comes, it must find us united.

And so the Council was to sift those ideas which are essential from those which are nonessential, to develop a new attitude toward *know how* by bringing back *know why*—in fact, increasing it and developing it in new terms, with new cogency—in the hope that, when the new spring comes, as come it will, *know why* and *know how* will work together and not against each other, and the philosophers, mystics, poets, and saints will have more common dealings with the scientists and the technicians.

Kucherov: Are you confident that this will actually happen?

Wright: I felt confident that this would be the eventual outcome during the synod Pope Paul VI held in October of last year.

A high point of that synod was the talk he invited the astronauts to give to the cardinals and bishops who had gathered for the synod. It was a remarkable talk, a magnificent talk. And the message that came through to me was: "We—top types of the age of technology, its best examples—are very eager to see this a holy world as well as an efficient one. And that is why we read the Bible from the face of the moon, instead of some political document or some page out of a scientific manual."

Kucherov: How does the Church reconcile her opposition to birth control with the danger that uncontrolled population growth in underdeveloped countries will lead to more and more poverty and misery?

Wright: The Church's answer to this, as to most questions when she speaks her authentic mind, is that, in any case and in any problem, persons and people are more important than things.

The Church has a very serious complaint to make—indeed an indictment—against a civilization that is capable of polluting the air, polluting the rivers, polluting the lakes, but not finding the *know how* to take care of this pollution problem and of greater exploitation of the resources of the earth in behalf of persons.

The Church doesn't believe for a single moment that a woman who goes downtown in, let's say, some Midwestern town in the United States to buy contraceptives is making a contribution to the population problem in India or Latin America. She is doing it for quite other motives, which are not concerned with the things that the Church holds dear.

Kucherov: How serious is the threat of overpopulation?

Wright: There has been an enormous amount of scare talk about the exploding population. Ours is an age of exploding everything. It's an age of exploding knowledge, and that knowledge should yield means of exploiting the earth, the sea—in fact, that's already beginning—so as to produce the food needed to sustain as many people as people wish to have around.

Old Joe Kennedy once remarked that there couldn't be too many Kennedys. I think that instinct is at the bottom of every natural human heart: "There can't be too many of my people." And therefore the decision in the matter must always rest with the people.

The Church's main complaint at the moment about this *exploding population* argument and the related arguments is that there isn't any serious effort being made—again, along the lines of *know why*—to teach family planning consistent with human dignity and moral standards. Quite the contrary: there is an obvious, open conspiracy at politically controlled family limitation.

We Americans even seek to link family limitation to our foreign aid. We have population experts with consular offices all over the world, especially in Latin America. We have senators now proposing that precisely the poor—for whom they are supposed to be, or pretend to be, speaking—are going to be taxed if they have more than two children.

This whole campaign, from beginning to end, adds up to something which a recent magazine article has called "the nonsense explosion". It's the making of a tyranny the likes of which we have never seen: the tyranny that will make it necessary to get a license to have a baby, or to get permission from public authority to remain fertile and capable of having children. It is this that the Church is fighting, and it is for the development in vastly greater degree of the *know how* that produces food and space.

Kucherov: Does the earth have enough land resources for this?

Wright: If you fly across the United States by plane, once you leave Kennedy Airport [in New York City] and put down in Chicago's O'Hare and then later perhaps in Los Angeles or San Francisco, it looks like an empty continent. The Church's position is not that the number of people be cut down but that there be efforts to make life in the vast open areas that remain on the globe both livable and pleasant.

Take for example, Peru: Peru is a nation which, irrigated, could produce more than enough food — in Peru alone, on its own — to support a population indefinitely greater than the present under-population of Peru. When we are told about the problem of overpopulation, we are told about it in terms of the *barrios* and all the crowded slums around Lima. But from Lima north to Chimbote it's a ride of 285 miles across absolutely open space which could be irrigated once they would take the trouble to perfect the desalinization of the Pacific and thus support a population many, many times its present size.

As a matter of fact, the bishops from India tell me the same thing applies there. Bananas and other fruits die on the tree because nobody has developed the *know how* or is moved by the *know why* which would prompt them to a redistribution of the goods of the earth.

Kucherov: Can the so-called rhythm method of birth control be made to work among uneducated people?

Wright: I don't know, because I'm not a gynecologist. And the only person for whom I have less respect than I have for the priest who plays the doctor, who plays obstetrician and passes out advice on gynecology, is the gynecologist who plays theologian. I find both of them out of their fields. I think they should get together and discover what each other has to contribute in the way of *know why* and *know how.*

That is precisely the invitation Pope Paul made in his much-abused encyclical on birth control: that those who are supposed to be experts in *know why,* such as the theologians and philosophers, should sit down with those who are experts in *know how,* the gynecologists and obstetricians, and find a way to make rhythm work in a manner which is consistent with the dignity of a woman and the dignity of a man.

As I've said, I don't know how to make rhythm work—first of all, because I'm not a gynecologist. However, there are people who may know how to make it work, but they find it considerably more profitable to leave things as they are—with the mark-up rate on birth-control pills and on everything in that particular area, and the high price of the ugly thing that is abortion.

Kucherov: How does the Church feel about the current trend in the United States toward liberalization of abortion laws?

Wright: I would observe in the beginning that the Church has an initial prejudice in favor of life; she is biased toward all life. That is why Pope Paul VI is prepared to talk out of his window Sunday mornings to Saint Peter's Square against the spread of the war and in favor of the controlling—if not the stopping—of war: because life is at issue.

We are opposed to murder in all its forms, and we should not care to see liberalized the laws against murder, whether the person killed is sixty years old, six years old, six months old, or a six-month-old fetus. We see here a living person with all the rights of a person.

In the case of the unborn, there is the right to be born, the right to come to maturity. The American courts, as the English courts, always recognized the right of the unborn child to inherit if he is born after the death of his father, and that for the simple reason that he is a person.

Therefore, we look upon abortion as murder.

Sometimes the public relations people tell us to be careful about the use of this ugly word. But I use the word, nevertheless. The destruction of life is murder, and, as Cal Coolidge said about sin, "We're agin it."

We look upon this as a general decadence in the attitude of respect for life. We ask ourselves: If any science—medicine included, surgery included—can become so autonomous that it can decide who will be born and who will not be born, what is going to happen even to those who manage to get themselves born? Suppose it is then decided that there are certain types of people that we do not like to have around. At first, it will be people who are obvious nuisances, as, for example, the mentally handicapped, or the criminal in varied degrees, or the insane.

Once upon a time, you could be put to death for religious reasons, as, for example, in Elizabethan or Tudor England. Once upon a time you could be put to death for political reasons. We are scared of this. And when we read, for example, a United States senator saying that he would like to see the population at, say, one hundred million, our temptation is to say: "O.K., provided we pick the committee that chooses who is to survive—both before and after birth." So we do not make any distinction between those who have already managed to get themselves born—and a kid is pretty smart if he gets himself born these days—and those who are not yet born, once they are real humans, real persons.

I have here in the office a picture sent to me from America which is certainly the most horrible thing I have ever seen, and that makes Hitler seem like an amateur. It is the fetus of a baby—seven months—lying in the bottom of a waste basket, waiting to be thrown into the sewer, having just been aborted at the decision of the doctor alone. And I have had a letter from a nurse saying that a baby who had been aborted in a room she was working in—but not in a case she was working on—cried as it was being killed.

Kucherov: Will the Church ever permit divorce, or remarriage by the non-guilty party to a divorce?

Wright: This phrase—the non-guilty party or innocent party— presents a bit of a problem. In all matters of disaster, there is an innocent party, but it does not alter the disaster.

For example, a woman who is walking in town late at night with her bag and is robbed of her bag is the innocent victim of something done by a thug. In this sense, she is an innocent party. What rights she thereby gains or what change this effects in her status it is a little hard for me to see.

In the case of the Church, which sees the marriage bond, once it has been entered into and duly consummated, as a permanent thing, it is hard to say about the innocent party anything more than the fact that she is innocent and that therefore her case is the more pathetic. Whether this gives her the right to marry again is quite another matter, given our idea of the permanence and exclusiveness of the marriage bond.

Now there is a considerable movement within the Church, however—quite apart from the question of the party's innocence, because innocence is a matter of degree—to see if perhaps with our new knowledge of psychiatry and psychology, of what makes the human tick, there may be people who go through the marriage contract—or, for that matter, the priestly ordination ceremony—unfit to do so.

It is in this area that one might look for an eventual broadening of the attitude of the Church. That is to say, we may come to see that some marriages really were not valid from the beginning —because of the immaturity of the people who got married, because of their lack of freedom in any full sense, or because of their incapacity for marriage.

Innocence makes the situation pathetic, as does the innocence of the kid sent to Vietnam, but it does not on that account make the marriage invalid.

Kucherov: Could any broadening of attitude take place in the Church's attitude on celibacy for priests?

Wright: The idea of celibacy in the Church is a very old one. As a matter of fact, contrary to many things widely said, it is a discipline, a custom which has foundations in Scripture, where both Christ and Saint Paul speak of remaining unmarried, as they say, "for the sake of the Kingdom".

Well, if there was ever a period in history when it was necessary to do whatever one can "for the sake of the Kingdom", that period is right now. So the traditional argument for celibacy—or at least the essential traditional argument for celibacy— seems to me more valid now than it has been in a long time. Now, what is that argument?

The argument comes back again to the terrible need that our civilization, that the world has of people who will bear a witness along the lines of *know why* as to why we are here, in preparation for the life to come; of why we must be a disciplined people instead of the kind of people you see if you look out any downtown window during, say, rush hours or traffic jams. There have to be a few men—and they'll always be very few; the number of priests in the world will never be a threat to the population—who must be self-disciplined "for the sake of the Kingdom".

Kucherov: How long has celibacy been required for priesthood?

Wright: As a matter of history, celibacy has been in the Church on a regional basis since about the year three hundred. By the sixth century, it was fairly universal as a requirement—though I need hardly say, human nature being what it is, it wasn't perfectly observed. But it was entrenched by then as the Church's ideal.

Finally, the Lateran Council in 1123 made it obligatory for the universal Church. The Council of Trent, four hundred years ago, reaffirmed that universal discipline. The Second Vatican Council in the 1960s reaffirmed it again, and Pope Paul has also done so.

No one pretends that this is an intrinsic requirement of the notion of the priesthood, because priests of the Eastern Church do marry. But then, they're in a very different culture from ours. Ours is a culture which is saturated with sex on the commercial level, on the billboards, every place you turn. And therefore there is needed a witness to a certain renunciation and discipline "for the sake of the Kingdom".

Another reason—and I think it's been present from the beginning, but it's more important now in the light of the things we've been talking about—is the fact that the Church needs the total devotion, the total love of any man who offers himself for the priesthood.

It is not an exaggeration to say that he has to be prepared to work twenty-four hours a day, seven days a week, fifty-two weeks a year. Even a woman who marries a doctor who has that kind of idealism has problems enough on her hands. No one has any right to ask a woman to marry a man who is thus committed, with his full heart, to the Kingdom of God.

Kucherov: Is the Church concerned that this may discourage otherwise qualified individuals from becoming priests?

Wright: Yes, she is—not only that, but the Church has the fullest sympathy with those who have discovered that they are incapable of making this particular renunciation.

By the same token, the Church has the greatest sympathy for people who discover that they are caught in a marriage which they shouldn't have contracted, or who were born and brought up in a country where it's now very uncomfortable to live but to which you have a commitment through a natural virtue which is patriotism.

The Church can only regret this and worry about it, because we need priests and we need them badly.

However, we need priests of unqualified commitment, and one man of unqualified commitment and undivided love is worth ten whose commitment is qualified or whose love is divided.

You know, in a conflict between the needs of his parish and the needs of his wife and children in the case of any man, according to justice he'd have to give the preference to his wife and children.

114

And, therefore, we could find ourselves even more embarrassed with a married clergy than with the shortage that comes out of the fact that celibacy is, in fact, something that makes a terrible demand on the nature of the normal man.

But so does every state in life. I happen to be a priest, and I have the worries that belong to a priest. My brothers are not priests. They are married, they have children, and they have other worries. Everyone has his own cross, and that is the Church's philosophy in the matter.

Kucherov: Do considerations against marriage apply to deacons?

Wright: No, they do not. The Vatican Council decided that there could be, according to the judgment of the need by the hierarchies of the different parts of the world, a provision for married deacons — in the case of men who had reached a certain maturity, who brought a special expertise to the work of the Church that in the ancient Church was confided to deacons.

There are whole areas of Church life which in the ancient Church were confided to deacons. It has been decided that it might be well to go back to that: for example, the administration of temporalities. Deacons have other duties they can perform, and in fact, the Church gives like permission for laymen to perform certain duties in special circumstances: as, for example, the administration of Communion. The deacon is also empowered to preach. He is empowered to do many things.

When I refer to those things which the priest and the priest alone can do, I am, of course, referring to the offering of the Mass, the hearing of confessions, and similar sacerdotal duties.

So I, for one, see no objection to married

deacons— given the concept of the diaconate. And this does not mean that either I or the Church hold marriage in contempt.

As a matter of fact, the Church sees marriage, even as the priesthood, as a sacrament and a holy thing. And in the case of the deacon, the Church is prepared in given circumstances, when the need requires, to see the two sacraments in the same person.

Kucherov: Are you worried by the shortage of priests?

Wright: We would have been more worried about the shortage, I think, if this crisis had come one hundred years ago, though there was a debate on the matter then, too, as there has been off and on from the beginning. The reason for less worry now is that at that time the laity didn't have the part in the life of the Church which they do have today as a result of the Second Vatican Council.

We are now, with the developed role of the laity, reaching a point—and, in my mind, we should reach an even further point—where many things which were formerly done by priests can and should be done by laity as active members of their parishes, their dioceses, and the total Church. We need the priests to do all that—and only that—which a priest is ordained to do.

In the United States, for example, two generations ago, a priest was expected to do just about everything, including finding jobs for immigrants and taking care of all sorts of local problems of a completely non-ecclesiastical kind. That situation has changed.

The laity has reached not merely maturity in the general community but also an increased level of responsibility in the life of the Church herself. Where there used to be five priests in, say, a large

	city parish, you now can get along very well indeed with two, if the laity are given their proper place in the life of the parish.
Kucherov:	What is the worldwide situation in the number of priests?
Wright:	In some parts of the world, there has been a grave shortage of priests for a long, long time, notably, Latin American and probably large areas of Africa—although there vocations are on the increase—and parts of Asia.

In many European countries, there are not only enough priests but in some countries there are too many.

A very interesting phenomenon, by the way, is that in Yugoslavia, which belongs to what we generally think of as the Iron Curtain zone, there is an excessive number of priests.

In Holland, which is thought of as agitated about this and related problems, I think it fair to say that there may be an excessive number of priests. I have had Dutch laity and clergy suggest that there are possibly too many priests and there is not always enough work for them to do.

On the other hand, to be fair and objective, we do see a serious falling off in vocations.

Kucherov:	Is this due to the celibacy requirement?
Wright:	No, I am not prepared to say that it is, because celibacy has been around, as we have just seen, for many, many centuries, and men have not changed that much in those centuries.

The sexual desire is here to stay, and it was stronger in some centuries gone by than it is even now, because now we live in an age of other diversions which ease or divert the sexual direction. Study is one; gold—or work—is another.

117

I think the explanation of the shortage of vocations lies in the fascination of an affluent society and a technological society, and for that reason I await—as I said before—the *second spring,* which will bring the synthesis. In the meantime, we will see it through, if only because we have to.

As a matter of fact, our Congregation of the Clergy devoted an entire week at Malta to a discussion with men from approximately twenty-four different countries, ranging all the way from Holland to Yugoslavia, from Poland to Latin America, in order to face up to this question of shortage of priests—or, as we word it, distribution of clergy—in the world. We wanted to find out exactly what the facts are. We had a modest objective: to discuss those facts and sketch broad guidelines toward their solution.

I have read about half a dozen sociological surveys. They contradict one another totally. I don't know whether we have slightly less or slightly more than the number of priests that we had at the beginning of the Council—say, in 1960. I suspect that in some parts of the world—America, for example—we have less. In other parts of the world, we have about the same. In some parts of the world, we have more.

And so we made our discussion a discussion of the present distribution of the clergy: it is unequal. And we are going to try and see by what means we can equalize it.

Kucherov: How serious is the decline of US parochial schools?

Wright: About half a dozen elements enter into this problem. It would be very difficult to isolate any one of them and to say that this is it. It varies from one part of the country to the other. Let's consider a few of these elements:

We originally built our separate school system for positive reasons—to include the Catholic Faith in the general formation of the child—but also for defensive reasons. I don't think it is unfair or unecumenical to say that in many parts of the United States in the last century—and in parts of the United States even now—the public schools were, in effect, Protestant.

I, by the way, never went to a Catholic school. I went to public school and to a Catholic college. My reasons were not particularly defensive, but in those days the public school was a very different thing from what it is now. Our teachers, most of whom were Protestants, read the Bible to us every morning, and to this day, I remember the phrases of the Bible that they read, and I remember them with gratitude. They could not do it now without being sent to jail or brought to court. As a result of recent Supreme Court decisions—resented more by Protestants than by us—the schools have become strictly neutral as far as religion is concerned.

So this defensive element has always been present and is still, but now it is less necessary perhaps, because the anti-Catholicism that characterized, let us say, my native city of Boston in the 1840s has entirely disappeared. There is no longer any danger that any little boy will be given the rattan for refusing to say the Lord's Prayer or recite the Ten Commandments in accordance with the Protestant formula.[2] And so many Catholic people are sending their children to public schools because public schools, supported by taxes, can offer courses that are consistent with this new culture we are talking about.

Kucherov: Do parochial schools offer the same courses?

Wright: The laboratories for technology, for engineering, for the space age are very expensive. We have tended in our schools to stick to the liberal arts tradition. So the cultural change is one of the explanations for the shift on the schools.

The second explanation is that schools are supported by what you might call the *charity dollar* — the dollar freely given. Nowadays it is very hard, if not impossible — in schools, in old folks' homes — for the charity dollar to compete against the tax dollar. The tax dollar has become cancerous — not only in the United States but all over the world.

This is not a problem peculiar to Catholics; it is a problem which goes across the board. I don't know what Protestants have to do without in order to pay their taxes, but I know what some Catholics have to do without in order to pay their taxes — and that is supporting their schools.

Third, there is a crisis of personnel. Among us, religious teachers have not increased at the same rate that our population has increased. This is also true in some degree in the public schools. Teaching has become an unpopular profession, and there is a great shortage of teachers, as there is of nurses and of doctors — of anything that requires what they have to take nowadays.

Finally, a very serious question of a philosophical kind has arisen — namely: Where is the best place and what is the best method to teach religion? There are those who see it in the so-called Confraternity of Christian Doctrine, which is given over entirely to religion, rather than in the schools, where it is a departmentalized thing. I have met many people who think it would be wiser to put more money into the Confraternity of Christian Doctrine rather than into the terribly expensive school system that has been built up.

Nonetheless, in America, at least, the hierarchy have served notice that they intend to hang on to the schools as long as they can, and the mail that I get from laity seems to indicate that a substantial number of the laity are behind them. I limit that observation to the United States, because in most European countries the so-called confessional schools —Catholic, Protestant, Jewish—are supported by the state.

Kucherov: Do you see any possibility of parochial schools in the United States receiving cash support directly from the Vatican or from government?

Wright: Well, I can't imagine any way that they can expect support from the Vatican, because—a couple of sensational articles to the contrary notwithstanding —the Vatican has all it can do to keep afloat with the commitments it has to the missionary world and that world throughout which Vatican diplomats are dispersed to work for peace and to help build a more peaceful society. I would not look for any help from the Vatican—rather, the other way around.[3]

As for support from the states and the federal government, in some states it is already underway— under the so-called formula of purchase of service, whereby the state purchases the teaching of secular subjects in the Catholic school.

The reasons are strictly realistic. They have nothing to do with an increased love of the state for the Catholic schools. It is that these states have no school space left, and they have problems enough in their own schools, so they have decided that it would be cheaper to throw a couple of bucks in our direction in order to keep the children where they are, rather than have all the children in the Catholic schools suddenly unloaded on the public school system.

And the public schools are having a tough time getting teachers and paying their own bills. I don't see any great idealism in the programs for federal aid — the more so because they come precisely when we, too, are embarrassed with personnel.

Kucherov: Why does the Church still prohibit joint ceremonies for mixed marriages?

Wright: The difficulty here is that marriage is a sacrament. In the Catholic Church, it is one of the seven sacraments — together with priesthood, baptism, confirmation. In many of the Protestant churches, marriage is not viewed as a sacrament at all. As a matter of fact, it is called an *ordinance*. It is not seen as sacramental in its nature.

Now, I don't wish to be misunderstood. Protestants, including my Protestant friends, see their marriages as a sacred thing. But they have theological ideas concerning marriage which are very different from those of us who see marriage as a sacrament.

For example, they are broader — and some of them extremely broad — in their idea of how permanent it is. Even those who use the phrase "until death do us part" have managed to substitute the divorce-court judge for death a little more rapidly than we think healthy. Certain other aspects of the matter — contraception included — have made mixed marriage a problem for us.

Having said that, it is only fair to add that it is a

Kucherov: problem we are working on in collaboration with them—to see what our irreducible minimum is and what their maximum concession may be.

Kucherov: Often a distinction is made between *liberal* prelates such as Leon Cardinal Suenens, of Belgium, and *conservative* prelates such as yourself. Is that distinction valid?

Wright: I think I can suggest to you the value of that distinction if I tell you that, within the week, a group of people came to me to complain about how conservative one of the so-called liberal cardinals had been on a matter, and if I tell you that the year I left Pittsburgh I was burned in effigy by conservatives in front of my cathedral for being excessively liberal on social questions, more particularly on relations between white people and black people.[4]

I do not know what the word *conservative* means any more. I know what it used to mean. It used to mean those who wanted to conserve certain values. I don't know what the word *liberal* means now. Here in Europe, by the way, it means the reverse of what it means in the United States. A member of the Liberal Party here in Italy is someone who is an industrialist, has millions of dollars, and who does not want any change in the *status quo.* So in England, so in France, so elsewhere. So I tend to avoid these two words, and when either of them is applied to me—as both of them are—I attribute no significance to this.

I think there is a distinction among members of the hierarchy—as among those of the *lowerarchy* and the general community, Republicans and Democrats included—and that is the distinction between those who are open-minded and those who are

123

closed-minded. I have never met anyone more closed-minded than a totally closed-minded liberal. And I have met many people labeled *conservative* who are fairly open-minded and who are prepared to talk things over with people who are, or tend to be, at the other end of a polarized society.

For my own part, in the Church as in the civil community, I favor what Arthur Schlesinger, Sr., at Harvard used to call "the vital center"—the place where people meet to find out how much is true in each position and how the common good of the person will be served by both, not by either alone.

Kucherov: Do you foresee the possibility of the Pope's being chosen by all the bishops instead of by the College of Cardinals?

Wright: I don't quite know how to answer that. There are about two thousand, five hundred bishops in the world. They're scattered all over the world. We had trouble enough getting them here for the Vatican Council. In all affection and friendship, I'd have to give a lot of thought as to how prepared some of them would be to take part in that kind of election.

Another thing: Professor Jacques Maritain, probably the best of our living lay philosophers, has said that for him one of the proofs of the presence of the Holy Spirit in the Church in our times is the high quality of the last six popes. What remarkable men they were in a world of mediocrity! Well, they were elected by the College of Cardinals—which means to me that the College didn't do a bad job. I'd have to have very impressive evidence to the contrary before I'd be too enthusiastic about a change.

Kucherov: How would you characterize these years of the last six popes, so far as the Church is concerned?

Wright: It's one of those periods in the history of the world—there have been at least five such periods in the Western world in the last two thousand years—where a whole new culture, technological or technocratic, is replacing an old and long-established culture: broadly speaking, the liberal arts culture, which has been ours almost from the Greek and Roman days, but certainly from the Renaissance. Talking superficially, people sometimes speak of the present crisis as one in faith. I don't believe it's that deep. I think it's a crisis in theology, and theology is part of culture.

However, theology and faith are quite distinct. Just as at the time of Saint Augustine and the collapse of the Roman Empire there was a like chaos, just as at the time of the Huns and Pope Leo the Great there was a like chaos, just as at the time of the Renaissance and the rise of Protestantism there was a similar chaos, so now we have a cultural crisis which is taking various forms of challenges to authority, to received traditions, education, and a lot of other things.

Kucherov: Would you say the present crisis is more serious than that of the Reformation era?

Wright: No, I would not. I couldn't possibly bring myself to say that—if only for one reason: at the time of the Reformation, all the flow was in the precisely opposite direction—that is, toward division. At that time, the tendency was toward fragmentation among those who believed in God at all; toward division among Christians. Excommunication was running from Rome to the east and to the north and to various other parts of the world, and counterdenunciations were coming from them.

Today, the tendency is entirely in the other direction. In the last year alone, I have seen in Saint Peter's, embracing the Holy Father, the heads of religions of the East and of the West. I have seen the head of the Lutherans sitting in his reserved seat in Saint Peter's to attend the Council. Last Sunday, I saw the ranking patriarch of the Armenians—who are typical of the Orthodox autonomous nationalistic churches—walking in procession at Saint Peter's with Pope Paul.

I wouldn't be surprised if at the end of the present crisis—which is a real one—there would be fewer Christians and fewer believers in the world. But they'll be more nearly united, they'll be stronger, and they'll be much clearer in their own heads.

VI

Cardinal Richard J. Cushing, 1895–1970

And God will wipe away every tear from their eyes. And death shall be no more; neither shall there be mourning, nor crying, nor pain any more, for the former things have passed away. And He who was sitting on the throne said: "Behold; I make all things new!"[1]

The lamented Cardinal-Archbishop of Boston was a man of many contradictions—some within minutes of each other. He was a man of not a few controversial words and actions—some bitter, some bewildering, some almost amusing to himself and to us who loved him. But one single, overriding, constant purpose integrated his entire life and to that abiding constancy he was totally committed unto death.

That one constant purpose was his determination, stubborn and untiring, to serve, with whatever genius or frailty, the one, holy, universal, apostolic Church, in communion with Rome, and to do everything else in his power, at all times, in all places, on every level, to advance that Kingdom of God of which he knew the visible, organized Church to be the beginning and the principal agent on earth.

To this unchanging motivation, he was faithful all the days of his life and through all the mysteries—joyful, sorrowful, and glorious—of that life otherwise shot through with superficial contradictions and occasional controversy.

I am grateful to Archbishop Medeiros and to the bishops and priests of this truly holy church of Boston for the privilege of speaking, in behalf of all present and millions not able to be

This eulogy was preached at the Holy Cross Cathedral, Boston, Massachusetts, on November 7, 1970.

present, some words of affectionate remembrance of Richard Cardinal Cushing.[2]

The text I read a moment ago was one I heard on his lips on many occasions, some of them occasions so bound up with his goodness to me that they came instinctively to mind when, by a curious providence, I arrived the other night in the New York airport to be handed a scribbled note that Archbishop Medeiros and Bishop Minihan had phoned that our Cardinal was dead.

When Archbishop Cushing was installed in this cathedral over a quarter of a century ago, he thought of choosing the last part of today's text—"Behold, I make all things new!"—as the theme of his first sermon.[3] A last-minute decision, expressed by him with a characteristic comic touch, prompted him to choose another text, but he returned to this theme time and again in those early years of his pontificate, as he went about the diocese where he was welcomed and loved so passionately.

When he preached at the Mass establishing the new Diocese of Worcester twenty years ago, he used the last words of this text, as he did nine years later when, with paternal solicitude he installed me as Bishop of Pittsburgh. This is a purely personal reason why I am grateful to be able to repeat those words as he is laid to rest, since in all of my life as a brother bishop, as in the lives of thousands of bishops, priests, and lay collaborators, these words, the aspiration of his own life, became our dynamic ideal: "Behold, I make all things new!"

These words coming from him were no heady, empty boast concerning any charismatic gifts or special talents Richard Cardinal Cushing thought he possessed or wished the rest of us, all of us, to share. It is an echo of words which Scripture places on the lips of that Christ, the Alpha and Omega of all things, who alone could possibly pronounce such powerful words, that Christ of whom every believer in one way, every priest in a most especial way, every bishop in a preeminent way, is called to be the agent.

And so, from the day of his ordination as a priest, indeed before, and unmistakably from the springtime of his archbishopric in the exciting years of the 1940s, Richard Cushing, fired by the energies of Christ and inspired by the word of the Lord of all, sought to "make all things new". For years this aspiration had identified him with the work of the missionary Church as few in history and none in our times have given themselves to the spread of the Kingdom to the ends of the earth. Seeking to build on the firm foundations of solid faith and holy pride left by Cardinal O'Connell and his predecessors in the local church of Boston, Archbishop Cushing aspired to bring fresh vitality — to "make all things new" again — in the diocese committed to his care. Those were the days — the latter 1940s and the early 1950s — of the joyous mysteries in the life of our beloved leader. He stood so tall, so confident, so radiant, so energetic, so indefatigable, and, if one may dare to say it, so *debonair,* as America's youngest archbishop and one of the Church's most articulate, open-handed, and prophetic witnesses to God's truth.

In those days of the joyful mysteries of his high priesthood, Archbishop Cushing was everywhere. He preached everywhere. He was at work building everywhere. He sought to encourage everywhere, at home and abroad. It was wartime when he began this omnipresent apostolic action. He combined with the all-out service of his own flock an amazing apostolate to soldiers and sailors, to men and women in the service, not only here on local ships and bases, but also wherever in the land he was asked to confirm, to offer the Mass, to comfort, or to say the word of encouragement for those caught up in the war.

The moment the war ended he began, again with all-out effort and in worldwide fashion, to labor for the things which make for peace. He was among the first, together with the late Cardinal Dougherty of Philadelphia, to take a clear stand against future compulsory peacetime military service. But at the same time, he braved the wrath of the more equivocal, if not disloyal, at home and abroad by pinpointing in his public addresses those whom he saw as enemies of faith, freedom, and the prospects of abiding peace, no matter how much some of them may have, at the time, presented themselves as allies of freedom, lovers of peace, and, on at least one occasion, spokesmen for religious faith.

Much more positively and unforgettably, before rebuilding from the devastation of war had even begun in Europe, he projected and personally led a series of pilgrimages to European nations, shrines, and peoples from whom we had been estranged during the years of the war. This was among the greatest of the joyful mysteries of this man's life, and how it rejoiced us all to see him leading a thousand of his people to Canada, before any political personality even dreamed of doing anything, to walk through the streets, to preach and to pray in witness to the unity of spirit which must bind neighboring nations. How proud we were a year later to see him standing, erect and confident, in the pulpit of crowded Notre Dame of Paris, before the altar of Lourdes, surrounded by five hundred of his Boston flock and thousands of the French eager to hear him speak of the indestructible ties between our countries. As in France he spoke of new hope, so later in Spain he pleaded for new ways, in Ireland for new courage, in Germany for new understanding. Never were the joyful mysteries of his life so symbolized than when we priests and people of Boston went with him to Rome to present to Pope Pius XII our petition for the canonization of Pius X, whose motto had been, "Restore all things in Christ", as Richard Cushing's inspiration had been, "Behold, I make all things new!"

That was the springtime, the season of joyful mysteries as the Rosary, which he delighted to recite on trains abroad, over the radio at home, at religious gatherings everywhere, as he would call them. That was the season that saw him consecrating new bishops, especially missionary bishops, not only here in Boston but in the chapels of the motherhouses of great missionary orders all over the land and beyond. His theme was always the same: new worlds to conquer for Christ, new hope to bring to men, new energy and openness in the profession of the Faith, "all things made new".

It was in this period of the joyful mysteries that he began to dream of concentrating his energy and his vision especially on Latin America, toward which as a neighbor continent he felt that we had special obligations in affection, generosity, and faith.

Before anyone, known to me, was using the words *Third World,* the indomitable Cushing in the years of his joyful mysteries was launching, with the aid of the priests and people who shared his vision, Latin American programs all his own, typified by but not limited to the Society of Saint James—the name of which had dawned on him as he stood at the shrine of Saint James, one of his patron saints, at Compostella in Spain. "The Spaniards", he said, "were chief among those who brought the Faith to South America. They did a wonderful work. The job of bringing back the Faith, *of making all things new* must now be ours!"

Yet none of his worldwide activities distracted him, during that springtime of the joyful mysteries, from his duties here at home. He multiplied, in plain fact, he pioneered locally, new educational work for handicapped children; there are those who say that it was he who coined the tender phrase *exceptional children* to describe those born with all the odds against them. He made his own an especial apostolate to old folks, and, in a mixture of pathos and comedy, he planned festive visits not only to institutional homes for the poor, but to public restaurants, even night clubs, to which he invited those who had no one else to entertain them on national family feasts, like Thanksgiving. He was the host and he was the entertainment. He built institutions for the aged and the poor, the sick and the abandoned, but, what was more important, he *identified* himself personally with his brethren, whether they were in the institutions of the Church or those of the state, they were in whatever we now call poor houses or were in prisons.

It was in this period, again the springtime of his joyous mysteries, that he revealed his highly publicized flair for hats of varied and marvelous design, as well as his disarming, not to say sometimes disconcerting, delight in uttering the unexpected phrase, the unstuffy remark, or a frequently astonishing bit of self-heckling and self-deprecating humor.

And thus, in the midst of laughter, intense activity, and resilient indifference to either flattery or adverse criticism, he lived out the joyful mysteries of his springtime as a prelate, reproducing in deeds, something, at least, of what only Christ could promise: "Behold, I make all things new!"

Then came the season of his sorrowful mysteries. It is a little difficult to place a date; it doesn't make much difference. It is even more difficult to assign clear causes, particularly for the contradiction, confusion, and sometimes personal attack that left his spirit sorrowful, even broken, more than ravaging diseases made painful his flesh. Suddenly, the seemingly carefree, contagiously enthusiastic young archbishop of the early days, began, manifestly, to share the priesthood of the Man of Sorrows, as once, not less manifestly, he had exemplified the priesthood of the Son of the Cause of our Joy.

He became like to no one so much as to Job. His telephone calls, his letters to friends, his private conversations sometimes, when affliction of spirit and pain of the flesh were especially acute, and his unguarded public remarks began to echo the very vocabulary of Job. He spoke, as many of the bishops who are our fathers in Christ have been obliged to speak, of abandonment, repudiation, unconcealed contempt for what he loved and what he tried, at least, to do.

Words from the lips of Job, words of ulcers and tumors, of desolation of spirit and utter heartbreak, began to be heard from his lips. Once, apologizing half-jokingly, half-ruefully for his shrunken physical condition and his inability to eat anything but clear soup and a little ice cream, he quoted in a letter a line from Job: "My flesh is consumed, my bone is cleaved to my skin, and nothing but lips are left above my teeth!"[4] The years of the sorrowful mysteries had unmistakably descended upon him.

Unlike Job, his personal possessions had never been of a financial kind. He had never held on to money, and so he couldn't lose that. He owned no camp, no villa, no hideaway from the pressures of life: any place he stayed, perhaps for a day or two, he stayed as a guest, usually a paying guest, but in any case, a grateful guest. As his secretary, I wrote the draft of his first will after he became archbishop. His instructions were very simple. He said, "So far as my job is concerned, include everything that canon law requires. *So far as my personal effects are concerned, find some legal, high-faluting way to say that I haven't got a dime. I came into the world poor, and I shall go out the same way!"*

Neither did he suffer, as did Job, from neglect or indifference by his family. Since they are present, and we understand one another in this hour of grief, I must acknowledge, as did the late Cardinal, that it sometimes seemed quite the other way round. His people loved him deeply, but he apparently felt that by giving his own family even a day of his time he might neglect the work for all God's children. His parents had taught him to love Christ and His Church above all else. His kin understood this perfectly, and so they were content, but not surprised, that only in the year before he died he at last took time to visit home on the family feasts of Thanksgiving and Christmas. His nephew followed in his footsteps as a priest and a missionary, and the Cardinal was very proud of that fact, but he never told him. On the one occasion that he invited his family to rejoice with him in Rome, the news of a death in the family, the death of one who had remained at home, disrupted the Roman reunion at its height. He was already sick, wracked with pain, in no small degree frustrated—but his comment at the hotel in Rome that day might have been a line out of Job.

In the season of his sorrowful mysteries, it became common for him to faint at public events or to show utter exhaustion in ceremonies or at meetings. By then, the rumor began that he had cancer together with asthma and other afflictions. A loose-lipped woman started the cancer rumor. Her phone lines sizzled with the grizzly news. Finally, he heard the rumor himself, as all evil reports finally reach those whom they are intended to disturb. His doctor had been discreet, but a writer whom the Cardinal had helped, when no one else would, helped spread the rumor that he was taking means to kill pain and showing symptoms of metastasis and sclerosis.

This was indeed the season of sorrowful mysteries, but he never stopped going. He never stopped preaching. He never stopped wiping away tears, though they were invariably the tears of others.

It was then that the pilgrimages for peace gave way to pilgrimages of prayer for the physical healing of others. He chartered airplanes to bring crippled and handicapped boys and girls—*his exceptional children*—close to some of whom he will be buried this afternoon—to Lourdes and to Ireland. All that was most beloved about him is summed up, not in the funny stories in his popular biographies, but in a poignant piece of sheer poetry that was uttered at two o'clock in the morning, forty thousand feet above the Atlantic, in the darkness of a plane filled with afflicted children, their afflicted Father in Christ and the sisters and doctor who took care of both. In the midst of the midnight silence, a small boy called out, "Cardinal!" An exhausted Prince of the Holy Roman Church, to give him one of his exact titles, sleepily but promptly murmured: "What do you want, Bobby?" The small boy answered with a demand that Christ gave the poor and afflicted the right to make of all Christians, princes and peasants alike: "Cardinal," the small boy said, "I can't sleep. Come hold me!"

Lest any of the captious describe the Cardinal's prompt response that night as sentimental or untypical, let me quote from an article by the librarian of the Boston Athenaeum, to which, by the way, the first bishop of Boston, a Frenchman, left his library.[5] The quote again involves an airplane and Cardinal Cushing at the height of the season of his sorrowful mysteries, but still hard at work making all things new. Here is what Walter Muir

Whitehill tells us in an article about Massachusetts entitled, *Who Rules Us?*

> Never underestimate the role played by that remarkable prelate, Cardinal Cushing, in breaking down fences in Boston. . . . Few cardinals have been as simple or as indefatigable. . . . Undeterred by illnesses that would have defeated an ordinary man, he carries on tirelessly. One stormy winter night in 1968 I went to LaGuardia Airport to take a shuttle to Boston. The plane was at the gate, receiving passengers, but both the time and the likelihood of its departure were uncertain. A moment after I had taken my seat, I was relieved to see Cardinal Cushing come aboard, for his presence inspired confidence that Eastern Airlines would get us safely to Boston. They did, and on time, at that. But throughout the flight the Cardinal—at the end of a long day—was chatting and joking with everyone, trying on pilots' caps and stewardesses' hats, as if he had not a care in the world. Once on the ground at Logan, he had a friendly word, a joke, or a blessing for half the people he passed until he strode out of view into the snowy night.[6]

What sustained this paradoxical man as he disappeared into the dark after his antics, some might say—his apostolate you and I will say—on the airplane where Walter Whitehill watched him with such sympathy and admiration? It was, of course, the conquering joy of those words of Christ: "Behold, I make all things new!" But joy and confidence are not always the well-springs of energy, nor certainly of holy entertainment in the midst of the sorrowful mysteries of one who is wracked with pain and exhausted by contestation and picketing demands for *instant solutions* of evils one had fought all his life—and such had become the humiliating destiny of our Cardinal. Now only *faith,* indomitable faith, is adequate to keep alive the joy and to spark the laughter of the sick at heart. There is no one in this Church who does not know the nature of that *faith* as it kept strong in spirit this man of broken flesh, now that the sorrowful mysteries of his beloved Rosary overwhelmed him.

Oddly enough, a classic affirmation of that faith is in the very chapter of the Book of Job that I have already recalled him as once quoting. What Job said of old, Richard Cushing said now, without, perhaps, speaking the words but by the way he carried on in the midst of infirmity and desolation: "I know that my Redeemer liveth, and on the last day I shall rise out of the earth. And I shall be clothed again with my skin; and in my flesh I shall see my God. Whom I myself shall see, and my own eyes shall behold, and not another. *This is the hope that is hid in my bosom!*"[7]

It was my privilege to come to Brighton with His Excellency the Apostolic Delegate, when the personal representative of our Holy Father in the United States brought to Cardinal Cushing the letter from Pope Paul accepting the Cardinal's resignation and sending him warm and loving greetings on his birthday. I wanted to be with him when the news that the work we all had seen begin was at length ended, and I wanted to have lunch with him on his birthday. He read the letter from the Holy Father; he read it out loud in his bedroom as a young boy might read an affectionate letter from his father writing from a distant place. It was a beautiful letter; you all saw it reproduced in the *Pilot.*[8]

Cardinal Cushing used to say, in the midst of his years of sorrow, that he thought good Pope John was the only Pope who understood him. But this was not true. Pope Paul understood him well, and with exquisite sensitivity he obviously delayed as long as he dared the acceptance of the resignation on which, in fact, the exhausted warrior insisted. He deliberately waited until the birthday, which would make the resignation not only the more gracious in the eyes of the public, but also the more welcome to the suffering Cardinal.

The luncheon prepared by the devoted Sisters of Saint Joan of Arc for the Apostolic Delegate, for Monsignor McGuire who served him so loyally, and for me was a steak and a bit of birthday cake. But the Cardinal could eat only ice cream, and not much of that, so far advanced were the lesions, the tumors, and the pain. After lunch and a little bit of laughter recalling the joyful mysteries, and some invisible tears at the thought of the sorrowful mysteries, the Apostolic Delegate withdrew to phone his office concerning his travel plans. I was left alone with the Cardinal. It was a terrible minute but, characteristically, it was he who broke the melancholy. He said: "John, I am through now, and I am glad. But when I am gone, if anyone asks if anything I ever said or did may somehow have hurt the Church, what do you think the answer will be?"

I said, as everyone here would have told me to, "Archbishop, everyone will say that if you ever seemed to hurt the Church, even a little, it was in your loving desire to *serve* it—to make it stronger and more beloved, to build it up as a more powerful means to the Kingdom of God!"

He thought for a moment and then he said: "I hope so! Now we have to pray for the man who is coming, to pick up some of the broken pieces, maybe, but above all to build higher and better!"

Then he smiled painfully with a face that showed signs of the beginnings of the glorious mysteries, the glorious mysteries in the life, the death, and the victory of everyone who loves God and his neighbor as did Cardinal Cushing. He obviously was thinking back to things as they had been thirty years before, and he said: "The next man will make it all new again, won't he?"

This was less than three months ago, and it was the beginning of the end, but not quite the end. He was dictating letters, and adding his scrawled chatty postscripts, two nights before he died; he had arranged with Joe Sullivan for his Christmas cards just a little earlier. "Don't charge me much!" he warned. But most glorious of all, the promise of Christ and the faith of Job had enabled him just a month ago to walk, *head high,* out of this cathedral after he had thrilled to the glorious mystery of seeing his successor installed, *firmly and unchallenged,* in the sanctuary from which the now dead Cardinal's voice rang out so often, as priest, later as prelate, the promises of Jesus and the Faith of the Fathers.

On that wonderful day, so recent and so proud, your applause of the dying man helped him to persevere, joyful and glorious, to the end, all sorrow being left behind. Your applause of his successor was heard around the world. It told our new Archbishop to fear not, that the way will be made straight, the wilderness will be broken open with new paths and new directions, and that as God was with our Fathers, so will He be with us. God now wipes away all tears from the eyes of Richard Cushing, since death for him shall be no more nor pain nor evil anymore, for the former things have passed away—and by that same power God gives to Archbishop Medeiros the full share of divine power needed to make all things new again!

This is the point of the Church; there is no other. This is the point of the apostolic succession; there is no other. This is the point of the priesthood; there is no other. This is the point of the Christian Faith and of all the people who share it or whose lives it touches; there is no other that matters enough to mention. This is why all mysteries—joyful, sorrowful, and glorious—blend in the exultant cry: "I know that my Redeemer liveth, and in the last day I shall rise out of the earth . . . and in my flesh I shall see my God!"[9]

Confirmed in this Faith, we commend this valiant newsmaker to history, this holy man, zealous priest, uncommon prelate to the God who gave joy to his youth, the Christ who consoled his age, the angels and saints with whom he will share eternal life, undying love!

VII

Priestly Maturity

The recent instruction *Ratio fundamentalis institutionis sacerdotalis,* published by the Sacred Congregation for Catholic Education, indicates as the purpose of seminary formation the attainment of *sacerdotal maturity,* which maturity presupposes, as essential and integral to it, the presence of certain human elements which guarantee a greater efficacy, fruitfulness, and stability of the priestly ministry in the Church.[1]

It appears opportune, therefore, to focus our attention, as we intend to do in this paper, on one single affirmation of the instruction. "The building of a total priest is by its very nature such that *throughout his* life, but especially in the first years after *his sacred ordination, his formation should be continued and perfected ever more completely.*"[2]

This argues that the mature priest must also be a mature man, and it suggests, by inevitable implications, that whenever a defective priest, a man unstable in his priesthood, appears in the Christian community, underneath the unfulfilled priest, there may well be an immature man. Priestly defections, priestly unhappiness, priestly crises of whatever kind may have various explanations, as they do in the lives of other men; but the most common one that shows up in the priest who loses or compromises his commitment to the priesthood, especially in the area of alcoholism, uncontrolled sexuality, and such complications of priestly efficiency as hypochondria, is not so much lack of idealism as a priest—this remains as a further torment in such cases—but personal and priestly immaturity.

It is our present purpose, then, to present the figure of

This article was written for and published in the September 1970 issue of *Seminarium.*

priesthood in terms of priestly maturity, both human and supernatural, and to argue that the realization of maturity constitutes the principal objective of seminary formation.

The purpose of seminary formation for the priesthood and of the continuation of that formation after the seminary, particularly for young priests but also for all us priests, is the formation of a *mature man, a responsible man, a priest who is therefore fulfilled and faithful.*

All men are called by God to that self-realization that we call maturity and that constitutes perfection; Christians, but above all *priests,* are the objects of a special call in this regard. Early in the Old Testament, Yahweh charged His people to be mature, perfect, and holy: "You shall be holy unto me, because I the Lord am holy, and I have separated you from other people, that you should be mine."[3] Likewise, the Lord Jesus in His first public sermon on the mountain of the Beatitudes renewed this call: "You therefore are to be perfect, even as your heavenly Father is perfect."[4] As a consequence, all Christians, and, one repeats, above all the apostles and their successors, together with their priestly collaborators, are called to be perfect. Their vocation is not to a perfection like to that of the angels, but like to God Himself, like to the heavenly Father, like to His beloved Son, their eternal and High Priest, the likeness constituting in the fact that they seek and, by God's grace, attain the total fulfillment of the being that is theirs as God possesses the total perfection of the Being that is His.

This maturity and perfection of a man is also the theme of the apostolic exhortations of Saint Paul:

> But to each one of us grace was given according to the measure of Christ's bestowal. Thus it says, "Ascending on high, he led away captives; he gave gifts to men." Now this, "he ascended", what does it mean but that he also first descended into the lower parts of the earth? He who descended, he it is who ascended also above all the heavens, that he might fill all things. And he himself gave some men as apostles, and some

as prophets, others again as evangelists, and others as pastors and teachers, in order to perfect the saints for a work of ministry, for building up the body of Christ, until we all attain to the unity of the faith and of the deep knowledge of the Son of God, to perfect manhood, to the mature measure of the fullness of Christ.[5]

Hence the end of seminary and postseminary formation is the formation of a mature man who will thus become the basis of a complete priest "in the mature measure of the fullness of Christ."[6] Himself, for the priest is truly *another Christ;* he is the minister and *servant of Christ* and of the Church, as he is the guardian and dispenser of the mysteries of God.[7]

Certain aspects of contemporary culture and civilization, more particularly perhaps within the family community itself, but certainly in the general community, do not make easy a ready response to a priestly vocation and its equally easy realization. Even less do these circumstances of our times lend aid to that coming to maturity, even as a man, which priestly perfection presupposes. The situation in which the contemporary priestly personality finds himself as a man must therefore be described as *negative* in terms of his prospects for priestly maturity, if only because it so greatly increases the personal responsibility of the young candidate for the priesthood for his own formation. Responsibility for bringing to attainment his own personal progress, for drawing out of himself (we must never forget that the root meaning of education comes from *educere*) his own personal potential and thus achieving maturity falls back almost entirely upon himself, the priestly aspirant, in an age of technology and a culture chiefly concerned with the world outside the person rather than within. Seminarians and young priests of another generation had an advantage that came with the very education constitutive of the liberal arts tradition, a tradition involving a humanism which was more concerned with the person than with the machinery of his life and which summed up and transmitted the wisdom and the discipline of the ages as a counteractive to the preoccupations of a bewildering knowledge explosion, especially with regard to things, and a technology preoccupied with externals, however convenient and however useful.

This humanism, particularly when it became influenced and elevated by Christianity, transmitted to the seminarian and the priest not merely the knowledge but, what is much more important, the wisdom accumulated in the Western world by the learning of Greek civilization, the discipline of the Roman heritage, and the mystical insights of the Judeo-Christian tradition. I hasten to note that the philosophical, literary, and religious traditions of the Eastern world had like normative elements, but in the Western world, most assuredly the liberal arts tradition plus religious faith provided a heritage which may be summed up, somewhat over-simply perhaps but with real point, in three norms for which we were indebted to the Greek, Roman, and Judeo-Christian traditions, almost in successive stages, which added up to the Christian culture and, in no small measure, to the culture of the Western world.

Each of those norms could be expressed in two words. The Greeks, intellectual and philosophical, left to us the formula: *Know thyself.* In this formula, the philosopher who transmitted to us the two major streams of Greek philosophy summed up the contribution of that world to our maturity as men and, in the case of those who pursued an ecclesiastical vocation, as priests. All knowledge begins with knowledge of oneself, and whatever other knowledge we may possess, however vast, however erudite, may easily prove a force of personal disintegration unless he who possesses the knowledge first of all *knows himself:* his capacities, his limitations, his virtues, and those inclinations toward evil which traditional spirituality called his *dominant passion.* It is as true in our own day as it was in the day of Socrates: all knowledge begins with self-knowledge.

In no one is this more true than it is in the candidate for the priesthood. From the first days of his formation, he must necessarily know more about himself than any outsider, however keen his discernment of spirits, can possibly know. Indeed, only to the extent that he knows himself can he provide the essential elements of the knowledge which those who advise him, guide him, help form him, can possess. He must know himself in depth, perceiving clearly his own motivation and weighing carefully his own potentialities toward the realization of that motivation. He must have gazed within himself and reflected upon himself sincerely and realistically in order to evaluate his physical condition, his psychological aptitudes, his moral potential, his religious, emotional, and intellectual capacities. Only on the basis of his self-knowledge can he answer for himself or provide others with the elements of the answer as to how prepared he is to respond to a seeming call to the priesthood with a decision that is carefully weighed, responsible, and, to return to our key word, mature.

If he thinks himself to hear the voice of the Lord saying, "Follow Me", "Come, follow Me, and I will make you fishers of men", he can respond with at least the beginnings of maturity, "Behold, I come . . . to do Thy will, O God", which means on the basis of a self-knowledge which has traditionally been part of a demand of our culture and the heritage available to us.[8]

A knowledge of what constitutes a divine vocation — the vocation of Christ Himself to the priesthood — is, of course, indispensable. But the response to such a vocation presupposes a human *self-knowledge* which, realistically, humbly, and objectively, brings under one's own study and one's own eventual control forces within oneself which make for maturity. The blend of these two forms of knowledge, knowledge of Christ and knowledge of oneself, yields the indispensable conditions of human maturity both in the seminarian and in the priest. The former will provide the characteristic *difference* in the man who becomes a priest, another Christ; but the latter must be prior in time if the blend of the two is to be effective.

If the Greeks were intellectuals and thus contributed to our heritage and intellectual formula *know thyself,* the Roman world was more nearly what we would probably call *voluntarist.* Its culture was largely derived and its characteristic contribution to the liberal arts tradition and the civilization of the Western world was typified by its *planning,* its purposefulness, its road-building, its genius for law and for empire. We can, again with a certain but not excessive simplicity, summarize its contribution in the two words: *rule thyself.* Added to the Greek *know thyself,* this norm provided the basis of a humanism which was at the heart of the culture of the Mediterranean world and which was later to give wise and disciplined Christians of every kind, but especially priests, the advantage of self-knowledge and self-discipline.

Jesus was to say quite simply: "Deny thyself", by which He made the admonition to rule thyself and the perfection that is self-discipline even more effective and programmatic. In the Gospel of Saint Matthew, we read the following words of the Lord: "If anyone wishes to come after me, let him deny himself, and take up his cross, and follow me. For he who would save his life will lose it; but he who loses his life for my sake will find it."[9]

These words of the Master became the foundation of priestly self-discipline for generations; they gave a greater nobility to what might otherwise have been the mere stoicism of the Roman quality at its best. The doctrine of Jesus concerning obedience and the manner in which He linked obedience to His commands to love for His Person ("You are my friends if you do those things that I have commanded") are His form of the Roman insistence on the formation of the will and of the centrality of law.[10] Whenever Jesus spoke of Love, He did so in terms of Law, a new commandment, an act of the will, involving the entire self, to be sure, but depending on the measure in which we have blended self-discipline with self-knowledge.

The observance of the commandments of the Lord and of the

discipline of the Church early became, on the basis of the words of Jesus Himself, the guarantee of the authenticity of any Christian's love for Christ and for the Church; *a fortiori,* it became the essence of the priesthood and the evidence of the maturity of a priest.

The contemporary man who becomes a priest may have little patience with this contribution of the Roman heritage or the requirements which Christ, personally or through His Church, includes under His Law of Love. Our generation increasingly seeks wider and more diverting highways, broad highways with new frontiers made possible more by machinery than by personal requirements or considered motivation. But for the Christian, and again, most especially for the seminarian and the priest, such *autostrade* or many-planed turnpikes are part of the conveniences of this world, to be used when needed but not serving as a norm for the spiritual life. For these the words of the Lord, demanding self-discipline, remain as pertinent as they were before the age of superhighways: "Enter by the narrow gate. For wide is the gate and broad is the way that leads to destruction, and many there are who enter that way. How narrow the gate and close the way that leads to life! And few there are who find it."[11]

These are the words in which Christ still addresses His seminarians and His priests. There is nothing stoic about them, as their contemporary critics pretend, for they are charged with love and call out to love, a love which expressed itself, thanks to self-discipline, with free and loving obedience to the will of the Father. Such obedience, even unto the death of the Cross, was a divine form of the human instinct to *rule thyself* and self-discipline which the Romans transmitted to us. It constituted the very essence of the priesthood of Christ and His title to glory: "He humbled himself . . . becoming obedient even unto death, even the death of the cross."[12] This obedience was obedience to a mandate, a law imposed upon Him by His Father, but it was a free obedience made possible by that self-discipline which was preeminent in Christ and indispensable in the priest.

145

If it be true, as I take it to be, that the Greek and Roman heritage, on the natural level of our Western liberal arts tradition, with their respective contributions of *know thyself* and *rule thyself,* contribute mightily not merely to the climate but the content of growth unto maturity in the candidates to the priesthood in the pretechnological, prephenomenological period in our cultural history, it is not less true that the Hebrew prophetic tradition and certainly the Christian revelation integrated these and lifted them to the level where maturity in Christ became possible. The Judeo-Christian tradition added its two-word formula of *give thyself.*

It did so in terms of the spirit of self-giving in the form of the acceptance of divine election by the Jews, the voluntary segregation and commitment of a people for the sake of an ideal which constituted the Jews a nation. It did so by the symbolic gift of himself in total obedience and unquestioning generosity by the symbolic action of Abraham, prepared to give himself in his son at the request of God. The rule of life summed up in *give thyself* was, of course, perfectly demonstrated and exemplified for all time by the emptying of Himself, the unwavering commitment and the gift of Himself on the Cross of the Incarnate Son of God.

In terms of the vocation to the priesthood, self-knowledge and self-discipline made possible a self-giving in response to one's vocation that was at once, *total, free, definitive,* and, which is the point of our present considerations, *fully mature.* It involved commitment to Christ, the eternal High Priest, to His Church, and to the service of God's people as basically structured and planned by Him, and to the portion of the flock committed to one's unselfish care.

To this total and conscious self-giving to Christ and to the unqualified manner in which one made himself available to the service of the Church, a young man was prepared during all the time of his stay in the seminary not merely by spiritual guidance and by the grace that came from the sacramental life of a

146

seminarian, nor merely from his philosophical-theological cultural formation, but also by the integration of all three of the formulae we have been discussing: self-knowledge, self-discipline, self-giving. It was a personal preparation, at once humane (humanistic) and Christian. It made it possible for grace to build on nature, and it reduced the terrible danger of a conflict between nature and grace, between faith and reason, between the committed priest and the cultivated man such as has been the menace not only to priestly perseverance but to personal integrity since the distinctions of Descartes split the level of human preparation and of reason from that of priestly preparation and faith.

Self-giving must always be a *definitive* offering of oneself; it was traditionally symbolized in many ways, from the clipping of one's hair at tonsure to the symbolic step in subdiaconate and the prostration of oneself in the sanctuary on the day of priestly ordination. New cultural forms will require and suggest new symbols, and it appears almost certain that some, at least, of the traditional symbols may disappear entirely. But the heart of the matter remains perennial and constant. There is no self-knowledge which hides from oneself any area of his being; there is no self-discipline which exempts one from any area of his instinctual, physical, or spiritual life; there is no self-giving that is done with fingers crossed, mental reservations, divided heart, or looking back over one's shoulder. Jesus, using the last figure of speech, made that perfectly clear from the beginning of the Christian order; the Church, in her official teaching, at least, has never contradicted Him or been unfaithful to His mandate that priestly self-giving be integral, namely, an offering of one's entire person, with all his gifts, charismatic and other, as these were received from God and as God asked them back in the form of service to others in the moment that He gave the Christian man his special vocation to the ministerial priesthood. Self-giving requires the gift of all one's soul and all one's body: one's hands for the offering of the sacrifice of Christ and the administration of the sacraments, one's mouth for the proclaiming of the Word of

God, one's heart and all its affections for the unqualified and undivided love of the things of God, beginning with the humanity of His Son and extending, without exception based on personal considerations, to all God's people, most particularly those, as one's parish or school or other group, to whom one is assigned, not so much as the result of self-preference or expression, but as part of one's self-giving.

A further motive which renders indispensable the offering of one's very body is the necessity that mature priests play a special part in that *completion* of Christ by the building up of His Mystical Body, which is the Church, in accordance with the plea of Saint Paul: "I rejoice now in the sufferings I bear for your sake; and what is lacking of the sufferings of Christ *I fill up in my flesh* for his body, which is the Church."[13] For all this, Paul described himself as having been *crucified* once and for all with Christ. He could express his own self-giving in terms of an identification with Christ so intimate as to make it possible for him to say that he lived no longer as one apart or on his own, but in such fashion that Christ lived in him. By this, he meant no merely mystical presence of Christ in his spirit, in his obedient will or his devoted mind; he meant that Christ lived in his very flesh and did so because he himself, knowing that flesh in all its potential for good or evil and dominating it in all the same potentials, responded by total self-giving to that gift of Himself by Christ which had made possible his life as a Christian and a priest. In his Epistle to the Romans, Paul addresses himself to all Christians, but in an especial fashion, one cannot doubt, to the priests who must be the models to Christians: "I exhort you therefore, brethren, by the mercy of God, *to present* your bodies as a sacrifice, living, holy, pleasing to God—your spiritual service."[14]

Somehow our new culture, our changing civilization, our new historical patterns of life and thought must make possible that self-knowledge, self-discipline, and self-giving which were once produced through the happy combination of the liberal arts culture, a theology based on the Gospels and faith constant in the Christian community. For it is only with the realization of these three essential elements of maturity—self-knowledge, self-discipline, and self-giving—that it becomes possible to talk of the *authenticity* of the ministerial priesthood as Catholicism has understood it from the beginning. It is only when these three elements have been verified in modern terms that we can speak of the priestly *identity,* the reality and efficacy of which in the contemporary world is so earnestly sought.[15]

Pope Pius XI, in his still valid encyclical on the priesthood, *Ad Catholici Sacerdotii,* summing up all the tradition of the Church from the beginning, felt prepared to draw a conclusion which may have to become the premise of the planning of contemporary bishops until the three formulae we have been dwelling upon are once again realized. Pope Pius said that if we cannot secure a sufficient number of the type of priests we have been describing, "then it is better to have a few good priests in the service of the Church than a multitude of bad ones."[16] Better a few priests and these mature, than hosts of priests and these immature, knowing neither themselves nor God, unprepared to rule themselves and therefore unfit to rule others, qualified in their self-giving and therefore inefficacious in their labors personal or official.

We have touched upon certain essential elements of seminary life and of the formation of young priests in the light of Sacred Scripture and the humanistic tradition. Vatican Council II has this to say: "By the power of the sacrament of orders, and in the image of Christ the eternal High Priest, they [priests] are consecrated to *preach the gospel, shepherd the faithful,* and *celebrate divine worship* as true priests of the New Testament."[17] To realize these objectives of their sacred vocation, priests are called continually to cultivate and develop their *self-giving* and *self-discipline,* as well as their *self-knowledge.* The requirements of this call have been developed by recent documents of the Sacred Congregation for Catholic Education, by repeated discourses of the Holy

Father, as these are summarized in a single book and in a programmatic way by the recent directives published both by the Congregation for Education and the Congregation for the Clergy.[18]

The Council speaks clearly of the need for priestly maturity and perfection in the decree *Optatam totius,* especially when it calls upon episcopal conferences in the various parts of the world to provide for the *gradual* introduction of their young clergy into priestly life and action, with a constant provision for the renewal and increase of the spiritual, intellectual, and pastoral resources of the clergy.[19] The documents published by not a few episcopal conferences give hope, sometimes strong, sometimes wistful, that new directions of life, thought, and action are being linked to the ancient, perennial requirement of *priestly maturity.*

Intellectual maturity, above all in the sacred sciences, is solidly demanded by the ordaining bishop of the candidate for the priesthood during the ordination ceremony. Priests, it is said, should be mature in their learning. Their doctrine, evangelical and patristic in its roots, should include a knowledge of the declarations of the Magisterium of the Church, above all of the councils and of the chief shepherds of Christendom, as well as a secure and balanced grasp of theological principles, out of all of which they must blend "a spiritual medicine for the People of God".[20]

Spiritual maturity expresses itself in a continued renewal of that self-giving which we have seen to be the specifically Christian contribution to the trinity of formulae we have suggested. It becomes possible in the renunciation of *oneself, one's life, one's time,* all that one is and does. Such self-giving is possible only with Christ and in Christ and through Christ; it is liturgically expressed in the eucharistic celebration of the Paschal Mystery during Holy Mass, but it does not end with the final words of the Mass. It is a program of three hundred sixty-five days a year all the years of one's life.

Priests can seek perfection, indeed they are bound to seek it, in obedience to the precept of the Lord: "You therefore are to be perfect, even as your heavenly Father is perfect."[21] This special obligation to seek perfection on the part of priests derives from the fact that they, by means of their ordination, which is a further and distinct consecration to God beyond those made in baptism and confirmation, are lifted to the level of living instruments of Christ, the eternal High Priest, to continue in time His literally divine work, which has caught up into itself all the efficacies of human nature to put these at the disposition of divine power and divine purposes. Thus consecrated with the annointing of the Holy Spirit and mandated by Christ, they mortify themselves in the flesh and give themselves over entirely to the service of men, establishing thus the possibility of their progress and sanctity unto the realization of the perfect man, which means the fully mature man.[22]

For the attainment of this maturity, specifically priestly, one must see as indispensable *total gift of oneself* not only to God and to Christ, *but also to the faithful, to one's own local church and to the Church universal.* The priest must consider himself an oblation even as did Christ. He must pattern himself upon the Christ of the Cross (there is no other known to Christian theology or to history), to the suffering Church (again, there is no other known to history or to theology), and there is no true priest without the Cross and suffering at the heart of his life and the heart of his ministry.

In the decree *Presbyterorum Ordinis,* the Council clearly affirms, with no little force:

> Christ, whom the Father sanctified and consecrated, and sent into the world, "gave himself for us that he might redeem us from all iniquity and cleanse for himself an acceptable people, pursuing good works". . . . Since in their own measure, priests participate in the office of the apostles, God gives them the grace to be ministers of Christ Jesus among the people. They shoulder the sacred task of the Gospel, so that the offering of

the people can be made acceptable through the sanctifying power of the Holy Spirit. For, through the apostolic proclamation of the gospel, the People of God is called together and assembled so that when all who belong to this People have been sanctified by the Holy Spirit, they can offer themselves as "a sacrifice, living, holy, pleasing to God". Through the ministry of priests, the spiritual sacrifice of the faithful is made perfect in union with the sacrifice of Christ, the sole Mediator. Through the hands of priests and in the name of the whole Church, the Lord's sacrifice is offered in the Eucharist in an unbloody and sacramental manner until he Himself returns.[23]

In the twelfth section of the same decree, the Council drives home this point once again:

And so it is that they are grounded in the life of the Spirit while they exercise the ministry of the Spirit and of justice, as long as they are docile to Christ's Spirit, who vivifies and leads them. For by their everyday sacred actions themselves, as by the entire ministry which they exercise in union with the bishop and their fellow priests, they are being directed toward perfection of life.[24]

Furthermore, the self-giving of the priest, the oblation of himself, of his entire life and all his energies, is continually renewed in the daily eucharistic celebration of the Paschal Mystery of Christ and becomes the foundation of the efficacious pastoral action of his priestly ministry:

Priestly holiness itself contributes very greatly to a fruitful fulfillment of the priestly ministry. True, the grace of God can complete the work of salvation even through unworthy ministers. Yet ordinarily God desires to manifest His wonders through those who have been made particularly docile to the impulse and guidance of the Holy Spirit. Because of their intimate union with Christ and their holiness of life, these men can say with the Apostle: "It is now no longer I that live, but Christ lives in me."[25]

There is no point in denying that at the present moment in history we find ourselves confronted by a certain infantilism, physical, moral, spiritual, sometimes even intellectual in the sense that this includes one's personal interests, even among priests. But the true modern priest, the mature and genuinely fulfilled priest, is, as always, *faithful* to his promises, to the obligations assumed at ordination, to the vocation which placed him in the ranks of the priesthood, provided only he responded to that presumed vocation with the *self-knowledge, self-discipline,* and *self-giving* that we have been discussing. As faithful even as was Saint Paul: "Let a man so account us, as servants of Christ and stewards of the mysteries of God. Now here it is required in stewards that a man be found trustworthy."[26]

Such is the priest who truly knows his own nature and mission, whatever the civilization around him and the culture through which he attained his self-knowledge; such is the priest whose loving act of self-oblation was made with self-discipline, whatever the techniques, consistent with the gospel, that he achieves his self-discipline and his abnegation for Christ. Thus does he express, as did his predecessors in the priesthood over the centuries, that fidelity which, in the eyes of the world, has always identified him as an authentic, ordained witness to Christ, distinct but not separate from his brethren in the Christian community, realizing the Paschal Mystery, diffusing the love of the Father for mankind, mankind called to share the dignity of the Son of God, the heritage of God as a co-heir with Christ, maturely, perseveringly, totally. Thus, and only thus, is formed, in the words of Paul, "the mature measure of the fullness of Christ".[27]

The mature man, certainly the mature priest, has for his hallmark fidelity to Christ and the Church. This is the reason for his poise and his joy in the Lord, a joy that extends to all things earthly and eternal.

Intellectual maturity, spiritual maturity, and pastoral maturity represent, then, indispensable conditions for the genuine and profound renewal of the postconciliar Church. How could such renewal be achieved on shifting sands and in the midst of the winds that blow in every direction those who have no firm roots in *self-knowledge, self-discipline,* and *self-giving?*

VIII

Interview with Jordan Aumann, O.P.

Aumann: What is the function of the Sacred Congregation for the Clergy?

Wright: Recently, I read in a purportedly scholarly book on the Church that the functions of our Congregation included everything not handled by other congregations! Like most of the things in the book in question (including the name attributed to our Congregation by the author), this information was misleading. The fact is that our Congregation, as reformed by Pope Paul VI, has two direct functions, both intimately interrelated.

The first of these is provision for the life and activities of diocesan clergy. The second is catechetics, the everyday parish teaching of the Faith. The priests of religious orders depend on the Congregation for Religious. Theology, in its more specialized, scientific aspects, depends on the Congregation for the Doctrine of the Faith. Our work is the problems of the priests who work in the parishes both on the level of teaching and on the level of parish administration.

Obviously, we have other functions in collaboration with the other congregations who share their proper aspects in this mighty task. Accordingly, we have *ad hoc* mixed commissions or study committees with various congregations according to the nature of the problem under review or planning. Nowadays, these involve us indirectly with the Con-

This interview was published in *The Priest* in March 1971.

gregation for the Liturgy, the Commission for the Laity (parish councils, for example, involve them), the Congregation for Bishops and that for Doctrine, not to mention occasional others. The interests of diocesan priests, their life, and their work constitute our overriding preoccupation.

Aumann: Do you think that bishops generally have been cooperative in adapting to the teaching and directives of Vatican II which touch upon the government of dioceses and the life and ministry of priests?

Wright: The background—historical, cultural, and psychological—of the answer to this question makes an unqualified *yes* or *no* reply difficult, if not impossible. On the other hand, the answer that the situation is *spotty* sounds ungenerous. I think that the bishops, like the clergy, laity, and religious, have been all but buried alive in new instructions, guidelines, decrees, and bibliography, not to mention recommended policies, following like an avalanche upon the basic doctrines setting forth the essential teachings and directives of Vatican II.

I often wonder how they open all their mail, let alone read it or act on it, particularly when every aspect of their responsibility has undergone bombardment and recommended revision during and since the Council. Considering, then, the amount of history and tradition from which they have had to liberate themselves and the elements of their history that they were bound in conscience to preserve and improve, I think that the bishops have been cooperative to a remarkable degree. Certainly, their desire to be so is unmistakable, if I may judge from the letters our Congregation gets from them. This goes double-barrelled for the United States, but is by no means limited to our country. Even

	there, it is not absolutely universal, but it is enheartening, with nine pluses for every negative.
Aumann:	To what extent do you think that diocesan pastoral councils can be effective in the adaptation and renewal of dioceses?
Wright:	I look upon diocesan pastoral councils as indispensable to the renewal of the diocese and the implementation of Vatican II. I cannot imagine any other channel through which a bishop can tap the spiritual and intellectual reserves of every segment of his diocese in an effective and orderly fashion.

In the Diocese of Pittsburgh, we had, even before the Council ended, a diocesan pastoral council blueprinted for immediate implementation along the lines—and a bit beyond the lines—suggested by the Council. It met regularly. We avoided *extremists,* both in the two-thirds voted by the priests, people, and religious and in the one-third appointed by the bishop. The reason was that we had important questions to discuss, and we hoped to reach something like viable consensus without having to listen either to tirades or highly personal manifestos or proclamations. Accordingly, the membership was representative, not only because every area and broad vocation in the diocese was represented, but also because the prevailing spirit was represented, due allowance being made for occasional spokesmen of points of view that tended to be polarized.[1]

I would have seen the continuing council as essential to the work of the bishop and the well-being of the diocese, even though a diocesan synod developed rather logically out of the council.[2] What provision for consultation, alternative to a pastoral council, may come out of the synod, I do not know. In any case, some form of council is a logical and psychological necessity. Self studies of our council revealed that, among other faults, the council was criticized as being too large and for meeting for too long a period (two days) four times a year.

I probably agree with these criticisms. But (and on this point I kid you not) the bishop and his immediate official family were probably more interested in the development of the pastoral council than were many of the laity and not a few of the clergy and religious. I hate to state the reason, but realism compels me to do so. Officialdom (the establishment and all that sort of jazz) were honestly looking for information; some of the individual groups were preoccupied with pushing for special interests, and once the special interest either failed or prevailed, such persons or groups tended to lose interest. Never make the mistake of supposing that resistance or indifference to pastoral councils is necessarily the fault of the diocesan *establishment,* unless the *establishment* is failing to do the education job needed to create that sense of community in the total diocese, which is the soul of the pastoral council.

Aumann: Do you see any danger in the practice of allowing seminarians to pursue their academic courses in a university of their choice and to live as resident students on campus?

Wright: The idea of seminarians pursuing academic courses in a general university has almost everything to recommend it, so long as they return home to a religious or theological college which serves as their shared residence and the center of a liturgical community to which they belong as to their special spiritual family. This, by the way, is an old tradition in the great European universities and in the so-called Roman *colleges.*

In Pittsburgh, we experimented with it along local lines. Saint Paul's Seminary (we were neither afraid nor ashamed of the word *seminary*) provided a liturgical community for our collegiate aspirants to the priesthood. At Saint Paul's, they took special courses, of particular interest to them, in Scripture, theology, and related subjects. However, they journeyed daily to Duquesne University for humanities, sciences, and the specialized subjects which might be of interest to them as to other members of the general intellectual community. Our students were encouraged to enter into the life of the campus community in maximum degree, though they wore a blazer with their own college shield to indicate that they were distinct but not separate from those with whom they wished to live in mutual study and service. We were open to the idea of attendance elsewhere for individual students where courses were available which corresponded at once with their personal interests and the various needs of our corner of the Kingdom of God.

We never did go in for students living on the campuses of the universities they frequented. We felt that this would sacrifice too much, especially the liturgical community, without proportionate advantages.

Aumann: It would seem that the success of renewal depends to a great extent on seminary formation and the type of men who teach in major seminaries. To what extent can there be a pluralistic presentation of theology?

Wright: The extent of a pluralistic presentation of theology is and should be very great. This is not only a fact of contemporary life; it is a part of the Catholic theological tradition, as anyone knows who has read that tradition beginning with the New Testament, running through the Church Fathers, flourishing in the so-called Middle Ages, and limping into our own days. The present confusion on the point results, in some part, from a somewhat artificial and not quite innocent attempt to pretend that in recent years there has grown up a sharp distinction and a consequent division between what the architects of this pretence call the *Roman position* and all the wide world of creative and untrammeled theological schools of thought.

I am inclined to find this nonsense, where it is not phony. When I was a student in Rome, even as now, there was abundant theological pluralism in the various Roman universities, Jesuit, Dominican, Franciscan, etc. In my own Roman university (Gregorian), some of us thought we detected imaginative and inspiring theological pluralism among our own professors, though all were Jesuits. I realize that this runs counter to the researchers of recent issues of the popular press as well as to the lamentations of critics of what they called the *Roman position,* but I encounter the need to refuse to conform with these voices of the moment on many matters which have nothing to do with theology. It hardly comes to me as a shock when I conceive theological pluralism as part of the normal Catholic tradition, even though some appear to find it somehow revolutionary, unheard of, and even a *breakthrough.*

The unity of the Catholic Church is not one of theological opinions or schools, but one of faith. One of the great illusions, not to say illiteracies, of our little minute in history is the confusion between faith and theology. Faith is the revelation made by Christ and therefore officially preserved by the

Church. Theologies and the speculations of men are worth as much as the reasons advanced for them. Sometimes that worth is tremendous, both in the service of the Faith and in the nourishing of culture; sometimes is neglible or nonexistent—though for reasons of courtesy and democratic egalitarianism, I suppose, it is always well to be careful how one phrases this latter criticism.

This said, I would think it impossible to have too many enlightened intuitions of a theological kind into the mysteries of the single faith—and therefore I accept, without any cavil, the suggestion that, so long as they are confirmed in the Faith, professors should be as theologically cosmopolitan as it is possible to be without exploding one's head.

Aumann: Some of the statements in the conciliar decrees seem to have reference to problems of priestly ministry in Europe rather than the United States. Does this not allow for a misconception of *aggiornamento* on the part of American priests?

Wright: I am not sure about the validity of the criticism that underlies this question. I would have thought that the emphasis in the conciliar documents is more often occidental as opposed to oriental and universal, rather than European as opposed to American. If any single segment of the clergy receives short shrift in the documents, it would appear to me to be the priests of the Third World, not those in the United States or any other single part of the Western world. I would wish to give this careful thought before making a final answer, if only because I do not personally draw the sharp distinction between European and American clergy that this question suggests to exist.

I recognize and rejoice in the experience and the opportunities of the New World, but I must confess that, by and large, I continue to think of our American, Canadian, Australian and New Zealand peoples, clergy included, as spill-overs from the various parts of Europe, for better or for worse, and perpetuators of the cultural, religious, and basic political patterns they brought with them from the Old World. I realize that this will not be forever true, but I still think we have more in common than we have dividing us. On the political front, we are reminded of this about every thirty years and become military allies, God help us. On the religious front, I think I detected in Vatican Council II that the lines of division were not *vertical* (national, so far as the West is concerned) but *horizontal* (that they cut across our national frontiers and found us more often divided *within* our respective nations than *among* them).

Aumann: Apart from the crises which individual priests have always encountered, what would you say is the root cause of the universal crisis in priestly identity and priestly ministry?

Wright: I am not so sure what the root cause of the universal crisis may be. I am almost afraid to declare what I often suspect it is: a preoccupation with the kingdom of this world and a forgetfulness of the life of the world to come. However, this may be a rather glib comment; it may well be that the Faith of our Fathers is burning still, but that does not explain most of the healthy tans we see among us. At a conference on clergy problems we held in Rome a year ago October, we decided that the dozen or more major crises and problems in contemporary priestly life take forms which can be included in one universal, all-embracing word. That word is *frustration.*

However, the *cause* of the frustration is by no means universal. In some places (southern Italy, Africa, others) it is economic. In some places (France, Britain, the United States, Canada) it has to do with structures and communications or even excessive affluence. In some places (Iron Curtain countries, Scandinavia) it has to do with a sense of irrelevance, not being wanted, or being positively excluded. In some places it is cultural, political, alas, even moral. But it seems to be, fairly generally, a sense of *frustration,* the jargon word for which is *identity crisis,* and the cure of which is a rediscovery of one's sublime dignity, purpose, and destiny, come what may.

Aumann: What are your hopes for the future regarding American priestly life and ministry?

Wright: All my hopes (and I think they are the hopes of all Christians) can be summed up in the prayer that our priests will be *mature men* — and then men apart, like Aaron was, or Melchizedek or, above all, Jesus Christ. Some months ago, I nearly had my block knocked off in a half a dozen angry mail bags for remarking that all too many of our priests who revealed their instability by leaving us are, in fact, immature men, not necessarily bad men or even bad priests. The conclusion was not really my own. It was based on the testimony of psychiatrists, parents, brother priests, students, and, sometimes, most pathetically of all, the immature girls who had married some immature priests. I received, in reaction to my remarks, some amazing mail. It went from serious, considered dissent from the opinion I offered to almost amusing (were the subject not so serious) letters of the type which run: " . . . I never read such a lousy opinion. You must be a nut. I cannot imagine a more stupid remark than the one you made. However, I admire you very much. I am forty-five years old and am in the third grade." I even received a formal resolution from a group which calls itself a *study club,* saying that one of their members had married *a priest* who was "the most mature man she had ever met". I wonder!

Seriously, there is a widespread emotional lack in our generation. Call it *infantilism,* call it *immaturity,* call it the result of hothouse seminaries, momism, or whatever you will, but the opposite of it is *mature men,* which in the priest, means a man who has achieved the fullness of Christ Jesus and who therefore, in work and truth, imitates Christ by going about doing good and by preaching, with integral faith, the truth revealed through Jesus by God.

IX

Defense of Man

The present front in the battle in defense of human life is that of *abortion*. The next will assuredly be *euthanasia*. God knows what euphemism we shall be asked to use for the termination of the lives deemed physically no longer fit, socially no longer useful, mentally, politically, or, perhaps, religiously no longer acceptable —situations we have faced neatly, though nastily, in centuries gone by—and will again if we can find a smooth word and an acceptable technique. In any case, most of the issues in the battle *for* and *against* life have been faced by Pope Paul.

Pope Paul's encyclical *Humanae Vitae* is a prophetic defense of man, of the human person and of the future of the race. This will come as a surprise to any who, influenced by the encyclical's critics, think of it in negative terms as merely another condemnation of contraception or in positive terms as only another defense of the Church's teaching authority.

In fact, it is in the tradition of Pope Pius XI's concept of the modern papacy, described by Henri Bordeaux, as called to be "the supreme guardian of the human person, of human liberty, and of the human conscience universally under attack by contemporary Statism".

Pope Paul develops the pattern of Christian personalism which Pius XII wove into his encyclopedic moral and social teaching, notably on problems of war and peace, conscience and authority, technology and culture.

He echoes the witness of Pope John, almost his very words, on the natural law and the person, and the vanity of seeking solutions to population problems in expedients which offend

This address was delivered at Anna Maria College, Paxton, Massachusetts, on May 2, 1971.

against the divinely established moral order and which attack human life at its very source (rather than) in a renewed scientific and technical effort on man's part to deepen and extend his dominion over nature.

Pope Paul himself, notably in his historic address at the United Nations, has consistently put the teachings of faith and reason in the perspective of the person fully considered. It is against the norm of a total view of man, the full range of the nature and needs of personality, that he defended life in his case for peace at the United Nations and, in his encyclical, pleads for the jealous preservation of the norms protective of both love and life, for the place of God Himself in human affairs.

The encyclical is, then, much more than a negative pronouncement on artificial contraception. It is a positive though admittedly incomplete, presentation on marriage morality; it says No only to a negative concept of man's vocation. In an age when almost all the means of social communication are used in greater or lesser degree to debase sexual love to erotic techniques or diversions, the Pope proclaims anew the positive values of love, marriage, parenthood, and family life. He does so against the authentic Christian background of the Cross, which all followers of Christ must carry, and the destiny of life everlasting to which all who live are called. Is it a sign of the times that such familiar truths of the gospel message and the inherited wisdom of mankind struck so many as strange and harsh? How else can one explain that a defense of the person's essential dignity was seen by some as an attack on his freedom?

It is even insinuated that the Holy Father, as if indifferent to every other value, human or divine, had sought, with unbecoming defensiveness, only to bolster his traditional teaching authority.

The plain fact is that Pope Paul would seem to have risked, humanly speaking, the divine authority of the papacy by putting it on the line in the defense of human life, nuptial love, and man himself.

Saint Augustine suggests that every man is somehow Adam

and Adam is every man. This is why the defense of the person is also the defense of the human race, even as the defense of the race is the defense of every person. This is the premise of the Christian humanism underlying Pope Paul's encyclicals on the progress of peoples and on the defense of life.

His humanism sees every person as being called, even as was mankind in Adam, to subdue creation and rule over it. Such a mandate forbids humanity or the person to surrender to nature, to be willingly overwhelmed by creation or dominated by its blind forces, including those at work within man himself. It calls all mankind and every free person to that self-knowledge, self-discipline, and self-giving essential to responsible stewardship over all that God has given us, beginning with our own instincts, faculties, and powers. This, from the beginning, has been the heart of morality.

Christian morality implies a hierarchy of values, an order at work throughout the moral universe. That order is succinctly stated by Saint Paul: "All things are yours, and you are Christ's and Christ is God's."[1] This is the substance of Pope Paul's defense of the dominion of God; it is not less the premise of his defense of the rights and duties of the person and the race.

One need not go as far as does Maritain, who fears that many Christians are prepared to genuflect in worship of the world, to see signs of an inverted order in contemporary humanism and, as a result, the moral order turned upside down. This is the case when Christians, rather than seeking to subdue creation and rule over it, yield to pressures to conform uncritically to the spirit of the age.

Against all such depersonalized submission to the dictates of the times in what pertains to sexual love, the Pope's encyclical raises the standards of the Church's long-considered understanding of the sanctity of life and the moral norms for its transmission. In the face of unrelenting propaganda for the acceptance of contraception, the Pope has reaffirmed neatly the Church's ban on interference with the natural processes resulting in human conception and birth when nature, obedient to God, is open to new life.

That ban is based on the natural moral law as that law is illumined by reflection on divine revelation. Faithful to his mandate to interpret these authentically and confronted with a growing threat to God's law and man's vocation, the Pope has given his authoritative judgment that the procreative significance of the conjugal act is not less sacrosanct than its value as an expression of mutual love. Indeed, given certain anti-life forces at work in our civilization, he has emphasized the special concern for its life-giving power which must surround consideration of that act. In so doing he has, again, come to the defense of life, of mankind, and of the person.

He has defended man against the fragmentation of his person, the isolation of sex from the spiritual elements of human destiny. It is this consideration which prompts the renowned British scholar, David Knowles, to ask a reverent, careful, and repeated reading of the encyclical by those who would discover the profundity and humanity of its message.[2]

The encyclical further defends the person against reduction to demographic digit, a mere consumer of the earth's natural resources, a burden to the political order intended to serve him, or a liability to the economy intended to sustain him.

Against these and more frivolous trends of the contraceptive society (the phrase, by the way, is from one of its partisans), the Pope argues for an ennobling sense of responsibility and awareness of the consequences of one's every action, specifically actions involving intelligent and free cooperation with the creative power of God Himself.

Essential to the self-mastery in the moral man's conduct of his life, including the use of marriage, is a saving asceticism proper to each one's state in life. The due asceticism called for in the Pope's analysis of the vocation to marriage is in the service of man and the defense of his liberty, for it is the indispensable condition of freedom from the interior tyranny of instinct and the external compulsions of circumstance.

Pro-life and pro-person, Pope Paul's encyclical may yet turn out to be also the defense of human sexuality against mere sex.

Father James Schall, writing on the long-range significance of the encyclical, is not the first to suspect that our age is in danger of sacrificing sexuality to sex. A like misgiving obviously disturbed the thoughtful minority in the Lambeth Conference of 1948 who fought the Anglican compromise on contraception to the end, insisting that it is, to say the least, suspicious that the age in which contraception has won its way is not one which has been conspicuously successful in managing its sexual life. Is it possible that, by claiming the right to manipulate his physical processes in this matter, man may, without knowing or intending it, be stepping over the boundary between the world of Christian marriage and what one might call the world of Aphrodite, the world of sterile eroticism? . . . Once submission to the *given* pattern is abandoned, all kinds of variations on the sexual theme which heighten satisfaction can appear to be enrichments of the sexual life.

Father Schall reflects on the irony that the Pope, celibate and aging as his critics lose no chance to point out, may finally prove to be the main defender of sexuality itself—and all as a result of teachings rejected as folly by those to whom sexuality means so much!

The reason for this, he argues, is that what is ultimately at stake in the current confusion over sex morality is the very nature of human bisexuality [that is, normal sexuality between man and woman, i.e., *both* sexes]. He contends that any knowledge of proposals for genetics experimentation and control (this threat passed the proposal stage in England in February last year!) or an analysis of the *philosophy* surrounding contemporary homosexual or lesbian theory will soon reveal that it is precisely bisexuality and its implications in love and the family that are now at stake.

Two urgent issues—a genetic control of human life and the meaning of perversion—therefore move to the front among the perennial problems behind the Pope's defense of the natural act in marriage. It is its defense of man as a naturally bisexual being, whose dignity rests in large part upon the *naturalness* of man as he is received from nature, that makes this encyclical important to our culture and all its citizens. Through his encyclical, the Holy Father has placed the Magisterium on the side of man's natural system of reproduction as ultimately superior to any contrived or perverted alternative.

Father Schall sees this same defense as implicit in the scriptural and traditional rejection of perversion as a normal or licit form of human sexual life, let alone the superior way of life for man that a whole school of writers pretend it to be. What fundamentally distinguishes *perversion*—as homosexuality, lesbianism, and bestiality—from the bisexual relationship is its fundamental lack of any relationship to the transmission of life and its consequent sense of natural frustration.

Hence Father Schall's conclusion that these threats to human life, which in fact abound in modern society, cannot be totally disassociated from the theory and practice of contraception. Population fear, genetic control, and perversion all contain serious menaces to the nature of man. In the context of these issues and their relation to human life and dignity, together with some of the totalitarian implications of population theory to which the Holy Father pointedly refers, the encyclical does a major service to man by warning against dangers in our intellectual and political environments which strike at the very structure of man, the nature of human love, and its *natural* exigencies, not only toward the transmission of life but also toward truly human fulfillment.

Dr. Victor G. Rosenblum, founder of Northwestern University's program in law and social sciences, finds the Pope's encyclical *a document of confrontation* for modern society and a service to multiple human values. Dr. Rosenblum considers the present preoccupation with contraception as a threat to social evolution along truly humanitarian lines because it tends to warp some of the most significant of our human traits—compassion and love.

The Jewish intellectual stresses that our preoccupation with birth limitation contains the seeds of some very troublesome attitudes, indifference, or callousness, to the needs of others and a very crass form of materialism.

The fruits of these seeds Dr. Rosenblum sees in contraceptive approaches to social problems, beginning with those of poverty in the inner city and among minority groups. If we believe these problems can be solved by cutting down the birth of children, said Dr. Rosenblum, we are modern Malthusians, not the humanitarians we think we are. Because the families of the black poor are larger than ours, we feel we must teach them contraceptive practices so they can conform to our standards. If they don't, we blame them for creating their own misery and say it is all their own fault.

If nothing else, the Pope's pronouncement is supportive of the poor man who has a large family right now. It says to him: We know your difficulties, and we don't think you should have to face them alone. Everyone must be concerned to see that your children are fed, educated, given their chance in life.

The fears of this sociologist appear to be confirmed by history as it is analyzed by a noted student of human civilization. Commenting on the effect of contraception once it sets in among a people, Dr. Will Durant asserted, long before the Pope's pronouncement, that the birth-control movement has already created in America a problem immeasurably more profound than any it purported to solve. Nor, as a historian of culture, was Durant surprised.

He said: I know what happened to Athens. . . . I know what happened to Rome. I know how Caesar almost scratched his head bald thinking how he might induce the Roman women to have children. He decreed that they should have no diamonds if they had no children, that they should have no jewels of one kind if they had none of the other. I know that Augustus passed law after law in the first decade of our Christian era almost 2,000 years ago, trying to stop this current of family limitation. I know, too, that all legislation failed. . . . It was the end of the Western Roman Empire. True, Dr. Durant later sought, by a letter to a Los Angeles paper, to explain that he had merely lamented the self-annihilation of superior *stocks* and then take-over by *lesser breeds,* but this kind of racism, not without its parallel in our own times, is socially and morally as sick as the genetic control which, in fact, Durant originally and more wisely opposed.

Pope Paul's encyclical also takes up the defense of the person and of mankind against the totalitarian tendencies of the modern secular state, especially when it turns to population control in order to solve domestic and foreign problems.

The fact is that already governments aggressively link contraceptive policies to welfare programs and (in the case of the United States) to aid to underdeveloped countries. The Church acts in the service of man when she resists invasion by the state in the autonomy of the family. Contraceptive requirements by the state run directly counter to the purpose for which governments exist: namely, the service of life, not its prevention; the provision of the means needed to sustain life when these are lacking, and the protection of the autonomy of the family, not its violation.

Parents lose none of their dignity nor their rights when they happen to be economically embarrassed. When they ask those in charge of the common good for food, education, shelter, or opportunity for their children, they should not be handed contraceptives by the political authorities.

Trends in the democracies give some idea of what may be expected in more grossly statist regimes. Already the federal government of the United States has a heavy investment in contraceptive projects, designed particularly for welfare clients and for poorer nations with claims in equity, charity, and common decency on American aid.

Not long ago, it was reported that the Department of Health, Education, and Welfare told authorities of two American states—Massachusetts and Wisconsin—to make contraceptives available to unmarried women or lose federal funds for aid to dependent children, and so much the worse for all concerned if local state laws prohibit the practice! Several American *planners,* some of them close to the shaping of public policy, have already declared for a punitive *baby tax* on the parents of families of more than two children.

Small wonder that Dr. Rosenblum sees the Pope's encyclical as a well-timed defense of man and of human freedom against statism! One gravely doubts how long free choice for families can survive in a society that accepts the use of contraception and the other forms of birth control condemned by the Pope—abortion and sterilization—as tools for human and social engineering.

To say these things flatly is to speak in the service of man; the Pope has done so. It is frightening that so many others, liberals and conservatives alike, remain silent while researchers (not all of them non-Catholic) in scores of laboratories are hard at work looking for what they would deem the ideal contraceptive— including something that could be implanted at adolescence to make women permanently infertile unless it is removed.

Use of such a contraceptive would, to be sure, make every child a *wanted child.* But Dr. Rosenblum raises the question: *Wanted by whom, the parents or the state?* For the illiterate (often the ancestors of the aristocracy), the disadvantaged (not less often the forefathers of a free society's leaders), and the ideologically suspect, the baby quota might always be full!

It is in its fundamental opposition to these anti-human possibilities—no longer Orwellian—that the Pope's encyclical takes on prophetic significance for the wider community than that of Catholic belief, in Dr. Rosenblum's judgment.

Nor is the word *prophetic* lightly used. Pope Paul's encyclical's speaking out on a question so widely treated by others with caution or downright cowardice makes him a prophet in the radical Greek sense of the word: *one who speaks out.*

His immovable stand, in the midst of cries demanding compromise or change in what he must see as God's law for life, for love, for man himself; his speaking courageously in the face of popular opinion; his destiny to be God's voice at whatever price, these make him a prophet in the fullest Hebrew sense.

His unambiguous call to conscience not as a merely instinctive self-contained, blind witness—one among many voices clamoring within a man—but as the internal judge of one's own conformity with God's law and with the faith that comes from hearing the Church—all this makes the Pope a prophet in the pattern once demanded for our times by Father Karl Rahner, writing precisely on the perils to individual conscience of just such moral problems as induced abortion and contraception.

Pope Paul's prophetic service of life and love has no taint of Puritanism or pessimism. He does not speak in terms of distinctions between sex and love, life and sex, or life and love. Quite the contrary, he proclaims the essential relationships among these at every point. It is not the Pope, it is the contraceptionists who speak of choosing between and therefore separating the expression of love and openness to life, the love-sharing and life-giving aspects of sexuality in marriage.

Pope Paul's defense of life and love in the interpersonal relationship that is marriage commits him also to optimism for the future of the race. Here too the pessimism is in the ranks of his critics.

Pleading for openness to life and to God's Providence, he puts faith at work with hope and enlists both in behalf of love, all in the service of man. He has done this with the optimism of Pius XII who, speaking of overpopulation panic, dared to say: As for the future, who can foresee what new and unsuspected resources may be found on our planet, and what surprises may be uncovered outside of it by the wonderful scientific achievements that have just barely begun? . . .

It is strange to find that the fears of some individuals are able to change well-founded hopes for prosperity into catastrophic spectres at the very moment when science is changing what used to be considered the dreams of wild imaginations into useful realities.

An age of breathtaking space science, astounding surgical service to life, and marvels in exploiting the riches of land, sea, and sky extend to fantastic frontiers the call to Adam—all mankind—to subdue creation and rule over it. It is no time to forget the primacy of life or the supremacy of the person. Hence Pope Paul's prayers for the new science and his defense of the life it should serve.

X

Contemporary Humanism

In recent addresses, Pope Paul has analyzed, with a sense of urgency shared by many, the threat of the secular humanism to the person and to spiritual values, beginning with the very ideas of the existence and Providence of God.

The menace of a humanism that excludes salvation history, the Incarnation, the mystery of the Cross, and the fact, together with the implications for the person and humanity, of the Resurrection, is far from new. However, contemporary forms of humanism reveal, together with an unwonted aggressiveness, a greater negativism, even nihilism, than the humanism of earlier generations. For historic humanism, *Homo sum et humani nihil a me alienum puto* may have left the humanist hazy or agnostic about the supernatural and the life of the world to come, but current secular humanism is hazy about the needs of the human spirit even here below and is met in its denial of the divine, at least as being what it would call *relevant*. [1]

Classical humanism, even as late as our first flare of modernism at the turn of the century and since, was characteristically centered on man, even on the person. It sometimes excluded the immortal longings and supernatural needs of the human spirit, but it did so as would deists rather than atheists. It retained a certain soothing Christian rhetoric, but it either prescinded from or avoided precision concerning the God of Jesus Christ. Christ himself came to be numbered with Socrates, Joan of Arc, John Hus, and, in due course (I remember well the day), Sacco and Vanzetti. But the point was that these were seen as persons, prepared to do battle for the human person. In this sense, the

This article was written for and published in the June 1971 issue of *The Sign*.

older humanism, however dubious about the claims and gifts of God, was crystal clear about the dignity and rights of man.

One may question how much of the fully human was left in the person surviving the exclusions and denials of the older humanism, including that of modernism. But drab and stoic though a person might be in a humanism thus limited and arid, he was still recognizable as a human, albeit a somewhat grim one.

It was precisely this grimness that gave some modernist humanists, especially those reared in the ancient, more relaxed Faith (for all their criticism of its formalism, structures, and institutionalism), a few significant second thoughts. Dr. William Lawrence Sullivan is a ready example.

Dr. Sullivan came to perceive the limitations of his relatively humane humanism in a contribution he made to the *Atlantic Monthly* early in the debate within the Unitarian fellowship between the deists and the theists in the late '20s and early '30s. Writing under the title: *Is Humanism a Religion?,* he described the unhappy plight of the mere humanist in that date, a truncated person, but still recognizably human: *The first curse of the Almighty on those who deny him is to deprive them of their sense of humor.*

That the curse is still working in these more emancipated days weeps from every page our latterday modernists write. Observe the stoic, sterile *courage* which is their claim to be honored. Note the saving patches of religious rhetoric with which they soften the blow of our impending doom. Particularly watch the sense of intellectual affront and emotional indignation with which they deplore (to say no more) believers, past or present, who make jokes about religious controversy or who laugh in the middle of a *theological* lecture or a *dialogue.* Read their reflections on Chesterton or listen (as I did recently with mingled pain and amusement) to one of them talk on Ronald Knox's translation of the Scripture wherein much was passed over except to recall that, as he [the writer] understood it, the

177

hierarchy never paid Knox for it. The thrust of the presentation was on Ronnie's satires and especially the *flip sarcasm* of *Reunion All Round* and the *contrived wit* of *The New Sin*.[2]

But the plight of the new secular humanist is considerably more pathetic for the person and perilous for civilization. It is that plight which Paul VI (first among many) is seeking to expose. The older humanist would not genuflect to a tabernacle, but he might tip his hat to a man or, at least, to a woman. He could and did attempt an occasional feeble joke; he became quite serious, even heroic, about the importance of the person. But who can *process* a joke into the formulae of the new scientific humanism? Moreover, the person is not the center nor the apex, under God, of the technological humanist's universe. Gone now is even the deadly earnest voluntaristic individual who thought of himself, with futile bravery, as the master of his fate and, bloody but unbowed, the captain of a figure of speech known as his soul.

In the new humanism, impersonal, calculated, technological, it is idle to talk of the Incarnate Person of the Son of God as the source and center of a fully personalist humanism. As for the shadow of the Cross over all creation and the hope-filled mystery of Easter; as for cruel conscience and personal immortality —ah, eat, drink, and be merry, or at least look merry, for tomorrow we die!

At the center of the new humanism is the machine, probably a computer and possibly a bomb. If a man is anywhere near that center, it is not man as the image of God, nor man the rational animal, nor the laughing animal, least of all the mystical animal— but man the economic unit, the useful citizen, *homo faber.* He is present not as a *soul,* central to the whole scheme of things, a *person* made in the image of God, but as a *statistic.*

Such is the crudely technological humanism which concerns Pope Paul (and not a few atheists); such, too, are its byproducts: the conformist culture of the standardized book clubs and manipulated thought controls: the contraceptive mentality with its slavery to sociological *findings* and antiseptic *techniques,* the military-industrial complex; the planned communities with their houses made of ticky-tacky and their *picture windows* looking out on other houses made of the same stuff. Sometimes the rationalizing process uses the traditional vocabulary of religious humanism (as did the earlier modernists), if only for forensic reasons. Sometimes it adopts the jargon of sociology, psychiatry, or politics (democracy today, fascism yesterday, collectivism tomorrow), to give the act a *grabber.* Sometimes, with greater inventiveness, it devises a vocabulary all its own (Teilhard?), to show the ineffable mystique and cosmic complexity of it all. But the net result is the same: the *person* becomes lost in the ideological shuffle, God ceases to be transcendent and absolute, man becomes a cog in the machinery, and Christ a *douce chimere* in the dictatorships and a constitutional deity in the democracies. You pay your taxes and you're assigned your choice.

Meanwhile, any gap between the world of political collectivism or Marxism (classical communism) and technological democracy is slowly but surely closing so far as concerns the rise of secular humanism, the eclipse of the person and the elimination of the factor of freedom or of spiritual values, human or divine. Christian humanism can look for little more than tactical tolerance from either of the major ideological or technological powers which confront it at the moment—tolerance, even flattery perhaps, but acceptance *never.* Coexistence, maybe; a measure of limited collaboration for specific secular purposes, probably; mutual comprehension and reciprocal interplay—well, only with great difficulty and violent if not suicidal compromises.

The reasons of this are common to both the systems of secular humanism which confront us: *dialectical materialism* and *technological impersonalism;* the reasons are also built into the very nature of the morality and view of the person and of his story which are the premises of Christian humanism.

It would be difficult to deny the conflict between personal

liberty and the rigid pretenses of technocracy, on the one hand, and of dialectical materialism on the other. He who runs can read that spiritual values and divine realities, in personal or human histories, are challenged or denied by ideologists in both camps, whatever their political stripe. As a result, human nature being what it is, and propaganda and public opinion polls being what they are, these values and realities are in grave danger of being practically forgotten by most. In plain fact, they are already ignored, if not forgotten, in polls on abortion, celibacy for the sake of the Kingdom, the work of the worship of God, the distinction between the sacred and the profane, no matter on which side of the iron, bamboo, or silk curtains the polls are taken.

This situation is due in no small part to two powerful forces which, as we have suggested, are dominant in our world today, save, perhaps, for small enclaves or something like truly human or Christian humanism which must strike our typical, and intellectual, leaders as *exotic, romantic,* or, worst of all, *medieval.*

Superficially, these two dominant forces seem to differ; indeed, they are sometimes regarded as mutually antagonistic, ultimate enemies, *two rival world powers,* largely because of differences in political rhetoric or economic structures. In fact (for whatever facts may be worth), careful study discloses that they have much more in common than in contrast; as a result, in the long run, there is little to choose between them so far as the dignity of the person and the primacy of the spiritual are concerned.

Again, I mean, of course, the two cultural and social controls represented by *dialectical materialism* (Marxism) and by a certain mentality which is the spiritual, above all moral—*de facto,* though not necessary—byproduct of an increasingly dominant *technological scientism.* This latter mentality is particularly the result of automation, the cult of the gadget and the facile solutions of scientific techniques without regard for more complex moral values, personal or community. The pill is a familiar and cheap example; the bomb is a less popular and more expensive *technique* for prompt, strictly practical solutions of annoying problems which complicate our convenience. All these artifacts—automation, the gadget, the efficient techniques, the pills, the abortion suction pump, and the bombs—have their rationalizations, some valid, some plausible, some perverse. All are aided and abetted by the apodictic *statistics* marshalled in their behalf as slippery syllogisms were once used to bolster other mentalities. Taken together, they constitute the degenerative *automative mentality* as opposed to the moral and cultural sense of responsibility which saw tools and techniques as *good* to the extent that they serve and perfect personality completely. It is already a long day since men have talked what must seem to them the sociological nonsense and democratic *heresy* about *one* man, *with God,* constituting a *majority!* Moreover, psychologically speaking, how long can the free will of one lonely Christian, who wishes to be thought of as *democratic* and *with it,* stand up under the bombardment of the Gallup Poll, the Kinsey Report, the monolithic press, and the researches of bipartisan Congressional commissions and *community* pressure groups?

The other form of secular humanism, *dialectical materialism,* typified but not limited in Marxism, involves a direct denial of God and of the human person as a subject of innate rights and powers (including free choice), plus an autonomy proper to an image of God. But even *democratic* secular humanism, conditioned by a certain *cult* of technocratic science (as opposed to reasoned *use* of science), and reinforced by the swift frozen certainties of the electronic computers, involves no less a materialism, at heart atheistic, even when departmentalized *liturgical* observance survive in the *democracy* for reasons atavistic or habitual.

Hence the necessity, if personality and a valid humanism are to survive, to bring into the battle against secular humanism not only a refreshed and vigorous religious faith, a lively awareness of the presence of God and the claims of Christ and his Kingdom (including his Church), but also a passionate love for the liberalizing arts—music, poetry, painting, creative art forms, divine philosophy, theology centered on God and eternity—to counterbalance and render humane the current apotheosis of the sciences and enslavement by their techniques and formulae. Only thus can materialism be cut down to size or, better still, transformed and humanized.

A world in which the choice, for the vast majority of mankind, would perforce lie between *dialectical materialism* (of the type of Marxism) and the mentality of automation and computerized controls would be—as the Protestant theologian Helmut Thielicke justly remarks—a world offering no choice: only secular human-ism, with two forms of materialism, neither entirely distinct from the other. The one is frankly atheist and Marxist; the other (that of the West) is implicitly atheist and what Thielicke calls *biological* and *technicized.* Again, in terms of spiritual liberty and moral freedom, the choice is no choice. The one explicitly denies whatever absolute values, above all God, provide the context of freedom; the other practically annuls the influence of these (some of its *theologians* even deny moral absolutes) by the exaltation of the physical and material, the measurable (at least by statistics!) and the technological.

Since our folklore and eloquence continue to repudiate the first and more explicit materialism, let us consider with care the more subtle (and perilous) mentality of technocratic materialism nearer home.

Christian morality, still the object of Western lip-service, is based on the concepts of human free will, the primacy of the spiritual, the dominion of God. It has always been a question as to how much we can talk of *free will,* not in the use of science, but in science itself. Charles Herzfeld, in *Science and the Church,* emphasized pointedly that there has never been elaborated an adequate philosophy (let alone moral theology) of the meta-physical principles concerning morality and freedom, on the one hand, and the more or less fixed and constant *facts* of science which imply a certain determinism, on the other. This reality, plus the increasing influence of computers and cybernetics in human relations and decisions, including moral choices, social planning, and public policies, constitutes an inevitable threat to attitudes toward and even awareness of personal freedom and individual responsibility. The threat lies precisely in the mentality which has become acclimated to an impersonal dependence on calculators, mass opinion, the tyranny of statistics (usually manipulated), and the seeming infallibility of electronic computers for the solution of those problems (they are already innumerable) where *human factors* (love, loyalty, hope, courage, faith, sympathy, passion for freedom) are not only directly or indirectly part of the equation, but are *precisely* the elements that cannot be programmed, processed, or otherwise fed into the computer!

Before a human factor can be used in the electronic calculator that settles problems of personnel, of assignment for military or other service, planning of population (and therefore love and marriage), together with God knows what, that human factor must first be reduced to an inanimate object, a mathematical measurably predetermined in its procedures, development, finality. Some forms of classifiable *knowledge* or *information* may fit into the machine; wisdom, virtue, heroism, sanctity haven't a chance ... I almost said a prayer!

History affords examples galore of the potential folly of this technological materialism; it offers consoling evidence that the final historical outcome may discredit the slavery to machinery. Suppose, for example, that in 1957 French experts in economy, sociology, demography, and the other tangible and measurable sciences had programmed all their future of France for the following ten years. The machinery would have fed back indications for policy premises which would have been precise, clear — and false. How could they have programmed into their computers the personality of General de Gaulle? How do you process into the formula the friendship of a moral giant like Adenauer? With what digits do you feed into the calculator the prayers of the saints, the self-sacrificing austerity of the people, the conniving of the politicians, the wave of the future, the debilitating sins of the past?

The simple fact is, then, that we ourselves become, in all but name, *dialectical materialists* if we exclude from our norms, our planning, and our procedures (moral included) that whole universe of values and realities that cannot be reduced to statistics, to handy little formulae, for feeding into computers. We, too, become, for all practical purposes, imprisoned in a world of materialistic predetermination, if, prescinding from divine faith, we accept the lie that nothing is valid or true which does not admit of demonstration from human experience or mechanical analysis.

Both forms of secular humanism—that of the atheist and that of the victims of the computers, cybernetics, and the ominous generalizations of statistics—by their very nature are *irreversible* and leap blindly from *facts* to *decisions* to *action* and to *moral reaction* in the light of values no political controls can safely admit or mechanical scientific controls can possibly absorb.

The brutal cruelty of all this is clear enough. Clemenceau once remarked that one death may seem a tragedy, but a million deaths are a mere statistic. Who does not sense a like outlook in our contraceptive society? One birth, especially among sentimentalists, may be a *happy event,* but a million births are a statistic with which to clobber governments into adopting immoral (I didn't say *illegal*) legislation and programs to justify a dubious political policy or piece of moral counseling and to drive the frantic citizens of Main Street to the nearest *boutique* of the Planned Parenthood League.

I have called this secular humanism a new materialistic phenomenon. In truth, it is not. It is at least as old as the Pharoahs, and its gods are those that Moses found the Chosen People flirting with when he came down from Sinai with the brief but God-inspired wisdom that our not less brief generation of pedagogues has found so negative, so inhibiting to the insurgent instincts of secular humanism. What has failed so often before, with better odds in its favor, is not likely to endure now when, in fact, the Spirit shows so many signs that God is not dead and does not intend to be mocked. Our God is not only constant; he also has a certain caprice and raises up saints who change the course of history, sometimes when we least expect or even welcome them. Saint Paul, Saint Ambrose, Saint Joan, Saint Dominic, Saint Thomas More, Saint Catherine of Siena. How many bright young rebels are still spitting with rage because of a few simple truths Saint Augustine told them about themselves one thousand, five hundred years ago! Saint Pius X, Saint John Fisher, Saint Paul of the Cross.

The power and Providence of God apart, the human spirit has more than enough resilience to pull the rug out from under the despots and to throw an occasional monkey wrench into the best of computers. Something deep in the human heart demands a bit of poetry and love much more than it is satisfied by logarithms, logistics, and the kind of junk turned out by the translating machine which, according to the *New Yorker,* blew its fuse with ecstasy when it rendered the English "out of sight, out of mind" into the Japanese for "invisible, insane". It is heartwarming to reflect that there is no calculating machine so omnicompetent but that a small baby, crawling around on all fours, can pull out the plug, as Bob Considine pointed out.

Finally, a coldly secular humanism is foredoomed when we reflect not only that the word of God abides forever, but that while our machinery has advanced marvelously from the primitive wheel and slingshot to the imposing UNIVAC, IBM, and H–Bomb, human nature has changed nary a whit.

This last point we have tended to forget, yet in it lies no small part of our hope that the ancient decencies will continually reassert themselves, and the essence of authentic humanism, person-centered and God-directed, will survive, wounded on occasion but fundamentally sound. One of the greatest frauds of all time, next to the primitive fib of the snake to Adam and Eve but pretty much like it ("Ye shall be as gods!"), is the transparently absurd *myth of progress,* when human progress is unrelated to that "Kingdom of God (that cometh not with observation)", i.e., the development of which cannot be photographed, measured, or reduced to flow charts.

The fact is that any form of Pelagian humanism is doomed in advance, as faith teaches, and disastrous in the event, as history would seem to confirm. Leftist or rightist, it leaves out the grace and guidance of God and therefore leaves human nature unchanged and basically unimproved, thus making eternal salvation impossible and the temporal achievement of eminent humanity unlikely or precarious. That is what Pope Paul is talking about in his strictures on secular humanism. His view of the world is necessarily in the light of eternity and the pattern of the gospel; it is, therefore, neither pessimistic nor detached from the human condition. It blends the common sense of historic experience with the prophetic insights of profound religious faith, both indispensable conditions of realistic hope or sane optimism about the well-being of the person or the future of the race.

The New Catechetical Directory and Initiation to the Sacraments of Penance and Eucharist

No one would have thought that half a century after Pope Saint Pius X issued his decree (*Quam Singulari*) on early confession and Communion, we would be discussing again the appropriate age for the admission of children to the sacraments of Eucharist and penance.

This has happened, however, in the midst of other marvels, and the problem has assumed such relevance that the Holy See has deemed it opportune to examine the issue once again, even if in somewhat nuanced terms, in its recently published *General Catechetical Directory.* [1]

Perhaps the authors of this new catechetical directory have found it necessary to reaffirm the norms of Pope Pius X, while at the same time recognizing the possibility of such experimentation as is made legitimate in Catholic Faith and order by the approval of local hierarchies in consultation with the Holy See. This partly may be due to the fact that many, perhaps most — clergy and laity alike — may not remember the luminous pastoral norms provided by Saint Pius X.

The present writer was taken aback to discover how little he realized certain aspects of the practical wisdom and pastoral theology which Saint Pius X wove into the decree *Quam Singulari.*

For example, this writer had supposed that Saint Pius X had left to the *pastor* of the child the determination of readiness to receive either the sacrament of penance or that of Holy Communion for the first time, although one had a vague recollection of hearing (and frequently recommending, particularly in the

This article was written for and published in the December 1971 issue of the *Homiletic and Pastoral Review.*

case of retarded children or special cases) that the parents of the youthful candidate be consulted. In fact, Saint Pius had a considerably more *personalist* approach to the question, an approach that must, one strongly feels, have been observed little if at all in the United States, Canada, or for that matter elsewhere.

Pope Pius X, in defining the *age of discretion,* did so at the same time and in the same terms for both sacraments. He did so largely on the basis of the understanding, the intuitions, and even the desires of the *child himself.* The final decision as to when the *age of discretion* might be present—and therefore the possibility and desirability of receiving both sacraments—was to rest not with the pastor nor any other random priest, sister, teacher, or special consultant of a professional kind. It was to lie with the child's *confessor*—a major acknowledgment of the maturity of a youngster, an assumption that he already will have established a spiritual relationship of a most intimate and fruitful kind with his confessor or spiritual director.

Moreover, it was indicated that the only other consultation that seemed indicated or appropriate was with the child's *parent.* The recollection of this fact should come as a shock of joy to those who, in recent years, have all by themselves discovered the important role of parents in the spiritual formation of their own children and their right to be heard when the juridical Church— which, one thinks, would probably mean the pastor, the bishop, or a committee of a *national* hierarchy, rather than a confessor or a spiritual director—are deciding matters of this kind.

A brief recollection of the situation in 1910 and the background, as well as content, of the teachings of Pius X are clearly in order.

The decree *Quam Singulari,* in treating the age at which children are to be initiated in their postbaptismal sacramental life had to face certain doctrinal and ascetical errors that had become deeply rooted in Catholic life at the opening of the century, at least in some parts of the world. (Similar problems had faced a decree on frequent Communion by the Sacred Congregation of the Council in 1905). One of these was the pretense that a greater discretion is required for first Communion than for first confession. This, like most of the other errors, was rooted in Jansenism: one example was the idea that reception of first Holy Communion requires a nearly complete knowledge of the Articles of Faith and, therefore, an extraordinary preparation. In effect, this means deferring first Communion for the riper age of twelve, fourteen, or even older. Another error was the pretense that the Holy Eucharist is a reward (for virtue) not a remedy for human frailty, a concept which is contrary to the teaching of the Council of Trent that Holy Communion is an antidote by which we are freed from our daily faults and preserved from mortal sins.

One remarks in passing that a twist on the aforesaid error is not entirely absent from the current contention that *little tots* are so incapable of sin that they do not need sacraments to release them from faults. In the light of the *theology* that now is attempting to replace that of *Quam Singulari,* it is difficult to see why first Communion in one sense is not as redundant as first confession in another, since both now are seen as means largely to preserve from fault *little tots* as well as adults.

In at least one *advanced* parish known to the writer, a *kerygmatic* preacher, theoretically the reverse of a Jansenist, strongly affirmed that, in accord with *his* theology and psychology, no one in his largely typical parish (ten thousand souls) ever had committed a serious sin. It was *foolish,* he said, for anyone in the parish to go to confession *even once a year;* all should approach Communion at any time without hesitation or scruple. All this in a parish notorious for racism; for the handy little *concordats with conscience* of political life in metropolitan America; a fairly serious drug problem among the young; and well-founded reasons for belief that marriage and family morality is about the same as in any other parish more responsive to the *new morality* than the *old commandments.*

It is of course not being argued that the children in this or like parishes who have not yet made their first Communion are racists. Neither is it suggested that they form part of any corrupt political machine, at least thus far, nor are they members of the *Mafia*. None of them, one expects, is addicted to drugs, alcoholism, or anything else save, perhaps, having his own way in the maximum possible degree. The infants are not themselves contraceptionists or abortionists, although euthanasia may understandably have passed through their minds as a solution to some of their problems.

All that is being argued is this: the mood and moral atmosphere is in favor of their becoming all these things and more too, in due course. It is suggested that the positive role of confession, including spiritual direction of an intensely personal kind, might prevent this by the development of solid preferences for virtue as against vice and the bringing to maturity of moral potential latent in every child. Alas, it is not enough to counter that the Eucharist, by itself, is a sufficient food for virtue in the absence of a contrite and humble heart. The proof of this melancholy fact might possibly be seen in the fact that, although confessions are fewer than ever in the parish, the number of Communions has boomed enormously, to the intense joy of the somewhat myopic pastor.

All this is, as anyone familiar with the religious history of the Western world well knows, an old story. It certainly was the case by the time of Saint Pius X. The errors pinpointed by him inevitably had led to grave abuses. One was depriving children, early in their lives, of the right of living in Christ through Holy Communion, a right given by baptism. Another not less serious abuse touched on both first Communion and first confession, undoubtedly causing the loss of angelic first innocence in many youngsters by concealing (and burying in the subconscious) the probability, perhaps the *beginning* at least, of faults, major or minor, which orient the child selfward rather than God-ward, toward love of self rather than love of neighbor, let alone of God. Such an orientation, once well underway, is as difficult to remedy as is the recovery of an overshot turn-off from a turnpike with its consequent steadily progressive journey further and further from one's goal.

A third abuse common in the days of Pius X and renewed today is the causing of children, by ill-conceived pastoral practice or by worldly social controls, to live in a dimly felt ("Cleanse me from my unknown faults!") or even conscious state of sin by not *allowing* them to go to confession until the age determined for first Communion. Pius X found priests even denying children absolution when they did confess (on the grounds often heard today: "He *may* think he has sinned, but you and I know he *cannot!*"). This is a singularly perverse abuse, destructive of the child's discretion, sense of responsibility, and spiritual rights. Other *utterly detestable* abuses along the same line were denounced by Pius X.

Particularly astonishing is the confusion of the moment concerning rational norms for first confession and first Communion in the light of the fact that the cogent and clear norms of Saint Pius X were proclaimed within the lifetime of living man. In fact, they were promulgated within the lifetime of grandparents at least, and of some pastors now seemingly completely at sea on the matter.

The conditions for the first confession and first Communion were interrelated in the mind of Saint Pius X. The age that he chose as the *age of discretion,* for initiation into both these sacraments, conforms roughly with the age that still is acknowledged as the time when the *discretion* of the boy or the girl is deemed adequate to begin an initiation into the influence of television, the absorption of comic-book philosophy, the personal and community aspects of schooling, movie attendance, and the initial forms, at least, of a considerably developed social and formal education program.

The writer three years ago had the fascinating experience of arbitrating a fight (it had passed the debating state) between two groups of suburbanite mothers who differed as to the age at which a country club dance, complete with expensive orchestra, should be planned for their primary school boys and girls so that they might come to know one another and be rid of sexual, social, and related *awkwardness.* One of the spokeswomen mounted the bastion defending *eight* years of age! Although in subsequent conversations she revealed her conviction that *fuddy-duddys* were responsible for Pius X's norms for first confession and Communion, she felt that, at least for chaperoned dances, eight years was an *age of discretion* in the particular township where she lived. The township later was the subject of a feature article in a national magazine as a sample of a good town to avoid for bringing up children or saving one's soul.

Pius X, as we have recalled, saw the *age of discretion* as applying equally to both sacraments, as it does to going to school. He saw this norm as being suggested by the first indications a child gives that he is using reasoning powers and therefore making decisions and choosing up sides not only within the family but on the battlefield of life. He thought that a child by that age could know the difference between ordinary bread and bread somehow identified with the Bread of Angels, Sacred Bread containing a Divine Mystery.

He also declared it his opinion that the same child knows what is right or wrong, whether it be a matter of torturing a cat (in due course, a prisoner of war), being caught with one's hand in the marmalade jar (in due course, the public treasury), or defying the authority of one's parent (in due course, of God himself). No absolute age is placed as a condition by Pius X; the age of seven is mentioned for the broad reasons indicated above and because the majority of children arrive at a certain responsible discretion at about this period, some even sooner, some later.

Quam Singulari held in high esteem the knowledge which a child, just beginning to reason, can have about God, not merely as One who rewards the good and punishes the wicked, but also as One who dwells in unutterable mystery, including the Triune God and certainly the God of the Incarnation. He nowhere suggested that it was necessary that the child should commit to memory and rotely repeat accurate but superficial theological definitions which convey no idea to the budding intellect. He simply recognized that at this age a child, in fact, usually so develops intellectually as to reveal frequent and astonishing intuitions not merely into human situations but also divine realities.

He indicated that the child must be able to distinguish the things of which he feels ashamed and those in which he takes a holy satisfaction; he must be able to distinguish the Eucharistic Bread from common bread, to recognize no more clearly than did Thomas Aquinas, but really not less so, that what looks like bread is, in this case, *not* bread but somehow nourishes us with very Life and Love of Christ, who is God. He spoke of other matters too, but most of these have not returned to the realm of controversy.

In a day which thinks of itself as having discovered the rights of parents and the wholesome claims of personalism, the contention of the 1910 decree that the formal admission of the child to first Communion rests with its parent, or the one taking his place, and with its confessor or spiritual director is most moving. The decree presupposes that these will act together, and when they agree on the matter, no one may interfere.

Where the parents are negligent, indifferent, or opposed to their child's first Communion, the father-confessor (note carefully that he is assumed to be *already* the child's confidant) can take on the entire responsibility. Even more, should the confessor oppose the admission of a child whose parents know that he already has begun to reason and make at least incipiently mature decisions, the prudent course, in practice, is to introduce the child to *another* confessor, perhaps one less Jansenistic, perhaps one more inclined to take him seriously as a *little man,* rather than lightly as a *little tot.* Every confessor has a right to admit a child to private first Communion. Let it be recalled that it is as *confessor* that he has this right, not as a friend of the family, not as a psychological consultant nor as the local accredited representative of a national liturgical commission or director of the catechetical bureaucracy.

Since the days of Pius X, a considerably larger cast of characters has been brought into the act as a result of behavioral sciences, testing and measurement programs, and a developed pedagogy that surrounds everything that a *little man or woman* must undergo in order to meet the complex requirements that stand between a simple soul and taking one's place in our well-planned society, civil or religious. One reads the straightforward, commonsense decree of Saint Pius X, so deferential to the confidential life and personal dignity of the child, so insistent on the responsibilities and requisite reserve of those *few* who have the slightest right to approach, even at a respectful distance, the inner sanctuary of conscience in a child, of which Pope Pius XII spoke so passionately; then one wonders how far the elaborate norms proposed nowadays are intended to serve the person of the child and how far they may be a pedagogical and religious development of Parkinson's Law.

The *General Catechetical Directory,* published in Rome this past spring, does not deal in depth with these problems. As a matter of fact, the question is raised in an appendix. This was done chiefly in order to present the question in fresh terms and to integrate anew some basic norms, while raising the question for appropriate discussion and action in an authentic Catholic fashion, i.e., consistent with Catholic faith and order, rather than social fads or a spirit of naturalism.

As a consequence of postconciliar reforms and a fresh eagerness to explore the full part in Christian life of all the sacramental rites, we recently have witnessed a revival and renewal of catechetics, which, in turn, has led to a rediscovery of the power of evangelization and formation present in the sacramental actions, especially those which, as penance and Eucharist, mark for most Christians the first salvific encounters with Christ.

As Bishop Tonini argues in his comments on the directory for

L'Osservatore Romano, it has become clear that, in a Christian community inserted in a Christless and decadent world, Eucharist and penance, since they are received in childhood, could assume the role that baptism had for the Christians living in the ancient pagan context. They can become the sacraments of Christian initiation, they can determine the first experience with God which, as we all know, when it is authentic, leaves a mark in the depths of the ego, or, better yet, in the total personality of the child.

Since together with the individual youngster we are dealing with an increasingly desacralized generation—a generation that in a few years will be harder and harder to evangelize—we have come to realize that this is a most decisive moment for the Church. This is so because it is exactly in Christian initiation that one generation evangelizes another and the Church of today generates the Church of tomorrow.

In the light of this connection between the sacraments of Christian initiation and the problem of the evangelization of the contemporary world, it is absolutely necessary that the time of the first encounter of the child with penance and Eucharist be an ecclesial event of primary importance. Therefore, it is vital that the care of pastors, the study of theologians, the researches of psychologists, and the attention of the whole Christian community should be centered around that moment.

It is in this context that the question of age has reappeared. In this search for better methods to make Eucharist and penance more relevant to the young Christian of the future, some have thought it best to separate the two moments, anticipating the first Communion in childhood and deferring the sacrament of confession until adolescence. The separation—it is said—would afford the possibility of receiving Communion in early years. It also would avoid psychical anxieties deriving from talking, sometimes awkwardly, about sin (always an embarrassing subject!); it would eliminate the rote repetitions resulting from the habit of going immaturely, perhaps, to confession; finally it would foster a more profound education to the penitential spirit and at the same time a more valid and efficacious catechesis in preparation for eventual confession. This time interval would in any case be legitimate since—this opinion is of course highly disputable—before adolescence and even afterward, man is, in the sanguine view of some, not really capable of deliberate serious sin.

As we can see, we would thus experience the fact of generations who, during their whole childhood or most of it, would go to Communion without confession, a custom which sometimes seems already to be returning for postadolescents—precisely the situation which sound spirituality and Pope Pius X sought to avoid. Hence the new questions, grave questions fraught with promise or menace for the future. Hence the cry for further experiments, though, since we are dealing with children, we find it difficult to believe that serious men, especially pastors of souls, would use children as spiritual *guinea pigs* or their consciences for areas of uncontrolled or unauthorized pedagogical *experimentation*.

An error in a child's first experience of God, even under the experimentation of the most expert liturgists and moralists, could lead to incalculable consequences for the people of God. It is precisely in these first mysterious experiences, in what happens in the virginal souls of children, that the mystery of salvation realizes itself. It is there that the Church is built, there that we witness the nuptials between the Church and God and sense the progress of that Kingdom that "cometh not with observation".

What then really is to be thought of the hypothesis, proposed by some and already realized here and there, which suggests the admission of children to first Communion without confession, deferring the latter to a later date, even several years after, even until adolescence?

We have to admit that going to confession for the first time in childhood involves difficulties, especially because of the delicate psychological structure of an age when inadequate education can provoke serious upsettings at the psychical as well as the religious level. In this sense, a delay of a few years in the practice of confession might imply fewer risks.

Furthermore, the coupling of confession with Communion, if on one hand it impresses and confirms in the conscience the central position of the Eucharist—which is one of the most beneficial truths for the Christian life—on the other hand presents disadvantages, because it could determine the beginning of the habit of not going to confession except when Communion is to be received.

The greatest disadvantage, though, lies in the danger that the child might not appreciate fully the value of the sacrament of penance, since his attention would be absorbed by the first Communion. This difficulty, however, does not necessarily imply a delay of confession; it can be overcome by anticipating confession, thus separating it from Communion at least for a month or so and making it the beginning of the preparatory phrase of first Communion.

In any case, the emphasis should be placed more on the way of preparing the children for the two sacraments, and, in general, on the initiation of the child for Christian life. Such preparation for the two sacraments should be faced in modern terms, keeping always in mind the confrontation of the Christian with today's world, sharing responsibility with the whole Christian community.

Merely moving the years does not help, unless we invite into action the whole Church, especially the families and in a very special way, the parents.

As far as age is concerned, the most suited age seems still to be seven to eight years, as we have it today. This is true for many reasons.

Pastoral experience tells us that the so-called *second infancy,* due to the development of the moral self, has the same decisive importance that the *first infancy* had for the unconscious ego, since it can determine those conditionings, anxieties, and impulses whose influence will remain during the whole future life of the person.

This is the age at which the child, if helped, can pass from the instinctive phase (tied to the stimulus of the binominal pleasure-sorrow) to the ethical phase, in which emerges, together and sometimes in contrast with the instinctive law, the attraction to good and disgust for evil.

It is a very delicate and precise moment, an opportunity which cannot be missed without serious consequences for the future. The awakening of ethical and moral life is not automatically linked to physiological and psychical growth; alas, as history proves in chapters writ with blood, moral sense does not necessarily develop with intelligence, least of all with mere knowledge. Without solicitous care from parents, priests, and educators, the instinctive life is prolonged through the *second infancy* and beyond, with disastrous consequences on the spiritual destiny of the individual.

To act in time to awaken the moral sense at the beginning of the age of discernment is to save the person at his roots, is to give him moral being, namely, full eventual personality. To do this, not only through the best available human means but through the pedagogy of the liturgy and the sacraments, in particular through the sacrament of penance (which has exactly the *conscience* as its object, and the purification, liberation, formation, elevation, and perfecting of the *conscience* for its proper contribution), constitutes—Bishop Tonini emphasizes—a very dramatic moment of *operative salvation* whose advantages we cannot renounce without serious danger.

The sacrament of penance, if well prepared, works wonders in this sense. A most beautiful experience comes to children when, receiving first Communion, they discover the existence of a Father who loves them and begin to examine their actions in answer to that love. They then become aware that they not only possess an interior treasure, namely, an upright conscience, but are themselves beings who are the objects of God's satisfaction,

His faithful children, His friends as was Adam before the fall. This is the beginning of the discovery of moral greatness and of the consciousness of the eternal value of their actions. Such an experience is a delicate one, which can be disastrous if not guided in a proper way; but, well guided, gives the whole future life an authentically supernatural tone, thus providing the one and only antidote to both religious formalism and religious apathy.

It may well be asked, however, whether the practice of delaying penance until after Communion and toward the last years of *second infancy* carries with it serious risks. One such would be the prolonging of the instinctive phase, the settling of habits more difficult to correct than to prevent. These are habits that Communion without previous confession will hardly help the child to discover and discontinue, since there will then be lacking the personal consultation with the priest which helps bring to the surface personal conflicts that the child does not confide even to his parents.

One suspects therefore that Communion without confession does not allow that work of personalization of the moral conscience which experience sees achieved through the practice of the sacrament of penance.

The beginning of the *second infancy* not only presents the conditions sufficient for the valid reception of the sacrament of penance, but it offers also the best dispositions needed for its integration into a harmonious and fruitful plan of Christian initiation.

Rightly, then, contemporary Catholic teachers underline the necessity of a wider participation and personal consciousness of the child in the liturgy and insist that admission to the sacraments not be an isolated action, but, while respecting the fact that every person, however young, is a *moral universe* in himself, should provide for the communitarian dimensions of Christian spiritual life. Again, the most suitable age for such a program appears to be, for various reasons, the age of seven to eight years, identified by Pius X.

All this necessarily brings the child to confront himself, namely, to examine his conscience on his actions and consequently to feel sorry for whatever offenses he has done to God or neighbor. It is the sense of sin that is awakening, in proportion and together with the sense of filial and fraternal love; so radical is the concomitance of the two—reverential fear and holy love—that *aut simul stabunt, aut simul cadent.*

How can we then deny the sacrament of penance to the child—since he possesses the ideal conditions—without ourselves sinning against his needs and spiritual rights?

Moreover, the proper effect of penance is not only liberation from guilt, but also stimulus to the perfection of the soul, namely, a passing not only from death to life or—in the child— from spiritual infirmity to greater strength, but also from a lower to a higher degree of love. Now there is no doubt that children seven to eight years of age—precisely because they are sensitive to the love of God—easily tend to interpret everything good that they received as a sign of God's love, and thus become capable of a sensitivity from which they derive the purest joys, joys whose remembrance in the years that follow will be an element of defense against temptation and, even after a long period of time, motive for going back to God.

A further observation: it has been said that for children seven to eight years old, confession is superfluous for the reason that they are incapable of serious sin. On the contrary, experience teaches that, aside from the subjective consciousness of evil, we frequently find among children at that age habits acquired through the example and instigation of other people. Such habits, if not corrected, could jeopardize forever the recuperating capacity of the child, placing him in radical conflict with the law of God, a law which will be very hard for him to observe when he will come to know it more fully.

It seems proper to conclude that the practice of confession at the beginning of the *second infancy* is something to be kept in the Church. It seems, moreover, something to be perfected. If, in fact, confession remains—as it often is—a mass operation, performed as a mechanical routine and without full personal participation on the part of the child or the part of the priest, the vitality of tomorrow's Church will be seriously jeopardized. Postponing confession to a later age might easily increase rather than solve difficulties. The chief remedy would be that the whole Catholic community gather around these sublime moments all its best energies, in particular, the attention of the family and the spiritual care of the priests. Priests, free from so many occupations not precisely sacerdotal, will find here ample possibilities for a full use of their time and wonderful occasions for appreciating, with joy and gratitude, what it is to be a priest—full time and fully available, even to the least of Christ's brethren.

Father John Hugo, for many years a seeker after means of realizing the fullest possible potential for the sanctification of the faithful, lay and clerical, finds in chapter V of the *Constitution on the Church* a truly integral perspective of the sacrament of penance in the life of all called to sanctity, which means called to salvation.[2] Father Hugo argues that the potentials of this great sacrament for spiritual direction have been universally neglected, with a consequent emphasis, in the sacrament of penance, on confession, seen merely as a remission of sins, a negative thing, mechanical, and, in terms of growth unto sanctity, as something too often important, unproductive, and irrelevant. All this, according to Father Hugo, has been to the great hurt of priests and penitents, penitents of every age and category. The sacrament of penance, an important means not merely of ridding oneself of the guilt of daily failures, great or small, is or should be the means of accomplishing Christian maturity, of *divinizing* through grace and bringing to supernatural maturity all the desires, gifts, and positive qualities which the individual under spiritual direction who turns to the sacrament of penance, adequately considered, can bring to the consecration of the secular and the promotion of the Kingdom of God.

Father Hugo observes: If laymen are to consecrate the secular, bringing it into the Kingdom of God, this will mean, besides human competence in carrying out their work, a consecration of this work to God and hence a continual self-purification that this consecration may be realized in fact. This self-purification, Father Hugo would agree, must include, above all, a continual purification of *motives*, information, and enlightenment of personal conscience and discovery of new and positive elements in progress toward personal perfection. The *Constitution on the Church*, with its historic universal call to sanctity among all classes and conditions of men, gives the sacrament of penance a greater role in Christian life and growth than it has had, perhaps ever, in the centuries of Christian sacramental development.

This is why Father Hugo argues in his scholarly, but above all pastoral, reflection on *Children and the Sacrament of Penance* that clearly the quest for holiness should begin as soon as possible and that children should be early introduced to the sacrament of penance. Childhood, with its relative innocence and receptiveness, is a most valuable time, a one and only time, he agrees, for developing the life of faith and charity which is at the heart of holiness. As Newman suggests, commenting on "the better part" and the "one thing necessary", childhood is providentially intended to provide for an accumulation of resources that will be needed when the person, no longer a child, takes up, in increasing stages best accomplished gradually and without sudden innovation and changes, the responsibilities of adult life.

Moreover, it would be a mistake to delay putting into the child's hands the weapons he needs in the struggle against evil until evil already has established a beachhead in his soul. The school of thought that sees the confession of children only as a bore to the priest and a burden to the *little tot* who has no *mortal sins* with which to worry himself or the bored confessor, makes no provision for the fact that the sacrament of penance, as both priest and penitent should understand it in terms of spiritual direction and growth in sanctity, is not merely a spiritual laundromat, but a means to spiritual refreshment, encouragement, and growth.

Hence Father Hugo's conclusion: The policy that would deprive children of the sacrament of penance in the name of a positive psychology approach is itself negative in supposing the Christian life to be only a warfare against rudimentary evil and in failing to realize the unity of this life as a development in holiness. No doubt it would be a waste of time, to say the least, to enlarge upon mortal sin for first graders—and in this respect past methods of instruction have been practically ill-advised as well as theologically unsound. (*But is it a waste of time for shepherds of souls to teach children personally and privately how to respond to God's grace in their daily lives and grow in love of God and of their neighbor?*)

No doubt the faults of children (from the standpoint of adults) are trivial. But they are faults, which from the beginning hinder the grace-filled soul from responding to the Spirit of God. Moreover, they are, or can be, beginnings: the first sly but potentially dangerous appearance, or reappearance, of the *old man:* the initial movements of that *law of the members,* which, as Saint Paul warns, unless countered by the *law of the Spirit,* will culminate in the *law of sin.* As the Christian life on its positive side must be viewed as a development, and therefore subject to the laws of life and growth, so on the negative side, the force that threatens this life must be seen from the start as incipient disease that will increase unless treated and removed.

Modern parents understand all this most protectively in terms of the bodily life of their *little tots.* Hence the universal activity of pediatricians, the prevalence, sometimes almost compulsive, of *shots, booster shots, inoculations* for specific and multiple purposes, and physical hygiene courses laudably designed not to fill teeth or cure the diseases of childhood but to *anticipate* cavities and *prevent,* so far as possible, the first beginnings of malady. The opposite number to scrupulosity on the level of the spirit and the conscience is, of course, hypochondria on the level of physical health and preoccupation with disease. For every priest or spiritual director whom I have met who seemed likely to induce morbid preoccupation with sin or scrupulosity, I have seen the advertisements of a hundred drug companies, infant panacea manufacturers, and toothpaste distributors clearly bent on turning children into hypochondriacs. One wonders if parents (is it ungracious to suggest particularly mothers?) who are terrified that their children have a crooked tooth or an unsocial adenoid, but avoid any word that might give them a scruple about incipient antisocial attitudes or a downright defect in their moral health, may possibly have forgotten the healthy as well as the holy counsel of Jesus: "Do not fear those who deprive the body of life but cannot destroy the soul. Rather, fear him so can destroy both body and soul. . . . "[3]

Throughout his reflections on years of profound scholarly study and incessant pastoral activity, Father Hugo reveals (in fact, invokes) the wisdom of Cardinal Newman. That wisdom, with respect to the faults, even the sins of children, was most cogently expressed in one of the *Parochial and Plain Sermons,* which Newman delivered as an Anglican.[4] It is not, therefore, open to the charge of reflecting a *Roman position* or *Italianate* or otherwise *European* and recessive point of view based on post-Tridentine excess, on magical concepts or otherworldly theories of nature and grace.

Newman is preaching on the moral consequences of single sins. In something of the spirit of the psalmist who wishes to be delivered from even those sins of which he is no longer aware, Newman is warning on the manner in which single sins, past or present, slight or even negligible, may have devastating effects on our eventual moral character in God's sight. He begins his reflections with the probable influence upon us of faults committed in our childhood, and even infancy, which we never realized or have altogether forgotten. His approach to this delicate problem, the problem at the heart of contemporary discussions about the age of first confession, is without morbidity, pessimism, or legalism; these do not happen to be Newmanian defects. It is realistic, perceptive, affectionately sympathetic, but, above all, positive. *It is indeed, a tract for the times and might well be read with profit for its affirmative content.* He meets the issue head-on:

Ignorant as we may be when children begin to be responsible beings, yet we are ignorant also when they are not so; nor can we assign a date ever so early at which they certainly are not. And even the latest assignable date is very early; and thenceforward, whatever they do exerts, we cannot doubt, a most momentous influence on their character. We know that two lines starting at a small angle, diverge to greater and greater distances, the further they are produced; and surely in like manner a soul living on into eternity may be infinitely changed for the better or the worse by very slight influences exerted on it in the beginning of its course. A very slight deviation at setting out may be the measure of the difference between tending to hell and tending to heaven.[5]

Newman goes on to indicate, with what many of us will see as psychological accuracy despite all the talk of little tots and the curious angelism in the discussion of children by people otherwise undistinguished for interest in or convictions concerning angels, that children's minds are impressible in a very singular way, such as is not common afterward.

The passing occurrences which meet them, these, whether from their novelty or other cause, rest upon their imagination as if they had duration; and days or hours, having to them the semblance, may do the work of years. Any one, on casting his thoughts back on his first years, may convince himself of this; the character which his childhood bears in his memory as a whole, being traceable to a few external circumstances, which lasted through a very small portion of it, a certain abode, or a visit to some particular place, or the presence of certain persons, or some one spring or summer — circumstances which he at first cannot believe to have been so transitory as on examination he finds they certainly were.[6]

Here Newman makes a parable, more urbane, perhaps, than the one we ventured above, between the physical effects of childhood and the indisputable theological and spiritual realities of the of the life of the child as a person, a psychophysical unity, whose soul in fact dominates his body, or he is a candidate for hell. This possible eventuality any priest, not merely a priest of pastoral bent but even (and especially) a *professional theologian* or *liturgist* would wish to prevent, however tedious he might find conversation with a child as opposed to a symposium of scholars. If the issue be fairly faced, so would the most apprehensive parent or pedagogue, fearful about a child discussing prematurely his personal problems, including the possibility that, just as he may be precocious in his vocabulary, so he may be precocious in response to the fascination of evil or in rejection of or indifference to potential virtue, love of God, and love of neighbor.

The English Cardinal presents this pertinent and impressive line of thought:

> On the other hand, let it be observed that we are certainly ignorant of a great deal that goes on in us in infancy and childhood; I mean our illnesses and sufferings as children, which we are either not conscious of at the time, or at any rate forget soon afterwards—which yet are of a very serious nature, and while they must have a moral cause, known or unknown, must, one would think, have a moral effect also; and while they suggest by their occurrence the possibility of other serious things going on in us also, have moreover a natural tendency to affect us in some other way. Mysterious as it is that infants and children should suffer pain, surely, it is not less so that, when they come to years of reason, they should forget it, as hardly to be able to believe, when told of it, that they themselves were the very sufferers; yet as sicknesses and accidents then happening permanently affect their body, though they recollect nothing of them, there is no extrava-

gance in the idea that passing sins then contracted and forgotten for ever afterwards, should so affect the soul as to cause those moral differences between man and man which, however originating, are too clear to be denied. And with this fearful thought before us of the responsibility attaching to the first years of our life, how miserable is it to reflect on the other hand that children are commonly treated as if they were not responsible, as if it did not matter what they did or were! They are indulged, honoured, spoiled or at best neglected. Bad examples are set them; things are done or said before them, which they understand and catch up, when others least think it, and store in their minds, or act upon; and thus the indelible hues of sin and error are imprinted on their souls, and become as really part of their nature as that original sin in which they were born.[7]

A somewhat appalling amount of recent writing runs counter to the wisdom, if not the knowledge, of the profound Anglican preacher and the immemorial insights of the Church, notably those of Saint Pius X, with which we began the present paper. There is less tendency to pay the normal child the tribute of seeing in him a *little man,* the child who is the father of the man, a tribute which was not merely sympathetic but affectionate, to the point of tears in some of us, more affectionate than the more sentimental but not particularly complimentary disposition to see him as a *little tot.*

A recent writer on this general subject in a series of opinions syndicated under the rubric *Know Your Faith* suggests that the problem of early confession of children was finally solved for him when he found himself confronted with the task of hearing the routine confessions of *little tots,* whom he suggests might well have been better occupied elsewhere, while he, too, was elsewhere, perhaps (in his own truly priestly and admirable case) in study, social action, or the intellectual work for which he happens to be richly equipped.

One sometimes wonders if this *little tot* approach to the

problems of children, an almost specifically American and Canadian approach, is not merely overdone but, in fact, a grave disservice, on just about every level, to the personalities of children and to essential aspects of our culture. Some recent sociological and psychological surveys of priestly problems, all of them certainly misleading and probably false in particular conclusions, have turned up a general, possibly accurate suggestion that American priests, like Americans generally, tend to be *immature* or underdeveloped. If this is true, it is not surprising; it is alarming, however, if the sociologists mean we are *retarded.*

The *perennial sophomore* is a familiar figure in American culture, sometimes including men who hold posts which should not merely presuppose but demand a maturity hardly consistent with fretting all year about Notre Dame's football prospects or the career of Mohammed Ali. Years in a marriage-consulting office revealed the anguish suffered by wives whose interests had moved on at least to a Book-of-the-Month Club and yet who found themselves chained for life to relatively successful business and professional men who, at the core of their being and interest, had not advanced beyond the sophomore year of college. One well recalls a totally disenchanted wife who first began to notice it when she was obliged to go directly home, seven hundred miles away, from her mother's funeral so that Freddy would not be obliged to miss the annual football game between the college from which he had been graduated sixteen years before and its *big rival,* a college which had had equally scant impact on the direction of history or the content of the times. She said that he was really Tom Swift or, perhaps, one of the Rover Boys.

One wonders if, in fact, he was not still a *little tot,* handled as such from the beginning of his life, in a familiar American pattern. One wonders if it would not have been healthier for the priest who was his spiritual director, the teachers who taught him, even in the earliest grades, his indulgent parents, and his doting aunts to take him, from the beginning, as seriously as he once doubtless took himself, seeing in him not a *little tot* to be

208

spared all contact with reality, together with the self-knowledge, self-discipline, and self-giving which constitute maturity at every stage of life, and treating him as a responsible person, in varying degrees, of course, but always as a man, even when a *little man*. This is not to suggest a Prussian or Spartan-like discipline, nor a certain British equivalent that demands *no nonsense, thank you,* from *little ones,* especially *little men.* It does not exclude the recognition that the joys, sorrows, performances, and irresponsibilities of children are real; it recognizes that they are small joys, small sorrows, small achievements, and small responsibilities, all proportionate to the age and capacity of the child. It remembers with deep feeling the wisdom of Francis Thompson's perception with respect of the *little hurts, little joys, little victories,* and *little treacheries* of children, but their proportionate *reality* all the same. It also remembers that the child is father to the man; that, also within his limits, he is sensitive to what shapes or deforms a personality in the process of coming to maturity, as he is also aware of the seriousness, not only to him but to the person that he knows himself to be, of the little faults, little perfections, and little disasters of which he is acutely aware and which he himself tends to take with great seriousness—as his resentment or satisfaction when these are ignored or praised abundantly indicates.

One wonders if we would not have more *mature men* if we talked with keen interest to the *little men* who come to us in confession—rather than seeing them as *little tots*—whose confidences in confession (so real to them) are, perhaps, so boring to some of us who have more important fish to fry or more exciting interests to pursue. It is worth asking, one thinks, in a civilization and a Church which laments her lack of fully developed, *mature men,* whether their coming to maturity would be better guaranteed if those we now think of as *little tots* were encouraged to be *little men* at the first dawn of their awareness that they stand in the presence of God and are capable of being intimately united with Him sacramentally or being alienated from Him, however passingly, by sin. This moment is when, no longer infants, they are budding personalities already subject to the influences which will eventually make for either immature, morally and psychologically underdeveloped citizens (priests included) or full, responsible persons.

We are told that we must face the fact that we are now called to catechize with basic Christian truths and norms of morality an entirely new generation, filled with a *new knowledge explosion,* new kinds of moral concepts and motivations. We are told that this new order constitutes a profound challenge to those who would seek to make Jesus Christ known to and loved by our coming generation.

The facts are all too evident. Pope Pius XII, twenty years ago, spoke of the decline and loss of the sense of sin; there is surely no room, let alone need, for further evidence of the effects of this personal and social, cultural, and religious disaster in the 1970s — a disaster with virtual universality and under every moral or ethical heading. That there is any sign, even possibility of an early recovery of a recognizable idealism is highly debatable.

The Christian response to this is not "love — and do what you will", ripped out of every context of spiritual sense and moral meaning.[8] It is the restoration of God and his Christ to the hierarchy of human loves — and the development of a healthy, saving sense *precisely* of what it is to pervert love. The initiation into *this* life of faith and this *level* of love cannot possibly begin too early — no matter how busy with less important things or bored with God knows what we priests may be, or tell the sociologists we think we are.

A priest-director of Canadian National Religious Education (speaking, one hopes as a private *expert,* not an official spokesman) announced promptly after the publication of the *General Catechetical Directory* that its argument would have no effect on Canadian thinking; they had said the last word on confession and Communion. One hopes that others will be more open-minded and more disposed not to instinctive contestation but to open-minded exchange of experience and insight, not only because where souls are at issue no one *ever* has said the last word, but also because the problem of renewing the sense of the presence of God, the primacy of faith and love and the awareness of the pervasive threat of sin is far greater than our Canadian friend may realize.

Somehow we—and he—must reteach a whole generation—perhaps more—that love is infinitely more positive—more nearly divine—than "not having to say you're sorry" for the fornication, blasphemy, impiety, and contempt which apparently constitute the most popular current *Love Story* known to millions, and which, in mere fact, is among the mildest of the literary and entertainment *signs of the times.*

We cannot begin the spiritual, educational, and sacramental battle against desacralization and degeneracy too soon in a person's life if we wish to forestall the day when, in Orwell's terrifying phrase, the watchers will be unable to tell the pigs from the men or the men from the pigs.

XII

Maritain's Two Most Recent Books

As at least two full generations of those indebted to France for their most cherished spiritual intuitions have spoken of *notre cher Péguy,* permit me to speak here, for parallel reasons of *notre cher Jacques.*

He presents a roughly similar image to that of Péguy, an old and familiar image: the young rebel who, as he grows older, appears to become transformed into a pious reactionary. We think perhaps, of Al Smith, starting off at the left or reform side of center in the Democratic Party and moving slowly across to the right wing of conservative reaction to the New Deal. We remember Wordsworth, discovering in his younger days the allied delights of revolution and of irresponsibility—"bliss it was in that dawn to be alive!"—but then becoming old and hidebound and writing the *Ecclesiastical Sonnets.*[1] In the history of the Church and of Christian philosophy, and also in public life and among the people we know, we find the same story often repeated: Augustine! Pio Nono? Some of the brightest and the best of our conciliar churchmen, now postconciliar prelates?

We need not be cynical about this. There are always certain truths of the radical or revolutionary kind, and on the whole, these will be most easily preceived and most hotly proclaimed by the young and the underprivileged; and there are always other truths as well, truths of the traditional or conservative sort, which will be mostly easily perceived and most sagely proclaimed by people somewhat older, somewhat more experienced. Knowledge comes early and in avalanches; Wisdom comes late and seeps in slowly through long study and suffering.

This address was delivered at Aquinas College, Nashville, Tennessee, on April 9, 1972.

Sound vision needs both heat and light, blood and judgment too: *crabbed age and youth* are entitled equally to a hearing, and if we desire a balanced and rounded view, we shall listen to both or be the poorer.

There is no reason, then, to despise and ignore the young rebel if he gives promise of contributing something worth the jealous instinct to preserve of the conservative—nor any reason to take the converse view. But, now, as Jacques Maritain approaches his ninetieth birthday, it seems necessary to say, with some emphasis, that he does *not* fit into this familiar pattern.

It is often suggested that he does. In the 1930s and later, he was both admired and distrusted as a high-powered spokesman for a progressive, liberal, and intellectually free Catholicism—as a voice of the Left as well, concerned for social justice and (on some views) quite insufficiently *Catholic* in his response to the Spanish Civil War and to the issues that were supposed to be at stake there. Given the Catholic *ambience* of the time, he was seen—plausibly enough—as something of a revolutionary. But that was before the Flood. The Council came, and it unsettled people as councils very often do; when Maritain surveyed the new situation thus created, after returning home from the Council where he was honored as the Catholic intellectual *par excellence,* he wrote *The Peasant of the Garonne.* [2]

At once, he began to be seen in a different light. There was something of a storm, affecting in the first instance the left and right wings of the French *intelligentsia,* but spreading rapidly as the book became better known. It shocked and disappointed a great many people. While still respecting the mind of one who is—on any reckoning—among the foremost philosophers of the age, they found it a deplorably negative book. There was talk of a lost leader, of a cause betrayed, of a pseudorevolutionary who liked theoretical plotting but took fright when the revolution actually began; it was whispered talk which many of us, of far lesser stature, have with varying degrees of accuracy, been obliged to endure for the Kingdom! There was slightly kinder talk of advancing years and hardening arteries. But very widely, this book was taken to express little beyond an elderly man's reactionary querulousness about a new period in the Church's life, different from what he was used to, but a period, indeed, of which he was a chief architect, a new period about which, with all its ambiguities, we all have every reason to feel enormous gratitude and hope.

Such response, to my mind, tells us more about the present habit of mind among the Catholic *intelligentsia* than about Maritain. This later work of his—*The Peasant of the Garonne*, and now *L'Eglise du Christ*, which we must hope before long to see in an English version—cannot be dismissed so easily.[3] Neither cliche-label fits their author: he was *never* a young rebel except in the most limited and relative sense, and he has *certainly* not changed sides and become a hidebound conservative now. Rather, he suggests to me—with one qualification, to which I will return in a moment—the wise and central man who has always listened to both extremes and has then synthesized and expressed the separate truths, the separate visions that are cherished in one-sided and incomplete versions on either side.

Certainly the intemperate criticisms, the violent reversals of character and conviction, the treacherous changes attributed to Maritain by left-wing erstwhile admirers (as François Biot in *Temoignage Chrétien*, and quoted in the *New York Times*, March 24, 1967) are not merely grossly unjust, but irrationally vituperative. With greater balance, Father William Clancy, of the Oratory, recorded his spontaneous *scandal* but enduring debt to the philosopher, turned peasant, whose point Father Clancy saw through all the polemic: undying resistance to all totalitarian monism and unobscure recognition that the secularization of religion or conformism with the spirit of this world empty of all meaning the warning of Maritain, past and present, which is the wisdom of Christ: "We must at all costs know a little of what it means to look at divine things with the eyes of a child, and in what school this is taught—and that God alone can teach us this."[4]

In anything like a central position, you are naturally likely (and happy) to get shot at from both sides, and Maritain seems to have expected this honorable destiny. "I have an idea that this book will displease everybody", he says at the end of *L'Eglise du Christ,* at least if by *everybody* we understand those who have taken up entrenched positions "on the right" or "on the left."[5] And in choosing a title for his earlier book, he took upon himself the role of La Fontaine's *Paysan de la Danube,* a character proverbial in all French-speaking countries for his blunt speaking, his inability to open his mouth without putting his foot in it.

It can be argued, of course, that annoying everybody is the same thing as pleasing everybody, since each partisan is glad and gratified to see his opponent annoyed; and we can thus see Maritain's near-central position, more positively, as one that ought to command at least a considerable degree of sympathy in every quarter. If you choose your topics carefully, you can represent him as agreeing with every sort of extremist who exists in the somewhat argumentative Church of today. The most vehemently *progressive* Catholic could hardly be more critical, more scathing than he is about the great follies and crimes of the historic Church—the Crusades, the Inquisition; the evil notion, more Moslem than Christian, of the *holy war;* the power-seeking pride of worldly prelates and Catholic *establishments,* leftist or rightist, new-rich social or self-consciously *intellectual,* the rigidity, the fossilization that has tended to cramp so much Catholic thought in recent centuries; the relative spiritual impoverishment of the laity, as though the high things of God were reserved to monks, nuns, and scholars alone; and then, by contrast with all this, the immense liberation and renewal now offered by the Second Vatican Council.

In connection with all such matters, Maritain makes it clear that he has in no sense abandoned the *progressive* way of thinking; charitable at every point, reluctant always to attribute formal guilt, he recognized and most vehemently scourges the alleged old tendency of the Catholic Church to become—at least in appearance, which is what most men will judge by—a narrow, stagnant, obscurantist, and reactionary thing.

He can thus be greeted as a still-faithful ally and prophet by most men of the Catholic Left—if, against his advice, we insist on using these quasi-political and always inadequate labels—and even, within limits, by the extremists on the other side, the people whom he calls "the Sheep of Panurge", a charitable designation of the leftist literary ghettos of so many *liberal* Catholic writers of, say, British *Slant,* France, the Benelux, and, of course, America's waspish *literary figgers* of the moment.

But it is also true, and notoriously, that he now offers aid and comfort to the more traditionally minded among us, and even (again, within limits) to our extremists of the Right, *"the Ruminators of the Holy Alliance,"* in his not less charitable and more romantic phrase. So long as such people confine themselves to strictly religious matters, resisting that tiresome tendency of theirs to associate orthodox Catholicism with political conservatism, they can rightly claim Maritain as an ally, an energetic defender of the things which they value and which are so widely under attack: the holiness, the unique privilege of the Church; the binding authority of her Magisterium: of the clergy; the permanent and irreformable truth of doctrinal definitions, as against all modernistic relativism; the transcendent and otherworldly purpose of the Church, as against all worship of the secular city; the literally crucial importance of the Cross, of prayer, penance, and especially of contemplation, as against the frenzied sociological *activisme* of the time; and the foolishness of many who, denying or belittling all these things, suppose themselves to be thereby following the *spirit* of the Second Vatican Council.

In a moderate and sometimes an extreme way, the people of either faction can thus claim Maritain as a powerful though partial ally. But in my view, it would be a mistake to see him as a precise neutral, a man of the precise center, finding equal quantities of good material and bad on his left and on his right, the Ying and Yang adept. If I understand him correctly, he is (so to speak) off-center, and desirably so; and I venture to warn those zealous traditionalists—the integralists, the die-hard "*Ruminators*" —that they would do well to invoke his name rather cautiously. It would embarrass them; and not only because, in temporal matters, he retains a political alignment that is well to the left of center, perhaps precisely as a corollary of his firm commitment to Catholic dogma.

It would be tragic if Maritain's passionate commentary on some theorizing and procedures surrounding Vatican Council II were seized upon by integralists or reactionaries as reluctant testimony to their cause from an unexpected witness. Maritain has suffered enough at the hands of integralist extremists in years gone by to be spared this indignity.

It would be no less grotesque if the philosopher who did more than any layman alive to create the mood and set the directions which resulted in the Council were to be dismissed now by those of progressive instinct who may find offensive his evaluation of tendencies which he sees as extreme, unfortunate, and fatal both for truth and for freedom.

The fact is that Maritain has earned his right to be heard by everyone who loves the Church, the person, the common good, and any values, human or divine, worth mentioning in genuinely intellectual conversation. All have plenty to learn from Maritain: Maritain the layman, the philosopher, the servant of humanity, and, now, the sometimes angry, sometimes anguished critic of postconciliar trends about which he speaks as would the peasant *who calls a spade a spade.*

My point is this. Maritain writes very fiercely indeed about the cataracts of un-Catholic and irrational nonsense that flow through our books and our periodicals. He has been called by a responsible Italian writer *"l'anti-futurologo della Chiesa",* a *"fecundo filosofo cristiano"* who has "remained *faithful,* never having relied on human realities—science, society, or culture—to make clear (least of all to take over) his faith, but has always depended on his faith to interpret and illumine human realities—quite the reverse of many current tendencies". But he is cautious, and increasingly so, about blaming the people directly and obviously responsible. Their foolishness is manifest enough, and (in all charity) he uses emphatic language about it. But he looks behind this and puts no small part of the ultimate blame upon the old negative pressures, against which all this foolishness was a sudden wild reaction—a temporary reaction, we must hope. Do some Catholics now bend the knee, absurdly, before this world and the passing moment, as Maritain asserts? Beyond doubt and quite plainly they do, and wrongly; but they are only disposed to such foolish excess because for centuries past they had seeped in an almost Manichaean distrust of this world, of God's creation, and in a rigidity that attempted to resist the mere facts of time and change. Do they now exaggerate the idea of ecumenism so far as to undermine the necessity, the given unity, the teaching office of the Church? Plainly; but largely because, in the past, a crude siege mentality discouraged them—rather forcibly—from thinking in any depth about what *the Church* might mean. Have some of them talked boundless, literally adolescent, nonsense about a recent encyclical? Plainly; but this was part of their reaction from an age of immaturity in which anything emanating from ancient, age-old Rome had in it the echo of the absolute voice of God.

In *The Peasant of the Garonne,* Maritain names and rebukes a number of serious evils—intellectual evils, for the most part— that flourish in the troubled Church of these postconciliar years. But to a degree that may offend the true-blue traditionalist, the *Ruminator,* he sees these latter-day errors and evils as deriving, by direct inheritance or (more often) by reaction, from equal but opposite evils in the Church of earlier days; and he is most anxious that we should face this situation, not applying two coats of whitewash and dishonesty in order to make our own past seem more perfect than it was, as though the blame could thus be made to fall squarely and wholly upon the mavericks and wind-blown prophets of today. That blame needs to be shared more widely; many illustrious figures of the Catholic past must share it, many popes and councils and even saints, lay and clerical, princely and proletarian, bright and dull, *conservative* and *liberal.*

To that true-blue traditionalist, if his theology is sufficiently muddled, all this will seem like flagrant, semi-Protestant disloyalty.

This, at least, is how I see the implied perspectives of this book, especially when read in conjunction with *L'Eglise du Christ.* Maritain is not uttering any kind of mere reactionary grumble, any crude lament about novelty and the abandonment of old proven ways. The shoe is on the other foot. People often say that the Church is now passing through a *revolutionary* phase. Very well: the peasants revolt, and they commit various follies and excesses and atrocities, for which they carry their own responsibility. But the more wildly and foolishly they behave, the more obvious it becomes that there was something seriously wrong with the *ancien régime* . . . and also some kind of a built-in need for some of its elements.

In these two books, Maritain seems to me to be making a point along this line. He is certainly not acting the part of the reactionary who wants the revolution to be tamed by harsh repressive measures; and he has not changed sides.

Granted so much, men have to cope with the problems of their own day, however caused; and do we not find ourselves in a situation in which, while the faults of the *ancien régime* are loudly proclaimed everywhere, the current and comparable failings of the other side get little mention? We are confronted with an embarrassingly blatant and rudely self-proclaimed *anti-establishment establishment,* which is confirming what every thoughtful person always knew: there is no choice between a monopoly or dictatorship of the Left and one of the Right so far as vulgarity, pretense, or the reduction of critics to nonpersons are concerned. As so often happens in real revolutions when they are systematically managed, the rebels have captured the *mike* and taken over the newspapers; we therefore get a one-sided account of things, a version that is in constant need of being scrutinized, challenged, and corrected.

If I were to be asked why I consider Maritain to be exceptionally well qualified for this task of correction, a voice that deserves special attention, I would reply that he stands out—not only among men in general, but among philosophers—for his passionate dedication to truth, and his conviction that truth can actually be attained—however incompletely—by imperfect men in a baffling world. Few have understood, as has he, that *magna est Veritas et praevalebit.*

Philosophically—but in a religious sense too—this is the heart of the matter. In these two books, he ranges widely, covering a great many subjects, with many parentheses and digressions; but he is always circling around the primacy of God and the primacy of objective truth, and these add up to one central subject, since *Truth* is one of the names of God. And when he finds something to regret in the present state of the world and the Church, this can always be described in terms of a departure from that *still center* --as a turning away from God, or sometimes (more conveniently) as a turning away from *Truth.*

The key question concerns the primacy of the first great commandment. Maritain writes, neatly and clearly, in love of his fellow men, in a fashion that would make one wish to meet him and know him—for mere pleasure—did not one have that privilege already.[6] There have been great thinkers who were splenetic and malevolent men, contemptuous of all who disagreed with them, and, indeed, of all humanity, but he is not one of them. If, by magic, I could confer one of his personal attributes upon the members of the Church at large, and especially upon her controversialists, I think I might forget about philosophy and choose instead his Chestertonian geniality, the charity with which he writes even when honesty compels him to use strong words—always with a touch of humor, a touch of self-deprecation.

Nobody who knows him, and his political outlook in particular, would suspect him of any undervaluing of charity toward one's neighbor, any downplaying of our consequently arduous duties toward our *pieté envers le Ciel.* But unlike many Christian writers today, he never forgets that the *first* commandment does come *first* — that the love of God is absolutely required, initially and overridingly, and is in any case the only sound basis for a love of neighbor that can hope to remain uncorrupted. Two timbers make up the Cross, and the vertical one is the greater, rooted in the earth and pointing to heaven: it carries the whole weight of that other timber, the one that points horizontally.

Maritain's great regret, in *The Peasant of the Garonne,* is that so many good men drift into a reversal of this basic priority, as though the love of men could realistically and safely be put first, before the love of God and of Truth, or as the chief and only medium of that greater love. He finds this tendency variously manifest: the best-intentioned version of it — and therefore perhaps the most dangerous — is familiar to most of us in the field of ecumenism. He distinguishes two sorts of ecumenism, a *true* kind and a *soft* kind; he reminds us that *the pleasures of togetherness* — that so-reassuring word in our so alienated and fragmented chapter of history — are too expensive, and are dishonestly enjoyed anyway, if they are purchased at the price of our intellectual integrity, our central concern for truth. He warns us against *"those brotherly dialogues in which everyone is in raptures while listening to the heresies, blasphemies, stuff and nonsense of the other. They are not brotherly at all."* Because *"it has never been recommended to confuse loving with 'seeking to please'."* [7] Life was never as simple as that. The salesman and (for that matter) the prostitute seek to please the customer, but seldom in the name of the high and crucifying motivation of *agape.*

The practical problem is never a simple one: Maritain was on the right lines, however, when he once said to Jean Cocteau, "We must have a tough mind and a tender heart" — adding sadly that the world is full of dried-up hearts and flabby minds. (It is entertaining to speculate about Cocteau's reply, which is not revealed to us.) Somehow, there has to be a harmony between these two loves, of God or Truth and of neighbor, so that we can then say *misericordia et veritas obviaverunt sibi.*[8] But there will often be difficulty, and Maritain is quite clear about the love that will then need to have priority, and also about the fact that by taking the high and honest road and putting first things first, we shall sometimes incur distrust and lose friends.

This may seem an impossibly austere doctrine, a "hard saying", indeed, and perhaps a proud one, in the eyes of a generation that likes to put *humanity first,* and this world, with humanity's comfort and prospects within this world. But it is the hardy perennial point of Maritain's message, before and after the Council, that *humanity* does not exist. *I* do. My *neighbor,* my human *brother,* does. Our *common good,* the bond among persons, does. Above all, God does. *Humanity* has no face, no address, no existence. On the other hand, a *personality,* each person, despite all his moral and community relations to other persons, is a *spiritual universe* in himself.

Maritain speaks repeatedly of the tendency to think otherwise, finding even among Catholics *a dangerous fever of veneration for this world* and the natural order at the expense of God, the supernatural order, the supernatural destiny of man, and the integrity of the person. Even where there is a longing for some specifically Christian kind of goodness and hope, we find men seeking it chiefly or only through their neighbor as a fellow citizen, concentrating in practice upon the secular city, making this the object of their faith, their hope, their charity.

He sees (of course) that in so behaving, they are exaggerating a necessary Christian principle. In a sense, one does meet God in one's neighbor. *That is true, but the fact remains that our brothers are mere creatures, confronting our eyes, and not* (to us who have not had the chance to see Him with our eyes) *God before the gaze of our soul, as is Jesus when we contemplate Him in His very humanity.*

It is not exactly in them, it is rather through them and behind them that we see Jesus and His love for them. And he certainly does not propose any kind of ivory-tower withdrawal, away from humanity and its daily problems into self-centered religiosity: the Christian has a temporal mission, he must *enter as deeply as possible into the agonies, the conflicts, and the earthly problems, social or political, of his age and not hesitate to get his feet wet.*

Even the Church—as such—has the task not only of rebuking moral evil but also of promoting temporal good. But all this needs to be kept in proportion, not being made into the object of any exaggerated hope. The Christian can, and must, ask for the coming of the Kingdom of God in glory, but he is not entitled to ask for—nor propose as the end of his temporal activity—a definite advent of justice and peace, and of human happiness, as the term of the progress of temporal history; for this progress is not capable of any final term.

In practice, he is gloomy about the temporal future that we seem likely to have; Maritain is altogether too erudite and sensitive to swallow the *myth of progress.* For him, civilization is plainly on the decline, with the human person threatened dreadfully by dehumanizing pressures, the pressure of technocracy in particular, so that only one hope remains to him in the temporal as well as in the supernatural order. "Let me say it once more, it is Christianity which will doubtless be the last resort for the human person, and for those poor adults who, after a too well-educated childhood, will have nevertheless retained concern for freedom, and will struggle to break from the universal conditioning."[9] But it will need to be a transcendental sort of Christianity; Maritain expects little from the social-welfare gospels of today, according to which the Church is to become a kind of public agency, charged with assuring the well-being of the world, universal peace, pay raises, and free room and board for all. It will also need to be—by some present-day standards—an *individualistic* (say better, *personalist*) sort of Christianity, at odds with the collectivizing trend of the times.

In that community of human persons which is a society, the Church, in keeping with the demands of truth, gives primacy to the person over the community; whereas today's world gives primacy to the community over the person—a highly interesting and significant disagreement. In our age of civilization the Church will increasingly become—bless Her—the refuge and support (perhaps the only one) of the person.[10]

Maritain here points to what is (in one sense) a secondary duty of the present-day Church, but a desperately important duty nonetheless; it grieves him to see an underlying principle eroded away by Christians, by Catholics, who are rather too anxious to be children of their times, and who therefore tend to see a statistical collectivity where they ought to see a personal membership in an organic and not merely organized community.

Widely, in many aspects of Christian life today, and notably in the field of liturgy, we see this tendency at work; and when this concentration upon people in the mass coincides with a strong emphasis upon worldly hopes and worldly endeavors and worldly methods, there follows—naturally enough—a keen and even frenzied concern for *activism* of a visible, audible, even clamorous kind, a consequent neglect of contemplation. Even the liturgy has become less personal and contemplative, more collective and more a matter of activity; and many people see this development as a wholly beneficial one, rejoicing also at the other kinds of *activism* that now absorb so much of Christianity's energy and good-will. Maritain has his doubts; he suspects that "the widespread infatuation that today prevails for action, technique, organization, inquiries, committees, mass movements, and the new possibilities that sociology and psychology are discovering . . . will some day give rise to a great deal of strong disappointment"[11]—and (he adds elsewhere) to many defections. There are depressing indications that this prophecy is not going to go unfulfilled. In fact, not a few feel that we can already document the damage done, that it is no longer a question of direful prophecy but one of disastrous history.

224

We shall have to think on different lines, locate our hope elsewhere. We face an immediate future that is going to be extremely difficult for the Church, and the practical advice offered by Maritain is both ancient and, to our ears, new. We are to put God first: few Christian writers today are more insistent upon this, and upon the idea—an impossibly bold and unfashionable idea, some might think—that our immediate and *practical* need is a widespread habit of contemplative prayer. "Be still, and know that I am God."[12] If the Church is to navigate the difficult waters that lie ahead, it will be—humanly speaking—by the power of many groups, many individuals who wait upon the Lord in silence, in the intuition of His being, each of them, like every person, in sympathy and affinity with one another, but each man, woman or child, even in the community of faith and love that is the Church, remaining a personal and distinct soul, *a spiritual universe,* as Maritain insists.

This is perhaps the heart of Maritain's book, which concludes with some very moving passages on this subject; it is certainly his chief recommendation, and it provides him with one of his chief grievances against spokesmen, some real, some self-chosen, for the official Church of recent centuries. The clergy, he says, have failed lamentably to encourage the life of contemplative prayer among the laity. Perhaps they believed that such heights were beyond the mere layman's reach: perhaps they undervalued contemplation itself, thinking it more urgent to organize all laymen of good will in the fascinating efficacy of collective action, as far as possible technically organized. For whatever reason, we failed in a prime duty, and Maritain begs us to take that duty more seriously in future at the peril of the Church's survival (humanly speaking) and our own personal salvation.

There are many people to whom this will seem unpractical advice, most unlikely to work out in practice, or not on any statistically efficacious scale. Wherever any such doubts are expressed, a tendency is illustrated that forms the other side of Maritain's central thesis. There has been a turning away from

God and toward this world: we can describe this in other terms, and say that too many people have ceased to see *Truth* as an absolute value, a name of God, making *efficacy* their ultimate criterion instead.

In my view, Maritain is certainly right here. Over these last few years, most of us will have encountered—in Catholic and theological circles—a rising tide of irritation and impatience, half-articulate but clear, toward the very idea of known truth, and especially toward any suggestion that dogmatic definitions might remain objectively and permanently true, despite changes in philosophical and linguistic fashion. A kind of basic scepticism is spreading among us, a distrust of language and reason as trustworthy avenues to reality, a strong preference for a kind of religion that will be strictly operational and pragmatic *experientially,* a matter of stimuli, responses, and efficacy. Here again, many go much too far in the redressing of an old one-sidedness, an excessive reliance upon formulae and definitions. There was probably need for wise change, but it needed to be sensitive and to remain sane. It often seems that some good Christians, by intention at least, have allowed themselves to become seriously infected by the philosophical scepticisms that prevail in the modern world.

Here, where the battlefield shifts from theology to philosophy, we find Maritain in the mood of the happy warrior, courteous to those sceptical thinkers who undermine our intuition of objectivity or truth, but pugnacious in his assertion that such people do not deserve to be called *philosophers* at all, least of all *theologians.* Not dismissively, by any means, but firmly, he calls them *ideosophers* instead, reserving the nobler title for those who—more realistically—believe that there is truth to be known, existing objectively, not created by our senses or our minds, capable of being known by ourselves, within limits but accurately, capable also of being described in sentences that shall remain objectively and permanently true, not to mention initially clear and reasonably grammatical.

It is Maritain the Thomist who speaks here—no mere cold mathematical logician, as some suppose, but a man passionately in love with the idea and the fact of objectivity, of Being, and full of jealous indignation at those *ideosophers* who seek to dissolve all Being into a flux of Subjectivity and Becoming. In this connection, he writes in something like the mood of a man who discovers a conspiracy to murder his true love. He sees all knowledge chopped fatally in two by the *Husserlian Parenthesis;* his anger reminds us of his great teacher's anger when a similar atrocity was proposed, long ago, by Siger of Brabant. Most of us will remember this story, if only from the third chapter of Chesterton's *St. Thomas Aquinas;* it is not only with respect to their geniality, but also—and more seriously—in terms of their shared and passionate intuition of Being, that Chesterton and Maritain constantly remind us of one another.

It is therefore in the spirit of a jealous lover—not in the spirit of a conservative philosopher, not in the spirit of a crude fundamentalist—that Maritain defends Being as against Becoming, against the essentially sceptical or nihilistic relativism and evolutionism of the day which ask: *Are There Moral Absolutes Today?* or *Do We Need the Church?,* as if in the hope that by the studied use of a seeming Socratic method in the title of his book, the author need assume responsibility for only the provocative question, while absolving himself of the murkiness left in the bewildered reaction of the reader. Even so, it is with great sympathy and understanding that Maritain considers the work of that great writer and deeply troubled poet, Teilhard de Chardin, whom he respects personally, though his *enraptured ecclesiastical retinue* comes in for some acid comment. In my view, his diagnosis here is an accurate one. He sees Teilhard as a gnostic at heart, who—in the style of the old gnostics—wrote *theology fiction* rather than theology, and who suffered interior conflict because this deep-seated instinct was not compatible with his powerful intuition of the fact that created Nature is a sacred thing. Teilhard (he suggests) had a deep and authentic

227

religious experience, but conceptualized it badly; this bad formulation could be passed on to other people—and *was* passed on, most widely, and in his view disastrously—while the authentic inner vision died with him.[13]

Sympathetic toward the man, Maritain has no time whatever for his *purely evolutive conception, where Being is replaced by Becoming and every essence or nature stably constituted in itself vanishes.* Such ideas are, as all know, popular today. If taken seriously, they seem to warrant a basic scepticism, an indifference to truth, fostering instead *an obsessive fixation upon the passing of time,* a habitual *adoration of the ephemeral,* of the process of mere change, contemporaneity. At many points in *The Peasant of the Garonne,* Maritain castigates this so-conspicuous element in the present-day mentality of the Catholic *intelligentsia,* the tendency to exalt the passing moment and its fashion into an absolute, as though it possessed—while it lasted—an infallibility beyond what the most rigorous ultramontane ever claimed for the Pope.

In every context of this sort, Maritain is sharply critical of what he considers an *intellectually degraded epoch,* and of *the powerful disgust with Reason, the joyous (no, it is not joyous) logophobia which is festering before our eyes.* In one sense, his central message is that we have a precisely *religious* duty of hard and rigorous thinking—with a suggestion that it is precisely failure in *this* duty that may well be the great religious fault of our generation.

There is some truth, then, in the idea of Maritain as a somewhat embittered conservative; he certainly writes nostalgically, looking back to an *age of faith* that he sees also as an age of authentic reason. But he has no sentimental illusions, and his nostalgia is carefully qualified; his conservatism is by no means merely instinctive, temperamental, or without profound reflection, even the meditation he practices as well as preaches. He castigates the faults of the medieval Church, its cruelty in particular, as fiercely as the most sensitive humanitarian, real or purported, could wish, and, while he remains a loyal Thomist, convinced that Thomism is *the* Christian philosophy, he detects a kind of childlikeness, even childishness, in the medieval mind, and he is (in the end) prepared to admit that the scholastic method has had its day, that our time calls for new approaches.

Nostalgic, then, in measured degree, he warns us against idealizing the past; evil, of one kind or another, has always been rampant within the household of the Church. In *The Peasant of the Garonne,* he discusses certain intellectual and spiritual evils that he detected in the Church of his own time, and he hoped to make this his last book; but now, in *L'Eglise du Christ,* he has returned to the subject, concerning himself for the most part with evil in the Church of earlier centuries. Significantly, his preoccupation with *personality* and with the *person* controls his concept of the Church. For Maritain, the Church is no mystical City, on the one hand, or holy but nomadic herd, on the other; she, for him as for Paul, is primarily a person.

He takes up his theme for a particular and deeply felt purpose, working out more fully an idea that was treated briefly in *The Peasant of the Garonne.* The mind of this great and faithful Thomist can hardly be in close sympathy with the linguistic or semantic point. It concerns our use of the word *Church,* in which he sees an ambiguity that we do not always recognize or allow for; and his last recommendation—his almost agonized plea—is that we should modify our vocabulary, our habitual way of talking and thinking, so as to eliminate a kind of confusion that has done immense damage in the past.

Putting it bluntly, this confusion arises whenever we talk as though *the Church* —theologically considered—were the same thing as the churchmen, the pontiffs and prelates and priests, whom we meet today and in the checkered pages of history. Maritain himself uses words that will hardly go into modern English: he wants us to distinguish the *personne* of the Church from her *personnel.* This second term is clear enough: he is speaking there, quite simply, of the clergy and the hierarchy and the Pope. The emerging layman, with his somewhat prickly sensitivity, should not smell clericalism here and take offence:

elsewhere, more keenly than any simple-minded progressive, Maritain has celebrated the priesthood of all believers, the equation — in one sense — of *the Church* with the whole people in God, organically and doctrinally as well. He is not here belittling the laity. If anything, his argument has a faintly anticlerical flavor. By way of contrast with the total goodness of the Church's *personne,* he is distinguishing and denouncing the imperfections — and often the gross wickedness and sheer folly — of her *personnel,* her appointed and ordained shepherds.

In each of these books, named individuals come in for some courteously rough handling; very few of them are Catholic laymen, though why, given the pretenses and profiteering of so many of these at the expense of their *Catholicism,* it is hard to decide. It remains to be seen who, in fact, will turn out to have done the greater damage to the historic image of the Church, the one-time *Most Catholic Majesties* or the present-day *representative Catholic enlightened citizens or lay theologians.* One wishes Maritain had reserved some of his ink for sprinkling these!

It is also a shade difficult to indicate what he means by the *personne* of the Church. The word *person* has become a weak word in English; it suggests a human being, vaguely and neutrally seen. And the alternative word *personality* has been so thoroughly vulgarized (*a television personality*) that it gives little help toward making Maritain's distinction part of our habitual way of thought. But it is an important distinction, and we need to make the effort.

Let us approach the task by considering our habitual way of talking about the Church. We see this (in the first instance) as all men do, as a structured society or organization of men and women, comparable to a nation or a club; being Catholics, we also — and more seriously — see her as the Body of Christ, His presence, as Christ in action within the world. Basing his argument upon the relevant texts of Scripture and acknowledging a deep indebtedness to Cardinal Journet, Maritain leads us to the point at which he proposes also a third and intermediate view of the Church. In no merely analogical sense, he sees it as a real *personne,* a created being, distinct from Christ (and so able to be called his *Bride*) and also from ourselves, and sharing with Christ and his Mother—though in a different mode from either— the privilege of being immaculate, of having no fault. And he sees this *personne* as existing, at once and in full continuity, in this world and the next. When we say that she speaks *infallibly,* we mean that she sees there and speaks here. In this sense, there is no distinction at all between the Church that *sees* and the Church that *believes,* the Church Triumphant and the Church *in via.* But between this *personne* of the Church on the one hand, and the life and thought and speech and behavior of any living man on the other, the relationship will be complex and often elusive. The great troublemaking confusion arises when we oversimplify this relationship. We can do this in various ways. In the past, we have often done it by equating the Church's *personne* with her *personnel,* and saying *The Church teaches* . . . when what we really mean is *The Pope thinks* . . . or even *Monsignor Hidebound insists* . . . or, more likely at the moment, *Yesterday at their annual meeting at Mumble Manor Country Club over 250 of America's greatest theologians unanimously resolved that.* . . . In these days, the latter source of confusion appears to be more widely felt.

We need clear concepts in this area, or at least an exact terminology, because our habitual way of talking about the Church—of failing to make the relevant distinctions—leads us constantly into two paradoxes, two apparent contradictions that make things harder for everyone concerned.

In the first place, we speak of our *Holy Mother* the Church; of Christ's Mystical Body, indwelt by the Holy Spirit, infallible and indefectible, *without spot or wrinkle or any such thing, but holy and immaculate.* But then, along comes some sardonic controversialist, or perhaps some secret part of our own awareness, to point out that the visible Church's record scarcely corresponds with the implications of such lofty and idealistic terminology. The point is a valid one; you cannot read any Church history, or even live for six months in a Catholic parish, campus, or club, without becoming painfully aware that the actual life of the Church—as we commonly understand that term—is an extremely human and mixed thing. It is not a matter of total depravity, but certainly it is not lacking in *spots and wrinkles*. And to the extent that the clergy have always been in practical command and in nominal control at least, they bear a special degree of responsibility for this situation. The controversialist need not suppose that we Catholics are unaware of the fact. For my part, I am haunted and made nervous by an observation that was made many centuries ago. "I do not say that a bishop cannot be saved," wrote Giraldus Cambrensis, "but I do say that it is in our days harder for them than for other men." While personally unshaken by the intellectual polemics surrounding Galileo—who, if he really said *"Eppure si muove"*, should have said it out loud and taken the consequences—I have studied too long and too lovingly the case of Saint Joan to have any illusions about my personal prelatial immunity from error or to be unduly upset by the openness to convenient compromises of *devout* prelates, princes, prime ministers, or candidates for public office who are, to be sure, Catholics (or other Christians) by baptism and *affiliation*, as one of the candidates used to word it in his campaign literature; but politicians still, and that in the pejorative sense,—he mere politicians or *intellectual spokesmen for the Catholic community*. Nor need things be any more unnerving for a prelate whose task—in the wrath of God—obliges him to be concerned, from day to day, with the problems, troubles, failures, and unrealized potential of the Catholic clergy throughout the world.

"If England was what England seems," said Kipling, " 'ow quick we'd drop 'er! But she ain't."[14] The Church also is not what she seems, not what the record suggests, and while she can be aptly discussed—on one side and within limits—in the language of history, psychology, and/or sociology, she remains essentially a mystery of faith. Maritain is very insistent about this, reminding us again and again that we shall be beating the air in all our discussions unless they are informed, through and through, with that awareness, of the Church as mystery—as *personne* and *personnel* at once, the relationship between the two becoming clear only at certain points.

He gives us here, and perhaps for the first time, an adequate terminology for describing the mystery of manifest evil in a Church that is—nonetheless—entirely good and holy. Maritain gives us at least a useful linguistic implement for exploring the depths of the mystery. *Personne* and *personnel* are distinct, but they are mutually involved, and Maritain draws on the old fourfold notion of *causes* to analyze their involvement. We see churchmen in action; at one extreme when a priest says Mass, and at the other when some medieval prelate (let us say) embarks upon some particularly nasty and bloodstained political adventure. In each case, a member of the Church's *personnel* is involved; in each case, the undistinguishing mind will see *the Church* at work. But in the latter case (we are being instructed here by Maritain the Thomist), that Pope acts as *principal cause* of what follows; whereas in the former case, the priest is only the instrumental cause of what actually happens at Mass, the principal cause being the Church herself, her *personne*—which was not involved to any degree whatever in that prelate's questionable rascality.

In practice, we see the Church *in confuso,* her perfect *personne* and her very imperfect *personnel* being often hard to distinguish when both are acting at the same time. The distinction will sometimes be easiest to make retrospectively; in spite of an unkind suggestion made by the anonymous critic who reviewed *L'Eglise du Christ* in London's *Times Literary Supplement,* there is nothing improper about that approach. Quite the contrary, a good deal of immediate certainty is available. When doctrines are solemnly defined *de fide* by a council, or by a Pope speaking *ex cathedra;* when a saint is canonized; when Mass is said or other sacraments conferred, and when the Divine Office is said or sung—at such moments we see and·hear the Church herself in action, her flawless *personne,* no matter how great and obvious the rubrical faults and moral limitations of the *personnel* whom she then uses instrumentally. With less clarity, and perhaps less certainty, we can say the same about certain other happenings when acts of churchmen seem to be also acts of the Church.

About other happenings, great and small, this will emphatically not be true. Maritain instances the Crusades, the *holy war,* the abuses of the Inquisition, the Church's frequent treatment of the Jews, and the condemnations of Galileo and of Jeanne d'Arc. We have to admit that these things were done by churchmen; Maritain now gives us a terminology, by the aid of which we can avoid the blasphemous suggestion that they were done by the Church, and without any use of whitewash or of sophistic distinctions and quibblings.

There is a second paradox, a second apparent contradiction that is eased by this approach. How are we to interpret the irenicism superficially embarrassing (to a pluriform age of ecumenism) principle of *No salvation outside the Church?* [15] In these ecumenical days, we are mostly disposed to dodge the question, or else to interpret that painfully apodictic principle very broadly indeed—so broadly, indeed, as to empty it of all meaning and utility. But if so, the controversialist will be ready with a charge of self-contradiction which—if taken seriously—would undermine the whole concept of a teaching and uniquely salvific Church, divinely safeguarded from error. He will invoke the bull *Unam Sanctam* and the Council of Florence, telling us that the Catholic Church has historically and plainly committed herself, with all due solemnity, to a doctrine which in more recent years she has not only abandoned, but even rebuked sharply when it returned as *the Boston Heresy*—the doctrine—(some would have expressed it) in the days of my youthful (and deeply involved) modest person—that all WASPS go to hell, in principle and quite properly. It was, by the way, not Maritain, though I was already his grateful disciple and friend by the time of the Boston Case, that alerted me to the dangers of the posi-

234

tion of my friend and confessor, Father Feeney; it was, in fact, *Pius the Ninth!*[16]

Maritain's approach to this question hinges upon the ambiguity of any such expression as *within the Church* or *outside the Church,* as applied to any individual. If we use such expressions, do we have in mind that person's relationship to the Church's *personne,* or to *personnel?* Maritain explores the various possibilities, and this takes him into a deeply interesting survey of the non-Catholic denominations and the non-Christian religions, and of the senses in which these various separated brethren can—perhaps to their astonishment, possibly even to ours—be said to be *within the Church,* despite appearance. (It may surprise some people to find him listing *Les Hippies* among the world's great religions; but when you think it over, it makes considerable sense. To say the least, these people constitute *a religion* quite as clearly as Confucianism or Buddhism does.) Maritain's central conclusion is that the expressions *to be in the Church* —that is to say, in the Church's *personne* —and *to be in the way of salvation* are (in the last analysis) synonymous. If we are attempting the unfruitful task of working out the probabilities and statistics of salvation, *Extra ecclesiam nulla salus* then becomes a mere tautology; but it regains positive and useful meaning if we see it as a pointer (at least) to what *the Church* means in terms of her special relationship to the Saving Person of Christ (sole source of salvation) even more than in terms of her relationship to any of her human *personnel,* not a few of whom, even when instrumental causes for salvation for others, may themselves be candidates for perdition. This is no new intuition of the enlightened *avant-garde;* it is sound Catholic doctrine as old as patrology or preaching. Maritain thus performs a useful task of salvage. We cannot possibly jettison that principle; however embarrassing, it is deeply and (if we believe in the Holy Spirit) rightly burned into our theology. But we did not wish to see it as an empty tautology, nor yet as a condemnation of each Protestant neighbor to fires that he may well not have merited.

Once again, the progressive mind can be wholly satisfied and can hail Maritain as an ally. The honest heretic, the saintly schismatic, the good pagan—such men, so long as they seek God in good conscience (though not necessarily with any explicit awareness that *God* is what they seek) will be in the *way of salvation* and will thus be *within the Church* in the sense that matters ultimately. Conversely, if you and I live in sin, we may still remain Catholics, within the Church in a limited sense; but so far as the *necessitas salutis* is concerned, we shall be fatally outside, cut off from the life of the *personne* until we repent, even though the Church's *personnel* (who can be wrong) may suppose us to be card-carrying members in good standing. Saint Augustine, not Maritain, said the final and briefest word on this.

Various objections can, however, be brought against this approach. For one thing, it does not seem *ecumenical* in the way that many of us would desire. Fairly warm toward the Orthodox Church, less warm toward the Anglican, Maritain is definitely frosty about most of the non-Catholic denominations and religions. His real ecumenism is profoundly universal, not so much a matter of affability toward our immediate institutional neighbors; it embraces the human condition as such, the whole race, all sinful, all redeemed by Christ, all capable of being gathered up into the life of a Church whose *personne* operates more broadly than some of her *personnel* are willing or able to recognize or function.

From a different point of view, it might also be objected that this approach proposes—in effect—an *invisible Church* of all good men everywhere, undermining the particularity of the gospel, the scripturally emphasized importance of baptism and of faith in Christ, the necessity of anything like a *visible Church,* even, to put it with brazen audacity an *institutional Church,* and a good man's objective duty of being in unity with that Church, organized historically and with a local habitation and a name. But Maritain has anticipated this objection and is not in fact proposing anything of that airy and formless, universalist kind;

he is insistent about the principle that the Roman Catholic Church—in all her particularity, and despite all the failing of her *personnel*—is the concrete presence on earth, the instrument, the mouthpiece of a *personne* that extends more widely, existing in this world and the next, her frontier running potentially through the hearts of all men. The importance of *being a Catholic* remains clear and compelling, and the consequent duty of the mission apostolate, of conversion where possible, warning us against a too statistical approach and an exaggerated concern for efficient organizational externals.

More, where the apostolate and the task of conversion are concerned, he does propose a certain shift of emphasis. Objectively or materially speaking, schism and heresy are still mortal sins, objectively evil, and the sinner who acts *sciens et volens* is lost unless he repents. This ugly fact remains: in this connection, we have not changed our theology, and we need not blush for *Unam Sanctam* or the Council of Florence. But we have changed our judgment of the consequent problem in applied pastoral psychology. Our forefathers tended to assume that the heretic or schismatic would be in bad faith; we tend (in a historically different situation) to make the contrary assumption. This may be a shade unrealistic of us, since all of them are imperfectly sincere, but at the worst, it is an error in the correct, the charitable direction. Assuming, then—as we almost invariably should—that the other man is in good faith, we ought to love him for what he already is, not for what he may become; and if we try to convert him (as we should), this is not because we seek an alteration in his relationship to God and to the Church's *personne*, but because we seek a recognition, a visible enactment, of what that relationship already is and entails. We are told by impeccable authority that the repentance of a sinner occasions an ultimate joy in heaven; in the conversion of a good man to the Catholic Faith and the Church's unity, we should—in Maritain's view—usually see something not very different, the rectification of an anomaly, the recognition of a fact previously obscured, a happy victory for that truth which is always his chief concern, his chief passion. We can also rejoice, on obvious traditional lines, because a brother in Christ will now have covenanted help and light that was not available to him before.

Rather clumsily, hampered by the lack of any really suitable terminology, the Church's doctrine has been developing for a long time in this kind of direction. In my view, Maritain's treatment is not beyond all criticism; one may be uneasy, for example, about his resolution of the particular problem created by the Council of Florence—his suggestion that words can meaningfully be said to have meaning not merely distinct from, but flatly antithetical to, the conscious intention of those who have used them. Here—with the bashfulness proper to a very amateur philosopher—I suggest that in the exhilaration of a profoundly necessary philosophical battle, he has allowed himself to be swept forward onto possibly dangerous ground. Language cannot be quite so objective, quite such an absolute; only when God speaks does the word coincide precisely with Being. Most wisely did Dr. Johnson say, in the preface to his *Dictionary,* "I am not yet so lost in lexicography as to forget that words are the daughters of earth, and that things are the sons of heaven."[17]

But his general approach seems to me both sound and timely; and I admire it all the more for not being any kind of compromise. In the splendid fifth chapter of *Orthodoxy,* Chesterton emphasizes the principle that Christianity involves us—at every level—in a balanced tension of opposites: *not an amalgam or compromise, but both things at the top of their energy—love and wrath both burning.* The utterly holy Church, which is also a Church of sin and atrocity; the Ark of Salvation, narrowly defined and unique, the denouncing and excommunicating Bark of Peter, which yet bears all men to safety unless they choose to drown. Maritain does full justice to both extremes of either paradox.

As a matter of some urgency, I think we need to follow his advice and modify our habitual vocabulary, so that we can speak of *the Church* without ambiguity. As he says, this will be difficult but not impossible. How can we do it? Perhaps we could use words derived from *ecclesia* when we refer to the Church's *personnel*, the Christian assembly of clergy and laity, imperfect as any assembly of people *in via* must be. Then we could reserve such words as are derived from *kuriakos* for use when we are referring to the Church's *personne*, the Lord's own thing, holy, without stain or wrinkle. Alternatively, in the English language at least, we could subtly vary the gender of our pronouns: speaking of the Church, we could say that *it* has been guilty of follies and crimes, and that *she* is the perfect and unfailing Bride of Christ. But we need to do something. At present, we cannot—without inviting confusion—say that the Church is holy and divine, indefectible, infallible; or that the Church is perennially guilty, *semper reformanda,* and needs to repent. Both facts need assertion, but not less the exquisite clarification demanded by concepts so close at once to the human condition and the divine realities.

We can leave the practical question, perhaps, to a Sacred Congregation of Vocabulary and Semantics; the present scribe has long maintained that more than any new *Codex* or *Summa,* we need a new *Lexicon.* Until then, we are somewhat at the mercy of our kindly but capricious scholars and writers, theological and other. But in the meantime, we have something to celebrate: the fact that God has seen fit to privilege the Church of this day with the presence among us of a man so wise, a *doctor ecclesiae* in fact if not yet in title, and supremely *Catholic.*

XIII

Teaching the Faith

I welcome a chance to talk about the most important work of the Congregation in the Roman Curia, which the Holy Father has been kind enough, or reckless enough, to appoint me to as prefect. It happens also to be in my judgment, the most important work in the Church today, and I justify that seemingly universal remark by saying that I personally cannot think of a single problem facing the Catholic Church, the solution of which does not depend on how well you do the work I am talking about tonight. If you were to name the problems that you consider among the chief problems, I suppose you might say the problem of vocations. Well, you'll get no vocations unless this work is done. Or you might say the problem of family life. You won't have any families unless this work is done, so there won't be any problem of family life except the nonexistence of them. You might say peace and war, or something vertical or horizontal, whatever the phrases are these days, but *this* work is the work of teaching the Faith revealed in, through, and by Christ Jesus, who died for our salvation on a Cross that is the symbol of the Church. Its staff, the horizontal one, falls to the ground. So remind the horizontal boys of that the next time they ask you why you are not in the horizontal church!

In a word then, the present crisis is a crisis in a complicated word called catechetics. I will never be able to figure out why the holy Catholic Church, the truths of which are the simplest in the history of the world, has managed to pick out the most complicated word to describe them—but isn't it true? We wrap it all up in a mystery. Well, the fact of the matter is we're talking

This address was delivered at the Bishop Thomas Grant Comprehensive School, Streatham, London, England, on June 9, 1972.

tonight about the crisis in catechetics: the teaching of the Faith. By the way, we are not talking about theology—I'd like to emphasize that point. It's perfectly possible to have the Faith and know as little about theology as my mother did. You well remember Louis Pasteur, who said that if it came to a choice between having the faith of a whole faculty of theologians (even Germans), he preferred to have the faith of a Breton peasant. Faith saves, theology is a kind of a science (we'll come to that later), but they are not the same thing. Now there are undoubtedly some many and distinguished theologians in the hall tonight, and they are going to go home as indignant as blazes with me because they are going to say he sneered at the theologians. But if you'd give us a hand I'd embrace you and kiss you. All I am asking you to do is not replace that Faith with your theology, that's all. The Faith is revealed by Jesus Christ, theology was dreamed up by you. Faith is a total personal response to the Word of God, speaking through Jesus Christ. Theology is some smart guy's scientific systematization of his opinion about the matter and how he explains it to himself (*if* he does).

But we just touch on this in a glancing fashion. All I am saying is that, what with one thing and another, there exists in the world considerable confusion at the moment about catechetics. About what precisely is the Faith and how it should be transmitted—that used to be the old phrase: *The Faith transmitted by our Fathers,* do you remember? "Faith of our Fathers living still". The Faith of our Fathers was transmitted by the mandate of God, through the word of Jesus to the apostles and their accredited representatives, and those to whom their accredited representatives gave the faculty to perpetuate the Faith. Some of them were theologians and some of them weren't. I have known several bishops in my life who weren't great theologians. I know one bishop who is a much better real estate man than he is theologian, but he has the Faith—and that's what scares the real estate broker, because he does not know what the power of it may be. He knows he has the angels—by the way he believes in the angels! So does the real estate man when this guy is around! Well, there is a crisis: What is the Faith and how are we going to teach it? This crisis has been a long time coming on—so long that I could talk to you for six hours and a half on how it came about, but I am going to abbreviate it briefly lest you get into an even worse crisis.

First of all, I have a theory that this crisis began not with a crisis in faith. I have had lots of fellows come in to me—seminarians, priests, and others—saying "I'm suffering from a crisis in faith", and after a few minutes conversation you discover that they're not having a crisis in the faith at all. They have very profound faith. They have a crisis of a theological kind. They can't quite understand Hans Küng or someone like that—well translated it's rough stuff—but it isn't a crisis in the faith. And after a short conversation, you discover that in fact they don't have a crisis in faith. More often than not, I believe at any rate (this is purely personal and I offer it merely as such), that they are suffering from a crisis in *culture.* We are undergoing one of those great cultural revolutions which occur every four or five hundred years in history. For example, even I can remember when England was a liberal arts country. They taught Latin, English, history, including American history (badly rewritten but they taught it): they had what you call liberal arts minds. Now, liberal arts are a classical education and produce a certain kind of intellect. Cardinal Newman had it. Can you imagine him suffering a crisis of faith? He did not split infinitives. His mind was clear. He had read the Greek Fathers—he knew how it all seemed to the Fathers of the Church when the Church was young. He had read the Latin Fathers.

This evening as I entered the school and I kidded the headmaster: "I see that even you have gone technocratic—you're computerized." There's a huge board out front which tells where everybody is every minute. It's something like the spaceships. There's a fellow down in Houston who knows where the astronauts are all the time. The astronauts don't know! The astronauts are part of the machinery! Because ours is no longer a liberal arts, intellectual, personal, free-will civilization, its an automated, technological, scientific, mechanical civilization—and you'd better get used to it or you're going to be run over the next time you cross the street, and you're going to get your hand caught in the machinery. In a period of such crisis, when suddenly everybody is studying space mathematics and all manner of so-called positive sciences, and poetry is disappearing from the schools, and theatre (except in regrettable forms), and no one remembers ancient history, and they all have nervous fits every morning when they read in the headlines that finally after six years of debate the Irish have joined the European market and they forget that it took 250 years to form the Peloponnesian league (which is about one-eighth the extent of the European market)—you see they have no perspective. The machinery has their poor little heads pounding. So, they go into what I think is a cultural crisis.

The same thing happens in the Faith. The moment there is a crisis in the Faith you get an epidemic of theologians! To explain it, they start off by a theology called the *Theology of God is Dead.* That's not faith, it's a theology (as a matter of fact it's a lie). Or even worse, they begin to show, even on Catholic book stalls, not books about faith, hope, and charity but books entitled *Toward a Theology of Hope.* After 2,000 years since Calvary, what in the name of heaven does that title mean? *Toward a Theology of Hope! Toward* a Theology of Community—2,000 years after the Cenacle and the Last Supper! *Toward* a theology of this, and *toward* a theology of that—they are what they call searching. All this means is that in the crisis of faith they have lost their way and they thumb a ride from any guy driving along.

The last great crisis of this kind came, I think, in Europe with the Renaissance and the Enlightenment. All of a sudden the best part of a thousand years of Christian unity in the Faith was challenged by the revival of classical learning. Just as now people say, "I don't go in for that early 20th-Century religious art", so then, they said, "I go in for Greek and Roman art", and we were flooded with Greek and Roman art: Michelangelo, Bramante— you'll never catch me saying it isn't great art, but it came to the people as a kind of a shock. Then there came the Enlightenment, the encyclopedists, the new learning, and the new wisdom. Many of your best men died victims of it, fighting for the old learning. One was Thomas More. He continued to write in Latin. But this tradition was *not* the Faith. You must not confuse culture with faith. Belloc did that: "Europe is the Faith, and the Faith is Europe."[1] There was never a more silly line uttered! Europe is *not* the Faith. I can be a witness to that. I have been in Europe. I have also met magnificent Catholics in Taipei and Taiwan, and they never saw the Eiffel Tower or Notre Dame Cathedral, or things we think of as the representatives of Western culture, which is what Belloc had in mind. That was a great period of crisis, and out of it there came a flood of theologians. It's unecumenical to mention their names now, but nonetheless they flooded out of that particular period. There's a monument to them in Geneva—they're all made out of marble, and they stand near the roadway staring at you. One morning, I got out at seven o'clock in the morning and stood in front of the Reformation monument, and there were all these great theologians of the reform staring at me. You know what they were thinking? They were thinking, "You are a Roman Catholic, you've just got off the aeroplane from Rome, and I bet you played bingo last night!"

So, there was this little transition, first a crisis of faith, then a flood of theology, and then it settled down a little bit because there came a synthesis. Then there came the Industrial Revolution, and that caused a very great crisis, both in your country and mine, as you can tell whenever you read between the lines of Dickens or when you read about the terrible losses among the immigrants in my own country. Then in God's Providence, this new learning, sometimes even the new theology, and the new culture synthesized with the ancient Faith (because the Faith never actually died), and there came the Faith lived out—the same Faith, lived out in new forms.

So the Faith is going through a crisis—but the synthesis of the Faith, and for the Faith, is already under way. Let me give you a proof. What is the highest possible symbol of the new science, the new technology? Just as in the age of the classical renaissance you would have chosen a great painter or a great sculptor, so today you would choose a great technologist, a great technocrat—let's say an astronaut. He is a symbol of the new science, isn't he? But did you notice that when the astronauts were orbiting the moon on the Eve of Christmas four years ago, they read to the entire world by Telstar, not a page of politics, not a page of sociology (thank God), not a page of science. They read the first chapter of the Book of Genesis, "In the beginning God created heaven and earth . . .", and they took turns, the three of them each reading a verse until they reached the verse where it said, "and when He looked upon that which He had made, God found it good." Remember by doing so they violated the Constitution of my country. The Constitution of the United States is more sacred than the Ten Commandments, because not even the most advanced catechist has suggested that we tear up the Constitution, but the Ten Commandments have been removed from any book you care to look at. There was a nutty woman in our country who decided to sue them for violating the First Amendment of the Constitution. They had read the Bible from a tax-supported, government-owned machine. Well, a friend of mine, a constitutional lawyer, Bill Ball, saw a chance to get in on the act, and it was very attractive. He said:

I'll figure out a line of defence for you, and this is it. If you are finally called before the Supreme Court, I will put you in the prisoner's box, and I will ask you your name. Then I will ask you your occupation, and you will say: "Astronaut."

245

Then I will say: "Where were you on the 24th of December 1967?" And you'll say: "Several hundred miles above the moon, riding around it!"

"Did you or did you not read a book out loud into a microphone so that you were heard all throughout Creation from that machine?" And you will answer: "I did."

"What was the name of that book?" "The Bible!"

"Who owned that machine?" "The United States Government."

"Who paid for it?" "The taxpayers."

"Did you read that book to all the people in the nation: Catholic, Protestant, Jewish, Orthodox, Zoroastrian, Hindu, Buddhist—without reference to their religion?" "No."

"Did you just read it to the Catholics on a government-owned machine?" "No."

"Did you read it to the Communists—to make enemies?" "No."

"To whom did you read?" "I read it to my three kids sitting in front of the television."

So, you see that, in the most surprising circles, this little instinct to get back to God—and how things got started—is very much alive. When the Holy Father invited the astronauts to address the Synod of Bishops in 1969—their talk was the best speech delivered during the synod! It was certainly the most spiritual talk, because during the question period, one cardinal put up his hand and said: "There is no doubt about it, your scientific accomplishment—from a technological point of view—was unbelievable. Did it have any effect on your spiritual life?" And one fellow—of whom I was particularly proud, because I taught his wife in college, and she was sitting right there listening to him—said: "I answer for all three because we have talked about this many times. The deeper we went out into God's creation and looked back at the earth and out at the planets—for the first time I began to understand the meaning of the phrase: 'Eye hath not seen, ear hath not heard, nor has it entered into the heart of

246

man to conceive the wonders that God has prepared for those who love Him.' "

That was the effect that their technological adventure had on them as men who may have grown a little weak in the Faith—a little preoccupied in not shooting off beyond the sun. They had a lot on their mind that night, but nonetheless when they looked back, that's what came back to them. And you may be quite sure when we read in the papers that the Russian astronauts said, "Salute" to Comrade Krushev from the moon, underneath their breath I think they probably said, "Our Lady of Nizhniy Novgorod, have mercy on our kids", as certainly ours did.

So, the crisis in culture is, I think, beginning to synthesize. Another thing contributed to this crisis—a philosophical thing. Many philosophers contributed to it, but if you picked out one it would be Descartes. Descartes was a kind of French Jesuit theologian in his day, and he thumped up his own brand of theology and psychology. His theory was: there are some things which are the object of sheer scientific knowledge, and they're totally separate—and thus began this Cartesian philosophy that has dominated these last couple of centuries. That the things you know by faith are purely personal—kind of between you and God (as President Eisenhower once said at a press conference when he was more mixed up than usual, "I want each of you to pray to the God of your own choice"). The other things that are certain, are like this great division in the forms of knowledge, and the results of it have been very far-reaching. Very far-reaching indeed—especially in the nineteenth century, when books were written about *The Conflict between Religion and Science*. One of your boys wrote that, it's a big two-volume thing and has a total of 980 pages. It's a history of the conflict between religion and science. In those days, there was great gab about Galileo—how poor Galileo, because he was smart, was put to death by stupid guys who only had faith. Now the fact of the matter is that Galileo was wrong. Galileo thought that the sun was at the center of the solar system and that the earth went around the sun. Up to that point he was O.K., but as a matter of fact, the sun is on the edge of a galaxy that is one of several million galaxies that Galileo never heard about. So his knowledge was incomplete, as the knowledge of those who judged him was incomplete—but those who judged him didn't happen to be the Pope. They were Dominicans and Jesuits who then, as now, were scrapping among themselves about who had the right interpretation of the passage of Scripture that said the sun went in whatever direction it said the sun went in—and therefore he fought it out with the bunch of them. The Jesuits were with him, and the Dominicans were against him, and Galileo got life imprisonment. Well, really not a bad one; I've seen the villa where he lived, and I'll settle for it any day, right or wrong.

Then there was a third thing. It had a heavy influence in this country and throughout the world but mostly in Germany, France, and what are now called the Benelux nations. It had a little influence in Italy too. It was called modernism. It was an inevitable follow-up on Descartes—absolutely inevitable. It involved many and very lovely personalities. Have you noticed nowadays now when some people are criticized as theologians you'll hear people say, "How can they possibly criticize such a sweet and gentle and good priest as if he were mistaken?" Well, you could have said that about half the modernists—beginning with your own Father Tyrrell, who was gentle, sweet, friendly, and *wrong*. And running down into Italy to a man like, say, Fogazzaro, who was sympathetic, poetic, literary, gentle, kind, and *wrong*—because it is perfectly possible, just as you can be good-looking, gentle, kind, and *stupid*—or *cruel*. But in any case, this thing called modernism came along, and it divided everything between the subjective and the objective. The things which are objectively mine (which maybe are, maybe aren't) and the things which my subjective, personal conscience tells me are needed for my subjective, personal perfection—like things that used to be considered wrong and which if Mama had done them she would have been in serious trouble, but if I do them, I am elected class secretary, because it shows I'm forward-looking and have initiative and a sense of the future and so on. On the level of the classroom teaching, it is much more complicated than that because they too get everything gussied up with big words of one sort and another.

Then finally there came the heavy emphasis on so-called experimental sciences. Whereas Descartes really undermined reason when he thought he was exalting it, the modernists wiped it out. They reduced things to instinct, sentiment, and feeling. And so this feeling and instinct led to a great dependence on the experimental sciences. "I really can't believe this unless I've experienced it." Make a list of the things you can't believe unless you've experienced them, but don't show the list to the policeman because he'll follow you home! The experimental sciences went into the ascendancy, and with them went things like pedagogy, which is an experimental science, and methodology. And methodology began to become more important than the content. In the commonwealth of Pennsylvania where I was last bishop, every teacher can be as ignorant as Paddy's pig on the subject that she's teaching — but she must do a course in methodology. The only thing absolutely required is that she has a certificate in methodology. If she knows French, well, that's helpful too — then she can be assigned to the mathematics class — but the main thing is to make sure she has methodology. This, particularly in my own country, has contributed mightily to the catechetical crisis. Everybody found fault, not with the content at first, because they hadn't read it for many years, but they found fault with the methodology. They said this had been done by rote. They get asked questions and like Pavlov's dog, they give automatic answers. Now, that's not good methodology. The answers happened to be correct for the most part, but that's beside the point. The methodology was at fault; let's leave it at that.

Then in the whole world of methodology and pedagogy, there took place a revolution which made approximately a million bucks for a professor who was getting $7,000 a year at the University of Toronto up till that time. He discovered that we have undergone a great change. We have changed from a reading civilization into a visual and photographic civilization—so Fordham immediately hired him for $100,000 a year to explain to the students that they like to look at pictures better than they like to read books. The students hadn't discovered that yet, you see, and therefore he gave lectures all over the world, since he had made *the most important discovery since the invention of movable type* (that was in the *Time* magazine underneath his picture). Namely, that we live now in a visual or audio-visual civilization, and you can't learn anything unless you see pictures of it and it's reduced to charts and flow-charts and so on.

And so we entered into the marvelous thing we have now— audio-visual education. Now there too someone is going to go home sore—mad as blazes! They're going to say, "After all those charts I made and all those pictures I took, he stood up and made a plea for the old Baltimore catechism and the catechism published in England in 1885, when no one knew any religion and didn't know how to teach." Didn't know how to teach? Macaulay, Gladstone, Newman, Manning, Vaughan, Wiseman—those punkheads?! I'd like a list of the opposite numbers fifteen years from now! Pedagogy or methodology, like theology, is an *aid* to catechetics; a tool, an instrument to a far greater end—the knowledge and love of Jesus Christ and the service of Jesus Christ in his brethren. That's the end, that's the purpose. The rest are instruments toward that end, and have only that importance. But for a while we were in danger of forgetting this, and hence the crisis.

We all began taking methodology courses. Priests would come into the Chancery and say:

I'd like to go to such and such a university for a couple of months and study methodology.

Why Father?

Well, I want to learn how to teach the kids the catechism.

Well, look, I've been in your parish, and they seem to me to be marvelously well instructed.

I know, but it's in an old-fashioned way.

That was *before* the Council. I won't even go into what happened *after* the Council. Then along came the change. The children shouldn't learn by being asked questions and by being brainwashed by sisters and priests who in turn had been brainwashed in Tridentine seminaries, where they had been brainwashed by medieval theologians, who had been brainwashed by the Fathers of the Church—who had been brainwashed by Christ and the apostles. No! Instead of this rote education, education should contain a greater amount of dialogue. Dialogue is the new word for conversation. Do you remember when you used to have nice, pleasant conversations with your Protestant friends? Now I get formal invitations to a dialogue with people I've been having conversations with for forty years, and I write back saying: "Do you mind if I don't come—it sounds rather stuffy." Then, they write back and apologize for inviting me because they can see that I've become reactionary. And still I'm dying to have some conversation!—as in the old days. But it those days we used to say, as Saint Paul did: our conversation is in heaven.

The word *brainwashing* is the only word I know that has been translated into every single modern language. This has become the great indictment word against instruction. So instruction is to be replaced by real education—self-expression. My father used to say that you shouldn't be allowed to express yourself until you had something to express, but that was back in the Dark Ages when you were expected to make a contribution to the conversation. On the other hand, to be fair, there is a lot to be said for these people's point of view. They're right, the root meaning of the word education is from the Latin word *educere,* and it means *to draw out of the depths of someone* the things that in fact are there, and that you help him formulate and direct. So there's a lot in this business about the part of dialogue, and self-expression, and all the rest of it in total education—but there's still a lot in listening to what is said by those who have been around a long time, and who've gone through it and have seen the good results and the bad.

Finally and worse, and more or less contained in all that we have said, there grew up this tragic confusion between faith and theology. People go off to study theology so that they can teach the Faith, and they may come back prepared to teach the Faith, and they may come back to undermine it. It depends on who the professor is. Faith, I repeat, is a personal response to God revealing himself in Jesus Christ. The traditional object of faith we call revelation, and only God can give us revelation. Theology is exactly what the theologians want you to call it; it's a science. Sometimes they even want it to be thought of as an autonomous science, as if it weren't dependent upon what Christ had to say—and the Church. The Magisterium means those authorized to teach the Faith of the Church. That's what it means—with the Pope at the top of them, and the authorization going down to the last catechist in the Bantu, as long as the catechist is in communion with that one at the top and teaching the same Faith. Good, bad, indifferent; temporary, long-standing. It can last for centuries as gnosticism has. Gnosticism has been going on now for eighteen centuries—London's full of it!

So there grew up the idea that there should be a pluralism of Faith. There could be, can be, always has been from the days of the gospel, a pluralism of theology—ways of explaining Faith, clarifying it—but there's only one Faith. This little confusion about the word *pluralism* followed after the Council, particularly when people began to talk about doing things and thinking things *in the spirit of the Council.* Never mind the letter of the Council! Most of the people who talk to me about *the spirit of the Council* haven't read a paragraph of the documents of the Council. So there isn't much talk about the *letter* of the Council, but a lot of talk about the *spirit,* and out of this has come this confusion of the purely subjective and pluralistic and personalistic and individualistic nature of the Faith which is one: one Lord, one Faith, one baptism.[2] So in the first synod called by Pope Paul, the first question put to the synod fathers was: *What are we going to do about this confusion we now find in matters concerning the teaching of the Faith?* And there was a long discussion. Faced with this crisis, this confusion all over the world, some said there should be established a rule of Faith, and either you conform with it or you don't. Well, it would be so long you could never stand it — with all the new ideas that would be piled in. Others said: Why not, like Pius IX, have a *Syllabus of Errors?* Well, the list of errors would be as long as the *Encyclopaedia Britannica!* You wouldn't be able to find your error if you spent six months going through the thing! So instead, it was decided to put into the hands of the Congregation of the Clergy, under the then-Prefect, Cardinal Villot, the responsibility for drawing up the *General Catechetical Directory,* which would be the norm and standard for catechetical directories in the different languages of the different countries.

Already, there's been a little feedback that the standard for each country will be the catechetical directory in *that* country. The answer is *No!* It won't be! Each country has to say its directory is in concord with the *General Catechetical Directory* and includes the same Articles of Faith. The methodology? Well, that depends on the culture of the country. The pedagogy? That depends on the type of people you're teaching: the age group, the background, the vocabulary, the I.Q., a hundred things — but the *content* of the Faith is set forth in this little catechetical directory. It's now been translated into sixteen different languages, and nothing I shall say tonight makes me more proud than to be able to say that in all the English-speaking countries the same translation is used. The content is one and the same.

The question has come up many many times (it came up at the Congress we had in Rome to present the *Catechetical Directory*): How much of this is binding? (We don't like to be bound by much these days!) The answer is: Everything that was *always* binding is binding *now*. If it was *ever* part of the Faith it is *still* part of the Faith. Some practices, some observances, we raise discussion about, because apparently some people are a little backward, some are a little forward, some this way, that way, and there's been discussion about them. But the best explanation I have seen of what's binding and what's not binding was written by Father George Telford, who is located in the Diocese of Southward and is a member of the Catechetical Commission. He says in effect that when people say (as three-quarters of you say every other day) "We don't know what we are suppose to teach and believe these days", Father Telford says, "You'll find it in the *Catechetical Directory.*" And then to the question, "What parts are binding?", he says: "The foreword says those things which are said about revelation (the things Christ taught and the Church transmitted) and the criteria according to which the Christian message is to be expanded, are to be held by *all*" —even the Ph.D.s (*I* put that in—he's too kind to make a nasty crack like that). On the other hand, those things which are said about the present situation, methodology, and the form of catechesis for people of different ages are given as *suggestion* and *guidelines.* Now that's not the long, mean, domineering, controlling hand of Rome—it's just the finger of the traffic cop saying "Don't go down that street or you'll run into a fire wagon or go off an open bridge!" It's a healthy suggestion! So there is a distinction between those things which are of the Faith and those things which are of the method and the presentation of it, and very well made. They're suggestions and guides, and they are indeed subject to some evolution, some development. Sure, we learn things by meditation, by studying, by research, by 101 ways, and those things are fair ground for development—but *not* the Articles of the Faith.

So in order to discuss the *Catechetical Directory,* and to get feedback from the many nations and their delegates, we had a big international congress in Rome last October. Permit me here and now to thank the English hierarchy, in the person of Archbishop Cowderoy, for the cooperation they gave us in the attendance at the congress. There was still the funny little feeling that you find when people from different nations get together. For example a sister, a Catholic sister, with a Spanish name, from California, wrote me a letter saying: "How representative from a democratic point of view was that catechetical congress? I got the impression there were a lot of Italians there." I'll tell you a secret: Rome is in Italy and lots of Italians live in Rome. Now, there were actually a minority of Italians (200), and that was deliberately arranged so that the little sister could have a seat. You can't be more democratic than that! If I had to make a rearrangement, she'd be out, because she contributed nothing to the conversation, absolutely nothing.

What were the purposes of this congress? Considering that it was held only last October, the results are heartwarming. The nations of the world are now mailing into us the translations of the directory and textbooks based on it—and prepare yourselves for a shock! I naturally thought that since the Anglo-Saxons and Celts are the first and foremost of all the people in the world, the textbooks which would come from our countries would be the best. Of the sixty-seven textbooks that I personally have gone through, the best was from Ghana. How do you like that? Watch Africa! It's the continent of the next century. It has nothing but the future. It has cultures, new enthusiasm. Their archbishops in prison are in the same position that Becket was in the days of the Plantagenets. In other words, they're on the way up. The best book I found was the one from Ghana. Immediately on the first page, it establishes a relationship between the child and God—and faith and theology are primarily concerned with God, not with anthropology. Anthropology, psychology, zoology, and all the other sciences must, should, come in as helps—but this little book on the first page helps the child to establish his identity.

These kids are asked: "What is your Christian name? What does that name mean to you?" There's a lot of faith in the answer to that one! The whole communion of saints, your whole place in the Kingdom of God. Then after a few other questions, "Do you have any brothers and sisters?"—and in Africa they do by the way. So: "What are the names of your brothers and sisters?" Then there's a square thing, a blank space, and it says "Put your thumbprint here." Now in my developed nation, to put your thumbprint on anything means you are in jail—the cops are making a record for the FBI when they take your thumbprint! But this thumbprint has under it: "You are the only one in the world who has that thumbprint; you are the individual, special object of God's love, when He helped form the body that carries that thumbprint." Isn't that terrific! In an age of standardization, of technology, of computers, that a kid would look at his thumb and say, "I'm the only one who got that from God; that's a sign of the Image of God in me in the sense that God is unique. There's only one, and I'm the one that has that sign, that particular little mark." Isn't that beautiful? The whole book goes on in that vein. It moves on from that little point to others. "What will you do with that thumb?" And the first thing it tells the kid is the last thing you would normally think of—it says, "I will make the sign of the Cross with it, because that is how God's Son saved me"—and it goes on through salvation. "I will serve others with it." The Ghana kid also belongs to the horizontal Church, and he's prepared to go into the inner city and put his thumb in the work with everybody else. He'll bear his witness, he'll get the social gospel—but he's learning the first law first. Love the Lord God, and thy neighbor as thyself. The dogma, the Faith, first, and then the moral code, including social teaching.

Well, what was the purpose of our congress? To bring together people to learn their experiences; to stimulate them to bring the message to the ends of the earth in new terms—but the *same* message. To collaborate with Rome, compactly with Peter as did the apostles when they started out to the ends of the earth. And to do so with a single Love, a single Hope, and a single Charity, and I took the liberty then, as I take it now in concluding, to add one further thing. I hope that every family will become a school of catechetics. The family is the first school of catechetics. No sister, no priest, no bishop, nobody, taught me the place of prayer in my life as I learned it when I came in late and my father's bedroom door was ajar and the beam of light went into it, and I saw the soles of his feet as he was kneeling by the bed saying his prayers before he went to bed at night. The family is the first school of spirituality and the first school of faith. So the need for adult catechetics classes, in order that parents may be the teachers of their children, and the children may teach one another. We said that we will do it with Faith, with Hope, and with Love—but I add a fourth quality: *Joy!* Has anyone else besides me discovered how joy has disappeared from the face of the earth? It's disappeared from our music: "We shall overcome . . . We shall overcome. . . . " Overcome *what?* Overcome *whom?* We used to be told: "Overcome yourself, pal, and then you'll be in a position to overcome others and you'll have a right and title to be heard." "Where have all the flowers gone . . . Long time passing. . . . " Do you remember when you used to sing in May about the flowers? But you sang with joy! Do you remember that resounding music that used to practically shoot from the organ and fire the bride and groom down the aisle ecstatic with joy. Joy in what? Joy in the *Faith!* I have known people to save their money all their lives, working in factories, to go back to the old country and see the parish church where they learned the Faith—and it was the greatest joy of their life.

Every Wednesday, I see thousands of people pour out of Saint Peter's, their faces transformed with Joy because they have looked on the face of Jesus Christ. So there is needed this element of joy. Have you noticed, with all the contesters and protesters how dreary their faces are? Every week you buy your *Time* magazine and see a drip standing there bearing witness, as it's called. If they'd just stand up and laugh in the Lord! But they say, "There's so much suffering in the world: if God is good, the suffering in the world would break His heart. It breaks mine, because I'm serious and I'm decided and I'm committed." Well, He sent His Son into the world and His Son's heart *did* break, and that heart is at the heart of the Universe, in the risen Body of Jesus Christ.

XIV

Worcester

I remember Worcester in more ways than I can possibly compress into the space, albeit generous, that has been allowed me.

My memories begin with March 7, 1950, the day I was officially installed in Saint Paul's Cathedral as the first Bishop of Worcester.[1] No matter whatever crowds I ever see or whatever affectionate welcome I ever receive, I shall never forget the thousands of people jammed in High Street and Chatham Street to watch the procession from the cathedral rectory to Saint Paul's. I will never forget the silence of the crowd. I will never forget the tears in people's eyes. I will never forget how small their obvious love made me feel and how unbounded became my determination to be worthy of them.

I remember Worcester because of its community life and spirit, especially when a disaster like the tornado hit us. I remember what a thrill it was to come over the hill of Shrewsbury Street on the way back from Boston at eleven o'clock at night and hear the news broadcast which would bring me up to date on the local news of the day when I might have been away on business elsewhere. The newscast was preceded by majestic music concluding Raymond Morin's broadcast of classics. It usually ended as I was going by the Richardson Tower outside the old railroad station.

I was so furious when I heard that the tower was to be torn down that I maneuvered an innocent business whereby I purchased the rocks of which it was constructed. It was my intention to build a memorial chapel at Saint John's Cemetery, where were buried many of the people who built that superb tower

This article was written for and published in the June 11, 1972, issue of the *Worcester Sunday Telegram*.

and laid the railroad tracks that went by it. Alas, the chapel was never built, and I have no idea where the pile of rocks may now be.

I remember Worcester for the flag flying twenty-four hours a day, a highly exceptional privilege, in front of the Worcester Memorial Auditorium where the musical festivals and many superb congresses have given me memories enough to last me a lifetime.

I remember Worcester and the dedicated citizens like George Booth, Harry Stoddard (who never failed to pay me a courtesy visit at Christmas), and the many Swedish people who gave such gifted leaders to public life and industry and so many things of which Worcester was proud. I remember Worcester for the kind men and women, prosperous and poor, who built our beautiful churches and helped in running a new and problem-filled diocese, including Saint Vincent Hospital where I spent so many happy, happy hours.

I remember Worcester for the wonderful festival in honor of Our Lady of Mount Carmel, which paraded every year with bands blasting down Shrewsbury Street to the playground. I called up Mayor Andy Holmstrom one time to ask if permission was needed for the bands, the parade, and the fireworks the Italians were planning. "I suppose so," he said, "but if it is needed, it will be granted promptly. That is the most cheerful thing that happens in Worcester every year."

I remember Worcester for Elm Park, for Indian Lake, for gentle hills almost on the edges of downtown. I remember Worcester for the night that Archbishop Cushing was talking to the Hibernians in the Elm Street Theater, while I was talking to the Unitarians in the Courthouse Church. He collapsed in Worcester that night but not, as the wags asserted, because he had been told where I was talking! My theme was the close friendship and collaboration and communion of spirit between the first Catholic bishop of New England, John Cheverus, and the founder of Unitarianism, William Ellery Channing. I tried to drive home the point that intergroup affection and understanding did not begin with the present noisy pretensions at *togetherness* and mutual collaboration. There were many brave men before Agamemnon's time.[2]

I remember Worcester for our Catholic Youth Organization parades, hours long and electric with enthusiasms. I remember Worcester for the concerts sponsored by Monsignor David Sullivan, every year, to raise the money to solve our many social problems.

I remember Worcester because, without any public appeals for money, I was able to build many churches in nine years, most of them perfectly matching in design, style, and material, the mood and history of the lovely towns in which they were located.[3] I remember Worcester in terms of the Lord's Acre Day–Labor Day weekend. I remember Worcester for the fire department, of which I was an honorary member, and which brought a fire ladder to my house the day we had the unexpected blizzard so I could get out the window from the second floor of my so-pleasant house on Flagg Street to get downtown to keep an urgent appointment.

It would, of course, be absurd to pretend that I remember every boy and girl I ever met at church, school, or civic occasions at Worcester. But I think it significant that I am under the illusion that I do!

Add to this list the unrivaled Worcester Art Museum, the friendliness of the B'nai B'rith, the institutes on *The Person and the Common Good* that we Worcesterites started long before Vatican Council II and all the rest of it, the manner in which people smiled at one and spoke so pleasantly anywhere along Main Street or in any corner of Worcester County—and then you will know why I remember Worcester.

XV

The Pope and the Astronauts

In 1969, when the first men to orbit the moon were received by Pope Paul VI, those of us then taking part in the Synod of Bishops were granted the privilege of being addressed by them. The Holy Father's joy in receiving such primary representatives of the new space age was evident and unmitigated; we prelates who were gathered at the Synod of Bishops felt hardly less. Every one of us—cardinal, archbishop, or bishop—was moved by the recognition that the occasion, ceremonial though it might be, was a truly historic one: in the bestowal of the papacy's blessing on the new space technology, and the men who were coming ever more to be its masters, was contained religion's ultimate salute to science.

If there was something historic in the coming together of these two great traditions—so long vulgarly believed to be hostile to one another—it was not the prelates alone who seemed mindful of the fact. Indeed, on that afternoon, it was the men of science who struck the most unforgettable *spiritual* note. One of the cardinals asked the guests whether the journey into space, affording, after all, an unprecedented view of physical creation, had had any effect on their spiritual lives. One man answered for all three, in a less poetic but no less forceful reinvention of a passage from Scripture: "Eye hath not seen, nor ear heard, neither hath it entered into the heart of man to conceive, what things God has prepared for them that love him."[1] The astronauts, orbiting the moon on Christmas Eve, had read to their earthbound brothers the first verse of Genesis; the gesture, then, had not been a histrionic one.

This article was written for and published in the June 18, 1972, issue of *World*.

As for me, I could not help being reminded of another day, nearly a quarter of a century earlier, when, at the kind suggestion of Pius XII, I visited the astronomical observatory on the roof of the papal summer residence. The observatory was then in the care of Father Walter Miller, S.J. Fascinated by the observatory's maps of the sky and noting the countless stars identified by names chosen by their discoverers from everywhere in the world, I asked if there were any heavenly body which bore the name of Saint Joan of Arc. Father Miller promptly searched his books and learned that in the nineteenth century a Frenchman working at the observatory in Moscow had discovered an asteroid now catalogued as *Jeanne d'Arc*.

Later that year, there arrived at my office in Worcester a glossy photo of the area of the sky where the asteroid may be seen; *Jeanne d'Arc* was circled. On the reverse side of the print were all the mathematical indications needed to locate the asteroid. It can only be seen two nights a year, as I remember, and then only over that part of Russia.

Here was simply another example of the fraternity based on the patrimony of scientific knowledge that has its parallel in classical studies, the arts, and all things truly human which cross all boundaries of nation, ideology, and language. Those ties at once profoundly religious and genuinely scientific, that unite the lovers of the true, the beautiful, and the good remain firm despite political frontiers or military aspirations. That invisible thread which stretched from the Kremlin observatory to the Vatican observatory—and even to me in far-off Worcester—is their vivid symbol.

In every realm of authentic humanism, the satisfaction of all the faculties distinctive and worthy of a man, that mutuality and universal interest, is confirmed. And now, in the new age of space most of all, it is inevitable that religion and science should be kindred forces. The true vocation of science is that of helping man to fulfill the mandate of the Creator that he become the responsible steward of all creation: "Fill the earth and conquer it."[2] Religion, both in itself and as the mother of cultures, thus has an obligation both to bless our scientific achievement in the domination of outer space and to keep the earth a home worth coming back to.

Nor has religion (the *Person* of the Church, in Maritain's sage remark, as distinct from personnel) awaited the space age to direct our gaze toward the moon as a first stop on the journey into our outer space. Most of the great religious orders have had their special scientific as well as spiritual disciplines. I link the Jesuits, most especially, to the moon if only because one of them has taken the trouble to chronicle their part in its exploration. The first astronauts to reach the moon could not, if they had any respect for precedent, have given merely English names to places they visited. Indeed, their task was to examine certain areas of the moon long since identified by telescope and given Latin names. Thirty-two of these signs would end with the letters *S.J.* (Society of Jesus).

In the Garden of Eden, Adam was empowered by God to name animals and things, and his descendants undertook to name the heavens long before the telescope. As soon as the first lenses made possible an intenser kind of observation, Francesco Fontana, a Neapolitan, drew a sketch map of the moon—if one may so dignify his effort. Argolus reproduced it in his curious *Pandosium sphaericum,* and thus began a longstanding competition. A Capuchin, Anthony Mary Shirlaeus, put out a different map in his *Eye of Enoch* and *Elias,* followed by four others—all, of course, merely the falterings of beginners.

The first really scientific work appeared in 1645. Michael Florence Langraeus (van Langren), cosmographer to His Catholic Majesty in Spain, and later in Brussels, made such careful observations of the moon that he ventured the publication of thirty large plates engraved by himself. In these engravings, two hundred and seventy points of the moon's surface are named— the first guide to the moon. Van Langren used names of his contemporaries in the scientific world, though he also took names with a moral or civic flavor: the Land of Worthiness, the Land of Virtue, the Philippic Ocean, the Copernican Sea. Among van Langren's names were those of several Jesuits. He sent a copy of his work to Father John Baptist Riccioli, from Ferrara, who was equipping the observatory of the Roman College with all the latest apparatus and preparing a monumental work with the pretentious name of *The Almagest* (Arabic, *al:* the; Greek, *megiston:* the greatest), an echo of Ptolemy's work of that name. In his introduction, he thanked van Langren for his gesture of Belgian courtesy.

Progress was swift: that same year, 1645, van Langren's achievement was bettered by Hevelius, whose maps bore as many as five hundred and fifty names, more than those of his predecessor. Hevelius was in turn superseded by the publication in 1649 of a new map by Eustace de Divinis. Two years later, the first Jesuit came into the field when Jerome de Sirsalis published a plain map, faithful, but without either names or explanations.

Meanwhile, Father Riccioli was looking around and biding his time. Not content with getting his hands on the telescopes of Galileo, Fontana, Torricelli, and Manzini, either as gifts or loans, he bought a magnificent telescope from a Bavarian instrument-maker. This instrument was fifteen feet long and of higher magnification than any of its predecessors. He also managed to find an assistant, Francesco Maria Grimaldi, a man of more robust health than his own, who after twenty-five years of schoolmastering had thrown himself heart and soul into physics and astronomy and had to his credit a pioneer work on the diffraction of light that paved the way for Hooke, Newton, and Fresnel. With Grimaldi's help and after lengthy observation, Riccioli had a still better map, with six hundred details easily discernible and many others that were observable only at twilight. The publication of this map fell rather flat because the engraver brought a ploughman's touch to his task. Fine lines were not for him, and poor Riccioli had to be content with a mere half-dozen maps for *The Almagest*.

Riccioli's names are a mixture of the scientific, literary, and poetic. Famous astronomers from whom he had learned were honored. The moon's continental regions and seas were named by the impressions they gave him: van Langren's Mountains of Austria, which for Hevelius were the Apennines, became for him the Land of the Snows. There was also a Marsh of Dreams. For the names of persons, this lunar Dante divided the moon into octants, eight equal sections like slices of a cake. The scientists of antiquity were in the upper sections, their most recent successors in the lower, including twenty-five Jesuits. In the fifth octant: Furnerius, Petavius; in the sixth: Arzet, Bettinus, Blancanus, Cabaeus, Clavius, Cyasatus, Bartolius, Gruenberger, Kircher, Malapertius, Moretus, Scheinerus, Schomberger, Simpleus, Tannerus, Zucchius; in the seventh: Deriennes, Zupus, Billy; in the eighth: Grimaldus, Ricciolus, Siralis.

This lunar invasion by the Jesuits, so to speak, can be explained by the fact that the Society had from its very beginnings displayed the keenest interest in scientific matters. Saint Francis Xavier had barely reached Japan when he asked Saint Ignatius for someone who "knew the sphere", and Ricci, who had such missionary success in Peking, thanks to his astrolabe, was not the only astronomer-missionary to use his science to spread the Faith. Modern astronomy owes much to Jesuits, who at the time of the Suppression, 1773, were directing thirty of the world's one hundred and thirty observatories.

Three other Jesuit astronomers deserve particular mention. Christopher Clavius, at the Roman College from 1592, was called the Modern Euclid: on the tomb of Pope Gregory XIII in Saint Peter's, he is represented giving the Pope the scientific information that led to the reform of the calendar on October 5, 1582. Grienberger succeeded Clavius and is famed for his invention of the parabolic mounting of telescopes. And, finally, Athanasius Kircher (1634–1680), also a professor at the Roman College, who specialized in ocean currents and magnetism. In addition, he studied the plague and came to the conclusion that it was spread "by tiny animals in the blood stream, so tiny as to be visible only through a powerful microscope". He published forty-four books, and his letters fill one hundred and fourteen others. The Kircher Museum in Rome stands witness to the Jesuits' formidable passion for making collections.

All of this is not simply to praise the Jesuits of the sixteenth and seventeenth centuries, but rather to underline the observation that if a believer's reaction to breakthroughs of modern science is truly a religious one, it will be a positive—even an enthusiastic—one as well. The enthusiasm of the believer for the new discoveries of science will have roots of delight in the fresh stimulation and satisfaction of intellectual curiosity about the universe in which we live. It will also find springs of spiritual joy in the increased insight that scientific discoveries give into the omnipotence, majesty, and wonder of God. The devout believer, like the prudent man generally, will frequently have a healthy suspicion of the claims of individual scientists, as he will have to the claims of occasional individual statesman, artists, or theologians—but he will always be receptive to new contacts with truth, goodness, or beauty. Scientists may be woefully mistaken, as many other mortals in any field. But science is concerned with truth, as art with beauty, and new frontiers of truth or expressions of beauty cannot be opened up to us without enthusiasm, gratitude, and reverence.

The principal focus of scientific interest in the era before us, I believe, will be found literally in the heavens. A time of fascination with the skies, the planets, and the universe promises to lift the minds and hearts of men out of the more self-centered occupations of the behavioral sciences that have so largely taken up men's attention for more than a century. One sometimes suspects that we do not realize the extent to which psychiatry, experimental psychology, anthropology, and even sociology— the sciences that, together with biology and other *microscope sciences,* have tended to dominate recent decades—have riveted man's attention on himself. These disciplines turned his gaze inward, downward, and, in the case of psychiatry, backward as well, in a way that has tended, at the least, to make us morbid and, at the worst, nihilistic.

Now our gaze once more seems to be turning upward, and the shift may prove to be not only healthy but even holy. From the most ancient times, the contemplation of the stars has led men to speculation about God.

Therefore, this new era of science may be bringing a whole new supply of fresh air into modern thought. Astronomy, the prospect of interplanetary study and even journeying—these are far removed from the brooding and negative agnosticism that were the frequent byproducts of the recent sciences gone to seed. These new directions in science may easily recapture the mood of mingled joy and reverence in which the Hebrew psalmist wrote:

> O Lord, our Master, how the majesty of thy name fills all the earth! Thy greatness is high above heaven itself. . . . I look up at those heavens of thine, the works of thy hands, at the moon and the stars, which thou has set in their places; what is man that thou shouldst remember him? What is Adam's breed, that it should claim thy care? Thou hast placed him only a little below the angels, crowning him with glory and honor, and bidding him rule over the works of thy hands.[3]

A similar mood of mingled awe and joy in the face of the universe opening before us has already set in. Perhaps it will prove to be nothing less than a new manifestation of the human predisposition to divine faith.

Once the spirit of narrow national interest in the probings of space—the spirit which asks who first launched or landed—has passed, as I believe it surely will, the dynamics of the new scientific development will be all in the direction of human unity. The mere presence of all the various satellites in space, plus the prospect of exploring the depths beyond the margins of the skies, must tend to shrink the earth and in so doing, to

268

subordinate earth's divisions. Mankind should henceforth function in a perspective far more consistent with that moral law by which God desires—and religion seeks—the unity under law of all the tribes of men.

Small wonder, then, that it was not in the precincts of some great laboratory or some bustling engineering office that I first heard the phrase *the shores of space*—but in the ancient Vatican. With prophetic fervor, these words were on the lips of Pope Pius XII when he castigated the pessimism and defeatism of the age. He was shortly to die, and he bade the crowd before him to turn its gaze from the problems of the earth and look out in hope into the heavens. *We stand on the shores of space. This is no time for despair about the future of the race or of the earth.*

XVI

Joseph E. Sullivan, 1895–1972

As one would expect of Joe Sullivan, he is being buried today following the traditional Mass for the Dead in the revised form authorized by the Holy See. Joe would never wish to kid himself or the public by choosing anything but a Requiem Mass proclaiming that he was, regretfully but in fact, dead to the world.

I have chosen my text, however, from the Masses of his patron saint, Saint Joseph, the Feast of Saint Joseph on March 19, and the Mass of Saint Joseph the workman, May 1.

Certain coincidences—Joe, believing Catholic that he was, would call them acts of Divine Providence—find me in this pulpit this morning to speak for all present our loving remembrance of the amazing, admirable public citizen, rags-to-riches community leader, and exemplary Catholic to whom we all bid our affectionately grateful farewell this morning.

Joe put up a brave front here at home about the nature of his sickness for the past year. However, he wrote me some months ago and told me the truth about his condition, adding that if I happened to be home when God called him, he hoped I would be in the pulpit to say something good about him. He continued in typical fashion: "Please say something *good* even if you have to make it up!" Bishop Minihan kindly phoned *the very day* I arrived home to say that Joe's children confirmed the invitation when he passed away from us the night I reached home.

He had never made any secret of his desire to die on a feast of the Blessed Mother; he died in early morning of the Feast of her Assumption, a few hours after the feast day had begun, as

This eulogy was preached at the Immaculate Conception Church, Lowell, Massachusetts, on August 18, 1972.

always, right on schedule. It will add to his joy in heaven that he is being buried from a church that honors Mary, under the title of her Immaculate Conception. This, too, he would say is providential, no mere chance event.

The supreme loves of his life were his wife, present here by symbol in the altar he gave in her memory; his family, present here with their spouses, and their friends to surround him as they did in life; honored by the presence of so many priests, so many prelates, and fellow citizens whom he had always sought to strengthen and encourage in their respective works. Truly, he was dear to God by reason of his faith and constant championship of God's Church; surely, he was dear to man by reason of his friendship and generosity. His memory, now that he is dead, is held in benediction.[1]

Anyone here present could say about Joe all the things that I will say. He lived his life unashamedly in public and practically paraded before the world his faith and charity without any effort to conceal his attitude toward God, his joy in the Holy Catholic Faith and all its commandments, not one of which he presumed to interpret privately, his pride in his friends and his civil community; his particular delight in his children and their friends, and his wish to be generous to everything that would promote the glory of the Church or the welfare of man. To him one can apply without qualification the words of the psalmist: "Happy the man who fears the Lord, who greatly delights in his commands. His posterity shall be mighty upon the earth; the upright generation shall be blessed. Wealth and riches shall be in his house; his generosity shall endure forever."[2]

Joe Sullivan, bluff and hearty, forthright, and fearless, combined in himself all the characteristics — we might say the marks — of a complete Roman Catholic. He loved all men and shared the common concern of all the community — civic, philanthropic, business, and religious — in the most sound ecumenical sense. But no one, however dull or sanguine, ever had the slightest doubt that Joe Sullivan was a Roman Catholic. No one, how-

271

ever sensitive, ever found this fact abrasive, discriminatory, or a reason on Joe's part for failure to cooperate for the common good of all the people. Everyone recognized that he loved his spiritual family, the Holy Catholic Church, as he loved his personal family, his children and their mother. They recognized that, even above the loyalty to the community in which he lived, the ethnic group from which he came, was his attachment by faith to the Catholic Church. All perceived that his generosity was to *persons* at all times, even when it was through the institutional Church, which he recognized as divine. He loved his friends in the hierarchy, the clergy, and the organized religious life as *persons,* but also as representatives of the institution which is the Church.

Joe was never taken in by any of the loose talk against the Church as an institution; he saw the Church as the divinely organized society of all those persons who seek to follow fully, as did he, the teachings and the example of Jesus Christ, under the leadership of those, however imperfect, to whom Jesus Christ committed the care of his Church. He was proud to identify himself with these leaders of the Church and did all in his power to help, encourage, and console them, as, in his opinion, every decent Christian should. Sometimes he expressed this opinion with witty cards, sometimes with his righteous wrath at folly or malice.

A third mark of his authentic Catholicism was his manly piety. There is no single sight so beautiful, except that of a mother with her baby in her arms, as the sight of a man on his knees in prayer, a strong man, tall and square-shouldered, level-eyed, and even tough, on his knees in prayer. I have seen Joe Sullivan on his knees for hours before the Blessed Mother at Lourdes, his rosary in his hands and his eyes on the Mother of Christ. I have seen him on his knees at the Tomb of Saint Peter, which he loved not merely as a glorious monument of marble, but as the living dwelling place in eternal Rome of the Successor, in Pius XII, John XXIII, and Paul VI, to that Fisherman who

272

gazed on the very face of Christ and received from Christ supreme authority over all who believe in His Church. I have seen him on his knees before the tabernacle where Christ is really present in the Blessed Sacrament, Emmanuel, God present among us in His Christ.

He did not need to be told that Christ is also present, in another fashion, in the poor, in the sick, in the ignorant, and in all the brethren; he believed this fully and implemented that belief and paid his tribute to Christ in all these living forms by generosity and personal service. But, my memory of Joe Sullivan will always be that of Joe on his knees, humbly, confidently, in worship before Christ on the Cross, in the Eucharist, and the Mother who gave Christ flesh and blood, in His Vicar on earth, Peter and his Successors.

But his authentic faith was crowned and proved by his constant laughter and gaiety. This is the hallmark of the Faith, that one can joke about it and make fun about it while others whine and lament the way even the Church sometimes seems to let us down. While others groaned and quit, Joe made this fact of life, the frailty of the human side of the Church, a frequent theme of the uproarious cards, folders, and quips that he used to insert in envelopes sent out every month to the thousands of his clients and his friends.

The humor and hilarity of Joe gave proof of his faith. Those who lose their faith lose joy, which explains the sullen grimness of their faces, their lamentations, and most of what they say and write and do. Joe Sullivan was earnest and dedicated, not grim, and never loveless or dull. He was inevitably in close touch with the weaknesses of us all, and probably he was often the victim of our amazing ability to disappoint and even to shock people as devout as he. But he saw all this in the light of eternity and of the nature of the Church as well as of history, and so he never ceased to laugh, laughing sometimes in the sheer joy of faith undiminished by human weakness, or sometimes by the absurd folly of some of the flock, high and low.

He had a gift in the quips and quotations inserted in his mailings for making several points at once, always with lightness but sometimes with subtle and penetrating play on words. One of his insert cards that I most cherish summarized everything about Joe that made me and millions love him. It is the card he enclosed with his mailing during the month of Archbishop Medeiros' call for contributions to the desperately needed diocesan fund. Joe's single sentence card, by a play of words, combined devotion to the Archbishop, his desire to win for the Archbishop the love of all his people, and his determination to advertise the Archbishop's plea for indispensable financial help. The single sentence of Joe's card, at once poetic, persuasive, and proud was this: "Archbishop Medeiros Appeals to Us!" In that line was concentrated the faith, the loyalty, and the generosity of Joe Sullivan to the personal and institutional head of this Holy Church of Boston. The complete Catholic integrates his faith, generosity, piety, and all else by love in accord with the command of Saint Paul in the Epistle of the May 1st Feast of Saint Joseph:

> Brethren: Put on love, which binds all virtues together and makes them perfect. Let the peace of Christ rule over your hearts; for, as members of the one body, you have been called to that peace. Be thankful, and whatever you do in word or in work, do everything in the name of the Lord Jesus, giving thanks to God the Father through him. Whatever you do, work at it with your whole soul, doing it for the Lord rather than for men, because you know that you will receive the inheritance from him as your reward.[3]

Joe was rewarded by civil and ecclesiastical distinctions beyond number; tributes were paid him by prelates, academic and charitable communities, as well as the general public; Joe took these with great gratitude, but he took them lightly. He kidded about them constantly, but he never ceased to deserve them by his generosity. He was not, in fact, particularly impressed by the praise of man, though he welcomed it if it increased his power to be a force for good in the human community that was his Church. His supreme objective was his personal salvation and the spiritual good of his brethren and his family. In business he was always ready to experiment; experiments with the sacraments and the Faith left him cold. In business and human affairs he was always prepared to take a gamble; he never gambled with his soul or his prospects for salvation; quite the contrary: he scrupulously observed everything that held out the promise or even hope of salvation. One of his few boasts was that he had not missed a First Friday Communion since 1912, sixty years ago, when he was seventeen years old. That was Joe Sullivan, greedy for salvation and generous with everything else.

One could list the millions of dollars and other gifts he has given to persons and institutions. I am sure that these were important, and I wonder, except that he taught his children generosity, what some good works are going to do now that he is gone. But somehow these gifts are not the things that are uppermost in mind as I try to say *thank you* to Joe Sullivan for us all and myself. In the words of the dying central character of *The Last Hurrah,* a novel about Joe's generation and a history of Joe's people in this particular part of the world, "How do you thank a fellow for a million laughs?" Well, you can't! You can only thank God for giving us the fellow, in this case Joseph Edward Sullivan, "dear to God and men, his memory held in benediction".[4]

I hope those to whom Joe has entrusted his business and his influence will keep him alive even here on earth, especially his joy and his way of spreading joy. With his blood in their veins, they cannot fail to do so, and the name of Sullivan Brothers will be found on thousands of desks every month with a little bit of propaganda but a lot of laughter. For my own part, and I think for all the prelates, priests, and God-fearing men here present, I expect to get a mailing from Joe himself next Christmas. It will be postmarked *heaven,* not *Lowell.* The stamp will not be a picture of the government-proposed alleged ideal family, Mr. and Mrs. Nobody and their two carefully planned kids, plus Mommie's dog, but it will be a development of Joe's traditional Christmas card. That card never showed the results of coldly planned parenthood, but a joyful group of greatly loved sons, daughters, and in-laws around a proud and happy father. The only difference will be that the card we shall receive from Joe will show him this time smiling as ever, and surrounded by his children, but also a host of angels and saints for whom he will have already discovered how to be of help even in heaven. I would not be surprised if the card enclosed a check backed up by a million prayers that will certainly be heard when they are offered, as are Joe's, by a man dear to God and men, his memory in benediction!

> May the angels lead you into paradise; [dear Joe] may the martyrs come to welcome you on your way, and take you to the holy city, Jerusalem. May the choir of angels welcome you, and with Lazarus, *who once was poor,* may you have everlasting rest![5]

XVII

What Was the Real Mind of Pope John?

The manner in which Pope John XXIII (not to say Vatican
Council II) has been the object of a certain disservice at the
hands of some analysts of him and his leadership calls for comment at the height of Pope Paul's postconciliar effort to restore
the *pristine beauty* of the Church which Pope John declared to be
the purpose of his calling the Council.

The Lord only knows how much rubbish has been written as
alleged responses to the *spirit* of Pope John, without reference to
the *letter* of anything he ever said, wrote, or did. Only the Lord
will be able to forgive those who have pretended that their
doctrinal and disciplinary disorientations of the Church were
inspired by the example or the teachings of Pope John. Pope
John undoubtedly would forgive them; such was his nature.
Pope Paul undoubtedly forgives them; such is his nature. But
can history do so?

It might be well to pause for a moment to recall the personality,
especially in its dimensions of faith and piety, of Good Pope
John. It most certainly was *open, amiable,* even *tolerant;* whether
it was *liberal* or *conservative* no one has successfully established.

It also might be well to review what precisely Pope John said
on the many occasions when he exercised his office as Supreme
Teacher in the Church, fully aware of his primacy, prerogatives,
and authority, and lacking in any evidence whatsoever of that
identity crisis which is said to be so prevalent because of the
windows and *new frontiers* he opened up.

Pope John did open windows to let fresh air into corridors of
power which had long seemed obscure, if not faintly remote.

This article was written for and published in the November 1972 issue
of the *Homiletic and Pastoral Review.*

Like Moses, he sought promised lands that he was not destined to enter. But he never, not even once, compromised or repudiated the past roads which had led him to his point in history. His personal piety had about it no air of *futurism,* let alone folly, but rather the characteristics of the priests who came out from the Old World in Search of New Frontiers in the New World, though not always in the precise forms of generations long passed.

Every pope has had his own temperament, as Pope John had his. But whatever may be the inevitable contrasts due to inevitable and desirable differences in personality, there is neither discontinuity nor contradiction of doctrine or devotion between Pope John and his five modern-era predecessors, nor his successor, *happily reigning.* The visits of Pope John to Roman station churches and venerable Italian shrines were part of the passion for pastoral contacts that has brought Pope Paul to every corner of the world, to the United Nations, to the Geneva center of Protestant Christianity, and the Constantinople center of Orthodox Christianity, not to mention the Indian and Oriental centers of those who believe in God and ardently seek him, but are still *separated brethren,* to use the name Pope John himself always used. The new frontiers of ecumenism, social action, and ecclesiastical reform which Pope John dreamed of from afar, these are the frontiers to which Pope Paul has passionately, perseveringly, and effectively led the Church, personally and officially. Popes John and Paul have loved the Church with equal self-abnegation, with or without cooperation, with or without criticism and opposition.

Somewhat more circumstantial than the devout priestly practices of good Pope John (his personal piety and traditional devotions both as a priest and as a simple member of the faithful) is the recollection of precisely what Pope John said. His *spirit* is, of course, present in his pronouncements, his encyclicals, and his pastoral documents, and that *spirit* all the world professes to find congenial, as well they might, it being the authentic spirit of

Christ and His Church. Less well known and less likely to enchant some if they were to read it is the actual *letter* of what Papa Roncalli taught during the exciting years of his pontificate. It is with this latter point, the heart of the matter because concerned with the Faith, that our present brief paper is concerned.

It is impossible to imagine how many of those who invoke only the alleged *spirit* of Good Pope John can possibly contain their chagrin, even contempt, when (or if) they read his spiritual reflections, meditations, retreat notes, and unashamed diaries of personal piety from the day he entered the seminary until the day he closed his eyes in death. His devotion to the Rosary, to penitential observances, to saints who were exemplars of a sacerdotal piety now sometimes labeled *outmoded* and of orthodoxy now likely to be branded reactionary (Ignatius of Antioch, Saint Athanasius come to mind), his incessant references to the Blessed Mother and the angels, as well as to the most uncomplicated and literal mysteries of the life of Christ and of the Church—all these must appal many who praise him as a person and even claim in him the inspiration of their own totally contrary procedures and preachments.

One is often stupefied by the representation of this magnificent Pontiff as a simple country priest of purely pastoral instincts when one remembers how he accepted with grace the sophisticated burdens of the papal diplomatic service in three of the most complex and difficult diplomatic posts within the assignment of Pope Pius XII. Pius obviously understood him and availed himself of his services for the Church in a manner totally inconsistent with the caricature of Papa Roncalli offered by those who wish us to see in him a kind of papal Savonarola and pious revolutionary rather than the smiling Pope who restored the use of the *camauro,* familiar from the portraits of Renaissance pontiffs (Julius II!) and brocaded stole on his person and who chose for his motto the significant words: *Obedience and Peace,* clearly suggesting that these qualities were interrelated, not mutually antagonistic.

One remembers reading in the *Christian Century* a somewhat patronizing description of Pope John XXIII riding in the *sedia gestatoria,* as if his traditional papal vestments and willingness to be lifted above the crowd so that all the crowd might see him constituted a repudiation of his own better instincts! By the same token, one often wonders what would have been the reaction if Pius XII, who delighted to preach from the pulpits of the world's great cathedrals, or Paul VI, who has gone to the ends of the earth in a simple white cassock to make friends for Christ and the human family, had chosen, as did John XXIII, two highly Italianate shrines to visit on the eve of the ecumenical council: one the shrine of Saint Francis, whom everybody loves but who was 100 percent Italian, and the other, the Holy House of Loreto, which must be, of all stumbling blocks, the roughest for those who profess to find in Pope John XXIII the inspiration of their own rejection of shrines like Loreto and bits of Catholic legend and lore about which they are themselves remarkably silent. These, indeed, are not merely paradoxes; they are mysteries beyond uttering.

Even the jokes of Pope John XXIII were jokes which manifested a humility and self-deprecation many of his admirers must find a waste of time that might better be given to serious debate about the origins of the papacy, which he made so beloved, and the claims of the papacy, which he never once concealed, compromised, or failed to exercise—gently, sweetly, photogenically, but *firmly.*

With these wayward thoughts in mind, one feels led to a rapid but revealing review of John XXIII's publications as Pope. They are worth recalling if only to estimate what was the mind and intent of this so often misrepresented Pontiff, who initiated many projects which Pope Paul has been called upon to continue and to supplement. He has done so, all questions of personality properly and desirably apart, in the same spirit and with the same total commitment to the primacy of the Holy See, the continuity of Catholic Truth and the integrity of Catholic Faith, as had John.

The bibliography of the work of Pope John XXIII is easily available. So far as personal, priestly personality is concerned, it is to be found in his *Journal of a Soul,* his lifelong retreat notes, and the innumerable volumes, large and small, which contain his letters to his family, his ecclesiastical flocks, his friends, and his neighbors.[1] Above all, these spiritual and intimately personal, sometimes embarrassingly personal, meditations and prayers are to be found in the popular volumes of the spiritual thoughts of Pope John XXIII which are available at every price and in every popular Catholic bookstore. His official discourses, messages, and pronouncements are contained in a set of five volumes entitled *Discorsi, Messaggi, Colloqui del Santo Padre Giovanni XXIII,* with an index prepared by Father Igino Tubaldo and published by the Vatican Publishing House, Vatican City.[2]

Of this second group of writings, the most official and therefore significant are his encyclicals and his apostolic letters, as well as some selected exhortations. Their content will come as a surprise to many Catholics who have been led to look upon Pope John XXIII as a *nonconformist,* as regards the tradition of his predecessors in the teaching office of the Supreme Pontiff of the Holy Roman Church and as a kind of *window opener* not so much eager (as he was) to refresh the life of the Church and to create an atmosphere of benevolence, hospitality, and friendliness, but to bring in gusts of wind which would blow about the useless pages of long-dead tradition as discredited spirituality and an *irrelevant* message of the Church for our times.

His first encyclical letter, *Ad Petri Cathedram,* was addressed to the hierarchy, clergy, and faithful people of the Roman Catholic Church on the Feast of the Holy Apostles, Peter and Paul, historically thought of as the cofounders of the Roman Church precisely as such. The encyclical develops, as would have been done by any pope in any century, certain points concerning the *singleness* of truth, above all, the truth of *faith;* the unity that must prevail in the Catholic Christian community; the consequent unity of the Church. It concludes with some paternal exhortations which are profound, pointed, and thoroughly papal.

His second encyclical, entitled *Sacredotii Nostri Primordia,* was written to commemorate the centenary of the death of a priest, of all priests imaginable, the Curé of Ars. The introduction to the encyclical underscores how the early days of Pope John's own priesthood were associated with the beatification of the Curé of Ars and how the Curé of Ars became the inspiration of his own priestly life. The Curé of Ars, hero of the confessional, personal penance, and pastoral commitment! One has no recollection of ever seeing an extended treatment of this encyclical in recent theological and ascetical reviews; it is not difficult to imagine why, once one reads the encyclical, and then re-reads the articles commonplace in the same contemporary publications!

The first part of the encyclical is given over to the ascetical side of the priestly life. It obviously has had little effect on sociological polls, even those taken among those who claim Pope John XXIII as the inspiration of their new aspirations and the beginning of emancipation from ancient ascetical disciplines in the Roman Church.

The second part of the encyclical is concerned with prayer and its primacy in the life of the priest, but it dwells heavily on eucharistic prayer and not merely assumes but sets forth the constant Catholic tradition concerning the nature of the Eucharist, including the Real Presence and the Mass, as understood of old, at the center of the priesthood.

The third part of the encyclical is concerned with pastoral zeal, and it is totally sacerdotal, what might now be called *cultic,* in its emphasis. The service of the community and of the person, by every means and in every social form consistent with the Catholic notion of priesthood, is, of course, present in the encyclical—but it is present in that manner in which it has always been presented. The conclusion of the encyclical may be briefly summarized and, again, is a bit of a surprise, though it should not be: the Catholic priesthood is indispensable; the sanctity of the clergy is supremely necessary; both of these contentions are required if Christ is to reign in the world, as Christ should, must, and will.

The third encyclical is almost shocking, given the image of Pope John XXIII diffused, probably innocently and certainly in ignorance of his teaching, in whole areas of the Church. It is his encyclical *Grata Recordatio,* and it is on the recitation of the Rosary. Pope John XXIII takes his theme from Pope Leo XIII, who died at the beginning of this century, and the encyclical is an exemplar of devout doctrine, profound piety, and utter conformity with the theological and spiritual traditions of the Catholic people, not only prior to Vatican Council II, but also prior to the twentieth century.

The encyclical on the Rosary leaves no possible doubt concerning the spirit of Good Pope John's total commitment to the traditional Catholic belief and cult with respect to the Blessed Mother of Christ. It also suggests the consternation with which he would hear his name invoked as that of a man, a priest, and, above all, a Pope set on *liberating* us from preoccupations with and devotion to the Virgin Mary. A Protestant minister noted for his own mariological insights and erudition once remarked to me that it was Pope John XXIII who had caused him to choose the Rosary as one of his favorite private devotions. He had been struck by the manner in which the Pope frequently indicated publicly the intentions for which he offered each of the decades of the beads, all fifteen of them, every day of his life. The minister once took it into his head to write a letter to the Pope asking if some time when the Pope was saying his beads, perhaps when he was walking in the Vatican Gardens (as he was wont to do) enjoying the sheer beauty of the place and the consolations of reciting the Rosary, he would remember him, the minister, and his efforts to make better understood and more loved the Catholic tradition concerning Mary.

Recollection of the fourth encyclical of Pope John XXIII will be no less surprising, if not disconcerting, to some who invoke his name as the justification for their theological and intellectual skidding in all directions. A case comes to mind. While taking part in a program to encourage young people in Catholic schools to participate in the Foreign Mission Association, I was bound, for my sins, to sit through a talk by a missionologist. Let us recall with care that a missionologist is not a missionary nor, at least by virtue of his title, a contributor to the foreign missions. He is a relatively well-paid professor, as professors in Catholic institutions go, of what has come to be called *the theology of missions,* a course which Christ appears not to have taken the time to develop scientifically for the Twelve Apostles when they started out to convert the world, as, for a moment, it looked as if they would. This particular missionologist (now happily married, according to his own say-so) informed the children that the Catholic Church had put too much emphasis on the conversion of non-Catholics and particularly those in distant lands. I nearly bounced my breviary off his head at the thought of all the spearmint jelly candies I had *given up* to ransom Chinese babies during all the Lenten seasons from the time I reached the age of reason until the time I could substitute a mild drink before dinner instead of the spearmint leaves!

The children, with more profound insight, dismissed him as a fraud and in their subsequent conversations, which were a delight, they seemed to be quoting Pope John XXIII's fourth encyclical, *Princeps Pastorum,* though, of course, being simple youngsters, they had never read it. They were simply saturated with twenty centuries of Catholic tradition, the centuries which had prompted Benedict XV and other popes to propose certain new missionary techniques and to reform outmoded or self-defeating missionary procedures.

The circumstances of Pope John's plea for further reforms in the procedures of the Church in the missionary world were later elaborated by Pope Paul VI who, matching the teaching with his action and example, went personally to missionary countries all over the world. On his journeys as Pope, he drove home the urgency of the need for indigenous clergy and hierarchy; the norms for the formation of local clergy in missionary countries; the enormously increased importance of the laity in the missionary work of the Church, and, last but not least, the perennial, unchanging, essential missionary nature of the Church, together with or, God forbid, apart from other good works in underprivileged countries. He urged ecumenical cooperation wherever such might be forthcoming and consistent with the original mandate of Jesus Christ that the one gospel be preached to all men.

It was with his fifth encyclical, *Mater et Magistra,* that Pope John began to become a trifle controversial. Some devout Roman Catholics, who slanted slightly to the Right in the United States and elsewhere, found the Pope a bit on the *liberal* side in his social teaching. One of them (his identity has become obscured by subsequent research and efforts to swap credit) made a mildly witty observation to the effect that the Church might be his *Mater,* but she was not his *Magistra* in what pertained to social teaching. It provoked an argument something like that occasioned by Pope Paul's encyclical on birth control among the *progressives,* but since the exploding population and sex were only remotely involved, there was never the high tension around Pope John's encyclical that exploded after Pope Paul's.

Pope John XXIII, as if to head off the opposition he knew he would encounter, spent the first part of his encyclical recalling the constant preoccupation of the Church with the social well-being of people. He chose for the publication of his revolutionary doctrine the seventieth anniversary of Pope Leo's encyclical, *Rerum Novarum,* and described the happy changes but occasional failures which had followed on the encyclical, the directives of which he repeated and underlined. He then recalled Pius XI's *Quadragesimo Anno* and Pius XII's world broadcast of Pentecost 1941. He reviewed some of the changes between.

Obviously thinking himself now fairly safe (but, if one judges his character, not caring very much, since truth and justice were involved), Pope John devoted the second part of his encyclical to personal initiative in the business and economic realm, with some gentle hints about the rights and limits of public intervention should personal initiative become unduly personal and, as he seemed to think possible, forgetful of the common good. It was here that he used the word which really set off the firecrackers; it was the word *socialization,* which, apparently having read the newspapers as well as the history books, the Pope decided was a contemporary fact and phenomenon which required recognition, analysis, and evaluation.

It somehow crossed his mind, as the son of a poor family, to raise the question of a just remuneration for the working class, and he argued, clearly and cogently, that all these previous considerations called, in his mind, for a review of our economic structures. To the best of my knowledge, no politician running for office in any nation has failed to develop this argument, sometimes to a lesser degree, depending on his audience, sometimes to a greater degree, depending on similar factors. All have been obliged to face the question of the future of private property in any revised norms of justice in the reformation of economic structures. And so Pope John included a passage on the nature and inevitable rights as well as duties of those blessed by the acquisition of property.

The third part of the encyclical reviewed certain entirely new aspects of the social question and was justified by certain facts of history, perhaps the change from the barter system to the monetary system, from the institution of slavery to the system of freely contracted labor, or perhaps the rise of labor unions and even the potentially exaggerated power of labor unions in certain circumstances. The Pope even may have had a conversation or two with people who were worried about taxes in the new forms which taxation has taken, as, for example, income tax, social security tax, corporation taxes, property taxes, and what the British call, with their grim humor, *death rates,* and what Americans call, with greater optimism, *inheritance taxes.*

The Holy Father concluded with an eloquent passage which lifted all this theory, history, and abstract principle from the level of mere sociological speculation and erudite but sterile debate to the warmer level of human relations. He suggested that human persons were even more involved than material property or economic and political structures. Here he made a plea for a symphony of truth, justice, and love in such human relations. It is almost psychologically impossible to imagine how anyone could find fault with what he taught and still remain in even pretended communion with Rome — but, as in the days of Leo XIII, Pius XI, and Paul VI, there were those who found fault aplenty and went straight from writing letters of protest to the diocesan paper to the last Sunday Mass in the nearest parish church, removing from their faces all trace of indignation and assuming a properly pious mien.

The next encyclical of the Holy Father was written to commemorate the fifteenth centenary of Pope Saint Leo the Great, whom Pope Pius XII had called "the greatest among the great", John XXIII recalled. He lauded this valiant Pope of antiquity for his orthodoxy, his valiant courage, his pastoral gifts, and the fact that he was a Doctor of the Universal Church by reason of the firmness and soundness of his doctrine. He then went on to link Pope Saint Leo the Great to his own hopes for Vatican Council II, developing this affinity at considerable length.

If *Mater et Magistra* had made a few affectionate enemies among the rightists, their number was increased by his next encyclical, *Pacem in Terris. Pacem in Terris* has had a strange fate. In all probability, if any single encyclical contributed to the worldwide popularity of Pope John and to his ecumenical image, this is the one. The very title *Pacem in Terris* became, together with *aggiornamento,* part of the *lingua franca* of our time. I bought my best copy of it, a book which presented the papal teaching entirely in dramatic photographs, in a Protestant bookstore in New York. One of the conversation pieces in my private library is the Jewish translation of it sent me from Israel.

I have met one or two isolationists or nuthouse-bound nationalists who expressed violent reservations in its regard, but I have never met anyone who expressed regret that it had been written. The Pope, apparently basing his twentieth-century teaching on the first-century Gospels, implies that the song of the angels about peace on earth might be accomplished if there were sufficient men of good will. He goes on to imply that good will includes, in addition to being kind folks and gentle people, a generation devoted to truth, justice, charity, and the other traditional virtues long paid lip-service, at least in just about every movement that does not actively promote theft, murder, and hatred as a program and in principle.

On July 1, 1962, Pope John XXIII published another encyclical. One almost hesitates in these times of permissive manners and comfortable religion to recall the title, let alone the content. The title was *Paenitentiam Agere*, which is practically a translation of the message of Saint John the Baptist, who had his head cut off for criticizing, among other things, sexual excesses, high living, failure to do penance, and being unfaithful to your wife, even as a means of more complete personal fulfillment and of tribute to the beauty of a dancer who was merely obeying her mother when she asked for her opponent's decapitation. The Pope suggested that if we fail to follow the advice of John the Baptist, rigorous and austere though it be, we may not expect much authentic happiness in the world or any happiness in the world to come.

Such was the teaching of Pope John XXIII in the encyclicals which he actually published. That teaching in no way negates his good nature nor diminishes his affable good humor; its stability and serenity explain both.

His apostolic letters turn out to be much the same, as one goes through them to find out what Pope John actually taught in order to enjoy the more authentically his *spirit*. His first apostolic letter was entitled *Sanctitatis Altrix*, and he published it on the first centenary of the death of Saint Gabriel of Our Lady of

Sorrows. The very name of Saint Gabriel hardly creates a spirit of leaping mirth in the hearts of the *emancipated of spirit,* recalling as it does a rule of life whose heart is meditation on the Crucified Christ and the need that they who seek salvation be crucified together with Christ—in fact as well as in fancy writing.

The second apostolic letter, *Apostolorum Choro,* commemorated the nineteenth centenary of the martyrdom of the Apostle James the Less. Why he chose the *Less* witness deponeth not, but somehow one detects the *letter* of Pope John as well as his *spirit* in this brief but instructive missive.

A third apostolic letter recalled the lives, times, and examples of two Roman pontiffs, Innocent VI and Blessed Urban V, both of whom are recalled by heroic monuments in Rome. Five days later, and as if he couldn't wait, Pope John put out his apostolic letter *Causa Praeclara* to recall the lessons of the fourth centenary of the reform of the Carmelite Order under Saint Teresa, an order and a woman given to meditation, prayer, self-discipline, and an intense measure of intellectual life in accordance with the norms of the Church.

One will not wish to forget the apostolic letter of Pope John addressed to all the bishops of the Catholic world on the subject of devotion to the Precious Blood of Jesus; the choice of the theme makes one think of his spontaneous insertion of the name of Saint Joseph in the Canon of the Mass while the bishops were discussing the merits of the question during Vatican Council II: he acted by his own authority in a brief note sent down to the council hall.

Every bishop in the world received an apostolic letter on the approach of Vatican Council II, reminding him of its importance in the life of the Church and the necessity that each prepare for it profoundly and carefully. He added to his recommendations with respect to preparation for the Council in the apostolic letter *Oecumenicum Concilium* by urging, with passionate insistence, the devout recitation of the Rosary of the Blessed Mother (again, of all things!) for the happy outcome of the Council.

Apart from his encyclicals and apostolic letters, Good Pope John issued certain exhortations. I recall but one, *Sacrae Laudis,* his plea to the clergy of the entire world to be faithful in the recitation of the breviary, as indeed, was he, down to the very end. This carefully argued letter, passionate and persuasive, was clearly long in the heart and mind of the Pope. He linked the breviary not only to his hopes for the Council, but also to the whole concept of the reform or renewal of the Church as he understood these in terms of the priesthood and the religious life, of theology and of action—*aggiornamento* as he, in fact, understood it. Referring to *Sacrae Laudis* and its relation to the Council's purposes, the Pope once recalled these words from the Provincial Council of Aachen: "The priest must shine as much in his doctrine as in his life; for doctrine without life makes a man arrogant, but life without doctrine makes him useless." To which Pope John added: "The breviary is a wonderful compendium of doctrine and life for every priest."

None of the documents signed by Good Pope John has been the object of more cloak-and-dagger writing, with distortion of the background of the document and the character of the Pope, than the apostolic constitution of the Pontiff concerning the increased study of Latin, *Veterum Sapientia* and, its permanent importance notwithstanding, the adoption of the vernacular in the liturgy for pastoral reasons. It was never the mind of Pope John, a remarkably humanistic type himself, to abolish the cultural tradition of the world which produced him. But he recognized, as did the overwhelming majority of the Council Fathers, the fact that millions of his fellow Catholics did not share his cultural background. For many of these, particularly in the increasingly important African and Asian world, the basic language of that culture, Latin, not only would be an obstacle to their pastoral participation in the liturgy, but also, as the most convincing speech on the subject in the Council argued, would rob the liturgy in some parts of the world of its role in their instruction in the Faith. This latter consideration would have been of supreme importance to Pope John XXIII and would have won him over to a vernacular liturgy for pastoral reasons in the contemporary and coming cultural world.

Quite another consideration was his attitude toward the place of Latin in theological studies and the intellectual tradition of the Church and the world. Hence there was nothing whatsoever inconsistent about his pastoral option for the vernacular liturgy and his cultural determination to preserve Latin studies, not only as the heart of the liberal arts tradition, but also as the condition of the preservation of the thought and teaching of those Fathers of the Church and other theologians of the past to whom he was indebted for so much of his own formation and to whom he dedicated so much of his writing. It is, therefore, nonsense to represent a man of independent will and judgment like John XXIII as having been forced, practically physically, by reactionary members of the Curia (whom he is otherwise described as perpetually keeping at a distance) to sign the apostolic constitution *Veterum Sapientia*. The witty remarks about *Veterum si, Sapientia no* recall the earlier wisecracks about *Mater si, Magistra no* and have just about the same value, though they usually come from the other side of that narrow line which divides closed-minded liberals from closed-minded conservatives.

The plain fact is that Pope John, as those who pretend to be inspired by him should be the first to admit, was not a man to be pushed around nor to be dragged into secret corners of Saint Peter's to sign, under compulsion, documents in which he did not believe. One can read accounts of this fantastic piece of alleged skullduggery, in which the aged Pontiff had his hand guided by bad losers on the vernacular liturgy as he signed, with silent or screaming protest, the document which expressed the desire that Latin remain a major part of priestly training and an integrating principle of our disintegrating classical and Christian culture.

It may be that his hopes will prove vain, at least pending a renaissance, but the descriptions of the manner in which he expressed and gave his formal approbation to these hopes are sheer legend, unworthy of their authors and, of course, even more unworthy of a great Pontiff. The fact is that, far from signing the document in the secrecy and dark shadows of the confessional under the high altar of Saint Peter's at some obscure hour and surrounded by scheming curialists, Pope John himself was the author of the solemnity of the circumstances under which he signed his brief for the retention of Latin studies as a prime element in the theological and humanistic tradition of the Church, the heritage of which he loved as much as her structures and pastoral spirit.

The document was signed in Saint Peter's, a unique circumstance. Present in that baroque temple were, by his invitation, the Sacred College of Cardinals, the members of the Roman Curia in all its subdivisions, the Center Commission for the preparation of Vatican Council II, the academic authorities of all the universities and athenaeums of Rome, together with the students of the scattered colleges and seminaries and a great crowd of the faithful of every language and from every nation. The day chosen for the event—the signing at the high altar, the consignment of the document to the Cardinal Prefect of the Congregation for Studies, while a choir sang a Latin motet— gives some hint that Pope John was not a poor old man, badgered into acting against his will, humiliated into the defense of Latin in studies, particularly the study of authors who wrote in Latin and built the theological as well as literary tradition that formed so much of his own mind and temperament. Pope John XXIII was perfectly capable of distinguishing between things done for pastoral reasons and other things done for perennial reasons on the level of intellectual tools and cultural witness.

The letter and the spirit of Pope John are to be found beyond doubt in his opening speech to the ecumenical Council, as they were also found in his frequent allocutions and addresses, formal and informal, sometimes grave, more often jolly, to the weekly public audiences of the faithful from all over the world. We shall content ourselves with a summary of the opening speech to the Council; it is frequently quoted, in and out of context, and is familiar to the informed of our period in the history of the Church.

It is a buoyant document, but by no means casual. He announced his purposes in calling the Council and declared the first of the needs to be: "to assert once again the Magisterium (teaching authority of the Church), which is unfailing and perdures until the end of time". He saw it but *natural* that in opening such a Council we should first of all look to the past and listen to its voice, "whose echo we like to hear in the memories and the merits of the more recent and ancient Pontiffs, our predecessors". He described the voices of these as: "voices which proclaim in perennial fervor the triumph of that divine and human institution, the Church of Christ", and he added that, as a result, he approached the Council with motives for spiritual joy despite the accumulated cloud of sorrow and trials.[3]

He expressed the hope that as a result of the Council, the Church would become greater in spiritual riches, gaining new energies and looking to the future without fear. For all this, he wanted the Church *updated where required,* so that men, families, and peoples would at long last turn their minds really to *heavenly things.* He rebuked *prophets of gloom* who are always forecasting disaster, but he failed to identify these and left one with the impression that they belonged to parties in many directions from his own central position. He particularly lamented those who compare our era with past eras, as though the present were a time of unmitigated disaster and the past were a time of unqualified triumphs. He expressed his conviction that the Church and the world are headed toward a future beyond our expectations, certainly one of greater good for the Church and a greater care for spiritual realities, with which the Magisterium is concerned, but he did this in a spirit of theological faith and pastoral commitment, not any spirit of Doctor Coue ("Every day and in every way I'm getting better and better"), nor of a *myth of progress* based on either evolution or Pollyanna.

He declared the principal duty of the Council to be the defense and advance of the truth; that it should never depart from the sacred patrimony of truth received from the Fathers; but that it must seek ever-new avenues to the Catholic apostolate and profit from the discoveries of human genius in order to do so.

He insisted that the Church was to continue to oppose errors, but he argued that her opposition must be with the medicine of mercy rather than that of severity. He made a passionate plea for the realization of human unity and, above all, the ever-greater unity in sanctity and *great joy* of the churches. He declared that heaven and earth came together in the Council and then, having addressed the Council Fathers on earth and urged them to labor and work, he ended with a plea to Almighty God, to Mary Help of Christians, and, particularly, Help of Bishops, to Saint Joseph, the holy Apostles Peter and Paul, Saint John the Baptist and Saint John the Evangelist. Finally, he called upon Jesus Christ, our most amiable Redeemer, immortal King of peoples and of times, praying that glory and honor will be His forever and ever.

It is difficult to imagine how any pope, however rigid and relaxed, however smiling or sober, could have taught the Faith and practice of Catholicism other than did Pope John. Nor is it possible to discover popes in past history—or to observe a Pope in John's successor—more buoyant in faith, as prayerful in spirit, as affable and gregarious as was Papa Roncalli. Nor does temperament have anything to do with papal duty. The solicitudes of all popes with faith, hope, charity, and service of life are part of the office of the papacy, not the personality of the pope, though each gives the discharge of the office his characteristic touch.

That is why one does not understand those who sometimes seem to think that a temperament they see as somehow sentimental would not have made Pope John more *soft* in his teaching on problems they see as more *human* than matters of faith and morals. Nothing he ever said or wrote confirms this reflection on his integrity or on the compassion of those popes who have taught the authentic mind of the Church, as did he, on subjects like contraception, celibacy, abortion, or peace and war, always blending inflexible defense of the Faith (including the "hard sayings" of which Saint John reminds us) with pastoral compassion for those who must live, even with lapses of frailty, the creed and code of the Church.

The *softness* of Pope John was *pro-life* and *pro-God*. Whoever doubts either his teaching or his attitude on certain muddled subjects of the hour should read not only his priestly *Journal of a Soul,* but, above all, his spiritual testament to his own family, especially the last line: "Oh, the children, the children, what a wealth of children and what a blessing!"[4] This Pope has a smile not of cynical *planned parenthood, planned genocide,* or coldly planned anything else; his was a smile that was *pro-life, pro-hope, pro-human* — and therefore *pro-God*.

XVIII

Our Tainted Nature's Solitary Boast

The privileges of Mary in the dogma of faith which we celebrate today are nowhere better summed up than in the oft-quoted line of the English Protestant poet who spoke of the Immaculate Conception as "our tainted nature's solitary boast". The line of Wordsworth sums up generations of theological speculation and expresses in brief but accurate terms both the definition of Pope Pius IX concerning Mary's Immaculate Conception and the reasons for the proud faith with which we Catholic Americans, above all at the North American College, celebrate the feast of the patroness of our land and our college.

One has often reflected whether "the solitary boast" aspect of this cult of our patroness may not have helped to foster a certain sense of "solitary boast" or special self-consciousness on the part both of the Church in our country and, in a specific way which preoccupies me this morning, in the men, largely of another generation, who thought themselves privileged, as they were indeed privileged, to be *Romani,* alumni of the North American College in Rome.

This speculation concerning the special self-consciousness that Roman College priests had, or were accused of having, is suggested by remembrance of the prominent place in their traditional piety of Our Lady of Humility and the Immaculate Conception, as well as, of course, their special sense of having been formed in their priesthood so close to the person of the Vicar of her Son, our Holy Father the Pope.

One remembers evidences not only of this attitude to which I refer and which, for better or worse, can hardly be denied, at

This sermon was preached at the North American College, Rome, on December 8, 1972.

least so far as times gone by are concerned. For example, time was when the likeness of the Madonna dell'Umiltà would have been found in fully eighty percent of the rectories or private rooms of graduates of the North American College. It was a sign—right or wrong, realistic or romantic, pious or pretentious—that the priest who had placed the image there had certain ideas not only about the Blessed Mother but about *himself* as being somehow distinct from, but not separate from, even his brother priests in the common sacerdotal service of the parish, the diocese, and universal Church.

One can remember when certain corollaries of this collective self-consciousness of the *Romani* were resented—sometimes contemptuously, sometimes good-naturedly, sometimes enviously, sometimes ironically. In my own native archdiocese, an annual reunion of the American College alumni within the diocese was forbidden by the Ordinary, though he himself was proud alumnus and a former rector who died in a bed over which there hung a reproduction of the Madonna dell'Umiltà. The Cardinal acted as he did presumably because of the danger, as he saw it, of a certain *separatism,* rather than legitimate self-consciousness, within the presbyterium of the diocese, which priestly body for every reason should be compactly united around the bishop, without reference to the background, the education, or any other loyalties, interests, or offices of the priests constituting the diocesan presbyterium.

I sometimes suspect that there is no longer much danger of such a separating self-consciousness among our students and eventual alumni, even though I long suspected, and still do, that this special self-consciousness of the *Romani* was occasionally overdone—or expressed in the wrong way, or in dubious taste. There was, however, at the core of this sense of identity apart, two unimpeachable premises, perhaps not always conscious, though I think they were, nor always kept in context. We have alluded to them both: (1) the unique place of Rome and a Roman background in the life of the Church and of

297

the priest; (2) the college cult of "our tainted nature's solitary boast".

I am not suggesting, least of all confessing, that the claims of our patroness as "our tainted nature's solitary boast" somehow became transformed subtly into any pretense or illusion on the part of the Roman alumni that they were, while sharing all the *differences* of the priestly order, somehow our tainted priesthood's special boast in excellence, commitment, or erudition. The typical *Romani* were too realistic, if not cosmopolitan, for any such vanity; a Roman sense of perspective—it was acclaimed or denounced as *Romanità*—prevented such nonsense. But they did seek distinction of character; they were determined to remain *different* and to reject conformism with standards, styles, or tastes acceptable enough elsewhere in the seminary world. Their nonconformity expressed itself in shared details of traditions, common interests, house dress, devotions, and the like.

They shared the tainted nature and *virtue* of all priests, beyond doubt, but they did not *rejoice* in this fact and did not deliberately cultivate, with convenient theologies of the priesthood, sacerdotal or seminary mediocrity, or that *cult of conformism* which, among some priests and candidates for the priesthood, is expressed in the phrase: "My priesthood is a *function,* not a form of life and being, and I am like everyone else in all things, *sin included."* They would have seen such a theological or practical formula not as a confirmation of their *humanity,* but a confession of their *sacerdotal failure.*

Two small incidents in recent years, both confirmed by many others, have driven home to me the differences between that antique spirit in the college, if you will, and other attitudes. At a recent gathering of Roman alumni, the present speaker undertook to describe not only our special love for the Bishop of Rome, but also the historic and doctrinal grounds for certain unique natures of the attitudes of *Romani,* graduates of the North American College in Rome. A more recent alumnus at the college screamed out in protest that some have another understanding of all these matters. I later went to the rectory where he lived to make quite sure that the passing violent reaction and my own abstention from comment had not caused a rupture of priestly fraternity, whatever our obviously different understandings of Rome, the Bishop of Rome, and, by consequence, the American College. Our conversation was extremely pleasant, as it might have been between two insurance men, but I hope to be forgiven if I noted, perhaps with a certain unfairness, that the principal picture in his room (I think the *only* one) was not the image of the Madonna dell'Umiltà, so universal a hallmark of an older tradition, but a somewhat large, technically contrived, but photographically effective profile portrait of the Kennedy brothers, Jack and Bob. I understood and understand the preoccupation behind the choice of the picture; with qualifications, one even welcomes it, but the symbolism, and therefore the *reality,* are manifestly signs of a difference in the consciousness of *Romani.*

Another incident makes my point more plainly. I happened to be in the nation's capital the night that incendiary violence broke out a few years ago, pitting against one another two minority groups in the capital city. It chanced that an interfaith meeting on religion and race, so-called, had been held on the day in the capital, and I was representing the Catholic community. The ranking Protestant and Jew were asked, together with myself, to walk together through the most troubled area until well into the morning. The streets were flooded with water and the stores were on fire. Looting and violence were widespread, and it was suggested that the three of us, *wearing obviously clerical attire,* walk down the middle of the otherwise closed streets, speaking to whomever greeted us or would return a greeting. Many touching, tragic, and sometimes humorous incidents took place during the course of that nervous walk through streets of social terror.

The incident I shall not soon forget took place at the entrance of one of the closed and chaotic streets, just after midnight. A young policeman lifted aside the wooden barrier to permit the three of us, vested respectively as an obviously Catholic priest, an Episcopalian bishop, and a Jewish rabbi, to wade into the street. At that point, a person stepped forward from the sidewalk to follow us into the closed area. I recognized his face immediately; he was a priest, nationally known for his somewhat special views. He was dressed totally in nonclerical attire and was, in fact, a study in a calculated effort to look completely casual, exotic yet *relevant*. His necktie is the bit of Brooks Brothers that I remember best, though his bad taste in pants could not escape the admiring attention that he clearly sought.

The young policeman restrained him as he tried to enter the street, saying that only clergy and firemen were being permitted to walk through that area. "But *I am* a priest", the nationally known personality declared with an obvious disappointment at the policeman's ignorance of well-known personalities. The policeman replied: "You don't look like one from where I stand", to which, in the midst of the looting and flames, came a theological reply: "I have a different concept of the priesthood from older clergy. *I think a priest is just like everybody else* —and therefore so am I!"

The policeman closed the barrier with an observation that revealed him to be backward, perhaps, in his theology but determined in his intention to bring back something like peace to a deeply troubled neighborhood. He said: "Listen, mister, these streets are *filled* with people *just like everybody else* tonight. We need some people who are *not* like everybody else and I suggest that you go back to your monastery (clearly he *did* know him) before I whistle for the patrol car." His Reverence disappeared in the dark, though not without telling the policeman that he would hear more of this. I doubted it and still do.

If there was sometimes a certain unjustified elitism, an unnecessary *clericalism* in the tradition with which *the priest like everybody else* has broken, if there was what is now called *triumphalism* in the specific self-consciousness of *Romani* who were nonetheless conscious servants of the servants of God, in accordance with the phrase that has become a part of their Roman life, the new attitude *was* and *is* not merely untheological, but, quite simply, cheap and vulgar.

One realizes, of course, that much of this may be of minor importance. It is a matter of customs, manners, and modalities. But today's feast of "our tainted nature's solitary boast", patroness of our college, suggests to me a brief reflection in favor of a more lofty concept of the ministry of the priesthood on every level, in every form.

That reflection begins with the unqualified insistence that the priests of the old *Romanità* knew as well as anyone, and better than most, that they were weak and sinful men and knew it, though ministers of the word of God. They knew it because they had mastered lessons like that of Cardinal Newman's magnificent sermon on the theme: *Men, not angels, are the ministers of the gospel.* The English Cardinal linked his reflections on this realistic and consoling contention — that all ministers of the gospel are men, not angels — precisely to the feast we are celebrating at our college this morning.

I venture a summary of John Cardinal Newman's argument:

When Christ, the sole Priest of the New Covenant, came into the world, He came in the most holy, august, and glorious manner. He was born of an Immaculate mother, "our tainted nature's solitary boast". An archangel announced His Incarnation; a Virgin conceived, bore, and nursed Him; His foster-father was chaste Joseph; angels proclaimed His birth; a luminous star spread the news; the austere John the Baptist prepared his way.

Seeing that he came to introduce a new and final Dispensation into the world, He left behind Him preachers, teachers, and missionaries. One might say: since on His coming all about Him was glorious, such as He was, such also should His servants be, such His representatives, His ministers. As he was without sin, they too must be paragons of perfection. As He was the Son of God, they must surely be angels.

And yet, it is not so. He has sent forth for the ministry of

301

reconciliation, not angels, but men. He has appointed sons of Adam, men, like you and me, exposed to temptations, failure, and warfare within and without; with the same three deadly enemies—the world, the flesh, and the devil; with the same human, the same wayward heart as Adam's breed generally, differing only as the power of God has changed and rules that heart by grace. So it is; we are not angels from heaven that speak the word of God, but men, whom grace, and grace alone, has made to differ from others. We ministers, we preachers, we priests are not angels, not saints, not sinless, but those who would have lived and died in sin except for God's grace, and who, though through God's mercy are in training for the fellowship of saints hereafter, at present we are in the midst of infirmity and temptation, and have no hope, except from the unmerited grace of God, of persevering unto the end.

What a strange paradox is this! All is perfect, heavenly, and glorious, in the Dispensation Christ vouchsafed us, except the persons of His ministers. He dwells on our altars Himself, the Most Holy, the Most High, and angels (never forget it at the peril of your souls), fall down before Him around your altar and your tabernacle, and out of visible substances and forms he chooses what is choicest to represent and to hold Him. Altar and sanctuary are adorned decently or splendidly, as our means allow; and decent priests perform their office in befitting vestments, lifting up chaste hearts and consecrated hands; yet those very priests, so set apart, so consecrated, they, with the girdle of celibacy and the armor of discipline, are sons of Adam, sons of sinners, with fallen natures, which they have not put off, though it be renewed through grace so that every priest has sins of his own to offer for.

The apostle says: "Every high priest, taken from among men, is appointed of men, in the things that appertain unto God, that he may offer gifts and sacrifices for sins; who can condole with those who are in ignorance and error, because he also himself is compassed with infirmity. And therefore he ought, as for the people, so also for himself, to offer for sins."[1]

All this is not strange when you consider it is the appointment of an all-merciful God; not strange because of the reason that apostle gives in the passage I have quoted. The priests of the New Law are men in order that they may condole with those who are in ignorance and error, because they too are compassed with infirmity. Had angels been our priests, they could not have condoled with us, sympathized with us, have had compassion with us, felt tenderly for us, and made allowances for us, as do worthy priests. They could not have been our patterns and guides and could not have led us on from our old selves into a new life, as they can who come from the midst of us and respond to the special vocation of the ordained priest in holy orders. Therefore, God appoints men to be the ministers of reconciliation and intercession; as He Himself, though He could not sin, yet even He, by becoming man, took on Himself as far as was possible to God, man's burden of infirmity and trial in His own person. He could not be a sinner, but He could be a man, and He took to Himself a man's heart that we might entrust our hearts to Him, and He was tempted in all things, like as we are, yet without sin.

Let us consider this truth more narrowly. Since Adam fell, none of his seed but has been conceived in sin; none, save one. One exception there has been. Who is that one? not our Lord Jesus, for He was not conceived of man, but of the Holy Spirit; not our Lord, but His Virgin Mother, who, though conceived and born of human parents, as others, yet was rescued by anticipation from the common condition of mankind, and never was partaker of Adam's transgression, as were we. She was conceived in the way of nature, she was conceived as are others; but grace interfered beforehand; grace filled her soul from the first moment of her existence, so that the evil one breathed not on her to stain the work of God. *"Tota pulchra es, Maria; et macula originalis non est in te."* But putting aside the Most Blessed Mother of God, everyone else, the most glorious saint, and the most black and odious of sinners, were both born in one and the same original sin, all were children of wrath, unable to attain heaven by their natural powers, and with the prospect of meriting themselves hell. Yet all were still called to sanctity and eternal life.

My brothers, though your conscience witnesses against you, God can disburden it, whether you have sinned less or whether you have sinned more, He can make you as clean in His sight and as acceptable to Him as if you had never gone from Him. Gradually will He destroy your sinful habits, and at once will He restore you to His favor. Such is the power of the sacrament of penance, that, be your load of guilt heavier or be it lighter, it removes it, whatever it is. God can undo the past, He can realize the hopeless, helping us live and die in something of the angelic excellence of Mary Immaculate. Consider our centuries of saints to whom the very notion of any guilty imagination would have been as death; there is not one of these seraphic souls but might have been a servant of Satan, except for God's grace; not one but might, or rather would, have lived the life of a brute creature, and died a reprobate, to dwell in hell eternally, had not God put a new heart and a new spirit within him and made him what he could never make himself.

And, thus pursuing the special and distinctive quality of sanctity, the priest, still a man and not an angel, is fortified in his legitimate and necessary apartness by every self-consciousness of a natural or supernatural kind that makes him *distinct but not separate* from his fellows. Fortunately, it is not necessary to be angels to become saints. Fortunately, it is not even necessary to be a saint, as it is impossible to be an angel, in order to be a priest. But it is necessary to have certain witness called *angelic,* and it is necessary to be at one with all men—but *different.*

This is something the world, including, alas, part of the Church, not to say the clergy, cannot understand; not that it does not apprehend clearly enough that we are by nature of like passions with itself, but that, being so like itself by nature, we may and must be so *different*. Men of the world know the power of nature, some, perhaps most, know not the power of God's grace; and since they are not themselves acquainted with any power that can overcome nature, they think that none exists and therefore, consistently, they believe that everyone, priest or not, remains to the end such as nature made him, and they will not believe it possible that anyone can lead a supernatural life. Those who argue that the sacerdotal differences which the Church asks of us are hypocritical or impossible know or realize nothing of the presence of God, the merits of Christ, the intercession of the Blessed Virgin; the virtue of recurring prayers, of frequent confession, of daily Masses; they are strangers to the transforming power of the Most Holy Sacrament, the Bread of Angels; they do not contemplate the efficacy of salutary rules, of holy companions, of long-enduring habit, of ready spontaneous vigilance, of abhorrence of sin and rejection of Satan, to secure the soul of evil. He is irresistible; they only know that when the soul has exposed and surrendered itself to his malice, there is (so to speak) a *necessity* of sinning. They only know that when God has abandoned it, and good angels are withdrawn, and all safeguards, and protections, and preventives are neglected, that then (which is their own case), when the victory is all but gained already, it is sure to be gained altogether. They themselves have always, even at their best, been all but beaten by the evil one before they began to fight; this is the only state they have experienced; they know this, and they know nothing else.

But if we priests are deeply conscious of and have a *holy* pride, in our differences, we will remain, of course, men, not angels, in the ministry of Christ, but, oh, with what greater efficacy! Those to whom we minister will know our limitations (God knows they are obvious enough!), but they will understand us; they will react to us with faith, hope, and joy. They will be tender to us more than they are at the moment, and they will *instruct us in the spirit of meekness.*

They will hear us say for Christ: "Come then unto us, all ye that labor and are heavy laden, and ye shall find rest to your souls";[2] come unto us, who now stand to you in Christ's stead, and who speak in Christ's name; for we too, like you, have been saved by Christ's all-saving blood. We too, like you, should be lost sinners, unless Christ had had mercy on us, unless His grace had cleansed us, unless His Church had received us, unless His saints had interceded for us. Come, listen, all ye that fear God, and we will tell you what He has done for our souls. Listen to our testimony; behold our joy of heart, and increase it by partaking it in yourselves. Take our word for it, we who have a right and a duty to speak.

And we will be heard, they will hear us, believe me, not so much as, say, *theologians* or *professional* teachers and preachers, but as human heralds of a new Pentecost to men whose humanity, common to our own, keeps us close to all God's people, though we are called apart, as Aaron was, to a priesthood made *distinct, not separate,* by our sacred orders—orders the *distinction* of which from the common priesthood of all the faithful is *fortified* and *protected* by the *differences* that *Romani* (and others, in their other ways) cherished and cultivated.

XIX

Things Old and New

Seido: It is now a year and a half since the *General Catechetical Directory* was issued by the Sacred Congregation for the Clergy. Can you say that it is beginning to have a beneficial effect on the teaching of Christian doctrine?

Wright: The beginnings of the effect of the *General Directory* and the celebration in Rome of the World Catechetical Congress are already clear.[1] First of all, the *Directory* itself has been widely translated and diffused. The proceedings of the congress have been similarly widespread, and already a considerable literature of comment on, reaction, and extension of the proceedings has multiplied.[2]

Many hierarchies have already begun to prepare their own official national catechetical directories, and there are indications that, apart from the hierarchies, versions of the *General Directory* have begun to appear. They will have no official character unless they become authorized, but they indicate that the *Directory* filled a need and a vacuum.

There has been one interesting and not entirely pleasant effect of the publication of the *Directory,* although in the long run this effect may prove beneficial. As you know, the *Directory* was directed toward bishops, catechetical commissions, textbooks authors, and like official catechists. It was not designed for popular use, even by parents. However, one begins

This interview was published in *Catholic Position Papers* (Seido Foundation) in December 1972.

to think that there should have been some sort of handbook prepared for parents, because our congregation is being inundated with letters from parents who, in their anxiety over the fact that textbooks are being used in some places to disseminate dubious theology and currently fashionable psychological theories, have written to secure copies of the *General Catechetical Directory* in order to check against it the textbooks used by some sisters and other teachers of catechetics.

Some of their letters are sad. Investigation reveals not a few to be unfounded in their misgivings, the variations from the Faith delivered to our Fathers being verbal or pedagogical. But other complaints turn out to be altogether too true, and this means that the parents have discovered either that ignorance or partisan theology on the part of the catechist has distorted the content and presentation of the Faith.

This, though unpleasant and sometimes scandalous, has led to a happy result. It has awakened the realization of parents that they are and must be the first teachers of the Faith to their children. It has made the home and the family the fundamental school of catechetics and the Faith, as distinct from mere theological opinion. It has activated, in a manner long desired and necessary, the sense of responsibility in parents not only for the physical life of their children but for that eternal life which faith teaches and makes possible. I think it is this aspect of the publication of the *General Catechetical Directory* that I find most satisfactory; it makes the parents a control on the teacher where the bishop may lack the time or the awareness of the need for such control. Our parents love their children, and they do not wish them to be taught nonsense or to receive inadequate, incomplete, or vitiated presentations of the Faith. The *General Directory* has given them a means of control, although, I repeat, this was never one of the intentions of the publication. The mail proves that it has been.

Seido: Don't you think that it would be valuable from time to time to restate and clearly insist on the principles enunciated in the *Directory*? If so, what aspects of it would you emphasize?

Wright: I agree fully with the premise of this question. The old adage says that repetition is the mother of education. It is fashionable to pretend that by repetition we mean merely rote, chanting, or recital from memory of the same thing again and again, much as children learn the multiplication table.

This, of course, is a parody of the fact. Repetition in catechetics includes, as your question suggests, development by restatement and enrichment by new emphasis of truths enunciated in the *Directory* which might otherwise be taken for granted or neglected.

The *General Catechetical Directory* is centered on the Person and mystery of Jesus Christ in whom God and man, eternity and time, heaven and earth, are brought together. He is the Son of God and the Son of Man. Neither point can be restated or explored too much.

He is at home in what might be called two universes: the universe of space and time, where history takes place, including salvation history, and the universe of the spirit, where God transcends both space and time, where the angels dwell and whence they are sent to do God's bidding and to manifest His power where man's eternal destiny awaits him.

A few critics of the *General Directory* pretend that the book presents Christ as God and in His role as

Redeemer of the individual person more than it presents Christ as true Man, our Brother, and the source of the renewal of the earth, including human institutions and society generally. This criticism is, one feels, without foundation; in any case, constant restatement, exploration, and insistence on the principles enunciated in the *Directory* would clear up the difficulty. I would therefore emphasize everything in the *Directory* — the Church, the social order, all things terrestrial, even space and time, on the one hand, and everything pertaining to eternity, to faith, and to the Trinity, to the world to come, the sacraments by which we reach it, the angels (including the fallen angels), and the whole spiritual order — as brought together in Christ. This Christocentric dimension of Christianity is essential, fundamental, inescapable. It is in danger of being neglected and therefore calls for new and greater emphasis.

Such emphasis must be provided by repeated writing, sermons, devotions, and the effort to find Christ wherever He has Himself declared Himself to be in whatever form: the Real Presence in the Eucharist, the life and action of the Church, His saints and even His sinners, the least of the brethren, wherever there is true goodness and beauty, the sacred Scriptures, the organized Church, and the organic presence of the Paraclete throughout the world. In a word, we cannot think, speak, or proclaim sufficiently about Christ in all the forms in which we find Him or serve Him, human or divine. That is the point of the *General Catechetical Directory.*

Seido: Even after the *Directory* was issued, a number of new catechisms, programs, and courses of instruction which defy its guidelines have appeared — at times with official backing and even the *imprimatur.* It has been said that such publications often contain serious doctrinal or moral errors, that they omit or water down some fundamental truths of our Faith, and recommend unsafe bibliography. Would you say that pastors should not use them to teach their children?

Wright: Your contention is unfortunately true. It always has been, it always will be. The spirit of contradiction is as ancient as Satan, and there is something instinctive in the human condition which prompts many people to say "Ego autem contra", not as Saint Thomas did in order to contradict error, but to proclaim what they would undoubtedly represent as their *academic freedom* or intellectual independence, especially of any guidelines provided by the Church. We encountered this phenomenon for example at the International Catechetical Congress when some militants arrived at the sessions with a whole line of attack prepared before they even heard the presentation of the Holy See and the Congregation; it was at once instructive and delightful to see their chagrin when they discovered that the straw man they had invented to knock down did not even exist!

In a sense, this sort of thing is natural and always to be expected. However, it must always be resisted, by exposure and refutation. Such resistance is an obligation of our Congregation.

Such resistance is certainly a pastoral duty of all shepherds of souls, above all the bishops, as Pope Paul has repeatedly reminded us. As I mentioned above, parents are becoming more and more aggressive in this duty of resistance. Sometimes they are wrong, but quite as often they are right, and they show no intention, thank God, of desisting from the defense of the right of their children to the undiluted, unmuddied, and honest presentation of the clear water and rich wine of the blended reasoning and faith which constitute the religious teaching of children.

In all this work of vigilance and devotion, every form of paternity is involved: that of God, that of the Church, that of our bishops and priests, that of authentic teachers, and increasingly, thank God, that of parents.

Seido: Could you elaborate on the kind of obligation envisaged in the last paragraph of the *General Catechetical Directory* concerning the approval of directories and catechisms by the Sacred Congregation?

Wright: The approval of directories and catechisms by the Sacred Congregation of the Clergy is and will be always carried on in collegiate collaboration with the hierarchies in the various nations and their authorized agencies or catechetical commissions. On occasion, fortunately rare, the Congregation is bound to intervene when a catechism is published by a hierarchy or section of a hierarchy without corresponding collegiate consultation and cooperation on the part of a regional hierarchy or teaching group. Happily, this is rarely the case. Most hierarchies, if only as a part of their desire to promote unity of faith, however pluriform be the methods (theological, pedagogical, and other) of teaching that Faith, are only too glad to consult with us, as we with them. All parties have much to learn from one another, and we are deriving many insights which we can then share with others, from the review of national catechetical texts brought to us by individual hierarchies. By the same token, there is guaranteed unanimity of faith with the universal Catholic world, whatever their differences of theological schools and cultural expression.

There is a single Catholic Faith, despite the wide

variety of cultural and even occasionally theological expressions of that Faith. It is our duty to protect that single Faith so far as catechetics are concerned; it is the duty of national hierarchies to collaborate with us in doing so. Thus, unity and the universality of the Faith are guaranteed, if either quality be missing, the Faith is not present. Hence, the *coordinating* function of the Sacred Congregation.

Seido: The *General Directory* leaves considerable leeway for innovation in the field of methodology. In some catechisms, however, this aspect seems to be stressed at the expense of the specific content. While admitting the importance of a proper methodology, don't you think that the method must be subordinated to the goal of faithful transmission of the whole content of the Faith?

Wright: The *General Directory* deliberately left great leeway for a diversity of methodologies and of recourse to other sciences and systems. It did so because otherwise catechetics would be a sterile body of truths imposed without reference to local aptitudes, needs, means of expression, and inevitable differences of a personal, social, cultural, and even political kind, at least in the broad sense that the diverse political traditions of the people express their diverse cultures. However, as your question suggests, the methodology is a means to an end, that end being the need of instruction in the single Faith. Methodologies are many. They change from place to place and generation to generation. They come under the heading of means and instruments. The need, the great overriding purpose, is the transmission of the Faith and to this purpose methodology, as all things else, is necessarily subordinated.

The wrapper is, or should be, less important than

the gift—though I have encountered exceptions even to this rule. So it is with some catechisms. I have one lying on the desk before me which is poetic, deeply moving, the last word in pedagogy—and a total waste of time, because none of these advantages individually, nor all of them combined, convey the Faith. The package is fascinating; the content is banal and worthless.

An effective methodology is needed and, of course, that methodology is subject to constant change. But the methodology must convey Jesus Christ—and He is yesterday, today, and always the same.

Sometimes it is said, to the offense of sincere people who have worked very hard in pedagogical schools, that they have become *professionals,* not *prophets.* This is true in catechetics when the message of Jesus Christ is subordinated to the methodology of the teacher. But this is a phenomenon of our times and is bound to pass. In my own country, Winston Churchill would not be permitted to teach history in a secondary school (although he wrote a magnificent six-volume history of the English-speaking world) because he never took the course in methodology required by our state accreditation agencies. In my native state, no one is eligible to teach civics, French, mathematics, or anything else unless he has taken a course in the local state constitution—much of which has been unheeded for the best part of a century. This is, of course, utter nonsense and is bound to collapse. So will the contention between *content* and *methodology* in catechetics. The most perfect possible *methodology* must be devised in each place, but its perfection will consist in how speedily and faithfully it transmits the *content* of the Christian message. This is something that bishops, teachers, and parents should watch with special care.

314

Seido: In some of the most recent catechisms, or in their explanatory guides, you often find sentences such as, "Modern exegetical and theological research seems to indicate ..." or "According to modern theology ...", invariably followed by some weird— or at least unusual—ideas. The *Directory,* on the other hand, clearly says that explanations must be made *"sub ductu Magisterii".* Would it be right to say that the so-called modern theology cannot be counted among the authentic catechetical sources?

Wright: I know you did not make up the magic phrase quoted in your question, because I myself have seen it and marvelled at the gobbledygook of some of the phrases used in a sentence like: "Modern exegetical and theological research"—by whom? "Seem",—how clearly? To "indicate",—suggest? imply? demonstrate? etc., etc.

All this may be very well so far as theological or other private opinions are concerned. In fact, it is even desirable. Different times warrant different expressions, and further research may not merely "seem to indicate" but *actually require* further additions to those conclusions already reached during our revisions of long familiar propositions. All this is fine and to be applauded so long as it is in the field of theological exploration, study, and pluralism. But the *unity* of the Faith is always and necessarily dependent upon the decision of the teaching authority in the Church (the Magisterium), and therefore, apart from that Magisterium and its final decision, neither *modern theology* nor *Counter reformation theology* nor *Western theology* nor *Eastern theology* nor *medieval theology* nor even *patrology* or, for that matter, *Scripture* have any autonomy of a final kind, whatever they *seem to indicate.* Some points of modern theology may prove, like whole chapters of Saint Augustine, to be sources of catechetical clarity, but they must be coherent with revelation and the Faith as Catholics understand both. This is not to downgrade any modern theologian or Saint Augustine (or any other personality or school in the history of theology); it is merely to put theology in its proved and positive relation to the Faith. The Faith is a hardy perennial: many theologies are seasonal flowers, and some of them, while adding great beauty to Christian thought and culture, bloom very briefly indeed.

Seido: In deceptively simple statements such as "a complete set of official obligatory Catholic doctrine has never been promulgated", or "Catholic dogma and morals do not consist of a limited set of propositions", some authors stress fluidity, theological progress, and horror of *formulae,* as principles for the preparation of catechisms. Would you like to comment on this?

Wright: I do not suppose that any one of the great professions of faith (the Apostles' Creed, the Nicene Creed or any of the like) contain a *complete* set of propositions setting forth officially and fully all obligatory Catholic doctrine. But the propositions they do set forth are obligatory and are Catholic doctrine. How does one express ideas except in propositions? There is nothing *fluid* about Saint John's statement: "The Word became flesh and dwelt among us."[3] And neither is there anything *fluid* about the proposition: "He will come again to judge the living and the dead."[4] One may discuss details of timing, manner, and other circumstances of these flat propositions—but the propositions themselves remain flat, final, and uncompromising. They are articles of faith. One may call them *formulae,* if he chooses, but that does not destroy their finality. No one can pretend to understand them in their fullness; as articles of faith, they are, by definition, mysteries, but they are not on that account vague. The cult of vagueness may weaken faith in the propositions, but the *mystery* behind them calls out to faith and transcends the shifting aspects of those things of space and time which are easily recognized and comparatively unimportant.

Seido: Some catechisms used in preparation for baptism omit all mention of the Decalogue where the norms of Christian life are explained, alleging that the Decalogue is not a summary of Christian morality since some of its precepts are not reducible as such to the *dynamism of love.* What is your opinion of this approach?

Wright: This question touches on one of the great delusions (sometimes I fear the great deceit) of our times. Jesus said that He did not come to destroy the Law, but to fulfill it. He said precisely that if we wish to be perfect we must keep the commandments—and the commandments include the Decalogue. Jesus summarized the Decalogue or Ten Commandments in stating the underlying principles of the *two laws* which He imposed upon His disciples as obligations quite as binding as any precept of the Old Law and entirely consistent with the commandments of the Decalogue. He said that we must love God and also love our neighbor as ourselves—but he called these obligations to love God and neighbor "the sum of the Law".[5] He did not substitute vague love for precise obligation; He made the obligation a *law of love* and made love the basis of the law. I cannot imagine which precepts of the Decalogue are not an application of the love we owe God or our neighbor or a warning not to neglect in some respect either the commandment to love God or the commandment to love our neighbor.

317

I suspect that this tendency to pretend that Christ talked only of *love* in the New Testament (which He did *not*) and that the Old Testament talked only of *law* (which it did *not*) is due to one of the temptations or heresies of contemporary Christians who are guilty, as Karl Rahner pointed out, of trying to separate the *God of Redemption* from the *God of Creation*. This is rubbish. Jesus Christ brings us a God of Love, indeed; but it was the same love that moved God the Creator (the God of the Old Testament) to create the world and everything in it. It is love which is the bond by which God the Holy Spirit is diffused in the hearts of those who believe. *Dynamism of love* is a lovely piece of rhetoric, but it was present in the leadership of Moses and the preaching of Christ; it permeates the Psalms and the Beatitudes; it inflamed the prophets and the apostles; it is present in the words of Ruth in the Old Law and in those of all the holy souls in the New.

Seido: In the historical process of elucidating the principles of the Faith, the councils of the Church and the Magisterium have introduced many finely honed formulae which precisely define important truths. What is your reaction to new catechisms which disregard these traditional formulations?

Wright: Close examination might reveal that such catechisms as you describe are tainted by modernism, which includes a cult of vagueness. On the other hand, they might merely be efforts at a little poetry as a substitute for precision or a rhetorical style as a substitute for religious substance. I would never make a general denunciation of such books; each one should be treated separately in order to discover whether and how, if at all, it adds a touch of beauty and attractiveness to what might otherwise be, in some cases and places, an unduly cold statement of the Faith—exact but unattractive. I have discovered catechisms which at first glance seemed whipped cream; with more close acquaintance, however, they had merely added some sweet icing to an otherwise substantial cake.

Seido: Memorization has always played an important role in the learning process, particularly in the case of children, although adults are not necessarily exempted. It can hardly be said to be improper of our times. Most of the *new religions* in Japan have manuals which their faithful are required to memorize. Why should it be excluded as a means of catechetical instruction?

Wright: Memorization should never be excluded as a means of catechetical or any other instruction. Otherwise we would have to begin our knowledge of mathematics, languages, systems of thought, manners, and procedures every morning all over again. Failure to use and develop memory as a basic faculty can only produce a kind of *amnesia,* personal or collective. However, memory is not the only faculty with which God has blessed us. Imagination is another and it should not be starved. Intellectual intuition is a third, and it should be constantly challenged and at play. The various faculties through which we acquire fresh experiences are quite a part of the learning process in religion as in everything else. But memory provides *continuity,* and without it we start our day with an empty blackboard. Of course, it is important both in the individual life of the person and in the collective life of a people; no record machines have replaced it.

Seido: The *Catechism of Trent,* compiled under Pope Saint Pius V, has always been a valuable guide for the use of pastors, especially in the formation of adult Christians. According to some writers, "all that stuff has been cancelled by Vatican II". Would you care to comment on this?

Wright: Anyone who thinks that anything was cancelled by Vatican Council II has not the slightest idea of what he is talking about. Vatican Council II repeatedly appealed to the witness and content of previous Church councils. How could it do other than build on the foundations of our Fathers in the Faith—not blast them out of existence—if it intended to develop yet further our understanding of the Faith and our more full access to the Kingdom of God? Whether it kept, in every instance, the exact *words* of the *Catechism of Trent* is, of course, another question; it did not contradict a single *truth* of the Council of Trent or any other historic council. It could not do so—and be true to itself. And yet, of course, one does hear insane phrases like the one you quote, even from surprising lips.

Seido: Judging by your lectures and articles, Your Eminence seems to be particularly fond of the saintly Pope Pius X. He was, among other things, a champion of good catechetics: he even had a new catechism made—at two levels, for adults and for children—which still stands out among many others. Do you feel you could say a word of encouragement for those ordinaries who want it translated or reprinted as a classic example of what you once described as "the handy catechism which retains its use as a chart, providing the clear stars by which to plot our course . . ."?

Wright: Pope Saint Pius X is the patron saint of contemporary catechetics. He encouraged a new form of catechetics by instructing his generation and ours in the old Faith both by word and by example. So have his successors down to and including Pope Paul VI at his weekly instructions in the Faith, where he avoids theological disputations and emphasizes the deposit of the Faith.

History abounds in famous pastoral masters of catechetics. I shall never forget how touched I was when I stood on the very spot, under the square in front of the cathedral at Milan, where Saint Ambrose, centuries ago, personally conducted a class in catechetics and his parish choir. The teaching of Jesus was a continual course in catechetics, promulgation, and explanation by parables and formulae of the Faith He had been sent to reveal.

I would borrow, even still, right and left, from the historic catechisms for adults and for children. I would never cease to reprint them — but I would always be looking for ways to express the unchanging Faith in fresh terms, taking great care that the new terms or contemporary examples faithfully reflected the *ancient Faith*. Thus I would be imitating, in a Catholic way, the example of the householder whom Jesus praised for drawing from his treasury "new things and old".[6]

XX

Contemporary Preaching

Alonso: What do you consider as the principal role of the ordained priest in that work of *evangelization* which is the subject of the upcoming synod?[1]

Wright: By virtue of his ordination, the priest shares in the principal work of his bishop in whatever pertains to *evangelizing.*

The word *evangelizing* is a somewhat awkward word, at least in English, because it sometimes carries with it overtones of an almost denominational and *cultural imperialism,* rather than the concept of the pure and total proclamation of the Word of God given to His Church and through the Church to the world by Jesus Christ. It is something like the word *preachers;* sometimes it would seem that Catholic priests have defaulted the title *preacher* to members of denominations or sects which have placed a greater emphasis on *preaching* than on liturgy, an emphasis symbolized by the central position given the pulpit, rather than the altar of sacrifice, in some non-Catholic ecclesial communities.

In any case, the word *evangelist* should be a spontaneous word on the lips of those who share the work of the successors of the apostles. So is the word *preacher,* certainly when it is used in the context of the total offices and roles of the ordained priest. Other words are also very much in order: Saint Francis of Assisi, a deacon, thought of himself as a *herald "praeco magni Regis",* and every person ordained

This interview was conducted by Joaquin Alonso on January 24, 1974.

322

to preach the gospel should have the ideal of being a herald. *Evangelization* consists substantially in the promulgation of the message of Jesus Christ as transmitted through the Church.

In our day, it is very difficult to draw distinctions between mission countries, where that promulgation has been accomplished in minimal degree or not at all, and those countries where once the good news of the gospel was heard with joy and lived with enthusiasm, but now is half-forgotten or compromised. The whole world has become a missionary world, and every parish is a missionary parish, i.e., a place where the gospel must be heard and lived as a result of the all-out preaching of all priests, whatever their special assignments, offices, or duties, not of themselves, their cultural or other partisan prejudices, but of the gospel of Jesus Christ.

Another word would be the word *teaching,* not as a professional craft, but as the follow-up on the divine vocation to make known the mysteries of God revealed in Christ Jesus. Here, too, the bishop is the supreme teacher in the local church, as he is the supreme liturgist, and all his priests or teachers of the Word are called to communion with him as the bishops in turn are bound to communion with the Vicar of Christ in the total work of *evangelization,* whether on a world front or in the storefront of an inner-city center for proclaiming the freedom and the Faith of the children of God.

Alonso: What themes do you consider most important in contemporary *preaching?*

Wright: The same themes that Saint Paul found important, as did all the major preachers or heralds of the Word of God in the twenty centuries since Saint Paul.

These themes may be found developed in the New

Testament, in the Fathers of the Church, in the historic preachers of the East and the West and in the modern heralds of the message of Christ, who like Cardinal Newman in his English language, have continued Christ's original mandate to the apostles, their successors, and their collaborators.

The themes are obvious, and there is nothing novel about them, although there is always something fresh and topical about their presentation. *Non nova sed nove.* Paul preached Jesus Christ and Him crucified, risen, and forever present in His Church. So did Newman. So did the great traditions of every Eastern and Western nation and the missionaries of every religious order. The preaching of Christ crucified, always central and pertinent, is particularly demanded at the moment when all but Christ seems in process of change or dissolution. *"Stat crux dum volvitur orbis!" "Jesus heri, hodie, ipse et in saecula!" "Ecce ego vobiscum" "sum usque ad consummationem saeculi".* [2]

No themes could be more timely, although all three call for development in concepts and terms made opportune by our space-time circumstances. That is why the *General Catechetical Directory* underscores without equivocation or compromise that, even in an age preoccupied with anthropology and technology, with space and time, all authentic Christian catechesis (and therefore preaching) is *Christocentric,* seeking to relate everything in time and eternity to that Incarnate Son of God who brings together in a single Person all of heaven and of earth. Our preaching, then, must be *incarnational;* it must not hover bodiless over the world or the culture of men.

Closely related to our emphasis on Christ in preaching should be our emphasis on His living presence in history through the action of His Church. Behind this theme of preaching on the Church, her joyful, sorrowful, and glorious mysteries, is a tradition which, again, goes back to Saint Paul and, indeed, the preaching of Christ Himself. In every language and cultural tradition, it has found persuasive expression through the centuries, not only on the level of scientific theology, but also on the level of the most popular preaching. One thinks of Karl Adam, of Humbert Clerissac, of Olgiati, or of Robert Hugh Benson's sermons on *Christ in the Church,* all of them evidencing in terms of their recent times the confession of St. Augustine: "When I talk about her (the Church as Bride of Christ) I cannot stop."

An age in which *the bewitchery of trifles obscures good things* and in which *the world is too much with us* is certainly a time for preaching on the life of the world to come. I, for one, do not remember hearing in a quarter-century a sermon or a homily which made the world *invisible* anywhere as real to me, as is the *visible* world all around me. I recall retreat conferences on how I must face eternity and on the fact of immortality, but somehow they were a little too abstract to kindle in me a desire to be dissolved and to be with Christ in the undying life, belief in which we affirmed so ringingly in the concluding words of the polyphonic Latin *Credos* at Mass: *"et vitam venturi saeculi!"* [3]

Here is a theme that needs a refreshed, convinced, and convincing development in our preaching or *evangelization,* at home and abroad.

The full development of these three themes alone will perforce include preaching on the saints, above all the Blessed Virgin, Mother of the Church because Mother of Christ, the angels, the sacraments as means to eternal life, the Holy Spirit as the Paraclete sent by

Christ to be the Soul of the Church, and the life at the heart of all our living. I sometimes suspect that if these truths of the Christian message were heralded and heard with dynamic force, morality would almost take care of itself, since the Faith would be lived with such conviction and love that the power of evil would be nullified and the need for moral denunciation would be diminished. The knowledge of the Truth, as Christ insisted, makes us free, and therefore the preaching of the Faith could, if it led to the living of the Faith, spare us from excessive moral preachments, since the first freedom of the children of God is that from sin.

Alonso: If the priest as a preacher speaks in the name of the Church and as a spokesman for his bishop or the Magisterium, does not such an official role diminish or even destroy the spontaneity and the personal witness essential to effective communication of the message of the gospel?

Wright: The message is always that of the gospel of Christ and of the Church, but this does not mean that the style of him who proclaims the message is stereotyped or that his personality is *standardized.* Quite the contrary. The Catholic tradition is replete with names of great preachers of the Word who, like Saint Paul, did not preach themselves or any supposed revelations of their own, but poured out themselves, with lively personal insight and intense love, into the work of heralding the Faith transmitted to and by our Fathers. The *style* of successive popes, for example, is notably personal and bears an imprint which reflects their individual gifts and personal readings of the signs of the times from the singular vantage point of their place in the universal Magisterium. So it is with effective preachers of the eternal unchanging Word.

Saint John the Baptist preached penance; so did Saint Francis de Sales. Who can find the content substantially different and yet who can find the personalities and the styles *stereotyped?* Bossuet is not Robert Hugh Benson; their backgrounds, gifts, styles could not possibly be more different, but both preach Christ, the Cross, the Church, and the life of the world to come. Think of the priests who preached our parish missions in years gone by. Their personalities and manner were entirely their own and highly individual; the message, however, was always that of the Church. Some preachers have a special grasp of specific aspects of the *Great Tradition,* and this enables them to bring their unique spontaneity to their special apostolate of preaching. Once again it is a case of *non nova sed nove.*

The Catholic concept of the communion between the individual priest in his work and preaching and his bishop as chief teacher in the local church, a concept given concrete expression by the grant of *faculties* to preach, is not one that makes of the priest a *marionette* or an automaton. It is quite different from the policy and procedure of, let us say, the Christian Science Church, where the place of a homilist or preacher is taken by a reader who has an assigned subject each week on which he reads an assigned section of the official teaching manual of the church and its founder, doing so, if I am not mistaken, without personal comment or illustration. All individual testimonies to the effects of their belief in the personal lives of members are restricted to special mid-week testimonial services, but the preacher is, in fact, a Reader, and the bylaws written by Mrs. Mary Baker Eddy carefully protect her own presentation of the teaching from any individual development whether from experience or from personal reflection.

At the other extreme is the completely free-wheeling, totally individualistic prophetic preaching of the evangelical or camp-meeting, unfettered charismatic service, and the personality-cult tradition once more familiar in the United States, but not unknown elsewhere. The Catholic tradition, so far as content is concerned, has its stable norms and substantial dogmas, but it presents personalities in the history of preaching almost as widely diverse as the number of effective preachers. Could personalities and styles be more different than those whose discourses are brought together in a single anthology from Saint Paul to our own day: Paul, John Chrysostom, Saint Ambrose, Saint Bernardino of Siena, Savonarola, Father Segneri, Bossuet, Bourdaloue, Massillon, Lacordaire, Newman, Monsabre, Schuster, Father Riquet, Olgiati, Archbishop Sheen?

Alonso: Obviously, you are emphasizing that Catholic dogma based on Christ's message underlies all authentic Catholic preaching, and the themes you have suggested as opportune in our day are constant articles of the Faith. But surely there are some themes, bound up with social, or historical conditions, and corollaries of the Faith which call for greater emphasis in one generation or in one place more than in another. What would such themes be today?

Wright: For me, the principal two such themes would be *the dignity of the person* and the *claims of the common good*. I suppose that both are philosophical themes, in a sense, but they have roots deep in dogma. The first is bound up with the basic concept of the *person* as the object of God's creative power and redeeming grace. I was always deeply moved by sermons which emphasized how the love of God for each of us individually was such that if I were the only person in the world

328

who needed Him, Christ would have died for me. Tied in with all this emphasis on the person is the idea of *personal responsibility,* not only for individual sin, but also for whatever individual good may be accomplished, concepts which are under eclipse in our age which has lost the sense of sin, seeing sin not as the result of an evil choice by a person who would have chosen good, but as the result of the blind operation of impersonal forces, sociological or historical, in the face of which the person is powerless.

On the other hand, the false form of a Christian emphasis on the person is the social heresy of *individualism,* which forgets and destroys the common good. Collectivism of an un-Christian kind perverts the concept of the common good, exploits it, and turns it into a political rather than a moral value. Followers of the Sacred Scriptures never forget that God gave all creation into the care and stewardship of mankind. They remember the insistence of Saint Paul that God had made of *one* all mankind to dwell together on the face of the earth in order that *together* they may seek Him.

These concepts of the primacy of the person and the reality of the common good are practical corollaries of the Christian Faith and urgent needs of our generation. Maritain made them the theme of one of his major books on social philosophy. I think that they call for continually renewed appreciation and preaching in our day. I cannot think of a single moral problem which would not be resolved if our heads and hearts were clear on the *dignity of the person* and the *claims of the common good* as these are understood in sound reasoning *under the light of faith.*

All preaching is in the light of faith, and most problems arise when that light grows dim; which brings us back to the need for preaching Christ, the Cross, the Church, the indwelling of the Holy Spirit, and that Eternal Life which puts all things in perspective, whatever the techniques or examples we use in our preaching.

Alonso: Do you see any subject which urgently calls for doctrinal, moral, or *pastoral* preaching at the moment and which more or less brings together these perennial considerations?

Wright: Permanent among subjects which call for pastoral preaching of the most positive kind today is the Christian family.

The family remains the basic cell of society and its interests are bound up with the common good of every other society; even the pagan philosopher defined the common good *"res publica"* in terms of our firesides and altars *"in focis et aris est res publica"*.[4] The family has been the victim of whatever forces have perverted the common good on whatever level; therefore, it must be chiefly by family life, reinvigorated and held in new esteem, that the elements of the common good can be restored to society on every level.

In terms of the person, it is precisely through the family that the person not only enters society but normally enters life itself. For the person, particularly in formative years, the family is the first school of civilization, spirituality, religion, and social relations.

In adult years, the family remains one of the primary objects of piety (*pietas* in the root sense) because the family is a source *author* of our being. Preaching on family life, family liturgy, family loyalties, and even family pride has suddenly become an urgent need of the times. Such preaching need not be narrowly moralistic, but must be realistic, positive, and *pastoral.* This need is worldwide.

In connection with family liturgy and family celebrations, the place of name-saints, guardian angels, the patronage of the Blessed Mother and of Saint Joseph, the reading of Scripture with its constant emphasis on the family, the consecration of the family to the Sacred Heart, family Rosary, all these are a few of the many themes that must be brought back with lively faith and effective development to our pulpits, discussion clubs, and other places where the priest functions precisely as a preacher. Christ remains the invisible Guest at every family gathering, and the family is the Church in miniature *ecclesiola,* as the life the family begets and nurtures is the life of the world to come, elevated and ennobled.

Accordingly, preaching on family life brings us back to where we began: the Christocentric and ecclesial nature of all truly Catholic preaching, as well as the placing of all things here below in the perspective of eternity and the Providence of God. This latter theme, by the way, the Providence of God and history, has acquired a wholly new place and urgency in our times. It calls for long meditation, prayerful study, and courageous speech on the part of our preachers!

XXI

Crisis in the Priesthood

Schweinberg: Your Eminence, Cardinal Wright, our an-
                nouncer has already introduced you and your
                background. Your name is widely known
                and your fame is worldwide as Prefect of
                the Congregation of the Clergy. We know
                that the Holy Father and many others, includ-
                ing yourself as the prefect, have manifested
                a concern about the crisis in the priesthood.
                What in your opinion is the nature of this
                crisis?

Wright: The present crisis probably differs from all the
                hundred other crises in the history of the Church
                so far as priests are concerned in what some of
                the sociologists have called a *crisis of self-identity.*
                I think that perhaps the best expression of what
                has been and is ceasing to be the problem of
                priests is one word: *frustration.* Frustration some-
                times by, perhaps, structures . . . the changed
                nature of the civilization in which we live.
                This is not the kind they were educated for in
                the liberal arts tradition. Frustration about a
                technological age which is more interested in
                getting to the moon than getting to heaven:
                frustration in society . . . the priests don't rate
                socially as maybe once they did. I'm always
                inclined to believe that that is a kink in the
                fellow's personality. The frustration takes many

This interview was conducted by Fr. Cyril Schweinberg, C.P., on
February 3, 1974.

	forms. Happily, in my book at any rate, it is resolving itself.
Schweinberg:	Perhaps we could get back to that a little later in this interview. Your Eminence, have there been similar crises in the past?
Wright:	Scores of them. They began during the lifetime of Christ Himself. If you doubt it, read the sixth chapter of Saint John's Gospel when some of the boys found what He had to say and what He wanted them to do was so difficult that, says the Gospel, "they walked no more with Him."[1] They couldn't take it. Never forget that in the days of Talleyrand, which is only two centuries ago, four thousand priests quit in one year. We haven't yet hit that!
Schweinberg:	Speaking of numbers, would you care to give any number of priests who have left the priesthood?
Wright:	Figures vary. I don't trust the figures that come out of statistical surveys and question-and-answer surveys, because the answer is usually in the question. The merit of your question is that you merely asked for a rough guess. It varies from three to five percent across the world. To hit that medium average, in some places there would be a higher percent . . . up as far as eight to ten percent.
Schweinberg:	Well, thank you for that information. Now, there is another question. From the vantage point that you have had in Rome for the last several years, you are in a position to know perhaps better than anyone which way the wind is blowing as far as the priesthood is concerned? Which way is the wind blowing?
Wright:	The wind is blowing wonderfully. I can almost tell you the day I noticed the change in the

wind. In terms of the priesthood, a total of substantially more than 1,000 priests come into my office every year, uninvited and without previous appointment, just to sit down and talk about their priesthood. When I was a student in Rome, it would not have crossed my mind to walk into the Curia and ask to talk to the Prefect of the Congregation of the Clergy. There are some afternoons when I have to find time to get back and sign my mail. Now these fellows are from all over the world. A couple of them want to tell you how to do your job, but that's all right, too. You learn a lot. Most of them want to tell you what they want to do.

Schweinberg: The interesting thing I find there is the fact that they feel free to do this.

Wright: They'd better; it's their place.

Schweinberg: Your Eminence, do you think that the priesthood in the future, as far as ministry is concerned, will be different than what it has been in the lifetime of most of our listeners?

Wright: If by ministry you mean special works adapted to the times, applying in practical fashion to the unchanging substance of the priestly contribution and witness to the changing civilization and world, certainly it will change. It has already changed many times repeatedly in history. The image of the priest in the community in terms of his proximate contact with the people is always changing. I take it for granted that we are agreed that the essential, substantial, underlying ministry of the priest is to render God present wherever he talks, acts, walks, and functions. This is the special way that Saint

334

Paul used for an ordained *minister.* That's unchanging because that is the work of Jesus Christ yesterday, today, forever the same. Jesus did that work in His way in the narrow and by the very narrow confines of Palestine. We have to do that same work in the contexts of varied cultures, varied civilizations, varied circumstances, varied needs, and varied opportunities—not to mention our extremely varied human talents, which run from nothing to a little bit. The essential mission remains unchanged. If, on the other hand, you mean hyphenated priest, well, the only part that comes under my Congregation is the priest end of the hyphen. The other end is a local thing.

Schweinberg: May I ask you to explain a little more just what you mean by *hyphenated priest?*

Wright: I mean me, the priest-administrator in the Church; or someone else, the priest-sociologist or priest–guidance counselor, or priest-worker, or priest-engineer, or priest-tenor or more often baritone, or priest hyphen anything else. The priest part is unchanging. The other parts are subject to the discretion and prudence of the Church and the self-knowledge and competence of the man.

Schweinberg: Basically, then, there is no essential objection to a hyphenated priest?

Wright: You are a hyphenated priest; you are a priest–communications worker. I'm a hyphenated priest; I'm priest and cardinal, or as they word it in Rome, a cardinal-priest. The fact of the matter is that in the case of both of us, the essential thing is we are priests. If I let the cardinal part of it make me forget that, or you

	let the communications part of it make you forget that, we're in the soup.
Schweinberg:	You mentioned previously that a great number of priests come into your office daily. You have traveled around the world. You have met x number of priests and bishops. Is the crisis that we talked about at the beginning of the program general or is it more specifically an American problem?
Wright:	Well, it isn't specially American and it isn't general; it's *spotty*. In the spots where it shows up, it takes very different forms. The *crisis of the priest* is more acute in those areas where all roles are changing: political, cultural, scientific, and others. Moreover—and I hope no one will misunderstand this, but you mentioned America, I didn't—sometimes there are reasons to worry that both as a people and as a priestly group we can't stand prosperity. We tend to fall apart under it. We get affluent and comfortable and settled down. We sit easy. In the parts of the world where the Church is having it tough, there is no crisis in the priesthood and there is no lack of vocations. I have visited four of these countries, and they come to a little congress I run every year on the redistribution of clergy. It's from them that I get the priests to send elsewhere, wherever they need them.
Schweinberg:	Could we get back to that word you used in the beginning of this talk: *frustrated.*
Wright:	That's a big word. The kind of frustrations can be many. The celibacy kick is one of those, but you don't find that kick where the going is tough. They are working too hard and they go to bed tired.

Schweinberg:	Well, now that you've mentioned that, you know I'm sure that many of our people can't understand how a priest can be laicized and allowed to marry. We know also that there are many couples whose marriages just are not working out. They are held together with Scotch tape, and they are not allowed to get a divorce and remarry. I wonder if you could briefly give us an explanation of this.
Wright:	I have to say first that I buy their bewilderment. I can't understand it myself. In the first place, I don't understand what the word *laicized* means. How do you debaptize a baby? Suppose a bishop in a fit of anger said, "I unconfirm the whole pack of you." This reducing to the lay state, I don't get. First of all, it's not any compliment to the laity, who are a holy people by the way, and I don't know how you go about it. How do you take a fellow who is a priest and say, "Okay, you are laicized from now on." I can understand release from his priestly obligations because he's sick, fed up, or even because he's lost the Faith . . . if only the faith in himself as a priest. I don't understand laicization. On your other point, and by the way it's one on which people feel very strongly, as you obviously know, I don't know why it should be easier to get out of one commitment than out of another. If, in order to get out of the commitment that is the holy thing called marriage, you have to sit around for a couple of years and wait for them to figure out what the case is, well, we ought to be prepared to do at least as much or else come right out flat and say that they are better people than we are.

Schweinberg:	What you are saying is an awful lot and I wish we had more time to explore. However, there is another question I would like to ask.
Wright:	May I interrupt a minute, Father. May I say that dispensation from the priesthood does not come under my Congregation. I say that so I won't get any mail. It comes under another congregation.
Schweinberg:	We won't ask you the name of that congregation. The question I would like to ask you has to do with the great admiration that I personally and so many other priests have for our young men who have made a decision to enter the seminary and our young men who in these past few years have been ordained in critical times. There are others who are hesitant. They feel that they should or would, but there are other things that are making them hesitate. I wonder if you would have a word to say to them.
Wright:	Yes, I have. I have two words. Last summer I gave the priests' retreats in the Diocese of London, Ontario. In the previous spring's ordination class, there were only two priests ordained, and there used to be seventeen. So, during one recreation period, I was walking with these two and I said, "Do you fellows realize what a titanic job you're going to have in twenty-five years? All the rest of these guys will be dead or old and unless you find a lot of vocations, you'll have this place to handle yourself." I'll never forget the answer of a clean-cut little guy. He said, "Cardinal, the Scripture is right, 'They saved the best wine until last.'" I believe that. As for making his decision, I don't want to end on a personal note, and above all not on

a maudlin note, but I remember when I made my decision. My original intention was to be a newspaperman. One afternoon I said to my mother, "Ma, do you think I ought to go into the seminary?" She was reading the paper. As she threw it on the floor she said, "Don't you dare ask me a question like that. I gave you your life. That's on my conscience. What you do with it is on yours. Grow up! Make your decision and find out what you have to offer."[2]

Schweinberg: Your Eminence, that's a good note to end on. Right there, I say there is a sermon in itself ... your mother's words. Now, I wonder if you have one final word to say to all of our listeners, many of whom are not Catholics, but all interested in the priesthood.

Wright: The first one is pray for priests. Above all, you who are not Catholics, pray for priests because you probably see them as functionaries and servants of the Church. They are really not merely that. They are servants of civilizations, and you care very much about that, so pray for them. My second point is this: you remember about the peasant in a dictatorship who was being shown all the marvels of the regime, and they brought him into a radio studio just like this and they said, "One word into that microphone would go to the ends of the world." He said, "Even if I said it?" They said, "That's right." So he walked up to the microphone and he said, "Help!" Well, my word is "help". I hope anyone who is hearing this program will help by looking around to find a fellow who even looks like a possible priest. We've stopped doing that, and certainly no priest has a right

339

to die until he's found two priests to take his place.

Schweinberg: Thank you very much, your Eminence, Cardinal Wright.

XXII

The Invisible Cloud of Witnesses

The cardinal president of the American hierarchy, Cardinal Krol, has given us the great joy of concelebrating this historic Mass. I count it a great privilege that we stand side by side at this altar in that prayer with and for you. I am *sincerely* grateful to have been invited to concelebrate Mass and to offer you these reflections.

I have very few, but not unimportant, qualifications to speak to sisters with affection, admiration, sympathy, and objectivity. The last is because I never went to sisters' school, and, therefore, I have none of the hang-ups I sometimes *think* I detect in the writing and conversation of those who lament our sometimes "bare ruined choirs" and who venture to make some positive, though often enough destructive criticism of all of us, despite the fact that they *did* go to sisters' school![1]

On the other hand, I have learned, in my own case and in that of loved ones, how in their hospitals and social programs (as also in the homes of bishops, of whom I happen to be one) the sisters, precisely as religious women, ministers of Faith, bring a dimension of loving service and sacrifice which transcends all professional competence or *professionalism,* however burdened with degrees and however necessary at the height, for example, of a surgical operation. Finally, in the case of the *Consortium* specifically, here represented in congress, I have experienced personally, observed through documentation, and learned from others who had seen and suffered more than I of the ways of man with man, and woman with woman, how the modern religious, witnessing

This sermon was preached at the Church of Sant' Anna, Vatican City, Rome, on February 24, 1974, on the occasion of the First International Assembly of the Consortium Perfectae Caritatis.

to Faith, can, like the householder in the Gospel, draw forth from the treasury of the Faith, new things while not despising old things; can gaze at new frontiers without turning one's back totally on *everything* that produced one; can renew a great good without jettisoning old ones; can raise new and sturdy walls for the castles of the Kingdom without abandoning the firm foundations built by their predecessors; and all this with the love that presses forward eagerly to new horizons and yet cherish the loyalty that clings to the hills of home — to proven and perennial principles, and even procedures, when these latter are *linked* to principles, and provide the stability which is at the core of sanity and self-identity.

My overriding, dominant desire this afternoon is to put you on guard against the *only* thing that could bring to ruin these high aspirations of the *Consortium.* For there is only *one* thing that could do this. The only thing that could annul your effort to play a mighty part in the strengthening of the Church, vertical and horizontal — the Church that descends from and must rise to God, in loving Faith, and the Church that exists to serve the brethren, all God's children, in love that is prayerful, sincere, unqualified, heroic, and *specifically religious,* respectful of valid secular values, but inspired by sacred vision and commitment — the only *threat* to those aspirations and that determination could come not from outside yourselves, but only from within. It does not come from the critical or the unsympathetic, least of all from the hostile, but only from succumbing to something in yourselves. I mean, of course, *battle fatigue* — the *noonday devil* of discouragement.

Paul Claudel, in his marvelous meditations on the Stations of the Cross, describes the three falls of Jesus. The *first* came from surprise — the stone He didn't know was there. The *third,* and the most pathetic, came from tedium, ennui, *battle fatigue.* [2] Be on guard! This danger you will prevent by joyful growth in the three God-centered and therefore theological virtues, which prepare you to be safely and successfully world-directed, but which fastened you to God, the Source of life and love, and, therefore, which *force* you, having fastened you to God, to serve all whom God has made one family, that together they may seek Him on the face of the earth and, in happy consortium, may find Him. For these God-given and God-centered virtues, the greatest in glory and beauty, the Scripture tells us and experience confirms it, is *Charity,* divine Love, but the most *basic,* the indispensable firm foundation is *Faith.* Without faith, charity is in orbit, it's in a vacuum. Hope is the sustaining vital link between the other two, that keeps us *in there,* motivated by faith and active in charity.

The name of your movement—and it is a movement, by the way, it is not a clique—the name of your movement proclaims your desire to grow in charity. You are the *Consortium Perfectae Caritatis.* That desire is, in itself, an expression of hope. If we didn't have hope, we'd never go to work; we'd never leave the house! And growth in charity is a means to hope. But with charity and hope, we find ourselves grounded on faith, for the realistic reason I just mentioned. Otherwise you'd be in space; you'd hover, disincarnate, over the world that you are called to serve and apart from the God that you are called to glorify. Without faith, there is no enduring hope. With hope, you go forth in the morning, but with faith, you have strength to come back at night. Without faith, there is no hope that transcends the promise or the possibilities of ourselves, and our boundaries, narrow, if not petty, in space and time. It is *faith* that pulls us out of ourselves, to hope, to dare, and to do.

The Epistle to the Hebrews is, by all odds, the most magnificent description of the power of that *faith* which I call upon you to develop as the antidote to every *battle fatigue,* to every defect in hope, every coldness in charity. I ask you during these days together to read, time and again, if the speakers will leave you alone, as I will shortly do, the eleventh chapter of the Epistle to the Hebrews.[3] I choose it because it is particularly appropriate to any period of transition. That chapter is a link between the Old

Law and the New, the old way and the new way in the history of human salvation. All the saints mentioned in it are from the Old Testament. All those mandated to live by it will be the children of the New. It's the perfect chapter of the perfect epistle for a period of transition, in which faith is challenged, hope is fatigued, and charity is selective—in spite of all the court decisions to the contrary—perhaps, indeed, sometimes *because* of them. Charity is wide-ranging, as hope is unconquerable, and faith—well, for that let's turn to the eleventh chapter of the Epistle to the Hebrews, the perfect expression of the Judeo-Christian tradition of faith that goes back to our Father in the Faith, Abraham, indeed to the beginnings of our heritage of belief. The author of the epistle—it makes absolutely no difference who he was since it has the canonical approval of the Holy Catholic Church—begins by putting the pertinent question: And what is faith? He answers: Faith is the substance of the things we hope for. Faith gives substance to our hopes and makes us *certain* of the realities we do not see. It is for their faith that our people of old stand on their record. By faith, we perceive that the universe was fashioned by the Word of God, so that the visible came forth from the invisible.

By *faith*, Abel offered a sacrifice greater than Cain's. By *faith*, his goodness was attested and his offering won God's approval. Through faith, he continued to speak even after he was dead—*do you the same*—by faith.

It is clear from the eleventh chapter of the Epistle to the Hebrews, that faith is not an abstract thing; it is not a purely intellectual thing. Faith is something *lived*, lived unto death.

In the chapter which is the basis of our reflection, there runs like a refrain in every other line these words: *by faith, by faith, by faith*. By faith, Enoch achieved what he did. By faith, Noah, divinely warned about the unseen future, took good heart and built an ark to save the household. By faith, he proved the whole world to be wrong and made good his own claim to the righteousness which comes by faith.

By faith, Abraham obeyed the call to go out to a land destined for himself and his heirs. He left home without knowing where he was to go—just as every girl does who accepts a vocation, and every priest, and every prelate, and every Christian. (Those latter words are not in the epistle; a homiletic application!) By *faith,* he settled in an alien land. He lived in tents—as did Isaac and Jacob, heirs of the same promise—for he was looking forward to a city with firm foundations whose architect and builder would be God. No one, nothing less, however impressive.

By faith, Sarah received the strength to conceive, and from one man, and he as good as dead, says the epistle, there sprang descendants numerous as the stars, as the countless grains of sand on the seashore. You think vocations are becoming few? That we may become again a tiny flock? Oh, remember that perennial promise: as numerous as the stars and the sands on the seashore—if you speak and work by faith.

The epistle continues, all these persons *died* in faith. They were not yet in possession of the things promised, but they had already seen them from afar, and they hailed them, confessing themselves no more than strangers, passing travelers on the face of the earth. The epistle insists that people who use such language, as did they, show plainly that they are looking for a country. If their hearts had been in the country they had left (had they stayed in the world, in your case) they could have found opportunity to return; but, instead, they longed for a *better* country—I mean, a heavenly one—and that is why God Himself is not ashamed to be called their God. There is a city prepared for them; so the epistle confidently proclaims.

By faith, by faith, by faith. And then in an explosion of frustrated rhetoric, characteristic of the writings of Paul, and therefore, I assume, the thought of those influenced by him, the writer says, "Need I say more? Need I say more?" In effect, he says, "*How* can I say more?" Time is too short for me to tell the stories of the others who lived and died by faith—of Gideon, Barak, Samson, Jephthah, David, Samuel, the Prophets. Through faith,

345

they overthrew *kingdoms*, they established *justice*, they saw God's promises fulfilled; they muzzled lions, quenched the fury of fire, escaped death by sword. Their weakness was turned to strength, women received back their dead; and all these renewals and even resurrections were worked by faith. Others were tortured to death disdaining release, to win a life and a better resurrection. Others had to face jeers, fetters; they were stoned. The world was not worthy of them. Why? Only because of their faith.

So, Saint Paul, or the author of the epistle speaking obviously in the Judeo-Christian tradition of Paul, asks another question, a practical question. "But, what of ourselves?" With all this cloud of witnesses about us, we must throw off every encumbrance, everything to which we cling, and run with resolution the race we entered, our eyes fixed on Jesus, on whom faith depends from start to finish—no one else—on Jesus! Jesus who for the sake of the joy that lay ahead endured the Cross, made light of its disgrace, and has taken his seat at the right hand of the throne of the Father.

Then there follow a few lines relating this practical word to you, following this "What of ourselves?" Remember your leaders of old. Rejoice in the new nuns and the new insights, but remember your leaders. Remember your leaders, who first spoke God's message to you, and reflecting upon the outcome of their life and work, all over America and Canada, follow the example of their faith. "Jesus Christ is the same yesterday, today, and forever."[4] So, *do not* be swept off your course by all sorts of outlandish ideas. The very words are from this Scripture, and it's fashionable to be reminded that *all* Scripture, inspired by God, is profitable unto our instruction. Everything valid is traced back somehow to Scripture. Trace back your origins, and the first message and commands given you, to Scripture, and, I beg you, be not misled.

It is clear from this, I think, that faith is a thing that is *lived.* It is clear that it is a dynamic behind a search, and a pushing forward to ever new frontiers of knowledge, perhaps, but above all, of love and being, in service in and under God. They seek a country, a more *perfect* country, a *heavenly* country. They seek a perfection; so teach the words of this epistle.

It is also clear from this epistle concerning faith—its nature, its object, and its power—that, if Faith involves any species of *consensus,* any counting of heads, *democratic-fashion,* then that consensus must include the votes and the testimony of the dead, not merely the testimony of the visible, the tangible, and the very audible. It cannot be the result of a mere Gallup Poll or a sociological survey, unless the research workers are able to penetrate heaven itself and consult the dead all the way back to Abel: "the visible crowd of witnesses". Before we decide the permanent value of what we are doing or changing or thinking, we must answer honestly, and having in mind "the invisible witnesses", these questions in what pertains to our relationship to the God of Jesus Christ:

> Why did you do it?
> What God were you serving?
> What did you believe about Him?
> What was your motivation?

Any democratic counting less complete than that which includes the "invisible witnesses" provides incomplete and probably very temporary evidence concerning the Faith. The decision is apt to be reversed. We must consult that great majority who seem to the eyes of the unthinking as dead, but they live in God. They sustain our faith; they nourish our hope; they remain within the compass of our love, which is why we pray for them, and remember them, and wonder what they think of us, as well we often might.

In any democracy—even by analogy, however thin or however strong—in the formation of the mind of the Church, the testimony of the blessed dead back to Abel and Abraham, to the apostles, the disciples, the One Teacher, Christ, our religious founders, guides, and spiritual ancestors across the centuries,

347

must be reckoned and must be heard, or all you have is *current events,* not Christian Faith—surrounded as we are by such a *crowd* of "invisible witnesses", even when there may be few visible sharers of the vision and the dream.

From this epistle, too, it is clear that faith commits us to a witness which is the very *heart* of the role in the whole of the Church, and therefore the role of every last one of us in the Church—a greatly discussed point at the moment. But what is the essence of that role? A post? An interchange of offices? Rather, it involves the very work of Jesus. Why did Jesus come? He tells us in Saint John's Gospel: "You are a King, then", said Pilate, as if referring to a job, a post, a career; "You are a King, then", said Pilate. Jesus answered, "King is *your* word. *My* task is to be a witness to the *truth.* For *this* I was born, for *this* I came into the world, and all who are not deaf to truth hear my voice." And Pilate decided to have a discussion to debate what is truth, or a survey. Pilate answered, "What is truth?" "I am called to give witness to the truth. For this I came into the world: to give testimony to the truth." And then later, and indeed before, Christ mandated His believers to share this *role:* "Be ye witnesses unto Me."[5]

It is clear that this responsibility for witness to faith is given at a price that is at once terrifying and glorious—terrifying, because filled with all the loneliness and the torment described in the epistle; but glorious because it produces a people "of whom the world is not worthy".

The American bishops have reminded us that of all this—the joyful, sorrowful, glorious mysteries of the life of faith—the great exemplar is the Virgin, ever Virgin, Mother of Christ. Hence the title of their magnificent pastoral, *Behold Your Mother, Woman of Faith.* She is, of course, many, many other things— Mother of God, Mother of the Church, Mother of Sorrows, Cause of our Joy, Morning Star—you know the Litany as well as I do. But in *this* moment of history, it seems well to the hierarchy to remind us that she is the Woman of Faith, but also the minister of faith. And so they wrote: "First came Mary's faith, then her motherhood. Faith is the key also to the spiritual motherhood of Mary. By her faith she became the perfect example of what the Gospels mean by 'spiritual motherhood.' In the preaching of the Savior, His 'mother' is whoever hears God's word and keeps it. All who truly follow Christ become 'mothers' of Christ—'spiritual mothers, as are you'—for by their faith they bring Him to birth in others."[6]

And since we are under the very windows of our Holy Father, Pope Paul, suppose we concluded by recalling what he has said about faith so that his thought may be the premise of your theme: *Religious Woman, a Minister of Faith.* In recent talks on faith, the Holy Father has reminded us that although faith is obscure, it is not blind. It has many titles which justify it, exteriorly and interiorly. As has been said by many, echoing Saint Augustine: faith has its eyes.

Faith has its eyes! What a thought-provoking reflection! And so, the Holy Father underlines, it admits of being studied, of being made more profound, confronted, and even contradicted by the natural order, but nonetheless successfully defended and even applied to the natural order. It admits of being verified by the experiences of life. Experience is not a source of revelation, but it is a source of confirmation of things that have been revealed, things that we can know only by faith. And so also, remaining integral and pure, it can penetrate, with new and great transformations, all things in life and history—so long as it be that faith which is the principle of eternal life, the Gift of God.

XXIII

Witness of the Laity

It is fashionable to linger lovingly on all the crises which confront us now and to talk tediously. In any case, neither in Rome nor here at home do I find evidence of crisis or tension in the work of the Knights of Columbus. Quite the contrary: I gather that the Knights are very much alive and propose to remain so. Let the dead bury the dead, with all due lamentation; as for you, as Catholics and as a lay fraternal order, long life to you!

It is my privilege to be able to direct my thoughts on these topics to an audience composed of Knights, a privilege for which, as a Knight, as an American, as a Roman Catholic, I am profoundly grateful. Were I not this last, ecumenical and humane reasons would prompt my sense of privilege in talking to an order which perpetuates the memory of the Great Navigator who opened up a whole new world of opportunity and progress when, almost five hundred years ago, the pessimists were singing their dirges of civilization doomed.

I propose to address you first as a lay organization at work in total communion with the Church and second as laymen with a specific role of witnessing to the Faith as part of your mission in the general priesthood of our priestly Church. In both cases, I am speaking of the Knights of Columbus individually and as an order, as laymen, though thousands of us priests belong to the order. You are a Catholic lay order grateful to and for their chaplains, laymen with a remarkable history of loyalty to the Church, her hierarchy, and above all to her chief pastor, the Pope, but nonetheless laymen unqualified and unashamed.

This address was delivered at Detroit, Michigan, on August 21, 1974, during the ninety-second annual meeting of the Knights of Columbus Supreme Council.

I am not without some small qualifications to speak of the laity in the Church. In the Second Vatican Council, it was my honor to present on the Council floor not the document on the laity but the plea for the more basic concept of the need for a theology of the laity—an updated statement of the Catholic concept of the place of the laity not merely in the work but in the very notion of the Church.[1] There is still much development of doctrine needed under this heading.

We still need a spelled-out spirituality for the laity—some ascetical theology which will give the contemporary layman persuasive guidelines for his day-to-day spiritual life, personal and professional, much as *The Imitation of Christ* and the great rules of the religious orders have for centuries given to monks. Such a book, or better an entire literature of lay spiritual life, provided it be authentically Catholic, will be the work of minds more sophisticated than mine. Some excellent beginnings already have been made here and abroad, but the task is mighty and delicate and still has a long way to go. I commend the work not to *professionals,* but to those who live in the theory and think and act not as freelancers but within the Church—as do the Knights of Columbus.

Such a lay spirituality must not produce laymen with mentalities that are either *clerical* in any crude political sense or *anticlerical* in any forms occasionally encountered among the sour, the victims of inferiority complexes, or the defensive, political types, bright or boring, so often encountered among us.

It must be lay, but loyal; modern, if you like, but thoroughly consistent with Catholic Faith and order; as *popular* and *personal* as decent democracy, but as *papal* and responsible as the Holy Roman Catholic Church, open to all that is good, true, and beautiful and just, closed only to moral disorder and doctrinal nonsense. It should be humanistic in spirit, Christ-centered in piety, supernatural in divine faith.

In all this, the Knights of Columbus, while making, please God, no pretense at perfection, have much to contribute to our instruction and guidance. Frankly a fraternal order—and therefore with a chartered self-interest which has far from inhibited generosity—constitutionally lay in its leadership and its proper solidarity, the Knights have an unparalleled history of collaboration with the structured Church, from the papacy to parish priests and bishops, from scholarship to brick and mortar construction, from the defense of life to the discouragement of whatever threatens mischief to the Church, and, give or take a very few personality conflicts such as might occur among clerics or within organizations of sisters, all this has been in spirit of prompt response to the needs for support, financial or moral, for which responsible voices of the Church have appealed. If it is true, as it is, that only ordained priests validly may celebrate the liturgy at the National Shrine in Washington, for example, it also is true and symbolical that the Knights built the belltower that summons the people of God to the altar.

There have been publications bearing Catholic names and patronage which have tried to pull the Church to the left or the right of the direction set by her tradition and her supreme teachers; not the publication of the Knights of Columbus. There have been groups of various levels of the Church's thought and action which have undertaken, boasting of the number of their signatories or supporters, to obscure, undermine, or revise the clear teaching of the Holy See or the Vatican Council; not the Knights of Columbus. In their long history in the United States and abroad, they have demonstrated a sense of the Church and her spirit in what they have done and, almost equally important today, in what they have abstained from doing. One may raise questions about this or that possible *sin of omission* in their long history, but even in these matters, they were silent or inactive in the company of others who could or should have known better.

So much for the lay action of the order in the general community. Now some reflections on the broader question of the relation of the laity, typified in the Knights, their witness of faith precisely in the life of the Church.

Saint Paul, still a ranking theologian in the Christian community, reminds us that there are diversities of ministries, gifts, offices, and witnesses in the Church. He does so throughout his epistles. The contention therefore is not a recent *breakthrough;* it has on occasion been neglected, but it never has been denied. However, the organic and organized unity of the Church is such that there is a coordination of these diversified witnesses and responsibilities under a single overriding purpose and authority.

This unity is consistent with diversity, as Saint Paul pointed out in detail. The legitimate and inevitable diversity in the Church is not only consistent with Catholic order, but must be subject to and productive of vital unity in all essentials: doctrinal, disciplinary, and devotional in accordance with the mind and heart of the Church.

This does not mean that we are all alike; God forbid, except in faith. We differ in sanctity; there are saints and sinners in the Catholic Church: saints, because the Church exists to produce them; sinners, or else you and I would not be in it.

We differ in some of our opinions, even theological opinions, so long as such inevitable human pluralism does not violate or compromise divine faith and order.

We differ in gifts, intelligence, offices, and missions, not to mention merits, without reference to these other differences. A priest is not a layman, though a priest is not necessarily brighter or more holy than a layman or vice versa. A patriarch is not a head altar boy or vice versa; a preacher is not necessarily an organist; a theologian is not necessarily a bishop and again vice versa, though he may be a saint and the bishop may not be — or vice versa. A columnist is not, as such, a choirboy — and neither is he necessarily a martyr, and both may hit sour notes or sweet, each in his own particular category. A retired rural dean, working as a chaplain in an old folks' home, is not a professional coordinator of religious education or scriptwriter for a document, but both have their talents, their prejudices, and, alas, their limitations. Star differs from star in brilliance, but it is all one heaven. Office differs from office, but it is all one Church, one Body of Christ, one Faith, one Lord, one Baptism.[2] The temper of discussions arising out of our differences always must be one of love, mutual respect, and good humor. According to Saint Augustine, a great theologian and man, our rule must be: in things that are certain, unity; in those which are doubtful, freedom; in all things, charity.

The important point where Faith is even remotely at issue is unity, but perhaps certain points call for comment: despite the necessary unity in the Faith, there are no *second-class citizens* in the Church—whatever the rhetoric and occasional antics of some ethnic, sexual, or other partisan groups may pretend, and there are no *outsiders* in the Church so far as the valid and conscientious attempt to witness to the Faith is concerned. None! One is of course perfectly aware of the *sniping,* usually highly selective, according to the side of center of the snipers or the sniped, from all sides. These present remarks may occasion distortion and exploitations—but, dear Lord, bishops also have informed consciences and both the right and duty to speak.

The laity have a defined share in the priesthood of the Church, as have other and different shares archbishops and associate pastors, not to say pastors and bishops. There are laity in the Church, and they have various competences, graces, gifts, and ministries—but there are never mere *also-rans* among the believing laity any more than among the clergy, sisters, or coordinators of religious education, or theologians or healers. There are clergy in the Church, and they have various degrees of participation in the hierarchy appointed by Christ and made organic by the indwelling Holy Spirit, but no one of them is an *onlooker,* an *outsider* to the total work of faith and life in the Church—unless he puts himself out by schism, by persistent error, or sheer heresy of doctrine. For better or worse, bad manners or mere vulgarity on any side never puts one beyond the pale of Catholicism or even legitimate discussion.

There is criticism in the Church and the right to raise

questions—but these realities are not limited to *first* and *second* parties, to the exclusion of the body of baptized believers and doers of the Word—they are limited only by built-in, objective norms of deference to the Faith, fidelity to the traditions of our Fathers in the Faith, and a due measure of common decency, good taste, and urbanity in dialogue—or, say better, that *Christian conversation* which Saint Paul says, lifts us to the level of heaven, not the level of gutter-sniping from any direction. Moreover, all these norms yield to the voice of the supreme authority of teaching and direction in the one Church, ultimately the Pope.

Recently, it appears to have been suggested by several—it is hard to say in precisely what terms, so prompt and partisan were the editorializing and embellishments in the polarized press—that witness to the Faith is somehow to be served by collaborative action of the hierarchy and of professional theologians. There appears to have been a certain incompleteness in what was reported on this subject and about the consequent cooperation—needed in its way and within its proper limits—that must take place between the hierarchy, or teaching authority, and the *professionals,* or research people, in clearing up confusion in the Church within our blessed but bewildered land.

Such valid collaboration is all to the good, and may God prosper the project. There undoubtedly is a distinction between professional theologians and amateurs or *untrained* writers on theology. The distinction however is no greater than that between the academic competence of theologians and theological societies on the one hand, and the divinely established teaching authority in the Church on the other. Collaboration, however generous and loyal, does not destroy that distinction, nor does it complete the picture of total witness in the Church. It is with the part of the laity in this witness that I am concerned about here and not merely of the laity who may be *trained, accredited,* or even themselves professional theologians.

The Second Vatican Council puts it this way in the *Constitution on Divine Revelation:*

Sacred tradition and sacred scripture form one sacred deposit of the word of God, which is committed to the Church. Holding fast to this deposit, the entire holy people united with their shepherds, remain always steadfast in the teaching of the apostles, in the common life, in the breaking of the bread and in prayers, so that in holding to, practicing and professing the heritage of the faith, there results on the part of the bishops and the faithful a remarkable common effort.

The task of authentically interpreting the word of God, whether written or handed on, has been entrusted exclusively to the living teaching office of the Church, whose authority is exercised in the name of Jesus Christ.[3]

There is no possibility of doubt that all this is implicitly in the mind of the proposal quoted and misquoted recently, but circumstances of place and audience may have conditioned one reported proposal of collaboration between the teaching authority and *professional theologians.* In any case, one must applaud the proposed plan of the hierarchy to profit from *dialogue* with theologians and *experts,* particularly if these include (and equally) genuine exponents of all legitimate schools of theological thought. It is important to know what the theologians, not merely the most newsworthy ones, are saying, and one must welcome the intent of relaxing the tensions among theological schools of thought and between some of these and the hierarchy, or between some of both and some laity, leftist or rightist. Nonetheless, in the light of valid theological and historical realities, such a proposal and procedure may not be enough, not because of what it stated, but of what is left out, especially if the constant witness of the *simple faithful,* as the phrase used to be, namely, the laity who are the *nonprofessional* lovers and witnesses to the Faith, were even unintentionally neglected.

The exclusion of the witness of others than the *academic peers* of *professional* theologians from the consideration of any crisis in faith could seem to leave out the rich history of the Catholic understanding of the presence of truth in the total Church and of the place of the persevering *indefectibility* of the Faith, indeed even a form of *infallibility* among ordinary believers, as a partial norm at least, of clarification of the Faith.

When we are talking about the total witness of the Church, we must be very careful, if history or theology teach us anything, not to talk too lightly of nonacademic *believers* or to make too sharp distinctions between *professionals* and the *profane vulgar mob*, if by these we mean the believing laity. Wise indeed was the procedure of the Commission for the *American National Catechetical Directory,* which in accordance with sound norms and history, *consulted,* at least, parents and other laity as to the content as well as the methodology of our eventual national catechism. The reasons for such consultation, always within proper norms, are obvious. They boil down to this: responsibility for witness to the Faith is incumbent on every member of the Church; such responsibility presupposes sharing but also differentiation.

It is a little glib to talk univocally of across-the-board coresponsibility in the Church. The responsibility for the Church is shared, but differentiated and subordinated for reasons of common sense, orderly procedure, historical experience, and accurate theology. It is not the same for everybody, but it is real in each case, and no one is excluded, least of all for *academic* reasons. The Spirit is one; the responsibilities and works, ordinary and charismatic, are many and different. Saint Paul said it better than any later writer or orator in several places of his epistles, all of them happily frequently repeated in the liturgy — a reminder through prayer of our constant faith.

All of which leads to some thinking out loud about theologians and their academic or professional peers on the one hand, and the witness of the so-called *simple faithful* on the other. The teaching authority in the Church, above all that of the Pope and the body of the bishops in communion with him, is not at issue here; I know no reputable theologian or sane layman who thinks he himself is the Pope.

Theology includes speculation about the Faith and scientific study of the content and corollaries of the Faith. Faith itself, however, is quite another matter. For one thing, though free in the act by which it is expressed, faith is not autonomous and neither is theology. Though it may and should be mature, its salvific value does not depend on its critical acumen or its documentation. Faith is total acceptance of the Word of God, mandated by the Father through Jesus and transmitted through the Church. The Faith of the Church is Christocentric; the Lord Jesus is the Lord of eternity and the Lord of time, the Lord of history, the invisible Head of the community of believers who constitute His Church, as the Paraclete, the Holy Spirit, that was sent by Jesus, is her soul—which, by the way, is why you and I never must separate devotion to the Holy Spirit, however Pentecostal, from the Incarnation of Christ.

Some theologians offer theology as a human science like any other. In Catholic tradition, theology is the *Queen of the Sciences,* but a science of a unique kind because concerned primarily with God (or it should be) and with commentary on faith. It is a reflection on the gospel, but it is reflection by human reason, if it remains a science in the usual sense. It uses human logic to reach its conclusions. But if it stops there, it is that much less *divine;* it is like any other purely academic discipline. It is at most a species of natural theodicy unless it becomes operative in the service of the Faith and based on reflection in the light of the Faith. Some theologians may be willing to settle for this; the Church cannot.

Theology for the Church is a systematic reasoning on the Faith within the Church, within the Faith of the Church, and whatever polarized toward the extremes, right or left of the received Faith, may do violence not only to the Faith but to truth. One can fall off the edge in either direction from that received Faith, because one may fail to remain within the lines of the two protective forces which tradition recognizes as the infallible teaching authority and infallible believing charism within the Church.

358

A theology which proceeds merely according to the laws of human science—which does not live and move and have its being within the Faith—is a theology which has built-in seeds of self-destruction. Pope Paul has been eloquent and authoritative on this point, notably in his address to the Theological Commission, October 11, 1973, but there is nothing new or defensive or antiscientific in his position. It is not just a *Roman position,* as a curious current phrase has it, but a received Catholic tradition no doubt calling for clarification in occasional details, but not admitting of contradiction.

So exalted, when stated in exact terms, is the role of theologians both as research professionals in the service of the Magisterium and as guides in the service of the faithful, though under the teaching authority of the Church, that one might conclude that all our worries about the content and presentation of the Faith would vanish if the bishops would consult only the professional theologians. But neither history nor theology warrant this overly-simple approach.

Both bishops and professional theologians constantly must have in mind, among other sources of security in the Faith, the constant witness of the laity, the *simple faithful* in the Church. What is their responsibility? What is their *role* in time of doubt and confusion? What gift of the faithful abides in the Church? Theirs too is a constant profession of the substance of the Faith of the Church, a role recalled in Vatican Council II when it added many explicit insights into the theological status and apostolic role of the laity, some of these guided by the great convert, John Cardinal Newman, who frequently spoke and wrote about the witness of the laity. Newman himself was a theologian, probably the greatest one to speak our English language, when he spoke about the transmission of the Faith of the Fathers by the witness of the laity. The substance of Newman's contribution to the council earned him the title "the absent council father of Vatican Council II".

Indeed, together with development of doctrine, his great characteristic was the role of the laity in witness to the Faith. Cardinal Newman prayed for an intelligent and well-instructed laity. And he worked hard to enlarge their knowledge and cultivate their reason—in order to help the laity understand how faith and reason stand in relation to each other. This was the dominant theme of his Dublin lectures on the *Idea of a University* in the 1850s.

In 1859, after his return to England following the rejection by the hierarchy of his *Idea of a University,* he began to study more profoundly the witness of the laity in the Church. Then it was no longer of university people alone that he talked—to use his phrase, *the intelligent and well-instructed* Catholics—but he began to talk about the role of the *obscure, the unlearned, and the weak* in the Church and their role in preserving the Faith.

Mind you, Cardinal Newman never walked out on the proper role of scientific theology or trained theologians. For him, theology was, as we have said, the *Queen of the Sciences* —but man is not saved by theology; we are saved by faith. The just man lives by faith, and faith is the principle of the good works by which salvation is achieved. One may have all the degrees in the world and have scant faith! Everyone knows such people. But in Newman's own case—as in the ideal he held forth—lofty theology and humble faith were blended. Moreover, in the heart of the believer there is always the scriptural prayer: I believe, O Lord, help Thou my unbelief! There is need for courtesy, of course, and due deference on the part of the laity, as indeed of all the rest of us, but it is the mutual respect and due deference of brethren, not of *second-class citizens* or mere *bystanders.*

Next to theology and to the preaching of the Faith, Newman's great field was history. So he well knew and recorded how many times in history the seas have been turbulent for those who study theology and for the greater number who merely walk by faith. A clear corollary of Newman's life and writing is the way in which faith and history are our two anchors whenever the ship of the Church is tossed about because the winds that whirl about it are rough.

Newman, as a historian, wrote about the great Fathers of the Greek and Latin Church, and he liked to draw examples from their times for our guidance in the troubles we can get into, if faith grows dim and mere learning grows great—or put in this way, if theology becomes abstract from living faith and life becomes bewildered to the point of pointlessness. Such is a description of many periods of history—you may live to see one. Newman predicted that we would.

Newman especially recalled the age of the heresy of Arius of which Saint Jerome said: "Suddenly the whole world groaned and awoke to find itself Arian."[4] Everybody seemed to have abandoned the orthodox Faith. Everybody? No, but most of the *big* people, the experts, the powerful, all the way up to the emperor! The voice of orthodox sanity was the voice of the popes—notably Pope Saint Leo the Great—bearing witness to the divinity and humanity in one Person of Jesus Christ. In the diaspora of the bishops, one great man, Athanasius—calumniated, reviled—bore the same witness. He and others stood fast with the Pope, and with them there stood, scattered among the *great,* the ordinary people!

Newman drew from Arianism a lesson he also saw in later centuries recurring when the whole bench of bishops in England went against the Pope in *national apostasy* except one, Cardinal John Fisher.

Linked with Cardinal Fisher was a layman, Thomas More, who had the Faith, but who also knew theology. He had written a book defending, theologically, the Faith against Luther; it was called *The Defence of the Seven Sacraments.* Henry VIII put his name on it and so acquired the title *Defender of the Faith.* Henry played fast and loose with theology according to *circumstances,* however, as did indeed his theological as well as political consultants. But Thomas More and John Fisher, plus many martyrs, lay and clerical, had the Faith that saves and the theology that clarifies and applies faith to life and death. They lived and died by the law and the Faith.

Newman, thinking of the *national apostasy* in his beloved land, recalled the age of Arius and noted that in that time of immense confusion and heartbreak, the divine dogmas concerning our Lord were held to firmly by the silent masses of the people. That is what he meant by the *consensus of the faithful,* and it is to that which Newman appealed on the dogmas concerning Christ, points, by the way, that widely are called into discussion again to the left and to the right of equilibrium.

The Faith was retained, substantially, by the people as a whole, so that Newman felt bound to utter an extraordinary but suddenly timely observation—about how when he read the great writers he came away confused; but what revived and reinstated him (concerning history) was the faith of the people.

When he speaks of this great "infallibility of the total Church believing"— *"infallibilitas in credendo",* "infallibility in believing" —Newman speaks of the witness and role of the faithful as a whole, not a single group, class, or profession. And, as Cardinal Conway has rightly observed, remember that Newman was speaking about the faith of the people as a whole. For Newman, it was not the wise and powerful, but the obscure, the unlearned, and the weak who constituted the real strength of the Church. The people of God unlearned in theological niceties but still recoiling in horror from an Arianism which, they knew in their bones, conflicted with the Faith they had received.

Father Congar has described Arianism and its byproducts as *a heresy of the intellectuals* which was *resisted by a faithful people.* The crucial fact is that an aberration of the Faith which, in human terms, shook the Church to her foundations, was defeated not by the pronouncement of the Magisterium, many members of which were silent, or the explanations of the experts, who were debating with one another, but by the persistent faith of the people of God.

Such constancy in belief of the body of the faithful, so clearly recalled in Vatican Council II, is an infallibility not in teaching, like that of the Magisterium (the teaching authority in the Church), but in believing. It is something which inheres in the body of the faithful as a whole, not in the faithful of this or that region—but the *universitas fidelium,* as Vatican II says: "The whole body of the faithful who have an anointing that comes from the Holy One cannot err in matters of belief [*in credendo*] . . . [for] by this appreciation [sense] of faith, aroused and sustained by the Spirit of truth, the people of God guided by the sacred teaching authority (*magisterium*), and obeying it, receives not the mere word of men but truly the Word of God, the faith once for all delivered to the saints."[5]

So Newman argued that when he wanted to know what the Church teaches, he had the advantage of two forces guided by the Holy Spirit sent by Christ to be at work in the Church. One is the infallibility of the *teaching Church*—the successor to Peter and to Pope Saint Leo the Great, sometimes together with the body of bishops in communion with Rome—and the other is an *infallibility in believing,* present by virtue of the indwelling of the Spirit in the faithful. This latter is not an infallibility in teaching, but it is a sustaining presence of the Holy Spirit in the total Church as a result of which, as if instinct, they say: "That is not true because it is not the Faith we received from our Fathers."

This is what Vatican II meant when it spoke of *the sense of the faith* thanks to which the body of the faithful, as a whole, cannot err in believing—*in credendo.* They can talk nonsense individually or even in groups; they can express themselves with defective decorum or plain bad manners of a personal kind. But broad consensus, the Paraclete, sustains them *in believing,* just as the Spirit of God's truth sustains the teaching Church: the Pope and the bishops in the local churches promulgating the Faith in collegiate communion with him.

The role of the faithful in the Church is to bear witness, to check their *instincts,* as Newman checked his, against these norms:

What did the Fathers teach? To what did the saints bear witness? What is the constant voice of the Church?

The council speaks of *the sense of faith.* I rather regret the usual translation of that phrase as one, by the way, is free to regret many translations. One wishes that it had been translated not *the sense of the faith,* but rather *the instinct of the faith* — for that is what it usually turns out to be.

We already have used the phrase *a feeling in our bones.* There is another current popular phrase: *This isn't mink; this is schmink.* That's what that Latin phrase, the *sensus fidelium,* means in practice: the *instinct* that tells us when articles of faith are under challenge that there is something *fishy* here, *something is going on around here.* Sometimes if we confess to this misgiving, we are in danger of being called *paranoid,* even *divisive,* as were the opponents of Arianism, but we would be truly off-beam if we forgot those two controls: the infallible teaching Church centered squarely on the Pope; and the infallible believing Church identified with the entire faithful people.

One suspects that we need to remind ourselves of these facts today. I think the people especially need to be reminded of it, to be given more confidence in their own mature and loyal instinct as to what the Faith of our Fathers is, as we received it from those who have gone before us, especially in our families. The family is the first, if not the best, school of spirituality and civilization, the cell of every stable society. Hence the central responsibility of parents in passing on a living faith, spiritual formation not merely religious information, sacramental life from the earliest moments consistent with the norms appointed by the Church, the great family of which each family and person is a part.

A final word of caution: Cardinal Newman, in speaking of *consultation of the laity* on any part of faith and order, did not mean to sound out the constantly changing tides of opinion, controlled and measured by public opinion polls, or, for that matter, even the vote of pastoral councils or conventions of *experts.* He, like the Vatican Council, focuses on the living, constant witness of the Faith across the centuries.

Newman never would have believed in a *democracy* in the Faith of the Church unless even the dead voted! We, by the way, have a phrase that *the dead are the great majority.* There are a number of moot points on which the blessed dead might out-vote us! On matters of faith, Newman, like the English martyrs, was always aware of the *great democracy of the dead.*

A moving example of the appeal to *the great majority of the dead* when the Faith itself is in question may be found in Father Richard Reynolds' self-defense before the *new faith* put him to death. First, he called on all the majority of the living faithful in England to be his witness to the truth of the old religion over the new interpretation; then, as dead witnesses, he summoned all the great general councils, all historians, the holy doctors of the Church for the last fifteen hundred years, especially Saint Ambrose, Saint Jerome, Saint Augustine, and Saint Gregory. The trial ended in a vote of *guilty,* but his canonization cancels that momentary nonsense.

What I have been trying to say to the Knights, typical and tested laymen, is simply this: infallibility is indeed a gift of the Spirit to the total Church, but it is not given to each and all the members of the Church with equal title, ground, or purpose. Nonetheless, it manifests itself concretely in two different ways, consistent with one another and with the hierarchical patterns of the Church fashioned by Christ Himself. One is the infallibility of the teaching Church as defined authoritatively. The other is a divinely protected infallibility in the believing Church—an infallibility that is not merely passive, since the faithful, all of us, receive the word of Christ through the teaching authority in the Church, and those who share, directly or by delegation, the missions involved in that authority, in order that once the teaching has been heard and absorbed, the believers themselves may become active witnesses to the Faith which, under the influence of the Holy Spirit, they activate and intensify. The faithful are not only hearers but also doers of the Word, sharers in the infallibility of the Church in proportion to their callings and specific states, custodians of the Faith transmitted by their Fathers and their shepherds, a faith they themselves are called to nourish by lives of grace and in turn to witness, in truth and fidelity, to their children and heirs in the Faith.

In this sense, tradition speaks of *two channels of infallibility* in the Church: one in teaching, one in believing. The first is that of the hierarchy: the Pope in defined circumstances, the Pope and the collegiate body of the bishops in others, for the promulgations, protection, and propagation of the authentic Faith. Theologians have a special responsibility of fidelity to this authority that they may explore, apply, and clarify its teaching.

In the second participate the laity and all of the faithful (theologians and hierarchy included), in a manner at once active and passive, in the sense that they receive the content of the Faith from the authoritatively teaching Church and then live it, witness to it, share it, and defend it, enriching it by experience and demonstrating it by action.

Hence the need that all, especially nowadays the laity, understand that the Catholic Faith is not a kind of baseball game between the Pope or the hierarchy on the one hand, and the theologians on the other, at which the laity are present as *fans,* spectators, or mere partisans. Rather, all the faithful, in diverse degrees and ways, are involved as participants, vitally concerned, however diverse their roles, and none of them *outside* the ballpark so long as they are baptized, believe, and play their respective but full parts—the inspiring *Coach* being the Holy Spirit through the channels of His charisms, but the *Umpire* being always the Lord Jesus and His Vicar the Pope and those who are his confirmed brethren in governing and teaching Christ's Church.

Few organizations have understood this better and implemented it more effectively than the Knights of Columbus. God grant that they may do so for many and fruitful years to come. If the laity are to be a major force in saving the Faith, humanly speaking, in our chapter of history (and many believe they are), then the Knights of Columbus, one million, two hundred thousand strong, have an obvious and supreme part to play in making good the promise explicit in the entrance hymn of the convention's opening Mass: "Faith of our Fathers . . . we will be true to you till death."

But even such loyalty is not enough. You must be catalysts in dissolving the polarization that hurts the credibility of the Faith. The Faith is not conservative. The Faith is not liberal. The Faith just is. It is a *given,* dynamic reality. Live it. Spread it. Love it with all your hearts.

XXIV

The Sacred Heart of Jesus: Persuasive Symbol for Our Times

Men live by symbols. They live by bread and the labor, together with all else of which bread has become the symbol. They live by love in every form that ennobles and sustains the human person; their love has many symbols according to its nature: rings, crosses, emblems of multiple kinds to express feelings and values for which they cannot find adequate words.

Above all, men as mystical and immortal beings live by every word that proceeds from God and tells us those things about Him that most we crave to know because we were created by Him with a purpose, are sustained by His Providence, and must one day face Him. Hence our search for symbols of God.

No man has ever seen God as He is in His infinite and ineffable divinity; if we did, the Scriptures warn us, we would be consumed as by fire. Therefore, God caused His Son to become incarnate that He might dwell among us, and we might see His glory and something of Himself. Thus, through the Eternal Word made flesh, God became visible to us and a symbol of His merciful and loving nature.

But the Eternal Word, the Lord Jesus, having accomplished through loving obedience unto death the demonstration of the merciful compassion of God, and through His Resurrection and ascension, the power of God over evil and death, walks no more among us physically. Nonetheless, He is present among us not only in His Spirit in designated vicars (the poor, the sick, the outcast, the least of the brethren) and in the Church presided over by His Chief Vicar, the Successor to Peter, and His local

This address was delivered at Paray-le-Monial, France, on September 14, 1974, during the International Priests' Congress.

churches, even when two or three are gathered in His name, but also in two special effective symbols which not merely call for our service but speak to us constantly of what kind of God is our God and what is the relation to us of our Christ. They are symbols of the divine realities which most we need to know and to remember in times of crisis. They are the *Eucharist* (Emmanuel, God in Christ, and Christ really among us) and the *Sacred Heart*, the symbol of all love and in Christ the effective symbol of a human love permeated by the presence of Divine Love in the very Person of whom that heart is the organ of life and the symbol of love.

Our Holy Father, Pope Paul VI, linked these two symbols, the Eucharist, with its Real Presence of Jesus among us, and the Sacred Heart of Jesus, sign and source of God's merciful love, in his letter to Cardinal Baggio on the Eucharistic Congress in Ecuador. In this letter, explicitly appealing to the tradition of Pope Pius XII's encyclical *Haurietis Aquas,* the Holy Father linked devotion to the Blessed Sacrament to the cult of the Sacred Heart, which he described as *a living proof and symbol* of the love with which the Divine Redeemer pursues us, even as that "Hound of Heaven" of which the English poet speaks so poetically.

So also the *Pastoral Directory of the Congregation of Bishops,* published this year, associates these two great devotions as central to Catholic Faith and order: devotion to Jesus in the Sacrament of the Tabernacle and devotion to the Sacred Heart as the clear symbol of the love of God, present in Jesus, for all mankind, a love which expresses itself in so many and such different forms, but in the Sacred Heart as an effective, persuasive symbol.

If we priests are to be convincing *other Christs,* in the sense special to His ordained ministers, then the warmth and dedication of our *hearts* must be as persuasive a symbol of our flaming self-giving as the heart of Jesus is the symbol of His love and service. *"Cor Pauli, Cor Jesu",* this was the tribute of a Father of the Church to the Apostle to the Nations. It has been the ideal of priestly spirituality preached from the beginning by saints and theologians. It did not begin with the apparitions of Paray-le-Monial; it is merely refreshed by these for more modern applications.

His Holiness' choice could not have corresponded more with the anxieties and spiritual anguish of the times, nor could the symbols he chose be more persuasive. I shall, under the circumstances of this symposium, confine myself to the consideration of the cult of the Sacred Heart as corresponding with special doctrinal, pastoral, and psychological needs of our times.

Last year, it was my privilege to preach the Spiritual Exercises in the Diocese of London, Ontario. I asked the most recently ordained priests, therefore the youngest, to prepare the program of the Holy Hour. I limited my own suggestions to the inclusion of the Litany of the Sacred Heart, a prayer which, like litanies generally, has tended (temporarily) to be out of fashion in some circles. It was impressive to hear the comments of these truly admirable young priests after the Holy Hour, especially with reference to the litany. "It is marvelous", one said, "how this prayer brings together and identifies with the Heart of Jesus all the preoccupations presently most urgent in our own hearts." It is all there: "Heart of Jesus, furnace ablaze with charity . . . full of loving kindness . . . patient and full of pity . . . overwhelmed with reproaches . . . source of all consolation . . . Heart of Jesus, our peace and reconciliation . . . victim of sin . . . salvation of those who trust in thee". What one of contemporary concerns is not echoed there in the litany?

It has always been so. There is nothing of sentimentalism or mere pietism in the history of either the preaching or the cult of the Sacred Heart of Jesus. In every age those who preached this devotion did so because they found it so persuasive a symbol of the needs of the times and what should be our active, pastoral response to them. In an age of fear or at any rate refusal of new life and negative attitudes toward children, the Sacred Heart of Jesus is a symbol of the human and Christian openness to little

370

ones: His special love for them and accessibility to them; His embrace for them and establishment of deference to them as the norm for perfection according to His mind and heart.

In a period of wayward loves, divided hearts, and centrifugal social hatreds, may our prayer be: *Heart of Jesus, King and Center of all hearts, have mercy on us* — for His heart is the symbol of the centripetal forces of nature and grace, the source of the compassion we must develop in ourselves and somehow evoke in others.

In a day of great technological but often cold science, of knowledge explosion not always accompanied by proportionate wisdom—even of priestly erudition which sometimes threatens pastoral zeal—we priests must make our hearts the living libraries of Christ and our prayer, however great our works or gifts: *Jesus meek and humble of heart; make our hearts like unto thine!*

The special timeliness of the renewal of emphasis on the Sacred Heart is linked also to the invocation of the concept *heart* in the great humanitarian aspirations of the day. An example is the Holy Father's program for relief and development under the name *Cor Unum,* an appeal to the single heart of humanity which must be inspired by and included in the human heart of Christ now somehow, as a result of the Resurrection, immersed in the depths of divinity. The Sacred Heart is a persuasive symbol for our times for another reason. People constantly ask whether there can even *be* a God, above all, a God of love, in a world so filled with injustice, sin, and hatred. They say that a God of love would be moved to heartbreak at the contemplation of so much evil, personal and social, individual and institutional. It therefore becomes suddenly *relevant* to remember the doctrine of the Church that all this evil was *precisely* why God sent His only-begotten Son into the world—and *His Son's heart did break,* lanced by the sword of Caesar!

No layman of our times has brought more sensitivity and sophistication, more knowledge and wisdom, than Jacques Maritain to the exploration and expression of the mysteries of the Faith concerning God and Man, the hope and the temptations of our times. Neither has any one stated so succinctly the theme of my meditation. Let me conclude, then, by quoting Maritain:

> To choose the heart for emblem
> is to dedicate oneself
> to the only heart
> which does not lie—
> and it is encircled with thorns!

This last phrase says what every man knows, but our times profess to understand best of all, namely, that *not knowledge,* the brains, but *love.* Celibacy is a form of love, the love of an undivided heart. But there is *suffering* in all love. Marriage is the sacrament of nuptial love, but surely it has its anxieties and its pains. The love of all things created is touched with melancholy— *Sunt lachrymae rerum. . . .* But all this pain, anxiety, heartbreak is proof of the presence of true love and the source of its salvific power!

XXV

Dear Worcester: A Love Letter

This is frankly a love letter, and anyone who is annoyed by or distrusts sentiment had best stop reading right here in my reminiscence of the first days of the new diocese.

When I received my information from the apostolic delegate about our new Diocese of Worcester back in 1950, it was indicated that there would be almost two hundred thousand people in the diocese. I mentioned this to Maurice Tobin, the Massachusetts political leader, and he said there will be nearer three hundred thousand. *"You see,"* he added, "I have to know!"

Tobin was right—but I worked on the principle that I had been sent to the over five hundred thousand persons in Worcester County (the entire civil population) and that each of them had some claim on me as the Catholic bishop. To my knowledge, no one resented that attitude during our nine years together except, perhaps, one or two, and they cheered up in due course. Everyone understood, one way or another, and with complete mutuality of respect and sympathy, we came speedily to know and love one another in the common work. The future we left to God with open minds, and no hand was turned against us, and every ethnic and religious group helped us become a pulsating part of the heart of the commonwealth.

I left Boston for Worcester at 7:25 A.M. March 7, 1950. To be named bishop of that diocese will always be a flattering appointment, but no man on earth deserves the thrill that was mine when we drove up to High Street at 8:45. Thousands of parishioners and neighbors had gathered at the cathedral corner and on the lawns of the public and parochial schools opposite. It was in that tearful moment that I caught the point of Worcester, a

This letter was written for and published in the *Catholic Free Press.*

point I shall never forget. The crowd was massive, but it had not turned out in such numbers in order to see me. There had been no advance publicity—certainly no photos—likely to create glamor. I especially remember the *Wright to Worcester* photo that appeared in the paper the day the diocese was announced; it was one of the steamrollered faces I frequently leave on a news film so that all the chins get full treatment and the face achieves a one-dimensional blandness that only a mother would look at twice—and then reluctantly.

No, the emotion-charged turn-out that March 7th was not in tribute to the first bishop. In no small part, it was sheer friendliness on the part of our neighbors, as well as an outpouring of the faith of our own people, the faith and openness of a people who will take anyone who is sent *in the Name of the Lord.* The chief factor, the specifically Worcester factor in *both,* I was speedily to learn, was *pride,* a kind of local patriotism, that is and, please God, will remain one of the beauties of Worcester. Something historic was happening to and for Worcester and, by chance, I was part of that something. A privileged part, but a part. The ecclesiastical relation has changed, the sentimental never!

The special pride, the French call it *petit patriotisme,* is reflected in books like S. N. Behrman's *The Worcester Account:* few Worcesterites escape it. This Worcester quality, crossing all lines of creed or other background, George Sumner Barton and I talked about one evening; I talked about it at other times with Tony [Monsignor] Ciullo and with Monsignor Dave Sullivan's mother. Also with that other deeply spiritual woman, Mrs. Aldus Higgins. *Local patriotism* —pride when something new—in this case, the Catholic diocese—was being added to Worcester. That day Worcester, Massachusetts, was taking its place, like Worcester in old England, among the dioceses of the world, and the fact explained many things: (1) The extravagant cordiality of the part played (known and unknown), by the county press but elaborately by the *Telegram and Gazette;* I still have the albums which the *T.G.* beautifully bound for me. (2) The unbelievable activity of the radio stations; I still have the tapes, though I am *anti-cassette!* (3) The *total* — not *token* — participation of the mayor and the public authorities, from the highest-ranking public official to the most recently appointed policeman. (4) The bipartisan, unanimous petition of all the county representatives to the State Great and General Court for the civil charter the diocese needed to function. (5) The anonymous gift to my automobile of a Bermuda bell and a fire siren (usually used by the CYO kids, I'm afraid!), but permitted by a now dead public official so I could get all over the place in no time for anything and everything. (6) The superb mahogany coat-of-arms in place over the door of the cathedral as soon as that gentlest of woodcarvers, our Protestant neighbor, Gregory Wiggin, finished it for Jimmy Knowles, so Saint Paul's would be a "full and proper cathedral" from the first minutes, as Gregory said. The statues — small, but exquisite, from the same neighborly sources — of Saint Wulstan for Old England and Saint Patrick for Old Ireland. Eventually, *La Pucelle,* the Italian Madonna shrine and the Eastern Rite Cross. The crowds of children, always and every place . . . the children, the children, the children![1]

What a place and mood in which to start a diocese! Breathes there the man with soul so dead . . . ? That night I went to bed, unable to sleep, in the suite in the maternity ward Saint Vincent's loaned me until we found the modest but ever so pleasant house on Flagg Street. And no time later the busy nine years began for serious on a gateleg table in the then Mercy Mother House on High Street.

One day a man in a music store on Main Street told me he often wondered if I loved Worcester as much as I seemed to! I'm sure he meant no harm but I nearly challenged his sanity. The love among us in the general Worcester community was never a coldly *fellow citizen* thing; neither did it take any *let's look and see* period to bring it to pass. Thanks to the *openness* and *pride* of our neighbors and our own deep desire to match these in doing our own specific part, I think that, by and large, we all, as a new diocesan religious community, did our part to justify the cordial confidence and open-handed goodwill of the general community displayed so affectionately on March 7, 1950.

The editor's letter inviting me to provide these recollections speaks of three coinciding anniversaries of this season and suggested a brief thought on each in terms of Worcester. What does the Silver Jubilee of the diocese mean to me? The beginning of a joyful love adventure unforgettable in a life that has been blessed with love, activity, and adventure beyond my (or almost anyone else's) possible hopes. But of this, let me speak out of my heart in the homily Bishop Flanagan has so kindly invited me to preach in April.

The Holy Year, in the very form in which it was planned this year (local church and then the following year Rome), brought back memories of how so many of us rode in the buses in which Brother Brassard brought us by the hundreds from the cathedral to the designated churches and shrines all over our one-county diocese. We prayed together in scores of places, from Fiskdale to the Blessed Sacrament Shrine in Barre, from the Providence Valley to the New Hampshire line, all in our own periodic little *holy year* type trips. 1950 was the last Roman Holy Year, and many of us went along to that at the call of Pope Pius XII with Archbishop Cushing, who was then in his most ebullient prime. We had our own Worcester pilgrimage to the places made venerable by the birth, victories, and martyrdom of Saint Joan. We were surely a *pilgrim* people during all those nine restless years, but in all the snapshots I treasure we looked relaxed. And the work at home never suffered—diocesan, ecumenical, or community.

Worcester's part in the bicentennial is in its best possible intellectual, patriotic, and even spiritual tradition. It is personified and exemplified in Isaiah Thomas, a model of whose printing press is before me as I write. In a significant chapter on why the American colonial newspapers were *conservative* (and controlled, as of course, *liberal* papers, without exception, also are),

376

Daniel Boorstin singles out the exceptional role of Worcester's Isaiah Thomas in the *colonial experience*. Boorstin's observations tell us much about Worcester in the Revolution and since.

I suppose that there were Worcester garrisons, regiments, and a battle or two, but it is somehow warm to reflect that the Worcester characteristic contribution to the Revolution was on the level of *ideas* and that the ideas were substantially those proclaimed on the Worcester Court House and preached of old by the patron of the cathedral of the diocese.

Long may the flag that, by rare exceptional permission, flies continually day and night in Lincoln Square continue proudly to do so in the responsible freedom that Thomas expounded! Long may the faith and the friendship from every side and group, bar none, which made the birthday of our diocese so warm and wonderful, continue to flourish until faith becomes clear vision, and love has blended us into a single, strong, indivisible Body, with many members and ministries but one heart and head, as our cathedral's patron prophesied and preached!

I send you all my grateful love and ask you to share it with all your neighbors in Worcester County. Pray hard for me. Ask all to do the same, especially the children![2]

Faithfully and affectionately,

John Cardinal Wright,
First Bishop of Worcester

Vatican City

XXVI

Brothers Helping Brothers

"When brother helps brother, theirs is a strength of a fortress; their cause is like a city gate barred, unassailable."[1]

I need not tell most here present, sentimental as you know me to be, with what gratitude, nostalgia, not to admit tears, I accepted Bishop Flanagan's so-thoughtful invitation to preach at today's anniversary Mass. I promptly fell to thinking of the image that the Diocese of Worcester is suggested in the text I have announced as my theme: it is the image of a *family; brothers helping brothers!*

It has always been amazing to me how quickly we rallied together as a proud family in Christ, *eager to do everything together* and *better than anyone else,* always as brothers and sisters. Symbolically, and a little mischievously, the image began for me the very day that I presented myself to the diocesan consultors, and Monsignor John McCarthy loaned his eye-glasses to Monsignor Francis Phelan so that he could read my letters credential. Naturally, there was no Bible available in the common room, so Father George O'Rourke found his, upstairs in Saint Paul's Rectory, so that I might take my oath. The book fell open at a strange passage which Monsignor Walter Furlong duly whispered to my colleagues in the Boston Chancery, but which I think is being said out loud in Worcester for the first time now, and recorded the beginning of the reign of some wicked Old Testament king!

Unaware of the doom in store for them, people by no means confined to the household of the Catholic Faith began to busy

This sermon was preached at Saint Paul Cathedral, Worcester, Massachusetts, on April 19, 1975, on the occasion of the twenty-fifth anniversary of the diocese.

themselves in new apostolic, holy, community, and fraternal works of every kind.

They did so spontaneously but encouraged on every side, notably by the press and civil authorities; I treasure to this day the magnificent album of our first day as a diocese delivered to me by Mr. George Booth and Mr. Harry Stoddard as a token of the good will of the Worcester community press from the beginning; *it is a superb thing,* beautiful, affectionate, symbolic.

The sun was never up early enough in the morning, nor did it linger long enough in the evening to see all the work of the guilds and societies that spread with holy contagion, encouraged by our own diocesans, of course, but also by our Protestant and Jewish neighbors, by everybody in sight: — the Saint Christopher Guild of taxi drivers, who became volunteer city greeters and ambassadors of Good Will.

The Archangels' Guild, policemen banded to be more than enforcers of the law, but the special guardians of the young and symbols of collaboration in their behalf. I shall never forget the manner in which Captain Bill Mack's troopers lined up at the Connecticut state line March 16, 1959, when I drove to Pittsburgh; we all saluted one another and then cried like babies. *Not all tears are bitter!*

The Firefighters' Guild, first of the unpublicized group of blood donors for our new and shining Saint Vincent Hospital, groups of donors which came to include, on a regular and systematic basis, the Fourth Degree Knights of Columbus, the Freemasons, the B'nai Brith, and the Saint Thomas More Guild for members of the Bench and Bar. *Germs and viruses are nondenominational.*

How shall I speak of our adult courses in theology, which were among the joys of my life in the midst of the brick-and-mortar first years of the diocese. Back in 1952, when, we are told, people could at most repeat by rote a few questions from the *Baltimore Catechism* and were forbidden to think, we averaged two hundred and fifty at our special courses in theology for adults at two centers in the diocese, Pittsburgh and Fitchburg.

The Holy Spirit Guild for public school teachers, all over the diocese, who without compromise of any constitutional theories, demonstrated the affinity between every good teacher and the Divine Teacher; the magnificent concerts and other social events of the year, organized by Monsignor Sullivan and Father Battista for charities all over the diocese, and by the Guilds of Saint Vincent's, Saint Anne's, and Saint Francis. The Catholic Youth Association under Father John Martin and a score of curates (associate pastors!) and thousands of kids (totally dedicated young Christians) with its unforgettable annual parade and convention! The resurrection, Phoenix-like, of Assumption College from the ruins of the tornado. The first National Liturgical Convention—and one of the few successful ones, by the way, despite a wave of storms and floods, at which the Vernacular Society held a meeting in broad daylight. The Newman Symposium—Summer Schools of Catholic Action—Jean Baptiste Conventions, pilgrimages by bus all over the diocese set up by Brother Brassard—first meetings with ministerial associations and some of the Orthodox churches, all this in the 1950s—invitations in all directions to participate in that ecumenism of *friendship* and *common work* which is the necessary basis of common knowledge, and thence *love,* and eventually *prayer.* The pastor of All Saints' Episcopal Church who used to phone to check Latin catchphrases; Dr. Wallace Robbins of the Court House Unitarian Church, from whom I first learned the evil symbolized by company mill houses and company mill stores and who used to come into the chancery to warn me when it was time for him and Monsignor Joe Lynch to make a quiet visit to the Labor Relations Board in behalf of the workers, most of whom came from my parishes, while the owners frequently came from his! We were brothers helping brothers—at the Lord's Acre Day, for example, in civic affairs—all over the place.

When I left Worcester in 1959, I was under the illusion—I *know it was an illusion*—that I knew by name and had shaken hands with everyone in the county—nor has this illusion been dispelled by the cards I still receive at Christmas and anniversaries signed: Yours, Joey or Ted—or Love, Judy, Yvette, or Joan! And so it went for nine unforgettable years of ceaseless activity on everybody's part—with so much social work—Monsignor Sullivan's and Father Battista's Marillac Manor, that *dream* of hope and happiness reborn which one form of the new theology and the mentality of the Supreme Court have *killed—killed—killed*—with what future decay to faith, life, and fatherland, God only knows!

Our wonderful schools under Monsignor O'Brien and the French, Polish, Italian, Lithuanian, and other pastors. Monsignor Harrington's House for the Knights of the Road, the House of Our Lady of the Way. Even he is learning this for the first time, and no one—*but no one*—can identify who the man was of whom I speak—*no one*. A man during the weeks he stayed there came to visit me in the chancery every day. He was the superintendent of a major public school system who had taken without notice to the road. He was picked up from a bench in Elm Park and returned after a little therapy and a lot of prayers to his splendid family and professional post to go on to an educational career on the national level prior to his greatly and justly lamented death. The priest, a typical Worcester priest, who, as his confessor, really turned the trick spiritually, never knew who he was; the political personality who found him a post so he could work here for a while to go home looking like himself and with a plausible story was a Swedish Baptist in city politics who knew nothing about him but took the word of the Catholic bishop. Nor is the case unusual—nor is the Worcester priest, nor is the help from the neighbor. So why rehearse a thousand similar cases?

The question is *this*: starting a new diocese, as we did, on a gateleg table in a parlor of a convent and without a single dime of finances (but with the integrity and talent of priests like Monsignor John Gannon, Frank Manning, and Ed Haddad), in a countywide orchard of sisters, brothers, priests young and old (give or take a minor lemon or two)—and with laity in every town—bursting to beautify and nourish the new diocese and giving us lay advisory boards second to *none,* did any bishop assigned to create a new local church *ever* have so much going for him? So much love and loyalty behind him, sight unseen, from every section of the county and every class and condition of people and not least, be it said *again* as we said it so often back in those days: what Protestant and Jewish neighbors! I correspond with many of them still—scores of them—particularly when I visit the land of their ancestors like Sweden. Did ever any diocese give any bishop such support? The answer is *No! Never! Mai! Jamais!* I am ever grateful to Bishop Flanagan for giving me the chance to say so twenty-five years later.

But it goes without saying that as the one permitted in the Providence of God to be the founder of this great diocese, I am even more grateful to Bishop Flanagan for the leadership he has given, not without much personal pain in the midst of the problems of the times, and with which he has met the exacting demands of new and changing times. He has been willing to try anything to push forward the boundaries of the Kingdom of God, but always at the core of his decisions there is a bit of Proctor, Vermont, granite that has kept his corner of the land prevailingly serene, conspicuously sane, and safe from unplanned flights into orbit. He has been a model of persevering patience, kindness itself, but never a *patsy,* more venturesome, for the sake of the Kingdom, than most would dare to be.

Which brings me to the point on which I would like to touch briefly as our thought for this anniversary season, so great with worry and confusion as the last quarter of the century approaches. Everyone knows we live in times of confusion and contradiction: political, religious, educational, familial, personal. So we ask: is there perhaps waiting in the wings of the stage of history, is there likely to appear suddenly among us, some universal genius, some charismatic personality, as some of us would say today, some hero, some earthshaking saint, who will, of a sudden and dramatically, clear the smog that has undeniably settled in among us, rout the confusion, bring to fulfillment the hopes with which we began and in which we have, in fact, tried to persevere? Is there such a person? Who is he? Where is he or she? How will it be done? This is the half-spoken question in every area of our life: political, economic, cultural, social, moral, and religious. Who is the magician who will flick away our troubles, the charismatic who will depolarize us and make everything clear?

The answer, it seems to me, is that there is no such single person waiting off-stage. In secular human history—and that is where the crisis lies, for it is our *culture* that is superceded, not our Faith; some *theologies* perhaps and even civilizations have collapsed, but not the Faith—in human history it has never been the Napoleons, or the revolutionaries, or any other personalities who have changed the face of the earth and altered the direction of history. So there is only Christ, His Church, His Paraclete, His saints, and His people to whom we can look for any change that endures and matters. The most that can be said is that at time of crisis, some leader sent by Christ, has stood up and dramatized not his own genius or his own charismatic personality, but an *Idea,* an *Ideal,* a great *Truth,* present from the beginning in the dynamic Deposit of Faith, whose time had finally come, clearly and cleanly, and the *word* expressing this timely great truth galvanizes the people of God. In the beginning was the Word—the Word became Flesh—we are always saved by words, by the Eternal Word, the Word of God Incarnate!

Sometimes a great idea excites us, but then dies; the hero or guru who seized on it is remembered briefly; but it ceases to be a rallying cry—it no longer galvanizes. Liberty? Fraternity? Equality? Peace? Love? Progress? Prosperity? Each has its little day—and each goes its way, compromised or crushed or discredited because not rooted in the Faith that saves hereafter and produces good works here below.

The silence settles in around the tumult and the shouting. Doubt and confusion prevail for a spell, perhaps even despair and the morbid forms of what we now call *searching*. Then the Spirit of God moves over the chaos, and when all the experiences and adventures *less than faith* in Jesus Christ have had their brief season, when all the overly grim experiments with the souls of children and the spiritual lives of adults have been played out to their last whim, theory, and defiance, as if inexplicably, but in fact moved by the Holy Spirit, there happens something like the joyful event described in Carl Sandburg's buoyant phrase: "Suddenly everyone burst out singing!"

What will the song be that will so unite and exalt us? Certainly not that *God is dead* — nor *Where have all the flowers gone?* — nor the like. No, it will always be, in one form or another, a hymn of faith: *Innegiamo, il Signore non è morto. Innegiamo, il Signore è risorto!* Lift up our hearts! the Lord is not dead! Lift up our hearts! the Lord is risen! We bless Thee, we adore Thee, we glorify Thee, we praise Thee! *For Thou alone art holy* — we and our schemes are not. *Thou alone art the Lord* — we are instruments and earthbound. *Thou alone art most High.* Jesus Christ, with the Holy Spirit, in the Glory of the Father, amen. . . .

What will hasten that day of laughter renewed and God more manifest among us; in His Sacrament, in His people in His Church, in all creation?

A new theology of hope? *I think not* — there is no hope save in Jesus Christ, and we come to Him through faith. Faith not only is but provides the substance of things to be hoped for, the evidence of things that appear not.[2]

A new outpouring of charity? But this is always the saving expression of *faith*. A new sense of human unity and secular commitment? Again, I think not. All this, if it be vital must follow on that dogma which the patron of this Cathedral Church set forth for our belief: *God has made of one all mankind to dwell together on the face of the earth that they may seek Him!*

So in the meantime our prayer is: I believe, O God, help Thou my unbelief. And when finally through the sound of an angel, or the cry of a saint, or the voice of a child, perhaps, the note that clears the air is struck, and suddenly everyone bursts out singing, what will the song be? "We shall overcome"? "God Bless America"? Again, I think not! There *are* no impossible dreams where there is authentic faith! America is blessed when everyone else is blessed—there is nothing left to overcome—when all are singing again: *Te Deum Laudamus, I believe in One God! Glory to God in the Highest*—Holy, Holy, Holy, Lamb of God, Who takes away the sins of the world, have mercy on us. Grant us peace!!!

God save the Pope! God save this holy church of Worcester—not as part of a spurious national church, but as what it *is:* a local church, under its local bishop, with its local saints and sinners—but its unqualified loyalty to *Rome* and therefore the universal Church—and therefore *God!*

XXVII

Stat Crux

The Diocese of Boston was raised to the dignity of an archdiocese February 12, 1875; the investiture of Archbishop John Williams took place May 2, 1875, and was reported on the front page of the morning papers of Monday, May 3, a copy of one of which I hold in my hands. The dedication of the cathedral took place December 8, 1875, and is reported on the second page of the paper, December 9. We concentrate our reflections on the cathedral itself as the monumental symbol of all three events. The Mass sung at the dedication was Beethoven's Mass in C Major.

Why celebrate the anniversary of the dedication of a cathedral? For that matter, *why* a cathedral? The question is not factitious. It is, in fact, widely asked—together with such questions as *Why Life? Why Art? Why Beethoven? Why Kindness? Why bother?*

The patronage and the history of our Boston cathedral suggest the answers. Its patronal feast is that of the *Triumph of the Holy Cross* —and no one, in the context of theology or history, will dare ask that we apologize here for the word *triumph*. The history of the cathedral exemplifies once again and in a local context the truth of a phrase which echoes the liturgy: *"Stat crux dum volvitur orbis"* —the Cross stands fast while the world whirls and wobbles.

The hymn from the morning prayer of the feast of the Triumph of the Holy Cross puts it this way: "O faithful Cross, you stand unmoved While ages run their course...."

A few years ago, when government welfare agencies were cautiously beginning to impose childlessness as the price of

This sermon was preached at the Holy Cross Cathedral, Boston, Massachusetts, on April 20, 1975, on the occasion of the one hundredth anniversary of the cathedral's dedication.

further mothers' aid and decent housing, an evening national television film summed up the *pros* and *cons*. The last scene was unforgettable: an exhausted farmer's wife in California was asked if she approved of the government program that was forbidding further life for her family if she wished even minimal material aid and housing. She replied wearily: "No, of course I do not approve. But they have taken everything else away from me, why not children?"

At about that same time, a group were protesting the rebuilding of the destroyed cathedral of San Francisco, and inevitably there was a TV report on their protest. I recall no reason to believe that the picketers themselves were poor, nor do I know what they themselves ever did for the poor. Their great cry was: "With so much poverty in the world, why a cathedral here?"

A paradox, or is it? Most of our cathedrals were, in fact, built by the poor. Boston's certainly was. Others helped greatly, but make no mistake about it, our cathedral is a witness by the poor to the fact that the Church is like the Cross: it has a *vertical* beam and a *horizontal* beam; it *soars* toward heaven and it *embraces* the people, people who painfully understand the truth that not by bread alone does man live, but by beauty, by truth, by faith in every word that proceeds from the mouth of God. Men *subsist* by bread; they grow unto personal perfection by beauty, truth, and goodness, the gifts of faith.

Cardinal Newman describes the purpose of a cathedral as well as can be done. It is to proclaim the essential characteristics of Faith, two in particular: *stability* and *permanence*. It represents the beauty, the majestic calm, the mystery, and the sanctity of *religion,* and, together with these, speaks to us of *eternity*. It is, therefore, a symbol of that which is most lacking in contemporary thought: the very concept of transcendence. It is a monument to Him who is the beginning and the ending, the first and the last: "Jesus Christ, yesterday, today, and forever the same".[1]

Stability, permanence, and transcendence. All who take part in the building or commemoration of a cathedral dimly sense that they are somehow caught up in a symbol of God's eternity and humanity's enduring faith. The first planners of its erection, the hands that fashioned it, the pious persons who contributed to it, and the holy lips that consecrated it have long ago been taken from us; *yet we benefit by their good deeds.* Is it not a wonderful yet strange thing that *we* should be fed, and lodged, and clothed in *spiritual* things, by persons we never saw and of most of whom we never even heard their names, and who never saw us or could think of us, decades ago? *What a moving, marvelous proof this of the communion of saints!* A cathedral is the castle on earth of the communion of saints, even when it is filled with sinners, even, as it is fashionable to pretend, occasional hypocrites.

Cardinal Newman noted a religious perversion among partial— *selective*—believers, or what have come to be called *supermarket Christians,* who opt for what they call *internal sincerity unadorned* and reject the manmade adornments, rites, and symbols of cathedrals which, they assert, are *external religion* and therefore without value.

Persons who put aside beauty, even majesty, in the worship of God, on the pretense that thus they may pray more spiritually, forget that God is a Maker of *all* things, *visible* as well as *invisible;* that man is a creature composed of body and soul; that the person, including the believing person, is a psychosomatic unity; that God is the Lord of our bodies as well as of our souls; that He is to be worshipped in public as well as in secret. The Creator of this world is the Father of our Lord Jesus Christ; there are not two Gods, one of matter, one of spirit; one of Law, and one of the gospel of Love. There is *one* God, and He is Lord of all we are and all we have; and, therefore, all we do must be stamped with His seal and signature.

We must begin, to be sure, with the humble heart; for out of the heart proceed all good and evil; but while we begin with the heart, we must not end with the heart. We must consecrate the visible world, its art and treasures, even though *relatively,* as compared with eternity, they are as nothing. But it is our duty to manifest the Kingdom of heaven upon earth, in all the beauty, truth, and goodness of which we are capable. They who submit their wills to Christ, visibly bow their bodies; they who offer the heart, visibly bend the knees; they who honor His Cross inwardly, are not ashamed to proclaim it resplendently before men. They who rejoice *with* their brethren in their common salvation and desire to worship together build a cathedral in which together to worship Christ their Savior and hear His Truth authoritatively promulgated by their successor to His apostles, to have Christ's Person adored at the common altar.

This, then, is the real state of the case: when our Lord blamed the Pharisees as hypocrites, it was not merely for making resplendent the outside of the cup and not purifying the inside also; and when it is said, as sometimes it is, "I don't go to cathedrals and great sanctuaries—there are too many hypocrites there", the answer, all too exact, is simple: "Don't be embarrassed, dear fellow pilgrim on the face of the earth! *There is always room among us for one more hypocrite!*"

The story of Boston's present great cathedral dates back to Bishop Fitzpatrick, who was wont to say, echoing the patronage of the Cathedral of the Holy Cross, "I will follow the Cross to the end", referring to his personal and priestly life.

Somewhere around 1860, the bishop began to plan for the new cathedral, a bold undertaking for a man in his condition. But the joy of seeing Gothic walls and buttresses rise on the site he had purchased was denied Bishop Fitzpatrick and his people. The Civil War had brought financial distress, even disaster. Parishes suffered because of reduced incomes, and the bishop used the money he had collected for the cathedral to meet these problems.

However, with the exception of a few minor changes, Holy Cross Cathedral is Bishop Fitzpatrick's conception.

There is an interesting story connected with the building of the new cathedral. Monsignor Robert Lord, in his history of the archdiocese, asserts that he is telling it for the first time. It

389

involves the Bishop and the then apostolic delegate. It seems that when Archbishop Bedini came to Boston, he was anxious that Bishop Fitzpatrick erect a new cathedral immediately. In a report made by the delegate to Rome, he stated that the diocese possessed only a mediocre cathedral, one of which Catholics were not proud. It was, in fact, the work of Charles Bulfinch, but it was also undoubtedly inadequate to the changes from 1808 to 1868! In those days, Catholics understood fully the meaning of holy pride, and the delegate felt quite properly that the position of the Church in Boston called for a cathedral more worthy of the increased dignity of the diocese. It was all true enough, but it was a question of priorities, as it should always be.

Bishop Fitzpatrick pointed out that thousands of Catholics in the city could not hear Mass on Sunday because of the lack of churches. These he felt should be provided for, before a cathedral was built. And, finally, since the whole burden of a new cathedral would fall upon him, Bishop Fitzpatrick flatly refused to involve himself in difficulties out of which he could not, even indistinctly, see an issue.

It was only after his death and the accession of Bishop Williams that the cathedral began to be in 1866 and 1867, and so there were reserved for 1875 two great joys — Boston's elevation to an archbishopric and the dedication of the new cathedral.

The section of Boston chosen for the location of the new cathedral had a curious history behind it, one which helps explain the reasons for its selection and the subsequent fortunes of the cathedral parish. Throughout the colonial period and down to early in the nineteenth century, most of the site now occupied by the cathedral was still under water. The harbor shoreline, at low tide, was only one hundred and twenty feet east of the old highway (since 1879 called Washington Street). A little north of the site of the cathedral were the fortifications of colonial days: a little to the south was the town gallows, where many a pirate or mere dissident, including, I suspect, some of

390

our own and possibly potentially best diocesans, were hanged, down to the early nineteenth century.

At any rate, it was still believed that the South End was to be the center of the future Boston when Bishop Williams succeeded to the episcopate. On April 26, 1866, Keeley, the architect, came to Boston, and in a few hours' conference with the Bishop the plan was agreed upon. On June 25, the digging of the foundations began.

While it had originally been hoped that the cathedral could be built in three or four years, it actually required nine; even nine years seems a notable achievement, in view of the fact that the Philadelphia Cathedral was eighteen years in building and the new Saint Patrick's in New York twenty-one. There was, of course, no suspicion that eventually the local establishment would shoot the ungainly and noisy elevated train structure smack down the middle of Washington Street, unnecessarily ruining the acoustics within and the property around the cathedral. But such were the times and the taste of those who planned things in an age of little or no careful community planning for persons, or places, or things.

The cathedral impresses, first of all, by its immensity. It covers an area of forty-five thousand square feet and is almost as large as Notre Dame in Paris, Saint John Lateran in Rome, or Santa Sophia in Constantinople. It is larger than many of the famous cathedrals of Europe, such as Strasbourg, Pisa, Vienna, or Venice.

It is built in the English Gothic style of the early thirteenth century, but the walls are of Roxbury pudding stone, trimmed with granite and sandstone—a combination which gives them unusual warmth and variety of color, as well as the quality of coming out of the hills of home.

In a message read to the congregation at the last high Mass in the old cathedral, Bishop Fitzpatrick had exhorted his people henceforth to labor for the erection of the new Cathedral of the Holy Cross, which may promote for ages to come the glory of

God and the salvation of souls, set before the world the splendor and majesty of Catholic worship, and be to us, and to all who may come after us, a just reason of pious exultation and *holy pride.*

At the height of the building, the Panic of 1873 gravely harassed thousands of our people. It utterly destroyed our most prosperous Catholic benefactor, Mr. Patrick Donahue, who deserves mention with the Archbishop on this centenary as representative of the laity who built this cathedral. Donahue had built up the *Pilot* to one hundred thousand subscribers and directed the largest Catholic publishing house in America. He saw the *Pilot* burned out three times in as many years and was bankrupted by the Great Financial Panic. I mention all this because it has, or may yet have, a message even this century later.

I mention another matter because it parallels contemporary preoccupations, but I sometimes fear it has not always been remembered; in fact I know perfectly well that it has frequently been forgotten, to say no more, by some of our own people as well as by our critics. As part of the settlement of Mr. Donahue's problem, Archbishop Williams and John Boyle O'Reilly purchased the *Pilot,* the archdiocese putting up three-quarters of the money. Few journals of that time could have surpassed it for literary excellence, for dignity, sincerity, fairness, and true liberality, or for devotion to the highest ideals in religious, civic, and social life. O'Reilly interpreted and defended the Church's position and the cause of Ireland before the American public. But he was no less effective in preaching to his coreligionists of foreign birth the concepts of duty to the land of their adoption and the principles and ideals of America. He hated injustice in every form, and his heart and pen went out to every injured race, class, or individual, beginning with his own Irish, for whom he had suffered exile to the penal colonies of Australia.

Noteworthy, therefore, in the difficult years that saw the building of the cathedral was the role and influence of responsible, intelligent, and dedicated laity typified by, but far from limited to, journalists like James Jeffrey Roche and Katherine E. Conway.

One seriously questions whether any single part of the world in modern times has witnessed so imposing and so thoroughly admirable an array of adults attracted to the Faith from every class of society and walk of life as that in the generation that built the cathedral and that immediately thereafter. Monsignor Lord's history devotes seven pages to their listing and hints of something of their quality, natural and supernatural, by noting a remark of the Irish Dominican preacher Thomas Burke, on his return to Ireland in 1886.

Father Burke observed that of all the converts he had ever met—converts to Catholicism from many different nationalities— the most intellectual, fervent, and religious were those from New England Puritanism. In Burke's opinion, those converts brought all the energy of their Pilgrim forefathers with them into the Catholic Church. They brought their Anglo-Saxon determination and the conviction that having seen the truth they would stand by it, fight for it, and (if necessary) die for it.

This is a commentary on the truly Catholic Christian influence of our priests, prelates, and people in the generation surrounding the building of this cathedral!

But there were grave problems, too, and the problems have a contemporary air to them. The Panic of 1873 was followed by six years of business demoralization, unemployment, widespread suffering among the working classes, and sharply reduced immigration. The new wave of prosperity that came in 1880 lasted four years, and then came the Panic of 1884 and another depression, which continued through 1885 and 1886.

Nonetheless, churches multiplied, good works spread, religious orders brought their special charismatic gifts, and, having finished the cathedral, the diocese went on to the building of the seminary, where once each year, on the Feast of the Priesthood, in the midst of all his priests, the Archbishop, before the tabernacle of the Lord, renewed his ordination promises.

But through all these years, despite the harvest of distinguished conversions and the consolation of dedicated priests, religious, and laity, the worries of the world threatened the stability of the Cross. The early years of Archbishop Williams' era—those of the new archdiocese and the building of the cathedral—felt the reverberations of the national situation. It is important, by the way, to remember that *there is always a national situation* and that it inevitably plays a part in the whirling and swirling, the wheeling and dealing, in which the Holy Cross must stand fast.

After the Civil War, the Catholics of the North, justly proud of their record during the late struggle, had indulged the hope that isolated but real old discords were buried and that the days of *No Popery* crusades were over.

As a result, it came about that in the late 1860s Catholics began to seek religious liberty for their coreligionists in public institutions; to secure for their own charitable institutions some share in the state subsidies so generously doled out at that time to others; to effect a solution to the school question that would not do violence to the Catholic conscience nor impose upon them forever the burden of double taxation; and to end the situation in which a man who remained a Catholic was excluded from public office.

As a result, anti-Catholic sentiment flared up vehemently at the first attempts to vindicate Catholic rights—attempts that were, of course, construed to be a papal campaign to conquer America. Around the end of the 1860s and the beginning of the 1870s, precisely as the cathedral was abuilding, there were many signs that, stimulated further by the excitement over the First Vatican Council, a new anti-papal crusade was on.

What has recently come to be called *the anti-Roman complex or syndrome,* then limited to *outside* the Catholic fold, became a powerful force in the land. Naturally, there sprang up a crop, small but articulate, of ex-priests and *liberated* nuns, though, be it said, the laity by the large, took it all in stride even when they suffered most, as the laity usually do. The Canadian *new theologian* of the period, a moral theologian, one Father Chiniquy, did the Massachusetts lecture beat in that period, leaving behind him a limited enlightenment and a measure of progeny.

The anti-Roman syndrome, curiously enough, reached its nineteenth-century crest precisely a century ago, in 1875 and 1876. If any of the present generation are sometimes tempted to be disgusted by the attacks on the popes from Pius X to our present Holy Father, from whatever source, let them keep in mind that the years that saw this cathedral dedicated, the years of Pope Pius IX, were years in which any Catholics who went in for compromise or indifferentism did so because, in their poverty or disadvantages, they were forced to do so, as State Senator Patrick A. Collins pointed out in a historic speech in 1872 concerning religious liberty in public, charitable, penal, and educational institutions. There was no choice, option, academic freedom, or personal fulfillment about it; it was simple and clear: give in or give up.

On the national level, the whirling and confusion of the world around the Cross did not then take the form of a battle against *Life* and the basic *morality* involved. It was not this that occasioned the lampooning of the papacy and brought out the remnants of the Black Legend in the political world or caused faintheartedness in a few, *very few,* Catholics a century ago. People were allowed to have children according to their consciences in those days, but they were not allowed to educate them in accordance with the dictates of conscience, except at the crushing expense of double taxation. President Grant, who in general lent his aid to the cause of bigotry as no President of the United States before or since, typified the apprehensions of that time in a famous speech at Des Moines in September 1875, warning the country that if there was ever to be another civil war, he predicted that it would be between patriotism and intelligence on one side, and superstition, ambitions, and ignorance on the other; and that the best hope of averting this lay in

395

granting not a dollar of tax-raised money to religious educational institutions chosen by taxpayers.

The foremost cartoonist of the country, Thomas Nast, of *Harpers' Weekly,* was then pouring forth the worst of his venomous lampoons against the Catholic Church. His subject was usually the then Pope; in all such times, whatever the subject of division, the Pope is usually the sign of contradiction and in the eye of the storm. It is almost one of the credentials of the papacy.

How far away all this seems!—or does it? Are things better or are they worse? Probably about the same. If today we have a more popular ecumenical spirit to protect us and our neighbors against one another, which is good, remember Bishop Fitzpatrick and his place and work in the general community, educational and social, as he was dreaming of this cathedral and his generation of Catholics were seeking the good things and true that we might share with our neighbors. The years 1861 and 1862 brought great community honors to the Bishop. The groups that conferred these distinctions upon him were to some extent influenced by his active support of the Union in the Civil War, but their tokens of esteem, including his honorary degree from Harvard University, justify the statement that, while they were a recognition of his personality, they were also a recognition that, on the level of human differences and natural antagonisms, among the basically rational and decent people of a community, and nowhere more than in Boston, to the banquet of the wise all worthy persons come freely—in 1975 as in 1875.

We are told that the present season of the Cathedral Jubilee comes in times of financial anxieties; so did the season of its building. We are told that there are now hopes of great ecumenism; so there were here from the beginning. Never forget that it was Boston Protestants who financed the excavations of the historic archeological treasures under the titular church of Boston's first cardinal, William Henry O'Connell. There were many brave men before Agamemnon's time; the myth of progress is of all myths the most deluding will-o'-the-wisp. But, come fair time or foul, *"stat crux dum volvitur mundus"* ... and the Cathedral of the Holy Cross is the proof, if proof be needed, of the authentic *Boston Roman Catholic* determination to share the fate of the changing general community while bearing witness to the unchanging witness of Christ and His Cross in the midst of all the change. "O faithful Cross, you stand unmoved while ages run their course. . . . "

Nor can things ever be so tense or troubled here in Boston but what we remember the motto of our very city, chosen by our Protestant founders out of our ancient Latin: *Sicut cum patribus nostris, sic sit Deus nobiscum!*—As God was with our fathers, so will He be with us—as he was with Cheverus, Fenwick, Fitzpatrick, Williams, O'Connell, Cushing, and our fathers. So He *is* and *will be* with Umberto Medeiros and his flock and all his good neighbors.[2]

XXVIII

Crisis in Vocations: Causes and Solutions

Many suggestions have been made about how to solve the problem of the shortage of vocations for priestly life. It is often feared, however, that some suggestions could make the problem worse, at least for the time being, while others, obviously, could relieve the shortage of the clergy and consequently the diminution of the number of vocations. One of these is the widespread *special* participation of lay *ministers* in the life and mission of the Church, for example: in the proclamation of the gospel, the distribution of Holy Communion, and the pastoral life of the parish. Certainly, the role of laymen in all forms of the life of the Church must be increased, independently of the number of priestly vocations, because laymen, by virtue of baptism and confirmation, have various specific and subordinate tasks in bringing about the Kingdom of God in this world.

There is no doubt that the increasing number of *ministers* in the liturgical, homiletic, pastoral, and particularly catechetical action of the Church, can help to solve the problem of the shortage of priestly vocations in many parts of the world. Sometimes it is a question of a formal restoration of the activity of lay *ministers* in the Church; at other times of the intensification of the work of lay *ministers* in the hitherto neglected fields of the life of the Church; sometimes again of an explicit and real ratification of lay *ministers* in growing participation in the common priesthood of the Church.

We must recognize on the other hand that the danger always remains that this extension of lay *ministers* beyond the limit of

This article was written for and published in the June 12, 1975, issue of *L'Osservatore Romano.*

necessity and reasonable need could create a process of attrition, counterproductive to the increase of vocations for the ministerial priesthood.

More than one right-thinking person has found the *crise de démolition* in which liturgical, homiletic, and pastoral functions have been not so much shared by laymen, also with due canonical delegation, but *almost abdicated* by the priests and delegated to laymen for reasons of *pure convenience.*

Another cause of the shortage of priestly vocations is certainly confusion in the world about the real nature and dignity of the ministerial priesthood, the specific work of priests, and their presbyterial obligations. The document of the Synod of Bishops on the *Ministerial Priesthood* and the document of the Sacred Congregation for Catholic Education on formation to priestly celibacy are very important in this connection. A great many difficulties in the crisis of priestly vocations could be eliminated by laying stress on the special nature, dignity, and responsibility of the ministerial priesthood in comparison with the royal and common priesthood of the Church.

Another cause of the diminution of priestly vocations is certainly a momentary theological confusion due to a considerable extent to the great changes in the nature of our culture and consequently in the educational system. For a clarification of this confusion, the latest decree of the Sacred Congregation for the Doctrine of the Faith on the restoration of the *Imprimatur* for books to be used in the religious instruction of the young can help us a great deal.

There is yet another cause for the diminution of priestly vocations, that is, the depreciation of the importance of the sacrament of penance and of spiritual direction. In the past, many priestly vocations arose from the prudent care and the indefatigable concern of holy priests. Today, the concept of real spiritual direction has been replaced by *psychological guidance.* Thus from the schools of a lay society in which religion and spirituality are almost completely neglected owing to the lay spirit of our times, few priestly vocations emerge.

Finally — this may be the most important cause — the diminution of vocations for the priesthood, as well as of other *vocations* in social life, must be regarded on the basis of the general crisis, the lack of a real meaning of life, that is, the life of man considered as the offer of himself in response to God's call. The lack of the sense of this divine professional vocation is felt everywhere, for example, of dedicated doctors, of teachers in the schools who really feel called by God, and in other social services. Today, medicine, teaching, and the other forms of public service, instead of being considered as a real divine vocation, have become *careers,* work to *earn a living,* or mere jobs.

It seems to us that the world of today has lost the sense of divine vocation as man's response to the call of divine Providence, which calls each of us to do something special — something specific; on the contrary, it seems to us that modern civilization has paralyzed the reality and the mystery of man's divine vocation. This applies not only to priestly vocations, but also to their *professional* vocations and to the institution of marriage and the family itself. Once it was said that marriages were made *in heaven,* to stress a real vocation to marriage and family life as a committed response to implement the plan of Divine Providence, which guides the world and human history. Today, on the contrary, the indifference to priestly vocations is generally proportionate to the evil of divorce and frivolity in choice of marriage as a *real vocation.*

Other causes could also be listed: but the one fundamental basis of all this situation remains: that is, *the loss of the real sense of human life and therefore a personal vocation in our culture.*

It is obvious that in this age of materialism and self-sufficiency, hedonism, and the consumer society, it is the duty of those who are responsible for priestly vocations and for the stability and holiness of marriage and the family, not only to denounce these evils, but above all to teach in every possible way the mystery of Divine Providence and its operative existence in the history of the world, and consequently the true meaning of human life, at the service of God Himself in our brothers.

XXIX

Saint Elizabeth Ann Seton

Elizabeth Ann Bayley was born in New York City on August 28, 1774, two years before the outbreak of the Revolutionary War.[1] Her parents were of mixed French and English ancestry, Richard Bayley descending from a distinguished English lineage, combined with some French Huguenot blood, that immigrated to America in the seventeenth century. Her mother was the daughter of an Episcopalian minister, with ancestral roots in England. The couple had three children, all girls; Mary, Elizabeth Ann, and Catherine.

The American personality of Mother Seton was manifest in her outgoing, even aggressive, performance as a woman. She was the mother of five children, which was in a healthy American tradition, the grandmother and aunt of two archbishops; she became the spiritual mother of thousands of nuns and the inspiration, as of a few years ago, of eight colleges, 160 high schools and academies, 447 parochial schools, 91 hospitals, 69 schools for nursing, six orphanages, eighteen day nurseries, twenty-one infant asylums, three technical schools, six retreats for nervous diseases, five homes for working girls, one leper home, eight schools and asylums, two schools for deaf mutes, twenty commercial schools, and three normal schools under the direction of her Daughters of Charity; apart from the grace of God, there is no other reason to explain the phenomenon except the courage and spiritual inspiration of one American woman. For from her, whether in the white cornetts of the French peasant, or in the black caps of the Italian widow, or in other styles, stem directly or indirectly all the Sisters of Charity in the United States of America.

This sermon was preached at the Catacombs of Saint Calixtus, Rome, on September 15, 1975.

It is appropriate, when speaking of the American aspect of her story, to mention here that 154 of her spiritual daughters served on the battlefields of the Civil War; 189 of her merciful religious administered comfort and consolation to the American soldiers in the Spanish-American War. Clearly, a great spiritual force started this avalanche of self-sacrifice and charity.

Elizabeth Seton was the most beautiful debutante of New York in her day. Her father, Dr. Richard Bayley (her marriage name was Seton, her maiden name, Bayley), was the first governmental inspector of quarantine in New York and was also the first professor of anatomy at the medical school of Columbia University. Her stepmother was a Barclay, after whose family New York's famous Barclay Street is named. One of their descendant blood-relations was Franklin D. Roosevelt, President of the United States of America. "In my childhood," said Franklin D. Roosevelt, writing in 1931, when he was governor of New York, "my father often told me of Mother Seton, for she was a very close connection of the Roosevelt family, and her sister-in-law was, I think, my great-aunt. Her distinguished nephew, Archbishop Bayley, was a first cousin of my father, James Roosevelt, and they were very close friends. In our family, we have many traditions of the saintly character of Mother Seton."

Mother Seton began life as a Protestant and was not converted to the Catholic Church until she was a widow with five children. Thus, the leading vanguard of the Catholic sisterhood in America, the Sister of Charity, is the result of the courage and sacrifices of a one-time Protestant girl, debutante, a wife, a widow, a convert, a nun. The set-up is rather extraordinary. It may be profitable for us to inquire into the details of the strange career.

In this Year of the Woman, 1975, it would be difficult to imagine a more appropriate candidate for the honors of the altar than Mother Elizabeth Ann Seton, a woman who clearly excelled in just about every career to which historically a woman aspires and on which civilization itself depends for the special gifts uniquely present in a woman.

Mother Seton symbolizes so many vocations of the valiant and holy woman, so many experiences and attributes sometimes eclipsed in our day but essential to the good life: she was a devout Protestant who came to the fullness of the Holy Catholic Faith with no little suffering and great triumph over the noonday devil of human respect; she was a young woman of goodness and grace, of fine family background, but keenly conscious of the dignity and needs of the underprivileged, the sick, the immigrant, and the poor, braving in the service of these even as a young woman the human respect of her socialite kin and companions, especially her devoted but domineering father. A *belle-of-the-ball* in the manner of the early nineteenth century, she captured the heart of William Seton, a prosperous merchant seaman, in due course married, gave birth to children, and thus became the mother of a family.

Financial disaster and physical infirmity hit William Seton almost simultaneously early in their marriage. Mother Seton and her husband, together with one of the children, left for Italy to see if they could straighten out the fortunes of her husband's merchant marine business with the Filicchi family, whose business had gone bankrupt and suffered for the Barbary Wars then ravaging the seas. Mr. Seton, having been confined to the pest house in the harbor of Livorno, died of the plague. His widow found hospitality with the Filicchi Family, whose palace is now a school for girls and where there is a monument commemorating her stay. In that devout household and at the many shrines in the countryside and the mountains around the city, she found not only the consolation but the vision, courage, and determination of the Faith. She returned to New York preferring to be baptized and received into the Church in her own country. She declined the graciously offered services of Archbishop Carroll, preferring to receive her sacraments of initiation in the Church from the parish priest of Saint

Peter, in New York, the first Catholic American church into which she set foot.

Her story as the mother of two families, both of which she personally nurtured, the family of her husband's children and the family of her daughters in religion, is well known, and I need not repeat it to the many of her spiritual daughters, granddaughters, and American admirers here present for her canonization. She was, in the temper of the times, cut off by her conversion from any part she might have in the fortune of her own family, and she therefore decided to open a school, which she conducted with sufficient success to attract the attention of a benefactor who later helped implement her dream of a religious school and the acquisition of the property at Emmitsburg, where her story as a religious educator and foundress really began. Emmitsburg remains the spot to which our thoughts turn, from Rome to home, now that the work begun in the modest white house there has resulted in her being elevated to the honors of the altar of the universal Church by her canonization as a saint.

Wife, sterling character, complete woman, educator, foundress, pioneer in American education, and American, she is now a saint—but not for any one of these reasons alone. The saint's business, as a beloved priest pointed out in a book on Mother Seton some years ago, is to create a vent between time and eternity, between natural goodness and supernatural aspiration. The saint is not merely a noble character possessed of a number of sound, natural virtues; but rather a creature struck by the lightning of God's grace. And a person struck by lightning behaves, in the force of the impact, very strangely at times. Saints are neither conventional nor predictable. Mere *good citizens* are.

The canonization of saints, like the liturgy in its way, is also a form of pedagogy by which the Church teaches us what we should be in our respective vocations, whatever they may be, or condition of life, whatever it may be, lay or clerical, male or female, intellectual or, for that matter, perilously close to dull. Canonization is not so much a piece of triumphalism, though the unthinking may make it out to be, forgetting that triumphalistic celebration of saintly heroism is certainly, humanly speaking, perfectly legitimate in the presence of a personification of the triumphant Christ such as is the heroic virtue of a saint; canonization is a form of teaching, a part of the pedagogy of the Church.

What, then, is a saint and why do we Americans rejoice in the canonization of this particular saint even while insisting, if our theology is straight, that while here may be a saintly American, there is no such thing as an *American* saint and while there may be and assuredly are many Americans who are saints, there are no *saints* who depend on their *Americanism* or *Gallicanism* or *Italianism* or *Orientalism* for their sanctity. It merely means — *but this means very much* — that while her nationality may or may not contribute to the essence of her sanctity, her sanctity does very much for her nationality, and if we had enough citizens like her, her nation would become indeed a holy place as well as the beautiful and admirable place we know it to be.

The place of America in all this simply means that she has become the first native-born American saint, a Catholic saint in the American manner. She looked, acted, talked, worked, prayed in the American manner. There is a French manner in sanctity, and it has half filled the litany of modern saints. There is a Spanish manner, an Italian manner, an Irish manner, an African or Asiatic manner. Not so long ago, the Church paid tribute to the English manner in sanctity to the point of martyrdom. There is a German manner, and within the year we have seen it honored by canonization. There are all sorts of holy *ways of life* in the universal Church, because the Church is supranational, and in the matter of saints she has no one set style, any more than she has any one set architecture, being capable of using Byzantine, Gothic, Romanesque, Rococo, African and Asiatic, or contemporary patterns in the expression of Sacred Mysteries, which transcend the potential of any of these particular styles, American included.

It is no lack of patriotism—God forbid—nor excessive piety—
God well knows—that makes me insist on this point, but the
simple recognition that we all share in what is more than likely
to happen. Our mass media, including our Catholic American
mass media, will for the most part and quite understandably and
decently, given our flare for publicity, headline the news that
now the Church has an *American* saint, whereas the fact is that
America has a canonized saint who is the symbol of the millions
of uncanonized saints who go to work or tend their homes or
suffer in their hospitals or do their good works or beg the help
of their neighbors all over the United States. It does not mean
that the Church recognizes that a Catholic convert has *made
good* by American standards; it means that an American wife,
mother, educator, religious, convert to Catholicism, and heroic
woman has *made good* by God's much more exacting standards.
It is ample reason for *American* rejoicing, but it is a cause for
universal joy in the Church throughout the world and in heaven
itself. Let no one misunderstand my seeming playing down of
the *American* part in all this. It was very real in the production of
the personality of Mother Seton herself.

That she was an American in every sense naturally rejoices
Americans now that she has been formally numbered among the
canonized communion of saints. America has and has had millions of uncanonized saints, but none combined so many personal vocations and qualities proper to her sex.

She felt the first movings of the grace of the full Faith in Italy,
in the city we call Leghorn and the Italians know as Livorno;
her husband is buried there and his grave in the Protestant
cemetery has become practically a place of pilgrimage for us
who visit Livorno in memory of Mother Seton. Our debt to
him is very great.

It was my privilege, together with Bishop Guano of Livorno,
to have helped to start the first parish in the world in honor of
Mother Seton as soon as she was beatified. We began with a
temporary church.

Now the groundstone has been laid for the permanent church in Livorno. The ambassador to Italy from the United States, John Volpe, delivered a superb address, which made the American Sisters of Charity and us other Americans very proud.[2] He spoke of the concept of Charity, charity in the family, charity in the neighborhood, charity in the nation, charity in the international society, and charity in the Church. The throng was greatly impressed to have a grandson of Italy come back to speak of the work and the spirit made possible by a daughter of America who found the Faith in Italy. He added a touch of humor (and perhaps made a mild point) when he observed to the mayor of Livorno (a Communist) as the bishop invited him to stand with the rest of us when the traditional box was placed in the hole of the cornerstone, that no American Trade Union would have tolerated a hole so badly cut to receive the box. He noted further that he, more than the mayor who was a lawyer and university graduate, could make the criticism because he had been a cement carrier in the United States and rose to the top of the construction firm for which he carried the cement. No offense was taken, and the land of Mother Seton was *one up* so far as the opportunities for progress of working men are concerned, while Italy retained its historic priority in inspiring sanctity.

The mayor gave me a beautiful book of etchings of Livorno at the time of Mother Seton; it is in the Motherhouse at Seton Hill in Greensburg and greatly admired for its artistic beauty and the spirit in which it was given.

The last hours of Mother Seton have lessons worth brief recall because of the reminder that sanctity, even in the American manner, is based not merely on good will but on dogma.

Her last Communion was made on the last day of the year 1820: Sunday, December 31. To the sister who tended her during the night and prepared her for the final reception of the Blessed Sacrament, she exclaimed: *"One Communion more . . . then our eternity."*

Later when asked what counsel she would give them as the last from her lips, she exclaimed: "Be Children of the Church. . . . Be Children of the Church."

Shortly before the hour of two, on the morning of January 4, Mother Seton made a great struggle to enunciate three words. The ejaculation was clearly to have been, "Jesus, Mary, and Joseph." But only one word came, the faintest, the most difficult, yet the most definite that she had ever uttered in her life. It was "Jesus!"

And that was the last word of the first Catholic school nun in America, whose soul went before the judgment seat of God to plead not only for the remission of her own sins but also, and perpetually, for the spiritual needs of her fellow countrymen.

May God have mercy on anyone, American or other, who plays fast and loose with the Person, the message, or the Church of that *Jesus* Whom Mother Seton, like Saint Joan, invoked with her last breath!

XXX

Pope Pius XII: A Personal Reminiscence

During these days commemorative of the centennial of the birth of His Holiness, Pope Pius XII, all who ever saw him, and there are millions given the period in which he lived, will have their cherished reminiscences of the personality and accomplishments of this first Roman-born Pope in generations. For most, the majesty of the man will be recalled by his remarkable monument in Saint Peter's. For all, the brilliance of his intellect (he was a kind of one-man council) will be symbolized by the massive output of his writings and discourses, particularly to learned societies which gathered in Rome. To soldiers who occupied the city in the various phases of the horror that was World War II, he will be remembered for his affability and the non-paternalistic manner in which he made them feel at home at audiences. The undersigned once wrote a small book entitled *The Pope and the War;* it opened with the recollection of an English soldier who sought sanctuary in the Vatican when the city was occupied by other forces than those which had brought him to Rome.[1]

Everyone who had the privilege of audience with him will recall the incredible blend of aristocracy and simplicity which characterized this gracious man, truly a prince but, whatever his bearing, a man of the people. Again, the present writer had occasion to witness these aspects of his character. On the golden jubilee of my parents, I sought audience for them at Castelgandolfo. Certainly, Pope Pius XII had received hundreds of couples observing their anniversaries as were my simple parents, but he made the occasion so intimate and unforgettable that one writes of it with tears. My mother wore a bracelet from which

This article was written for and published in the March 11, 1976, issue of *L'Osservatore Romano.*

were suspended the silver images of the heads of all her children and grandchildren. Nothing in the world was more significant to her. The Pope noted the bracelet, as he must have noted many such on grandmothers proud of their numerous progeny, and he asked my mother to extend her arm so that he might examine individually each of the score or more of the medallions. He inquired after the name of each of the children and invited my mother to identify them: what they were studying, what were their qualities or problems in the family. At the mention that one of them was a doctor, the Pope said: "Tell him I bless his hands!" The mention that one was in the process of having a large family elicited from the Holy Father a special blessing for those children. The point is that everyone was mentioned, and my mother brought home a message for each.

The last Easter before the outbreak of World War II is still springlike in the memories of those of us who were in Rome that day. Before the Holy Father came out on the balcony of Saint Peter's to chant the Blessing to the City and the World, the famous Irish tenor, John McCormack, lifted up his voice in the music of *The Psalms* and his voice floated out of the crowd and over the heads of the scores of thousands in the square. When he had finished, another voice, in another corner of the square, sang out the *Agnus Dei;* I have never found out who it was, but some said Beniamino Gigli and others said Giacomo Lauro Volpe. In any case, neither voice was more celestial than that of the *Pastor Angelicus* who, a few seconds later, chanted the papal benediction.

In almost no time, all the world was at war, and I suppose it was the last occasion before that war that Saint Peter's Square was crowded with the sons and daughters of every nation.

But the reminiscence that is uppermost in my mind during this week is in a way more sombre and significant, but also more revealing of the personality of Pope Pacelli. In my native city, there had broken out, the Lord knows why or how against the background of the place, a *heresy,* the condemnation of which appears at length in Denziger, the compendium of historic *heresies, the Boston case.* It was a curious mixture of the crusading zeal of a thoroughly good priest and the tendency to be more Catholic than the Pope on the part of a few superardent converts, most of them connected with the nearby university. The group were joined by a thoroughly respectable but somewhat perfervid group of first-class intellectuals, about a half-dozen in number. They decided to denounce the archbishop and his auxiliary (myself) to Rome for undue liberalism in holding out the chance that a non-Catholic might conceivably, under due circumstances, one day gain heaven. The group then numbered perhaps some sixty or seventy adherents, men and women pledged to the most literal and extreme interpretation of the axiom *"extra ecclesiam nulla salus".*

The axiom, in its proper context, was and remains completely true, but the manner of its application and some of the excitement it caused created no little havoc in a city usually fairly serene in religious matters. I need hardly remark that the most devastating aspect of the entire affair, at that point at least, was the announcement on the front pages of the paper that the archbishop and his auxiliary bishop were both *heretics* and had been denounced to Rome.

It was suggested that I should make a trip to Rome to answer certain questions about the movement in the mind of the astonished Supreme Pontiff. *The Boston Heresy* was inevitably condemned by the then Holy Office over the signature of Cardinal Marchetti-Selvaggiani, but the Pope personally wished to supervise and, indeed, *make* the official English translation which would be sent to the archbishop of Boston for promulgation in the battle zone. As a result, I spent three hours one sunny morning in the Holy Father's study at Castelgandolfo while he personally, with infinite care, reviewed and revised a document which would mean so much to the peace of mind of thousands.

I shall never forget how painstaking, precise, and scholarly was the Chief Shepherd of Christendom as he labored on a document designed to restore peace to a relatively small corner of the Christian world.

However, in the midst of this intent and absorbing work, which the Pope was determined to do himself, he found time to be (if the word is not irreverent) mischievous, if only to relax the manifest seriousness he attached to the situation. He indicated, with a smile, as his eyeglasses glinted toward me, his conviction that we Americans, whatever other virtues we might have, did not, in fact, speak *the King's English*. He listed examples of words which, by British standards, we obviously mispronounced, and I held my breath when some matching spirit of mischief prompted me to say that the situation was considerably more grave than His Holiness supposed. I said that the British even had some words that we did *not* have, and when he asked me why we did not have them, I replied that they denoted posts we did not have in America, as, for example, *vergers* and *bobbies.* He laughed and replied that the Revolution has apparently had more results than was popularly supposed.

When the work of translation was done to his satisfaction, he read it through with great silence and, again, great solicitude. I remember that he closed his eyes as if in prayer when he had finished the reading of the English version and then, with a gesture of finality, he put it to one side. I asked his blessing, which he promptly gave. Then he told me that a fellow citizen of mine was in charge of the astronomical observatory on the roof of the papal summer residence. Glancing at the clock, the Holy Father said that he had audiences waiting for him but that I would be expected to join the Jesuit Father (Father Miller) in the observatory on the roof where we might have lunch together.

I returned to Rome that afternoon far more aware of what a pastor and teacher, spiritually close to souls and their confirmation in the truth, a Roman pontiff must be. Moreover, when I read the observation of Jacques Maritain some years later that the popes of the twentieth century are a clear manifestation of the presence of the Holy Spirit at work in the Church, as millions came to observe a few months ago in the Holy Year in the case of the present Holy Father, I knew exactly what Maritain meant.

XXXI

Jean Daniélou, S.J., 1905–1974

At the request of my good and dear friend Father R. Stephen Almagno, O.F.M., I have decided to write my recollections of that incomparable theologian (better, mystic) Cardinal Jean Daniélou, S.J. During the years of Vatican Council II, I acquired the conviction that the late Cardinal Daniélou—then called, and even now still lovingly remembered simply as, Father Daniélou—was a person upon whom one could count to attempt the impossible, if need be, in the service of the Church.

I little dreamed that the one major favor I would one day ask of him as a public speaker and theologian was very close to the impossible; certainly, I did not realize that the request presented personal difficulties of a paradoxical kind that, as will be seen, involved almost a self-revelation on his part which, for him, must have added spiritual embarrassment, yet which—in the light of the circumstances of his death, so soon after—now seem prophetic.

In 1972, Monsignor Luigi Novarese and I—on behalf of the Volontari della Sofferenza—planned a unique congress for several hundred bed- and chair-ridden arthritic, epileptic, and other men and women who had been confined by their afflictions for years. It was required that the suffering person should have been schooled in suffering over a long period and totally dependent on others for transportation from floor to floor in the hotel, or place to place in the Austrian town selected for a congress which would discuss with great seriousness the theme: *Lo Sviluppo della Persona dell'Ammalato,* that is: the integral development of the person (as a person) in the case of people thus afflicted. In a

This article was published in the June 1976 issue of the *Bulletin des Amis du Cardinal Daniélou.*

word: with great seriousness, as if it were a gathering of intellectuals, and not simply suffering people, we intended to present lecturers on and subsequent discussions about the manner in which the superior reality of suffering completes, rather than diminishes, the human person; the Christian vocation of suffering as a vocation among the *careers* open to the children of God; the Blessed Mother as the model and teacher of all who suffer; and suffering itself as a source of hope and joy in the life of the Church, society itself, the nation and—indeed!—the world, if the world would be made holy.[1]

In other words, the questions about which our bed- and chair-ridden guests were to hear not sympathetic, spiritual *fervorinos,* but serious intellectual discussion was quite simply this: Why suffering? Why physical evil in a world and a person created by a good and loving God? The speakers were to stimulate discussion among the suffering themselves, and this was all the seriousness usually found at a symposium on a far more superficial question and with far less significance to the most intimate depths of the person and lives of the discussants.

Now, obviously, such a symposium required a top-flight theologian; a theologian who would be prepared to discuss precisely the part in the plan of God of physical suffering. The first name to occur to me was that of Cardinal Daniélou, although in retrospect, it is difficult to say why, since his vast field of professional theological work was seemingly (in retrospect) to have been so far removed from so tortured a subject.[2] So, I wrote to Cardinal Daniélou, asking him to be our principal speaker. Now, the difficulties were obvious: the congress was to be held at Mariazell in Austria—and not in Paris, Rome, or New York City. It was going to meet in early June 1973—in the most busy season possible for a theology professor, a time of examinations and professional demands upon his time. The subject matter was hardly the ordinary preoccupation of a cardinal of the Holy Roman Catholic Church, at least in a cardinal's public discourses—and especially since I had made it clear to Cardinal

Daniélou in our correspondence and over the telephone that we would expect a truly theological discussion and not a consoling message or pastoral presentation! The distance and the inconvenient location of Mariazell, with respect to the Institut Catholique or Sévres are obvious. There was, moreover, a further detail that Daniélou turned into a joke.

The public authorities had, you see, just declared the region as unsanitary; for Mariazell had been hit by a hoof-and-mouth epidemic—a misfortune that had caused other scholars and prelates to justify their inability to be present. The shrine of Mariazell— where there is venerated the holy image of *Magna Mater Austriae*—and other public places were made antiseptic, but faintly ludicrous, by mats and even vats filled with disinfectant at every instance. And where Cardinal Daniélou finally arrived and was brought up to date on the hoof-and-mouth preoccupation, he exclaimed in his so characteristically shrill and almost mocking voice: "Mais où est le problème? Tout ça, c'est une histoire de vaches!"

However, his acceptance had not been all that ready and lighthearted. With reference to the hoof-and-mouth disease situation, he said nothing; but he very properly pointed out the problem of distance and the means of transportation, as there is no airport at Mariazell. And he made absolutely no reference to or mention of his own physical condition, which, in fact, made all these factors (distance and transportation) doubly difficult for him. This problem—his physical condition—I understood only later when I discovered the necessity that Cardinal Daniélou go to his room for periodic inactivity and complete rest, so far advanced and painful was the heart condition that later became the horrified interest of a whole world. Instead, Jean Daniélou had protested his lack of qualifications to give so basic a talk as that we had asked of him, namely: *The Ontological Necessity for the Church That Daily We Complete the Passion of Our Lord Jesus Christ.*[3] He protested with a vehemence, only partly feigned, that for him this was an impossible subject on which to speak in

French, to an audience composed of 90% Italians. "Remember!" he said, "it is my vocation to talk to university students and to conventions of theologians who haven't a care in the world, let alone a pain in their bodies—and both groups are used to the jargon of a professional theologian. For me to speak to the people you are bringing together would be a further infliction upon them and an impossibility for me. Call on me at any other time, but what you are now asking of me: C'est rigolo, c'est absurde. . . . "

Nonetheless, when my request was put in certain terms, which now seem to have been inspired by God Himself (so close was Cardinal Jean Daniélou to his own death), Daniélou the theologian, probably the most sublime member of his craft then alive, gave way to Jean Daniélou, S.J., the priest (certainly among the most sensitive of his day), and Cardinal Jean Daniélou, priest and theologian, gladly accepted to come to Mariazell. More, when once there at Mariazell, he remained beyond the time of his agreement.[4]

At Mariazell, in June of 1973—just a year prior to his own death on May 20, 1974—Cardinal Jean Daniélou gave what must have been one of the most remarkable theological lectures in our times. Since his audience was largely Italian—with some Austrians present—and since he could speak only in French—or, as he said: "If you prefer, in Latin!"—the problem of communication was rather formidable. It dissolved, however, in the very first minute of his lecture; by a judicious use of words, rendering French in its approximate Italian equivalents, by mimicry at which he proved a genius, by acting out even the most abstract theological propositions he had proposed, and above all, by his contagious personality, with a reservoir of personal suffering underneath it (of which I, at least, was not aware), Cardinal Daniélou so captivated and controlled his audience that the rest of the speakers stayed in the hall, away from the last-minute preparation of their own papers, in order to marvel and to learn. At the conclusion, people who could not applaud because of

418

physical disability, or because their arms were literally tied for years to their beds and chairs, gave him an *oral ovation* as a result of which he sank into his chair and buried his tearful face in his quivering hands.[5] When later he could speak at all, so great was his emotion at this totally unexpected success—within which he had made profound theology intelligible to people racked by pain—he said: "Jamais de ma vie je n'ai donné, jamais je ne donnerai à nouveau une conférence théologique qui purifie à ce point mon âme elle-même"—I have never given before and shall never again give a theological lecture which has so purged my very soul. His gratitude to me for the invitation, so reluctantly accepted (partly out of humility, partly out of realism) was profuse to the point of embarrassment. Daniélou then went among the sick who wished to thank him personally for a talk it was assumed they would never understand. And with that vivacious smile—which we now all realize was, in fact, in no small part charged with personal pain), he kept repeating: "Mais ce n'est rien du tout. Nous sommes tous théologiens, et tous malades."

And it is certain, as the text of the questions and subsequent discussion among and by the sick themselves confirms, that Cardinal Daniélou was not talking in the air or over their heads. Instead, a suffering man, with an angelic mind, had gotten through (as could no one else) to a physically anguished audience, with minds bewildered by years of lonely suffering. And, who probably never had been taken seriously as members of a deep theological discussion. This striking fact alone helped explain in retrospect the avocation about which those who only knew Daniélou the theologian were totally unaware. Once the professor's day was done, Jean Daniélou the Jesuit-priest-theologian was able, in a most remarkable way, to reach prisoners, the alienated, the outcasts, and the victims of so many species of spiritual as well as physical humiliation. When I heard the news of his death, the whole talk at Mariazell came flooding back to mind, not as in any way a paradoxical inconsistency with some of the insinuations which his enemies permitted themselves in their own false strength.[6] And my recollection of Cardinal Daniélou's presence and conference at Mariazell illumined, as nothing else could, the soul that could sustain the destiny that—not in a high moment of sunny triumph—for long years had been that of Cardinal Jean Daniélou.

XXXII

From Gallitzin to Weakland

"Let us now praise men of renown, and our fathers in their generation. . . . Let the people show forth their wisdom, and the Church declare their praise."[1]

I am afraid that my sermon today calls for a word of apology, perhaps to the jubilarian, perhaps to you all. The fault may be easily found in that it is not in any degree theological nor perhaps as spiritual as the occasion would suggest or even require; it might even be open to the charge of a certain chauvinism because I propose to speak, with a certain pride, of a part of my own country that has become particularly beloved by me.

Charles Péguy attaches great significance in the formation even of the spiritual personality to the influence of the geographical territory and the general community that produces the person. In one of his poems, he tells how the region whence one comes sets the character and general pattern of one's personality, producing even the temperament of a whole people and setting them somewhat apart.

This theory of the influence geography itself has on the formation of a people, while by no means offered as the sole explanation of their common characteristics, is supported in part by Pope Saint Pius X when he speaks with great feeling of the manner in which one's native region has the power to evoke the most cherished memories, the common land where people had their cradle and to which they are tied by bonds of affection and tradition, the land of their ancestors which has been the

This sermon was preached at the Church of Sant' Anselmo, Rome, Italy, on June 17, 1976, on the occasion of the Silver Jubilee of Abbot Primate (now Archbishop) Rembert Weakland, O.S.B.

421

scene and, in part, the source of their historical, cultural, and religious traditions.

I think of these things as I reflect on the background of the priest and prelate whose Silver Jubilee rejoices us today. Archabbot Weakland is descended from people of no uncommon place so far as its characteristics and the personalities who shaped its destinies are concerned. The origins of his family are in a corner of western Pennsylvania that I came to know relatively late in my own priestly life, but it made an impact on my sacerdotal imagination which I like to hope is permanent and which, in his case, is clear to all who know him.

Many of you have probably never heard of the region of Loretto nor, perhaps, of the truly royal and extraordinarily disciplined priest whose life and memory dominated the region of Loretto of which the Weakland family were long-time residents. I refer to Prince Demetrius Augustin Gallitzin, a Russian nobleman, the scion of a family which had produced generals, great statesmen, and at least one martyr to the Faith, and which had always held positions of importance at the Russian court. Prince Gallitzin, who is remembered affectionately as *Mitri,* chose to become a pioneer missionary of the Allegheny hills and valleys, passing up the associations of his family with Diderot, Voltaire, and D'Alembert, and the life of splendor and brilliance which surrounded the brilliant personality of his mother, who was much admired at the Hague as the *Star of Holland.* She was a woman of surpassing intellectual gifts and intensive studies, as his father was a man of wide influence and with vaunting ambitions for his son, Prince Demetrius Gallitzin, whose life his parents had carefully planned.

None of their plans were accepted by the young nobleman. When he came to America, he used none of the letters of introduction which would have brought him into the highest circles of the New World after he arrived in Baltimore in 1792. The only exception was his letter of presentation to Bishop Carroll, our first American bishop. The Bishop was frankly embarrassed by the resolve of Prince Demetrius to abandon the life so carefully planned for him by his parents, to renounce his position and estates in Russia, and to enter the Sulpician seminary in Baltimore, to choose a life of toil, privation, and self-denial, which would eventually bring him into what could then only be called the wilds of the Alleghenies in Pennsylvania.

However, although he could renounce his career, he could not and did not put aside the noble qualities, intellectual and other, which were the dynamic of his life as a priest and which he transmitted in remarkable degree to the families in the remote areas of Pennsylvania where he preached the gospel and impressed his powerful, indomitable personality.

It was on Christmas Eve, December 24, 1799, that Father Gallitzin celebrated the Mass and blessed the Church built of laurel boughs and hemlock, the only house of God from the Susquehanna River to the Mississippi, placing it under the protection of Saint Michael the Archangel. He lived simply, even rudely, in a log cabin, but he kept alive his active intellect with reading that left no field of knowledge untouched. The presence in the countryside and the woods around him of immigrants of many ethnic backgrounds enabled him to keep his proficiency in many languages. His capacity readily to make friends with the families he found along the Indian trails and his spontaneous, passionate love for the peoples of his adopted country eased the blow that came to him in 1808, when he learned that in consequence of having adopted the Catholic Faith and priesthood he was excluded from any share in his father's estate, this decision having been made by the Russian Senate and Council of State and sanctioned by the emperor.

He was tall and stately; his bearing was decidedly soldierly, his figure slender, his complexion clear, his eyes dark and flashing. His features were regular and eminently aristocratic. There are those who say, and not merely because of local patriotism, that the people of the region where he preached acquired not only his mentality of faith but also something of the force and character of his bearing.

One more bitter experience imposed by those of his own household followed close upon his domestic bereavement, and for a time Father Gallitzin's influence was again weakened and his soul tried by defamations and forged letters. It seems almost incredible that the self-denying and beautiful spirit, whose personality at this distance of so many years is still felt as a benediction wherever his name is known, should have suffered such distress and torment at the hands of those for whom he was giving his life; and it is horrible to relate that at the critical point of the battle that raged so fiercely around him, personal violence was attempted, and that but for the stout heart and strong arm of one John Weakland, Father Gallitzin would have met the fate of Becket. But the civil courts and the head of the Catholic Church in America upheld his authority and rendered legal decisions in his favor; some of his tormentors repented, publicly retracted their accusations, and apologized for their behavior, and the long, wearisome contest was over.

He entered into the amusements of his people with great zest, and the story is told that at harvest time he provided dinners for the laborers on the Church land, and toward evening would take his violin out into the fields and play for their entertainment while they brought the harvest home in rough wagons decorated with vines and wreaths.

He was most fastidious about the sanctuary and all things used for the service of the altar, and gave to them his personal care. Vestments and altar cloths were folded and put away without crease or wrinkle, and every article had its place. The materials were of the finest, and almost everything he used was made and sent to him by his mother and friends in Europe. A handsome painting, *The Adoration of the Magi,* received from the same source, still hangs over the chapel altar at Loretto.

He was fond of books and gathered together quite an imposing library for those days, and his thorough education, together with a fine command of his mental resources, rendered him formidable in argument and a controversialist of no mean ability.

Gallitzin vowed himself to the priesthood in America. Why in America? Here is a further proof of the grandeur of his soul, of his earnestness in the consecration of himself to the priesthood. He was told by his father and by his friends that if he wished to be a priest he should at least return to Europe where illustrious episcopal sees would fall to his lot. Had he hearkened to their prayers, he might one day have become a prince-bishop in Germany as his schoolmate Von Droste became the prince-bishop of Cologne. A relative of his became King of Holland; he would have opened to him avenues to highest preferment in his kingdom. Gallitzin could have been a priest in Europe and there gathered around his priesthood whatever earth could give to decorate, in the eyes of men, the priesthood. But he said: "I will be a priest in America, because here in America I take to myself the priesthood for its own merits; if I become a priest where earthly glory awaits me, I shall perhaps be tempted to think much of the earthly glory and little of the priesthood of Christ."

Gallitzin said, too: In bringing people to where they will find homes, I am benefiting the country; I am making of them useful citizens. The thousands and tens of thousands of people homeless in large cities are of little use to Church or country, while on the rich farming lands of America, they become independent, honored citizens, the strength of the country as well as of Church. He thought, too: Let me get them around me, away from the moral and religious perils of cities, and I will, God helping, build up amid the mountains an ideal Christian community, where Christian thought and Christian practice will dominate.

In the history of the parish and region of Loretto, we read that Prince Gallitzin finished his chapel of logs in 1799, and in 1819 we find a certain John Weakland settled in the area. He proved to be a staunch collaborator of *Prince Mitri,* but before he came, in fact from the first year of the parish, we find a litany of names of the Weakland family. In the period from 1800 to

1835, we find the names in the parish register of no less than 73 persons who bore the name of Weakland and therefore who came under the influence of Prince Gallitzin. It is from among these people that the Abbot Primate is descended and precisely from the son of John Weakland, who became known as John the Defender, his father having been known as John the Patriarch, and through John's son, Samuel.

The parish register reveals that the Weaklands married with members of many different ethnic groups in the Loretto area of Cambria County. Many of the names are English, as Gardner, Adams, and Harrison. Some are Irish, as Farrell, McKinney, Flannigan, and McAteer. In a word, here was a family who blended many traditions under the gentle influences of a princely priest and gentle architect of character.

It is one of the ironies of American history that the group of early Maryland Catholics fled to Pennsylvania to escape religious persecution. Tolerance has been the very life's breath of the Catholic Maryland Colony ever since its foundation in 1634, and in 1649, perhaps when stormclouds appeared on the horizon, this was made official in the Maryland Toleration Act. The religious freedom established and fostered by the Catholics soon disappeared, however, when Puritans, driven out of Virginia by the Episcopalian-established Church, seized the Maryland government in 1650 and forthwith repealed the Toleration Act.

When the heavy hand of intolerance hit Maryland in 1692 and there was little hope of relief in sight, a group of Catholics fled into the west Pennsylvania wilds. There in the priestless forest, the elders baptized the infants. Couples were married before the patriarchs. Registers of these baptisms and marriages were faithfully kept.

It was to be a century before the arrival of Father Gallitzin, perhaps the first priest to visit these people in their new home.

The residence of Father Gallitzin, and also his church, were somewhat separated from the rest of the community. One day, the priest was surprised by a band of ruffians and was forced to flee to the church. The party of agitators seized upon Gallitzin and taunted him with insults. Above all, they were bent upon forcing certain concessions from him by which he would have renounced his rights and his position of leadership. When he refused, they prepared to treat him with violence. He would have been subject to a veritable siege if John Weakland had not then chanced along.

John was the tallest and strongest man within a hundred miles. Once, when he was alone in the forest, he met and fought a furious bear for hours, his only weapon being the limb of a tree hastily snatched from the ground. When he saw what was afoot, John decided that here he should make an exception to his accustomed rule of life—that is, minding his own business. He quickly looked about him for a limb or its equivalent, seizing upon an oaken fence stake which neatly fitted his hand. With it, he calmly advanced upon the mob, which, awed and frightened, started to retreat, obviously thinking that without further ceremony he would strike loose at them. But this he did not for the nonce; instead he gave a speech, a longer one than they were accustomed to hearing from him. He spoke approximately as follows:

> I have fought with bears and other animals it is true, but to date I have never, thank God, done harm to a human being. But now it looks as something else might happen. Go home, therefore, for if there is any more monkey business or if anyone acts improperly about the House of God or dares to lay hands on the anointed of the Lord, let them beware! [And here he lifted up the fence stake.] As true as I live, I'll crush his skull for him!

This put a decisive end to the trouble.

A chronicler says that John Weakland did not die until fifteen years after Father Gallitzin had passed away, that he left a posterity of more than one hundred souls and that a great-granddaughter with her child in her arms followed him to his grave.

For twenty years, Father Gallitzin had labored alone in his vast mission territory. When the Prince died May 6, 1840, he had behind him forty-one years of labor on the frontier. Among his first parishioners in the wilderness were, as I have indicated, the Weakland clan. Already in 1770, a survey now filed in the state capitol in Harrisburg lists the Weakland property.

Their patriarch, John Weakland, was born in April 1758. He married Catherine Jackson at Hagerstown, Maryland, and brought her to Loretto. He first appears in the Loretto records in 1800 when Father Gallitzin baptized his son George. In 1802, he bought a hundred acres of land from Father Gallitzin and cleared it for farming.

One who knew the Weakland brothers described them as tall, broad men, powerful even in their old age, with coarse hair and high cheek bones, which plainly revealed their partial and proud Indian ancestry. The strength of John Weakland was to serve Father Gallitzin well in his work among the rough frontiers of the Pennsylvania wilds.

According to a tradition in all branches of the Weakland family of Cambria County, Pennsylvania, three Weakland brothers came to America with the first colony sent out by the second Lord Baltimore, which arrived in Maryland March 25, 1634. These three brothers settled near the present site of Baltimore, and one of them married an Indian princess. It is this latter couple who were ancestors of the John Weakland who migrated to Pennsylvania near the close of the 17th century.

It is from this same John Weakland, the Patriarch, and his son, the Defender, that through Samuel, as I have said, our beloved jubilarian is the direct descendant. What spiritual qualities of Prince Gallitzin, himself an abbatial figure, and what human qualities of his ancestors, influenced by and collaborating with Prince Gallitzin, I shall not embarrass him by attempting to sketch. I merely go back to my initial thesis and say that the

428

Abbot Primate, in his person and in his priesthood, has recapitulated and exemplified the qualities of an extraordinary family and the unique priest who has shaped the character of the region and the culture out of which he comes.

In so saying, I earnestly hope that I have not embarrassed the Abbot Primate or his loved ones here present, although I am well aware that I have spoken with regional patriotism and perhaps a touch of pride not entirely inconsistent with our bicentennial year in thus adopting the counsel of Scripture that we should praise men of renown and our fathers in their generation.[2] It has been a proud privilege to do so on the occasion of the Jubilee of the son of a spiritual ancestor and a physical ancestry so well deserving of the members of the Church and the civil community, a man who, as does Abbot Rembert Weakland, even perpetuates Prince Gallitzin's love for music and learning, on the one hand, and the self-discipline and steadfastness of his own forefathers, on the other.

XXXIII

My Two Most Cherished Documents

It is a special joy to have this privileged occasion to visit the Philadelphia Free Library, and I am profoundly grateful to all those who have made the visit possible and so extremely pleasant.

The chairman remarked that this event is obliquely connected with the Eucharistic Congress going on in Philadelphia this week. I am afraid that I must dissent concerning the word *obliquely.* The relationship is direct and, to me at least, completely clear.

Faith, reason, and freedom are intimately bound up with one another, not only by their respective natures but also by their mutual dependence. Faith is a free act, and freedom is not likely to endure when faith is restricted, denied, or lost. History confirms this proposition, and so during a week that some of us are here in Philadelphia to celebrate faith, it was a most keen intuition that prompted the planners of this event to remind us of the accumulated treasures of reason housed within these walls, and more particularly in these rare book rooms.

Moreover, these rooms are, in fact, a holy place. More, perhaps, than most other rooms of any library, the rare book rooms bring together the beauty, truth, and goodness which are reflections, at least, of attributes of God Himself. That is not only because of the quality and the contents of the books, but it is because of the spirit in which they were given by people who love learning and love Philadelphia.

I just had a pleasant conversation with one of those people. She is here present and is the donor of your remarkable Dickens Collection. I had the great happiness of fingering and reading

These remarks were made during a visit, on August 3, 1976, to the Rare Book Rooms of the Philadelphia Free Library, Philadelphia, Pennsylvania.

parts of one of the most prized items in that collection. It is the manuscript, in his own hand, of Charles Dickens' *Life of Christ,* written to be read by him to his children. Its inspiration is, of course, beautiful beyond compare; the passages I read are messages for our times and for always. The book is entirely unique, and the gift of it to the Philadelphia Free Library is typical of the spirit in which everything in these gracious rooms was given. They are contributions to the learning, the common good, and the holy pride of Philadelphia.

The very name of your library gives expression to something fundamental to the American tradition. I have frequently remarked that the two documents which most I cherish as important in my personal life are my baptismal record, which I count on, if I live up to it, to get me safely into eternal life, and my library card, which has in fact contributed as much as anything and more than most things, to my felicity in life here below. I do not remember the day I received my baptismal record; I was only two weeks old and in no position to appreciate the wonders which opened up to me. But I well remember the day I received my library card. It was the first day that I was eligible to do so, and I had looked forward to it for weeks. I also remember the number of my library card taken out over a half century ago, plus a year or two. It was 146125, and it was issued by the Boston Public Library, where I later worked in the stacks and of which, as a young priest, I was a member of the examining committee. Last fall, I preexecuted the clause of my will, which left to the most beautiful room in the Boston Public Library my collection, gathered since I was in the 6th grade, of some six thousand items pertaining to Saint Joan of Arc, the magnificent statue of whom faces the Art Museum here in Philadelphia and to which I made a pilgrimage on my way here this afternoon.[1]

Like most of the books in your superlative rare books collection, so most of the books in my collection of Saint Joan of Arc were gifts from generous people or organizations who, knowing that you cherished this particular subject, sent you, in my case from all over the world, items pertaining to the collection. There is a community among those who cherish the beautiful, the true, and the good, and these rooms are a sanctuary of such a community.

But I was speaking of the relationship of free public libraries to the specifically American tradition. I assume that you realize that free libraries are unique to the United States and to those nations which have been influenced by the American tradition. Other nations have magnificent libraries, but they belong to universities, princes, or great institutions and are necessarily restricted both in their appeal and in their accessibility. In America and nations which have followed our example, this is not so. I will go so far as to say that more than any other civic force or institution, the free public library has forged such greatness as we have attained, more even than the free school, because the library is visited freely by those with alert and eager intellects, and attendance at school is compulsory and, I kid you not, largely reluctant. That is why we have truant officers to make sure that children go to school at least until they have fulfilled the so-called *Peter Principle*. Libraries are quite another matter, and their very existence is a tribute to the presence of intelligence, freely used and eager to develop, in a community blessed by God and good people by a library as proud and as beneficent as the Free Public Library of Philadelphia.

I am, of course, grateful for the kindness you have paid me this afternoon during the week that finds me in Philadelphia for the Eucharistic Congress. But I am not less grateful and I bless God for the existence and the influence of this free institution, where no qualifications of any negatively discriminating kind would be tolerated and where the freedom, intelligence, and faith (for faith is a form of intelligence and of knowledge) of this great city and our nation are guaranteed.

Heartfelt thanks—and God bless you!

XXXIV

The Hunger for the Spirit and the Sense of Vocation

"And I heard the voice of the Lord, saying: Whom shall I send? And who shall go for us? And I said: Lo, here am I! Send me!"[1]

Everyone present at this meeting especially gathered for the Eucharistic Congress has at one time or another had the experience described by the Prophet Isaiah. Every *person,* as a matter of fact, came into existence in response to a vocation, for every life is a mission from God Himself. Certainly, all priests and religious may well recall the very moment of their reply to God's question: "Who shall go for us? — Here am I! Send me!"

But this is true of every way of life within which one responds to the Spirit and places oneself, in whatever form of service of God and Man, at the disposition of the Holy Spirit. Every life, I repeat, is a vocation, a response to a mission, a call to which came from the very Spirit and providential surveillance of God.

One is no longer certain that the appreciation of this fact is as vital and as profound at the moment as once it was among Christians. The sense of vocation itself, no matter to what mission or form of life and loving service it may find expression, seems to have been *paralyzed* in our increasingly standardized, impersonal, automated, and regimented culture, where *professional* consultors, not to say computing machines and cybernetics have so often replaced spiritual directors and personal self-analysis and study and even professional consultors. There is not as much of the sense that prompts one spontaneously to say, with conscious, personal self-dedication: "Here am I! Send me!" to the voice of

This sermon was preached, at Philadelphia, Pennsylvania, on August 4, 1976, on the occasion of the forty-first International Eucharistic Congress.

the Lord asking: "Whom shall I send and who will go for us?" in our programmed society.

I have suggested that the very nature of our present culture tends to paralyze this sense of personal vocation, of a response to a divine mission that transcends the regimented, automated, and depersonalized aspects of our civilization. But there is a more embarrassing consideration: perhaps we priests and religious have ourselves in a subtle but real way contributed to the *paralysis* and the *limitation* of the sense of vocation, individual, personal, and distinctive, among our young people. We have tended to confine the very word *vocation* to our particular form of seeking God's will and serving both the Spirit and our neighbor; when diocesan statistics are published, for example, the word *vocation* invariably means the number of those in the *seminary* or the *convent. It no longer seems to occur to us that every life is, or should be, a vocation; the response to a divine call, to fulfillment of a providential mission from God Himself.*

I repeat, it was not always so among people who believed in God and His Holy Providence. Saint Joan of Arc, for example, *knew* she had a vocation and proclaimed it vigorously and unashamedly; she knew that she was sent by God and was unshakable in her conviction that her vocation involved, among other things, a vow of virginity, the life of the battlefield, and the uncompromising recall to his sense of duty of an insipid king. Frederic Ozanam knew perfectly well that he was a man with a mission, a mission to teach, a vocation to bear witness to the Faith in an unbelieving university world, a call from God to the special service of the poor. Saint Catherine of Siena was obsessed by her sense of vocation; so was Saint Monica as the mother of a genius off on the wrong track; so were hosts of laymen and laywomen who as lovers and parents, as poets and scientists, as persons in political life or in the humblest of temporal pursuits were convinced that they were people with a mission within which they found themselves because they had heard the voice of God asking, "Whom shall I send? Who will go for us?"

—to which, in the particular circumstances of their lives and their circumstances, they had replied, "Here am I! Send me!"

Such people in political life, professional life, trades, and crafts were seekers after the Spirit rather than mere office or power seekers. They were consciously responding to a call from God Himself, not to a pressure group or a political party. They had careers, to be sure, some of them historic careers, but it was not the desire for a career that brought them to make a decision that was frequently heartbreaking, frustrating, and almost self-annihilating. They were persons who had said: "Here am I! Send me!" and therefore were living out a vocation—not merely functioning as cogs in the mechanism of a business enterprise or a mere professional set-up, not to say *racket*.

Think of a prelate like Saint John Fisher, who was called cheerfully into heaven when the rest of his nation's bishops walked out on the Pope. Think of a layman like Thomas More who loved life and learning and his family, but merrily said, *Send me!* when the call was for martyrdom. Think of a religious like Father Damien, at work among his lepers. Think of a nun like Saint Brigitte of Sweden, who founded a fantastic order in which the priests tended only the *spiritualities* and the *religious women* controlled all the *temporalities,* finances included; her "Here am I! Send me!" brought her all over Europe!

It used to be said that marriages were made in heaven. This was another way of saying that they involved a divine vocation, the very sense of which kept them permanent commitments, holy and fruitful forms of service of the Spirit and of the race. People who said such things understood better than the self-excusing Adam, "the woman Thou didst give me", and they knew that their marriage was literally a vocation from God, with eternal implications and immortal longings that far transcended the passions of the moment or the superficial interests that are no longer likely to preserve fidelity and personal attachment when all passion is spent. Perhaps the breakdown of the sense of vocation in marriage, of the idea that marriages are

435

made in heaven rather than the result of mere chance or of the sophisticated suggestions of a cybernetic computer designed, according to the ads, to find the allegedly ideal partner, is the explanation of why so many marriages break down in our day, just as the decline in the sense of vocation accounts, one cannot doubt it, for so many of the difficulties encountered in the lives of so many priests and religious or other disenchanted persons who have grown weary of the exercise of the skill which, recognizing it as a mission from God, they had put to work as their way of saying, "Here am I! Send me!"

Sometimes the concept of vocation has been replaced by the seemingly more pretentious concept of *professional excellence*. If this were not true, more doctors would take more night calls and more nurses would be available on holidays, as was the case when the healing arts involved not merely skills but a *vocation*. Most of our generation has the good fortune to have been taught by teachers who did not look upon their work as a mere trade or even a profession, but as a *vocation;* one thinks of these with admiration, reverence, and grateful tears. So it is for many other callings, indeed for all other forms of service to civilization and God from the sublime vocation of a saintly king or statesman to the seemingly ridiculous antics, if you will, of the Juggler of Notre Dame or those persons with the charisms of making people laugh and thus relaxing an uptight moment of history by singing, by entertaining, or by the arts, simple or highly developed, of the theater, the circus, and the world of entertainment. These people—one can name examples of some who are secretly saints—are fulfilling a *mission;* it is as if God had said: in this dismal hour for humanity, whom shall I send to make people laugh? Who will go for us to relax them? And each of them had replied: "Here am I! Send me!"

The policeman on the corner, the soldier on guard, the diplomat on an authentic humane mission, the mother of a family, the judge or therapist, male or female, curing the ills of a sick society—all of them have every bit as much of a *vocation* as do you or I. These attitudes, I repeat, were once characteristic of civilized people generally. In the case of the Church, the symphony of various and distinct vocations were summed up by Saint Paul once, for all, and forever when he wrote to the Corinthians: Now there are diversities of graces, but the same Spirit; and there are diversities of ministries but the same Lord; and there are diversities of operations by the same God who worketh all in all . . . and God indeed hath sent some in the Church: first the apostles, then doctors, then the graces of healings, helps, governments, of tongues, as their way of saying "Here am I! Send me!" Are all apostles? Are all prophets? Are all doctors? No! But, you are the body of Christ, many members indeed, but one body.

Saint Paul is not only the great exponent of the inevitable diversities of vocations and yet the unity of those who pursue these, but he is also the great exemplar of the total submission of one who hears the call of God and replies, as please God all of us have done, usually as blindly as did Saint Paul at the gate of Damascus: "Here am I! Send me!"

This present International Eucharistic Congress has set for our meditation and, please God, subsequent action, some but by no means all of the hungers of mankind. To each of these and to the other hungers of the race, there corresponds a vocation. The Vatican Council document on the religious life calls attention to the rich variety of vocations among religious themselves who have specifically sacred contributions to make, which are as various as the vocations given them; the decree *Perfectae Caritatis* puts it this way; "Some exercise a ministry of service, some teach doctrine, some encourage through exhortation, some give in simplicity or bring cheerfulness to the sorrowful."[2]

You and I are invited on this day of the congress to reflect on the Eucharist and the human hunger for the Spirit and the ways in which we, priests and religious, can serve those who suffer from that hunger. They constitute the overwhelming majority of mankind at the moment; in no area of concern is it more true

437

that the harvest indeed is great but the laborers few. Cardinal Cushing, in his characteristic fashion, used to say: the world is full of guys who will spare you a dime for a cup of coffee, particularly if you promise to go away and buy it immediately — but, alas, even among us, there are too few who will listen to people for half an hour and try to help them discover the voice of the Spirit!

All the other hungers involve one another, but they are all included in this universal hunger for the Spirit, a hunger toward the alleviation of which, clergy, religious, and laity, all have their respective roles to discharge and a contribution to make. Who shall *dare say* that leading people to God and opening their ears to the Spirit are limited to priests and religious? Many of us had our first insights into the glory of God from our parents, uncles, and aunts, from neighbors and strangers, even from playmates. But, on the other hand, who shall *dare deny* that the leading of people to God and the opening up of their ears to the Spirit are of the very essence of the sacerdotal and the consecrated life and should therefore find priests and religious in the advance guard of that desperately needed vocation.

The hunger for the Eucharist and the hunger for bread are other cases in point. It is the calling of the priests that provides the Eucharist and the calling of religious to teach and lead an unbelieving world to the Real Presence and the sacrificial table and tabernacle. Would to God that hunger for freedom and the hunger for justice were the only forms of hunger that plague our consciences and torment our society! Who will pretend that professionals, social service workers, diplomats, and relief distributors are the only ones called to take care of these hungers? In the forefront must be found the priests and religious. Who shall say that it is only the nurse, the doctor, or the technician who instantly answers, "Here am I! Send me!" to the cry of the aged, the cancer victim, the infirm, the lonely? At every bedside where there is suffering, the Christian scheme of things found, side by side with the healer, priests and the sisters all joining in the response "Here am I!"

The voice of the times is the voice of God. If by these words we mean not merely the voice of the angry headlines and the raucous newscasts but what the great Cardinal Faulhaber meant when he chose these words for his motto, namely, that there is no cry mingled in the voice of the times more urgent or more moving than the cry for understanding, a cry that comes not only from youth but from the throats of almost every group in the world, rich and poor, black and white and especially brown, as everyone knows who has tried to follow the fortunes of Asia. To whom is that cry addressed? Psychologists? Parents? Police? Politicians? *Surely* — but most especially to you and to me, to religious and priests. If we meant what we said when we entered upon our vocations — "Here am I, O Lord! Send me!" — it cannot be otherwise.

And yet, we have been told there is a drop in the number of those who, either as priests or religious, are disposed to live up to that answer or to make it in the first place. It is even said that some priests, some religious, some parents, actively and effectively, seek to prevent vocations to the priesthood and religious life. Almost all of us have met parents implacably opposed to the religious life for their children, and a few of us have encountered young people inhibited even by occasional clergy or religious from giving the positive and enthusiastic answer that was in fact forming on their very lips in response to the call of the Spirit: "Here am I! Send me!" — whether that response was to the priesthood or the religious life. A like weird opposition to marriages frequently shows up. I mention this last because every one of us has at one time or another met a boy or a girl whose vocation to the service of the Church was argued against by an unhappy priest or sister, but we have also met boys and girls who become young men and women pining away their lives because *Mom* or *Pop* did not wish them to marry the person that they had chosen and, more likely than not, God had sent into their lives.

This whole trend of obstructing the movement of the Spirit which is the dynamic behind every vocation to every form of life must be reversed—and you and I have no greater duty than to begin that reversal immediately. Every priest has an obligation before God and the Church, not to mention civilization, to see to it that he has found at least two persons with a vocation to take his place when he finally drops dead. All religious have a parallel obligation to be the instrument of the Spirit in producing at least two vocations as replacements for each of them when finally they die. Everyone has the obligation to encourage the marriage of couples who will obviously stay together in that permanent nuptial fidelity which characterizes Christian marriage and constitutes it as a vocation. It is no accident that the divorce rate grows apace with the defection from vocations of every kind; neither is it an accident that vocations to the priesthood and to the religious life come so often from generous families, thanks to which the sense of vocation permeates the whole of a society, rather than a society in which that sense of vocation has been attenuated or lost. Priests and religious, not merely producers and managers, should be on the constant lookout for artists who will sing the glory of God, craftsmen who will manifest some measure of His beauty, men and women for public life who will bind up the wounds of war and restore the unity of the worldwide human family. Believe me, it all depends on you!

The Spirit of God is not dead; neither is ours. We priests and religious, working as one in Christ, with our various gifts and ministries, this day dedicate ourselves to the guidance of a whole new generation which will answer in their respective ways: "Here am I, O Lord! Send me!" It is not any particular vocation that is in trouble; it is the *sense of vocation itself.* We no longer look upon ourselves as agents of God—in whatever we are called to do. Let us look to it—beginning with the call to the priesthood—but by no means ending there. "Here I am, O Lord! Send me!"

440

XXXV

In the Old North Church:
Reflections for the Bicentennial Year 1976

"When the Son of Man cometh, shall He find, think you, faith on earth?" [1]

I need not say how great a neighborly kindness Father Golledge has done me by the invitation to appear in the historic Old North Church. As a student, I worked for a little over a week as a guide on a sightseeing bus that included the North End; but I came to a serious disagreement with our chief of staff on some details I have now forgotten, possibly the number of nails in the door of Paul Revere's house, and was obliged (temporarily) to bid farewell to this beloved corner of the North End. I later frequented regularly the Saint Leonard Church where I joined the Third Order of Saint Francis of Assisi. When I returned from Rome as a young priest, I came to the North End on Saturday evenings to make my confession and to eat in one or another of the Italian restaurants, prompted by nostalgia for Rome and occasionally by sheer hunger, teaching, as I was, at Saint John Seminary. [2]

Through all these years, the Old North Church held a warm place in my local patriotism. In any case, I come as no stranger and with great pride, and I must begin, I repeat, by acknowledging the fraternal thoughtfulness of Father Golledge.

Perhaps I should emphasize the joy with which I come because the theme of my discourse this morning may strike some as characterized by less buoyancy than that which appears spasmodically among some Christians at the moment, a buoyancy the depth of which one sometimes questions. There is no hope or *theology of hope* without *faith;* Saint Paul told us that faith is

This sermon was preached in the historic Old North Church, Boston, Massachusetts, on August 22, 1976.

441

the substance of things to be hoped for, the evidence of things which appear not but after which we must strive in the face of obstacles. One is by no means pessimistic, but merely realistically laboring to make hope possible and charity effective when he points out the terrible peril that faith may be growing dim or less vital, less universal, less profound than it must be if hope is not to be diluted and charity, in the Christian sense, to be dead.

The relevance of religious faith in our day, its part in the lives of children and adults alike, even its authentic voice in our pulpits and seminaries, is worth a moment of meditation. Obviously, the survival of faith on the earth was a preoccupation of the Lord Jesus, as the text I have just read to you suggests: "When the Son of Man cometh, shall He find, think you, faith on earth?"

More closely to our own times, some of the most prophetic preachers who have made spiritually sound judgments of our times have seriously questioned the state of faith in our civilization, indeed, even among those who have retained a formal, almost rubrical, tie with Christianity. One such was the great cardinal of the last century, John Henry Newman, who preached in 1873 a sermon on the *infidelity of the future,* by which he meant precisely the period in which we are living. He did so in a sermon that no one can read without recognizing its prophetic character. Another was an American Episcopalian chaplain, writer, and preacher, probably the most effective preacher to universities in this country, as Newman was certainly the greatest preacher who ever spoke our sweet English tongue. I refer to Dr. Bernard Iddings Bell, who died not many years ago and left behind him several volumes of sermons which are indeed tracts for the times. I frankly confess that what I shall have to say this morning is largely influenced by these two incomparable witnesses to the state of religion and the place of effective faith in our times.

Now, all times are perilous to faith, and in every time, serious minds, alive to the honor of God and the needs of man, are apt to consider no times so perilous as their own. All times have their special traits, which others have not. But nonetheless, I think that the trials which lie before us are such as would appal and dizzy even such courageous hearts as Saint Athanasius, Pope Saint Gregory I, or Pope Saint Leo the Great. And they would confess that dark as the prospect of their own day was to them severally, ours has a darkness different in kind from any that has been before it.

"When the Son of Man cometh, shall He find, think you, faith on earth?" The special peril of the time before us in the spread of the plague of infidelity bears a frightening resemblance to what the apostles and our Lord Himself predicted as the calamity of the last times of the Church. I do not mean to say that these are the *last times*—they are not!—but they have the evil prerogative of being like to that more terrible season when, it is said, the elect themselves will be in danger of falling away.

There are many reasons for this, as Newman set forth. In all truth, the general intelligence of every class of society, general but shallow, is the means of circulating all through the population all the misrepresentations which the enemies of the Faith make of her faith and teaching. Most falsehoods have some truth in them; at least those falsehoods which are perversions of the truth are the most successful. Again, you know that the true religion must be full of mysteries—and therefore to Christianity applies especially the proverb that a fool may ask a hundred questions which a wise man cannot answer. It is scarcely possible so to answer inquiries or objections on a great number of points of our Faith or practice, as to be intelligible or persuasive to our generation. And hence the popular antipathy in faith seems, and will seem more and more, to be based upon reason, or common sense, so that first the charge will seem true that faith stifles the reason of man, and next that, since it is impossible for educated men, such as clergy, to believe what is so opposite to reason, they must be hypocrites, professing what in their hearts they reject.

There is more to say on this subject, again in the opinion of

443

Cardinal Newman. There are after all, real difficulties in revealed religion. There are questions, in answer to which we can only say, "I do not know." There are arguments which cannot be met satisfactorily, from the nature of the case—because our minds, which can easily enough understand the objections, are not in their present state able to receive adequately the true answer. Human language has not words in which to express it. Or again, perhaps the right answer is possible, and is set down in the books of theology, and you know it. But things look very different in the abstract and the concrete. You come into the world, and fall in with the living objector and inquirer, and your answer you find scattered to the winds. The objection comes to you now with the force of a living expositor of it, recommended by the earnestness and sincerity with which he holds it, with his simple conviction of its strength and accompanied by all the collateral or antecedent probabilities which he heaps around it.

I am speaking of the evils which in their intensity and breadth are peculiar to these times. But I have not yet spoken of the root of all these falsehoods—the root as it ever has been, but hidden; but in this age exposed to view and unblushingly avowed—I mean the *satanic spirit of infidelity itself.* The elementary proposition of this new philosophy which is now so threatening is this: that in all things we must go by reason, in nothing by faith, that things are known and are to be received so far as they can be proved to the satisfaction of the secular mind, the reasons of this world. Its advocates say, all other knowledge has proof—why should religion be an exception? And the mode of proof is to advance from what we know to what we do not know, from sensible and tangible facts to sound conclusions. There is no revelation from outside the visible, the tangible, the experience of sense. There is no exercise of faith. Seeing and proving by personal experience is the only ground for believing.

Accordingly you will find, certainly in the future, nay more— *even now, even now* —that writers and thinkers of the day do not even believe there is a God. They do not believe either the *object*—a God personal, a Providence, and a moral Governor; and secondly, what they *do* believe, viz., that there is some first cause or other, they do not believe with faith, absolutely, but as a probability or a practical hypothesis.

You will say that these theories have long been in the world and are no new things. No! Individuals have put them forth, but they have not been current and popular ideas. Christianity has never yet had experience of a world simply irreligious. Consider what the Roman and Greek world was when Christianity appeared. It was full of *superstition,* not of infidelity. But there was no casting off the idea of religion, and of unseen powers who governed the world. When they spoke of *Fate,* even here they considered *that there was a great moral governance of the world carried on by fated laws.* Their first principles were the same as ours. Even among the sceptics of Athens, Saint Paul could appeal to the Unknown God. Even to the ignorant populace of Lystra, he could speak of the Living God who did them good from heaven. And so when the northern barbarians came down at a later age, they, amid all their superstitions, were believers in an unseen Providence and in the moral law. But we are now coming to a time when the world does not acknowledge even the first principles.

Then comes the remedy—nothing less than the practice of the presence of God, the essence of that religious spirit the angels and saints exist to create among us. "Now this I consider to be the true weapon by which the infidelity of the world is to be met", said Cardinal Newman, emphasizing, as we must, the importance of a constant state of supernatural recollection, the recipe for a holy and effective belief. The constant awareness of the presence of God is essential to the total personality of every educated Christian. This is the primary weapon for meeting the age, not controversy and not polemic. Of course, every believer should have an intelligent appreciation of his religion, as Saint Peter says; he should be prepared to give reasons for the faith that is in him. But still controversy is not the instrument by which the world is to be resisted and overcome.

In this ecclesiastical spirit, I will but mention a spirit of seriousness or recollection. We must gain the habit of feeling that we are in God's presence, that He sees what we are doing: and a liking that He does so, a love of knowing it, a delight in the reflection, *Thou, God, seest me!*

This Newman considered the true weapon by which the infidelity of the world is to be met: the recollection that we are citizens of two worlds, the world invisible as well as that which is visible, and more really, because eternally, citizens of the world of the angels, the saints, the Queen of Heaven, the Lord of Life.

Next important in the same warfare is an accurate, complete grasp of the reasons for the faith that is in us: sound catechetics. This, though it is not controversial, is the best weapon (after a good life) in controversy. Any child, well instructed in the catechism, is, without intending it, a real missioner to an unbelieving world. And why? Because the world is full of doubtings and uncertainty, and of inconsistent doctrine—a clear, consistent idea of revealed truth, on the contrary, cannot be found outside of the Faith. Consistency, completeness, is a persuasive argument for a system being true. Certainly if it be inconsistent, it is not truth.

Thus far I have been summarizing the prophetic words of Cardinal John Henry Newman, speaking in the last century, in fact almost precisely a century ago, of what would be the condition of the faith in an age of unbounded technology, of permissiveness, and of a fascination with the things of this world, above all, its gadgets, so much as to make us forgetful of the good things of the world to come, that invisible world of which we are citizens, even as the angels, and, in the communion of saints, even while we are citizens of the political, professional, and consumer society which so completely absorbs, depersonalizes, and bewilders us.

Father Bernard Iddings Bell is not the only one, but he is

among the most eloquent and perceptive of those who saw the fulfillment of Newman's prophecy and proclaimed the things that he saw to all who would listen. When Father Bell said some of these things in a lecture I invited him to give in Worcester some twenty years ago, a good woman, disturbed by the directness and candor of the man, remarked on the way out of the hall: "My, he is discouraged, isn't he?" I took the liberty of saying that if we took the trouble to listen to *all* that he said we would suddenly discover that we had regained *courage* by the renaissance within us of that faith which is the substance of hope and the wellspring of charity—yet who will dare say, with all the talk about the *theology of hope* and the humanitarianism of the times that we are not in fact a discouraged lot. So much of what passes for charity in our day, including the energetic social services and carefully card-indexed welfare work, is in fact what a Boston poet once called "the organized charity, scrimped and iced, in the name of a cautious, statistical Christ".

Alas, when John Boyle O'Reilly wrote those dreadful lines, the name of Christ was still pronounced with piety, and there was still at least an atavistic memory that He, rather than a political commission or social service board, was the one to whom the eventual report of our deeds, good and bad, would have to be made.

Bernard Bell argued that Christ has today for the most part ceased to have any active influence worth mentioning over human affairs, particularly on men who are said *to think and to lead*. It is time this was recognized by those who are sure, as the genuinely thoughtful are, that society is in grave and immediate danger of disintegrating into confusion; those who are certain that human beings with every year that passes are increasingly unhappy and more dangerous to one another; those who are persuaded that the trouble is that our day has forgotten, if indeed it ever knew, the nature and purpose of human existence; those who believe that in Jesus Christ is the highest revelation of ultimate purpose and of how man is meant to behave himself. It

447

is time that Christians shake themselves free from that polite inertia of self-contained ecclesiastical routine, which matters not at all to most of those who carry on the world's business.

When it is pointed out to church people how little nowadays anyone heeds their message, the all-too-usual plea in self-defense is an insistence that the fault lies not with the Church but with the world in our era, a world so content with things as they are, so utterly conceited, so only of time and space, that it feels no need of God. While there can be no doubt that some men and women of the moment are all that is alleged, still there are two things wrong about that plea. The first thing wrong is this, as Newman argued, that in the long run the effectiveness of religion is not determined by its temporary popularity but rather by its sanity and sincerity. The second thing wrong is that those who advance this excuse ignore the pertinent fact that there are numerous intelligent people today who are not content with things as they are, they are not this-worldly, not conceited. It is the greater part of these that the Church has not reached; she has managed to convince them too that she is negligible or irrelevant. There are, as a matter of fact, plenty of able people ready and willing to listen to the Church if only she knows what the religion of Jesus means in impact on the world and is not afraid to proclaim it. In a sense, the generation in which Iddings Bell talked is both worse off and better off than that in which the Victorian cardinal talked.

There are today a good many, in every nation and in all classes of society, who realize quite well that modern man has failed and who in consequence are disillusioned and bewildered. They have grave doubts about the sufficiency either of man's competence to think or of his natural virtue. They are no longer confident about the ability of a secularized education to produce a sane and sturdy character in growing boys and girls; they more than suspect that unaided humanity is incompetent to arrive at any goal but bedlam; they are dubious about the possibility of a continuance of even democracy except it find

448

supernatural sanctions sufficiently strong and sure to justify a rigid self-discipline; they laugh when they think of what once was supposed to be the inevitability of automatic progress into a sure-to-come millennium of enlightenment and liberalism—in a single phrase, *the myth of progress* without reference to moral and spiritual values has proved a fraud, and it is *they,* not the preachers who admit it. Hence the thoughtful turn—or try to turn, however tardily—to religion.

When they do, they have the right to know what is the Church's proper work, without the doing of which she has no right to be called Christian and, indeed no excuse for being. It is the work which the Church in our day has often seemed least to know how to do or, having known it, has left it undone; and by that ignorance or neglect has caused herself to be held in a more or less genial contempt. If one reads the New Testament, the scriptural charter of the whole Christian order, or if one examines the nineteen centuries of Christian history in the light of the saints, it seems plain enough that the Church's business is the simple and yet difficult bearing witness, in terms of *creed* and *code* and *cult,* to the nature of God, His absolute dominion, the nature of man, the right relationship between the two, as they are revealed in the Person and teaching of Jesus called the Christ. In a word, to bring us into the presence of God and to make God present to us: *to give us God.*

A French layman, Jean Guitton, has been frank on this point in terms of what the sensitive layman expects of the clergy. He says (in summary): I fear that the priests of the future, in their noble aspiration to mix with us, may be tempted to draw too close to us, wasting time and energy trying to speak our peculiar jargon, to adopt our ways and attitudes, our flurried lives and worldly occupations. Listening to my young priest-friends, I feel uncomfortably conscious that they do not seem to appreciate sufficiently the dignity of their vocation. The priest is not a welfare officer.

And, Guitton continues: What we laymen ask of you is *to give*

449

us God, by means of your exclusive powers of absolution and consecration; that you remain constantly mindful that we look up to you as representatives amongst us of the Eternal, as ambassadors of the Absolute. Starved for the Absolute, we laymen need to have you in our midst as persons who will prove to us that He can exist, and is, in fact, closer to us than we can imagine. Thus far the thought of Professor Guitton.

Meanwhile, there has flourished the fact that *the modern world does not believe in God as much as it puts its ultimate trust in man.* In other words, to the divine will revealed in Jesus the Incarnate God, our world frequently prefers a wisdom of its own, a naive humanitarianism founded on romantic idealization of human beings—their moral worth, their cleverness, their supposedly natural impulses to fraternal self-sacrifice. Well, what price for this humanitarianism today, while modern civilization crashes into catastrophe?

Life is hard to live in times like ours, even for the man of low aim; but the troubles which bear down today on those who are humanity-loving, idealistic, are much more difficult to be borne than those afflicting less spiritually sensitive people. It is those who perceive in the life of man a something more innately noble than is in the lives the beasts possess, those who in consequence hope for a better, happier world than eyes as yet have seen—it is they who the more severely feel a stifling weight. It is they who know that pressure which quenches the spirit. And why? Because they now have come to realize how surely man's cupidity and arrogance—man's sin!—plunges the world into failure and self-destruction. Only the unthinking can find modern life hope-inspiring.

The saints are our models in this great tribulation. Here on earth they faced without consternation not only the fact of their own unaided helplessness, but also the harder fact of self-destructive impotence of the whole of an earthbound, unredeemed humanity; they felt the pressure of the ceaseless round of human folly, yet were not crushed. What is the secret of these holy ones, whose hope and vigor even the contemplation of man's sin was not able to destroy? What did God teach to them which as yet He has not taught, or has only begun to teach, to us, who are impatient and depressed?

This is the knowledge which made them free, as Doctor Bell points out: they came to understand that our little earth, where man by folly and sin thwarts the will of God, the little earth which seems at first glance so substantial, of such tremendous importance, is of no great cosmic significance. Though it could vanish like a mist at dawn, yet a man's heart need not know fear. That is what the saints knew.

Bernard Iddings Bell recalls the story of some third-century martyrs who were imprisoned in a cell beneath the Circus Maximus in Rome. They had been seized as Christians by the imperial authorities, tried, convicted, urged to renounce their religion. Firmly and gladly, they had refused to deny their Lord and had been condemned to die. That had not been too difficult, sustained as they had been by a certain theatrical quality in their profession of faith and defiance of the world. But that night, in the tomblike dungeon whence only one small window looked out and up toward the sky, sitting in total darkness, these men and women, boys and girls, who would be thrown to the beasts the very next day, found it hard to withstand despair.

One of their number spoke aloud a thought in many minds. Had the Christ really triumphed? Had Jesus really been right? Two centuries and more had elapsed since He had come to found His Kingdom, and still Rome ruled the world by force and fear; still the Prince of Peace was crucified by ever-recurring war; still mankind lived for gain, for sensual pleasure, for pursuit of ambition. Would it not, perhaps, have been as well if they had burned, that afternoon, the pinch of incense which proclaimed the reigning Caesar as the God to whom men's lives belong? —*Behold, the ungodly are in no peril of death. They come in no misfortune like other men. Surely, we have cleansed our hearts in vain, and washed our hands in innocence.*

So the speaker said, and it was hard not to agree. In silence, they sat then, for awhile, sunk in a great despondency; and then a lad who had half-listened, half-not-listened, as he gazed through the barred grating of the dungeon, beyond the six-foot wall, up and out into the little patch of sky, said quietly: "Look, brothers. Far above this darksome circus *still shine the stars!*"

They gazed, away from their miserable prison into those depths beside which the earth is nothing, those depths wherein the galaxies in silent sweep of motion do the will of Him who made them; and then at last, in a far corner of the dungeon, an old woman began to recite the words of David: "Whom have I in heaven but Thee; and there is none upon the earth that I desire in comparison to Thee. My flesh and my heart faileth; but God is the strength of my heart, and my portion forever."[3]

And with a quiet hope—even joy!—they laid themselves upon the beaten ground and waited for the day . . . confident, as must we be, that *still shine the stars.*

XXXVI

A Gift to the Boston Public Library

I first became interested in Saint Joan while still a boy, in grammar school, immediately after World War I. I was in the sixth grade, and the so-called troop trains—on their way from the ships that brought them back from France to the Boston harbor, from which they were then taken to a camp where they were mustered out—passed frequently nearby our local public school, stopping near there occasionally to take on water in the manner of those days. Now, the occasional stopping of the train was always an excuse for the pupils to rush out and cheer the returning troops.

While we waved with juvenile patriotism, they in turn responded by waving their khaki hats and singing, in their joy to be home, songs they had learned in France. Some of these, I suspect, it was just as well that we did not understand! But, one of them was a kind of hymn which the French soldiers in World War I sang to Jeanne d'Arc. In effect, it called upon her to intervene with the legions of heaven; and in the English translation, which became very popular—several people have given me the sheet music for my collection—it was called: "Joan of Arc, They Are Calling You."[1]

As a member of the Catholic minority, in our sixth grade, I was naturally curious about Joan; already called Blessed by the Church, and the clear object of cult on the part of the troops. So, I asked my spare and somewhat austere Protestant school-teacher, and she told me that, more than any others, we Catholic students should know and revere Joan of Arc, declaring that it was taken for granted that she would be canonized sometime in

This article was written for and published in the 1977 issue of the *Bulletin de la Société des Amis du Vieux Chinon.*

the years immediately after. Miss Burgess proved to be right. And Joan was duly canonized on May 9, 1920. What was particularly touching, however, was the fact that on the following day Miss Burgess gave me the first book of several thousand I was to accumulate in the years after—most of these being, like Miss Burgess' kind gesture, gifts from people all over the world, especially during the years of my priesthood and bishopric. The book Miss Burgess gave me was Mark Twain's alleged reminiscences of a young man who served as Joan's page during her battles. Mark Twain, who was already writing under a pseudonym, wrote the supposed recollections of her aide under a further pseudonym, pretending that his book was a translation of the recollections of this page. Now, it is a curious—but, noteworthy—fact that Saint Joan is the only heroine who appears in any of Mark Twain's books, an oddity paralleled by George Bernard Shaw who never wrote a book which put a woman character in a favorable light—with the exception of his play: *Saint Joan.*

One of the copies of Shaw's play, in my collection, was given me by a nun—herself a distinguished author and personality—who used to be visited in her own Benedictine monastery in the Malvern hills, just outside of Worcester, England, by Bernard Shaw himself when he was thinking out his play. The book she gave me had won a second prize in a typography contest, in England, that year; all the competing books being various editions of Shaw's *Saint Joan.*

I have already mentioned that the vast majority of the items in the collection are gifts; the purchase of the rest has been my substitute for cigarettes, during the 55 years that I have made Saint Joan a hobby, a pastime, and an object of cult. I once figured out how much it would have cost me in those years if I had smoked a pack of cigarettes a day, and I found that the amount would have exceeded what was invested in my gift to the library of my native city.

Most of the books I have purchased were accumulated as a

result of the habit of visiting the secondhand bookstores in every city of the world to which my assignments have brought me. And the adventure of this kind of book-collecting might well be the subject of a book. Those secondhand bookstore visits and adventures explain the wide diversity of the translations and the quality of the books in the collection. These range from the simple paper-covered books for children, as one I picked up in Korea, and a profound Swedish text, to almost miraculously marked-down, rare items for which I have kept a constant and vigilant eye. For example, for years I had corresponded with British booksellers for a book which researched the life and character of the man who put up the money for the support of Saint Joan's army, before and even after the King of France finally took her seriously. I saw an advertisement in an Oxford bookseller's catalogue which offered the book for seventy-five dollars; but, by the time I wrote the bookstore, this title had been purchased, presumably for seventy-five dollars.

One day, in Rochester, New York, I ducked into a secondhand bookstore to get out of a sudden rainstorm and leaned on a counter, or table, just inside the door. I asked the dealer if he had any books about Saint Joan. He gave me the name of a half-dozen familiar titles, all of which I had long since acquired. I then lifted my hand from the book on which I was actually leaning and found, to my astonishment, that it was the very book I had been seeking for so long. Now, a sign on the counter said that all books displayed on that table were available for fifty cents each! Hoping against hope, I asked the dealer if *that particular book* did, in fact, cost only fifty cents. Slightly impatient with my apparent inability to read, he said that if the book was on *that counter,* then its price was fifty cents. Loyal to my Scout's Oath—or my conscience, as the then Bishop of Pittsburgh), I said that I had seen that same book in the catalogue of an Oxford bookseller and that seventy-five dollars was being asked for it. He told me that Rochester, New York, was not Oxford,

England—and that the price of the book was fifty cents, which I paid.

The scope of the collection covers every aspect of the life of Saint Joan of Arc from her birth to her cruel death, by burning, at Rouen, France, on May 30, 1431, at the age of 19. I had the privilege of preaching the panegyric—held annually at the cathedral in Rouen on the anniversary of the liberation of Normandy in World War II. Since 1905, there have been two commemorations of Saint Jeanne d'Arc throughout France each May—one ecclesiastical in the local cathedral, the other secular or civil in the local marketplace or public square. The year I preached in Rouen, Winston Churchill's daughter—then wife of the British ambassador to France—gave the talk in the marketplace at the very spot where Saint Joan was burned to death. I had the great honor of presiding at a precedent-breaking ceremony at which, for the first time, ecclesiastics were invited to the civil ceremony. Mary Churchill Soames' address—delivered in impeccable French to a spellbound audience of almost ten thousand people—was a magnificent analysis precisely of the sanctity of Jeanne d'Arc. At the mayor's luncheon, she learned for the *first time* —and from an American Roman Catholic bishop—that her father had written what is one of the most touching books about Saint Joan in the English language. Winston Churchill's book was published in New York, a few years ago, with illustrations by Lauren Ford, and no better book could be given an adolescent searching for an heroic model than Churchill's book on Saint Joan.

The collection includes, naturally, the books written by royalists to exploit the devotion of Joan to the crown of France and to the king—whom she turned from an insipid and indifferent character to a man longing to fight for his kingdom and who was eventually crowned (thanks to Saint Joan) at Rheims. Not less tendentious, and even more unfactual, are the books put out by the communists exploiting the fact that Joan was a peasant and making her out to be a kind of familiar revolutionary fighting for the proletariat in order to expel an unwelcome

456

conquerer of her native land—a dangerous thesis, it would seem, for communists to be developing in the light of the conditions in Eastern European countries where a Joan of Arc would be the answer to prayers! Nonetheless, the collection includes a remarkable life of Saint Joan published by the Kremlin to inspire young proletarians. I cannot read the Russian book, but Helene Iswolsky of Pittsburgh, who can, has prepared a summary of the book and says that—except for the inevitable cracks at the Roman Catholic hierarchy—it is a book highly laudatory of the saint. Now, it goes without saying that a representative collection of books about Saint Joan of Arc also includes the *debunking* literature which began to appear around 1870 and is having a bit of rage at the moment. These books are written by anticlericals who represent her as a tool of the Franciscans, or of the royalists, or of any other group whose mention serves their curious purposes. Such books include the recent run of publications suggesting that Saint Jeanne was not a peasant at all, at least by descent, but that she was the illegitimate sister of the king himself, whose parents farmed her out for upbringing by some worthy family in Domremy. This alleged royal blood of the Maid of Orleans is supposed to explain her native powers of leadership—powers strangely absent in the legitimate king, her alleged brother! It is also supposed to explain her prowess at horseback-riding and her poise, the kind of royal bearing found in storybook princesses. Finally, it is also offered as the famed secret which she whispered to the king at Chinon and thus prevailed upon Charles VII to turn over to her the command of his royal, but sadly scattered, army.

The facts concerning her life are attested in the several trials which she underwent before she was condemned. Her life is probably the only life in history which we have completely under oath; the British and their collaborators having caused to be written down every question put to her, together with the answers—confident that the consequent record would damn her, forever, in the name of history. Sir Winston Churchill made a pilgrimage to the National Archives in Paris to study the record of the trial. The facts of her childhood and her conduct in the battles are included in the rehabilitation trial twenty-five years later, wherein her playmates, relatives, and a string of godparents, together with Saint Joan's own mother, testified before the papal legate. The facts are also present in the processes for her beatification (April 18, 1909) and canonization (May 9, 1920) together with the testimony of the Devil's Advocate. All these are in the Boston Public Library collection—some of them original texts, others in exact facsimile.

There are books, too, about the literally supernatural collaboration between this virginal saint and the man who rode beside her into battle, as well as slept beside her in the fields at night—the infamous Gilles de Retz (known to history as Bluebeard). His testimony to her sanctity is in the *Procès de Réhabilitation de Jeanne d'Arc* (five volumes). Gilles de Retz himself was condemned to death—though a marshal of France—for his infamous impurities. This whole story is told in Frances Winwar's remarkable book: *The Saint and the Devil.*

Of course, the collection includes not only a preponderant part by authors of books in French on Saint Joan, but almost all the books written about her in the language which, next only to French, she is most remembered: English. Every aspect of her personal and military career has been the subject of research by English and Scotch scholars, at least one of whom hails her as the foundress of the British Navy—since she drove the English from continental Europe to the high seas and the lands beyond. In this Bicentennial Year, it is interesting, too, to recall that, if the British people whom she drove westward and eastward to establish the empire reached also to North America, it is to Saint Joan that we are indebted for the Free French Fleet, as well as army, which made our own American Revolution possible. Several hundred soldiers are buried at Yorktown and, appropriately enough, a statue of Saint Joan, by Fred Shrady, looks out on the battlefield. The French fleet which made possible the evacuation of Boston under George Washington and rode off the coast of Philadelphia and New York was there thanks to Saint Jeanne d'Arc, and thus statues of her are in dominant places of all the cities where the French fleet or army came to the aid of the colonies. By the same token, the monument of Joan in Orleans, France, is the gift of New Orleans, Louisiana. The story of all this background, as well as copies of the statues, are in the Boston collection.

The trustees of the Boston Public Library welcomed enthusiastically the idea that such a collection should be placed in a room which would bear the name of the first Catholic bishop of New England, a Frenchman, and so they turned over the former Fine Arts Room, one of the most beautiful in the Renaissance building on Copley Square in Boston, to be known henceforth as *The Cheverus Room;* and there scholars interested in the crucial period of history in which Saint Joan lived and died have ready access to the library which symbolized the French contribution to all America, but particularly New England.[2] The director of the Boston Public Library, Mr. Philip McNiff, made the dedication of *The Cheverus Room* and the Joan of Arc Library the first event in a series of educational programs to last all through the Bicentennial Year, commemorating the representative contributions of other ethnic groups to the greater Boston community. The month following the dedication of *The Cheverus Room* there were held observances of the contributions of Italy and the Italians to the American community we all share.

When asked why one chose the Boston Public Library to be the repository of so cherished a collection, the answer for me is extremely easy. First of all, there is precisely the memory of Cheverus, one of the Catholic missionaries who founded so many American dioceses and whose spirit still hovers over Boston, as was symbolized by the fact that the lecture given at the dedication was by the scholarly gentleman who has come to be known as *Mr. Boston* — Walter Muir Whitehill, who has for years written on Cheverus (partly because on leaving Boston to return to France where he died as the cardinal-archbishop of Bordeaux, Cheverus left his library and archives to the Boston Athenaeum of which Mr. Whitehill has, for years, been the director).[3] Saint Joan made Cheverus' presence in Boston, at the opening of the nineteenth century, possible.

Second, I worked as a stack boy at the Boston Public Library, and it was kind of a thrill to return years later with a benefaction that represented sacrifices on my part, but much more generosity on the part of the most disparate people—ranging from the Kremlin, the French embassy in Washington, scores of friends in many nations, and the parishoners of the first parish I ever tended, a small parish in a de-Christianized and remote region of France where the only parish organization was the Cercle Jeanne d'Arc—who have sent me books and souvenirs.[4]

Finally, it was my hope that the collection, treating as it does of her times as well as her personality, would be accessible to students on every level in the Boston community where, as a matter of fact and except for occasional fallings from grace under influences, I dare say it, of outsiders, we have always admired one another's heroes and heroines and have lived by the principle that all come equally welcome to the banquet of the good, the true, and the beautiful.

That was the tradition of the Boston public schools that I attended; and, of course, the libraries and museums. And the tradition still stands and holds—whatever publicity hounds may pretend to the contrary. It is symbolized by the carvings all over the walls of the library building of the great names of literature, music, and art of every nation in the Western world from classical times to the day the Boston Public Library was built.

I treasure a paragraph from the preface of a book by a Harvard professor who was a Jewish contemporary of mine in the Boston Public Latin School, recently under fire for alleged racial discrimination. The preface speaks of the extraordinary intellectual gifts of Arnold Isenberg even as a student of the Boston school which was also mine, as it was that of many

Anglo-Saxons, negroes, and other ethnic groups. There is a description, in the preface, of a typical gathering of the students at the school who published its monthly magazine. I am given an honorable mention in the club, which shows that the Catholics were there, though I find it difficult to recognize myself as a "gaunt, young Irishman" who debated ethical and theological propositions with a dialectical ingenuity that was diabolically effective. Another student mentioned was "black, frail, humorous, and a delightful companion"—he later became a leader in a political party which would never have been mine nor Isenberg's.

The description of the cosmopolitan nature of the school back in the 1920s mentions that the "gaunt, young Irishman" is now a cardinal of the Roman Catholic Church. That Cardinal thought of the easy access to learning, by all who desire it, that characterized and still does those who are willing to seek to qualify for the schools and colleges of his native city when he chose its Boston Public Library as the permanent home of his only lifelong hobby and purely personal pursuit.

I do not deny the vanity of saying that, in addition to Rouen, I have also preached the panegyric of Saint Jeanne at Orleans (Archbishop John Ireland was the previous American who did so) and at Chinon, where Joan took command of the army out of the hands of the king—and where I am an honorary citizen.[5] Mindful of the role of Saint Joan in the eventual French explorations in America—I used gifts received on my silver jubilee of priesthood to construct a Chapel of Saint Joan in Saint Paul Cathedral, Pittsburgh. Pittsburgh was originally called Duquesne, and the first Mass celebrated in precolonial times was offered in the place that is now called The Golden Triangle (the source of the Ohio River) by a French Franciscan. French tourists—who come to Pittsburgh—declare that the Saint Joan Chapel in the cathedral is the most exquisite and imposing tribute to Saint Joan they have encountered in their travels.[6] And *The Pittsburgh Bibliophiles,* a group which takes books and libraries very seriously indeed, used to hold one meeting every year in my house in Pittsburgh so they could enjoy the Joan of Arc Collection. Finally, the memory of Saint Jeanne d'Arc is in the accents of 35% of the Catholics of my first diocese, Worcester, and the first parish I founded there which was dedicated to her.

Sometimes I am asked the reason for this strange cult on the part of a bishop for someone who died at the hands of a bishop, condemned as a witch, heretic, and sorceress. My reply is now automatic: What saint could be more appropriate as a reminder to a bishop to be very careful when he is passing judgment— particularly where conscience is involved and where the alleged *heretic* is appealing over his head to the Pope?

The only thing the collection does not have is the manuscript— only two-thirds complete—of a book I began years ago, before my days as a priest and bishop obliged me to put personal interests in subordination to official duties and pastoral work; which, I must confess, has been every bit as happy as trying to write a book on Saint Joan . . . and, please God, perhaps more profitable to the salvation of my soul and the service of others. However, I still count on almighty God, who according to an old proverb accomplished His greatest deeds through the French— *Gesta Dei per Francos!* — to give my sufficient old age to complete the book, probably working in *The Cheverus Room,* and certainly eager to add to it.

XXXVII

Confirmation: The Layperson's Ordination

Few experiences in the pastoral life of a bishop are more consoling or more happy than the administration of confirmation. Anyone who has served as a confirming bishop cannot possibly disagree and will not fail to be dismayed when he hears it suggested that the wrecking crews, who have succeeded in downgrading first confession, if not confession itself, the special status of the ministerial priesthood, and of marriage may turn their attention and talents to an attack on confirmation. In fact, one already hears rumor of *coordinators of religious education* who are at a loss to where to fit confirmation into their scheme of things.

Confirmation, as Cardinal Cushing once pointed out some years ago, has always been more or less *the Cinderella of the sacraments, neglected and little understood.* The Cardinal argued that unless one is very clear about the nature of grace, it is particularly hard to explain confirmation. The other six sacraments almost explain themselves. Baptism creates in us a new life, the life of God himself, and purges us of original sin. Penance purifies us of the sins we commit ourselves. The sacrament of the sick is explained by its very name and ushers us into the life of the world to come. Matrimony and holy orders establish us sacramentally in two diverse forms of Christian vocation. The Blessed Eucharist nourishes us with the very Body and Blood of Christ himself and makes Him present in our very midst.

As contrasted with these other six sacraments, confirmation has perhaps seemed a little vague. With the contemporary renewed

This article was written for and published in the June 1, 1978, issue of *L'Osservatore Romano.*

emphasis on the Holy Spirit and in the light of certain trials and temptations of the Christian life, its relevance and its meaning should become more clear. It cannot be easily identified with a clearly spelled out act or state, and yet it is the sacrament, in a way, of everyday Christian vitality because it gives us the Holy Spirit in a special manner to fortify us in the day-to-day struggle with the powers of darkness, to enable us to answer the enemy, to come to maturity, prepared to show our faith in word and action, to live it and defend it, to persevere as defenders and witnesses to that faith and, as the old definition put it, "strong and perfect Christians, soldiers of Jesus Christ".

One hears this idea of militancy sometimes soft-toned in these days of dreams and programs of peace, but the Christian life remains a battle from the beginning to the end, and confirmation provides the special grace to wage that battle and to remain faithful to the graces of the other sacraments.

The effects, so called, of confirmation are described or expressed in the *seven gifts of the Holy Spirit.* These are familiar, but they are not always remembered as they should be. They are Wisdom, which enables us to relish spiritual things above earthly things; Understanding, which helps us to know more clearly the mysteries of faith; Knowledge, which enables us to discover promptly the will of God; Counsel, which warns us against spiritual dangers; Piety, which inclines us to a tender love of God and His holy religion, fostering sound devotion and eliminating emotionalism in our living of the Faith; Fear of the Lord, which gives us a saving dread of sin; Fortitude, perhaps the most characteristic gift that confirmation gives, which strengthens us to do God's will, especially in the face of difficulties and temptation.

To elicit all these gifts, confirmation imprints on the soul a *sacred character,* like baptism and holy orders. These three sacraments can never be, as it were, erased or repeated.

Again, it is Cardinal Cushing who relates an example of the reason for the embrace or kiss of peace, so common in the liturgy, that we receive in confirmation. Some say it is to remind us, however casually, that we must be prepared to suffer for the Faith, and this is why we always braced ourselves a bit for the so-called *slight tap* on the cheek of the days of our youth. In either case, it is a reminder that should we be called upon to suffer for Christ, he will give us peace of mind in the midst of our trials. The Cardinal recalled the case of Saint John Fisher. Saint John Fisher, Bishop of Rochester in England, was condemned to be beheaded for opposing King Henry VIII, who wanted to divorce his lawful wife. His jailer in the Tower of London was attentive to his needs, but one day didn't bring the Cardinal's dinner to his cell. When he came the next day, the saint asked him why. "Sir", said the jailer, "I heard that you were going to the block yesterday afternoon and I thought you would not care to eat dinner." The old saint laughed, "You see me still alive. In the future, let me have dinner at the regular time. If you see me dead when you come, then eat it yourself. But as long as I live, I will by God's grace never to eat a bit less." Saint John's mind was at peace; he had fought for the right, and his life was in God's hands to do with as He pleased.

There is a widespread lack of appreciation about the necessity of receiving confirmation. We are not *perfect Christians* without it. It may well be that it is not in itself necessary for salvation, like baptism, but a Christian could not without sin neglect to receive it when opportunity presents itself.

Moreover, it might well be argued that in our day the fortitude in which confirmation strengthens us is more needed than it has been even in times of more dramatic and violent persecution of the Faith. It has never been easy to persevere in the Faith, but our own moment of history, while retaining the various forms of organized pressure for the destruction of the Faith, has added new forms of terrorism, violence, and occasions of sin to reduce the effectiveness of sanctifying grace and to increase the occasions of sin, even apostasy, and certainly the sensuality which is almost the characteristic of our culture. Indeed, one might assert that it is thanks to confirmation that the Church retains the indwelling of the Spirit and therefore His identity and efficacy among us.

Baptism and confirmation may be said to create the Church, giving her her structure and uniting her with Christ and the Holy Spirit. It is by baptism that we receive the paschal graces Christ brought us by His birth, life, death, and Resurrection. It is by confirmation that we receive the gifts of Pentecost that Christ sent us in order to make us His agents, the builders of His Kingdom. That is what people mean by the slight oversimplification that baptism was given us for ourselves, that we might live in God, while confirmation was given us for others that we might share the Faith and cooperate with Christ in building His Kingdom on earth. That is why it is so unfortunate that relatively little attention is paid to confirmation, apart from its being almost incidental in our sacramental lives, or a purely social occasion in the life of an infant, or at most a young adolescent. Confirmation should enable the recipient to transcend the canonical and institutional structures of the Church in order to become himself, with all loyalty to the organized Church, a living agent of what Christ became incarnate and sent the Holy Spirit to accomplish to the ends of the earth and to the end of time.

The place of confirmation in our personal lives has been the victim, in part, of the tendency in many times and places to identify it too closely with baptism, from which other sacrament of initiation into the Christian life it differs in nature of the sanctifying grace which confirmation exists to give us at the precise moments in life when we need it. The Holy Spirit, formerly called almost as a symbol of what we are here talking about, the *Holy Ghost,* is a principle of certitude, a source of hope, a principle of unity between the believer and God and among believers. It is therefore a principle of action that makes us restless to reach all those whom Christ came to save and to mature constantly in our own personal spiritual lives.

466

Without confirmation, the Church would be timid, as were the apostles, hidden away before Pentecost. Are we, too, sometimes timid Catholics today, attempting to *understand* the world, to *come to terms* with society, to *blend* Faith and heathen culture, to eschew *divisiveness?* Confirmation puts sinews into our good intentions and enables us to proclaim and live the Faith regardless of the consequences, and to become strong enough to pay for our courage. That is no doubt why there is frequently question in the pastoral life of the Church concerning the appropriate age for confirmation. Without polemic, one ventures to raise the question of a more precise description of confirmation and choice of the appropriate age for its reception in our day. The differences in the ages set at various times and places for the confirmation of young people, all suggest that the question of age for confirmation is primarily pastoral and should be seen, like confirmation itself, in the context of the total pastoral life of the Church. True, as we noted at the beginning, confirmation provides a pleasant and profitable occasion for the visitation of parishes by the bishop, and for conversation with young people under unique, heartwarming, and frequently consoling circumstances. It provides the joy of dialogue with the children and not merely preaching to or at them. In a most especial way, it gives the bishop personally and officially the chance to make what may be his principal contribution to the development of the future life of his diocese by concentration on explaining the very nature of confirmation and the question of *vocations.*

Obviously, at the moment one means particularly vocations to the priesthood, but by no means only vocations to the priesthood. In a way, confirmation might be thought of as a kind of ordination of the young lay man or lay woman to a place in the total life of the Church, to a specific calling in the life of the Church. Pope Pius XI was eloquent on this point and stressed that confirmation was the sacrament of *Catholic Action.* He obviously was not speaking of any partisan political action positive or negative, but he was merely underscoring that confirmation more and more comes at the age when young people are choosing their life careers.

After all, one can detect in confirmation a kind of lay ordination or reception of the Spirit precisely for one's part in the life of the Church. So many of the elements of confirmation recall parallels with ordination: the imposition of hands, the signing with the seal, the special anointing. Lay people are on the way to a fuller consciousness of being organically active members, whatever the due subordinations, by right and in fact, in the life of the Church. We can see signs of this everywhere, particularly in teaching and action in private and publicly, even ratified by a mission within the structures of Catholic Action.

One speaks in our day of the *apostolate of the laity.* One sees a wider recognition, on the part of lay people who take seriously their spiritual lives, that one earns eternal life in the vocation or career by which one earns one's living. There is less emphasis on the need for a specific *mandate* to involve the devout person in Catholic Action and more understanding that Catholic Action is less a separate kind of organization and more what Pius X meant when he spoke of it as the Catholic life lived.

The *subordination* of the laity in the Christian pursuit of their service of the Church is of a kind befitting faithful people endowed with intelligence, who have abilities and a sense of Christian responsibility, and who are fit and prepared to conduct their own enterprises, not as lay curates, but as strong and perfect Christians called by Christ to specific vocations in baptism and strengthened and clarified in their vocations at confirmation.

Hence the case for thinking of confirmation more and more in terms of the *sacrament of Catholic Action.* Hence too the wisdom, perhaps, of linking the age of confirmation to adolescence rather than childhood, the time when life decisions are being made.

The question remains, when is the best time in adolescence to bring into play the forces and the effects of confirmation? There is a case for early adolescence when young people are headed,

468

more and more as our culture develops along the lines it has apparently taken, toward crises in the maturity of the flesh, the pride of life, the relative evanescence of the awareness of the life of the world to come, the company of the saints, the sheer joy of having the Faith and being a Catholic. The middle years of adolescence are years of peril to these ancient and essential Catholic qualities.

There is, of course, also a strong case for linking confirmation and the sense of one's place in the active life of the Church, whatever one's vocation, to the later years of adolescence when one is making holy and prayerful decisions as to what one will do with one's life, whether one marries, remains single, or seeks a religious vocation. The point is that confirmation was instituted precisely to clarify and fortify the one who is choosing his vocation in the life of the Church.

Father Congar in his book *Lay People in the Church* devotes considerable reflection to this manner of relating confirmation to the prophetic office of the faithful in the general priesthood of the Church. It may be time to take a second look at the *Cinderella of the sacraments* so that she can grow to full maturity in a Church which desperately needs all members to be aware of their responsibilities in and to the total community of the Holy Catholic Church as well as to the salvation of their individual souls.

XXXVIII

Last Will and Testament

I, John J. Wright, also known as John Cardinal Wright of the Title of Christ the Divine Teacher, declare that I am a citizen of the City of Pittsburgh, County of Allegheny, Commonwealth of Pennsylvania, although temporarily residing in Rome, Italy, and I do hereby make, publish, and declare this to be my Last Will and Testament, hereby revoking any and all wills heretofore made by me at any place or time.

I commend my soul to the merciful judgment of God and to the charitable prayers of all who know me. I ask pardon of all those whom I have injured or offended by word, deed, or omission; I gladly forgive any who have trespassed against me.

If acceptable to the Holy See, and notwithstanding any and all understandings heretofore made in or with appropriate authorities of the Diocese of Worcester or that of Pittsburgh, I desire to be buried with my father and mother in Holywood Cemetery, Brookline, Massachusetts. I ask that, in addition to the inscription of my name consistent with the inscription of theirs, there be carved on the stone marking our graves my motto, under my name, but enlarged to include two further words from the poem by Paulinus of Nola from which the motto is taken so as to read: "Resonare Christum corde Romano."

After the payment of my just debts and burial and other expenses, I give, devise, bequeath, and appoint as follows:

First: I direct my Executors hereinafter named to give all my chalices, episcopal crosses, regalia, and other ecclesiastical equipment to the bishops of any Roman Catholic dioceses at home or in the missions, who would welcome their use by reason of need, friendship, or taste, with the exception of items for which provision is made in Articles *Second* and *Third* hereunder.

Second: My brothers and sisters have never at any time sought any financial or like advantages as a result of my priesthood or my episcopate. They and I have always been closely united in enduring affectionate understanding on matters of this kind, and therefore I realize that they would expect no bequest under this my Will other than such tokens of affection as I have placed in individual envelopes addressed to each of them, and to friends, and which are rings or other articles which friends or relatives of them and me gave me in the course of my life. These envelopes are principally in a safety deposit box at the New England Merchants National Bank, Boston, Massachusetts, or in my residence at Rome.

Third: Chiefly in my residence at Rome and in the room reserved for my residence at St. Paul Seminary in Pittsburgh, there are many other items of my own personal property, including but not limited to vestments, books, medallions, statues, objects of art, pictures, clothing and other personal effects, and these I give as follows subject, however, to the provisions of Article *Fourth* hereunder:

a. The white cape with the coat-of-arms of Pope John XXIII and Pope Paul VI and the matching mitre used by me at Vatican Council II, I give to the Rector of St. Paul Cathedral, Pittsburgh, Pennsylvania, for the benefit of that Cathedral of which I was the Bishop during the years of that Council.

b. My stained glass medallions, except those pertaining to St. Joan of Arc, I give to the North American College in Rome.

c. I give the books in my residence in Rome to the library of the North American College in Rome and those in my residence at St. Paul Seminary in Pittsburgh to the library of said Seminary except for those pertaining to Vatican Council II and subsequent Episcopal Synods and those books containing articles by me, inscribed to me, or referring to me or my activities, which books are disposed of in Paragraph (d) hereinbelow.

d. I give to the Diocese of Pittsburgh for placement in its Diocesan Archives, or other appropriate place at St. Paul Seminary or elsewhere, the books excepted in Paragraph (c) hereinabove, together with all my personal papers, records, and personal archives, clipping files, medallions, stamp collections, photo albums, and like souvenirs and the bound albums of the Worcester Catholic Free Press and the Pittsburgh Catholic, including but not limited to all such items in my residence in Rome and my residence in St. Paul Seminary in Pittsburgh. This gift is made with the confidence that, in the event of the appointment by my Executors of a Literary Executor as hereinafter provided for, the said Diocese will make available to my Executors all such papers, records, and other material as they may request for the purpose of the Literary Executor which are acceptable to them. This gift further includes papers boxed for storage, located in a special room set apart therefor in the Administration Building of St. Paul Seminary and which by their nature should be returned to the dioceses to which they pertain.

e. The set of twenty-five consecutive pontifical annual medallions commemorating the years of the pontificates of those Popes under whom I served as a Bishop (which collection, boxed in red, may be located in my residence in Rome or in my safety deposit box in the New England Merchants National Bank, Boston, Massachusetts) and given to me by the members of the Congregation for the Clergy on the Silver Jubilee of my consecration as a Bishop, I give to the Diocese of Pittsburgh for placement in its Diocesan Archives or any other appropriate place chosen by the Bishop of Pittsburgh.

f. Any items of personal property not distributable under any of the foregoing provisions of this Article *Third* I give and bequeath to those individuals and institutions designated to receive them as indicated by me in a memorandum dated April 2, 1977. To the extent that items are not so disposed of or cannot be transferred because a designated individual does not survive me or a designated institution is not in existence at the time of my death, I authorize my Executors to dispose of such items as they deem suitable in their discretion, provided that a gift to an institution cannot be replaced by a gift to an individual.

Fourth: In accordance with an exchange of letters between myself and the Trustees of the Boston Public Library, I hereby ratify and confirm my gift of books, objects of art, medals, medallions, stained glass pieces, or other items pertaining to the life, work, and memory of Saint Joan of Arc, wherever located (including the altarpiece reredos and the original sculpture of Saint Joan of Arc given by me to St. Paul Cathedral, Pittsburgh, Pennsylvania, if at any time and for whatever reason these are no longer used in the Saint Joan of Arc Chapel therein), to the Boston Public Library of Boston, Massachusetts, to be kept in the Bishop Cheverus Room as a reminder of the French first Bishop of Boston and the French missionaries of Catholicism in New England, as well as the French influence, thanks to Catholics and Protestants, in the city of my birth. I further give to the said Trustees, to be kept in the said Room, all articles relating to Saint Joan of Arc, Chinon, or related items located in my residence in Rome.

Fifth: If at the time of my death I am the owner of an automobile located in the Vatican City State or the Republic of Italy, I give such automobile to the pastor of my titular church in Rome, Christ the Divine Teacher, to serve the pastoral needs of that parish.

Sixth: I direct my Executors to dispose of any items of my tangible personal property not distributable under any of the foregoing Articles *First, Second, Third, Fourth,* and *Fifth* as they may determine in their discretion, whether by way of gift or otherwise.

473

Seventh: I give to the Pittsburgh diocesan offices of the Society for the Propagation of the Faith:

    a. The sum of three thousand dollars ($3,000) to be distributed among priests in offerings of five dollars ($5.00) apiece for special Masses for the repose of my soul and reparation for my sins of commission or omission while in the service of the Church.

    b. The sum of two thousand dollars ($2,000) to be transmitted to the pastor of my titular church in Rome, Christ the Divine Teacher, for the general purposes of the parish.

Eighth: Any balances I may have in the Pie Opere Bank of the Vatican I give to the Holy See, for the charitable purposes of the Holy Father.

Ninth: Because I owe to the Boston Latin School my introduction to the traditions of Western civilization that I like to think of as my own, and in the hope that what the School does for its students may be in some degree supplemented hereby, I direct my Executors to purchase for the School Library one complete set of Migne's *Latin and Greek* Church Fathers.

Tenth: All the rest and residue of my estate, real, personal or mixed, of which I shall die seized or possessed, or to which I may be in any way entitled at the time of my death, or over which I may then have any power of appointment (excluding that referred to in Article *Twelfth* hereunder), I give, devise, and bequeath as follows:

    a. One-twentieth (1/20th) thereof to La Roche College, Allison Park, Pennsylvania.

    b. One-twentieth (1/20th) thereof to Anna Maria College, Paxton, Massachusetts.

    c. One-twentieth (1/20th) thereof to the Pittsburgh diocesan office of the Society for the Propagation of the Faith.

    d. One-twentieth (1/20th) thereof to McGuire Memorial, Mercer Road, New Brighton, Pennsylvania.

e. One-twentieth (1/20th) thereof to Boston College for the use of its library.

f. The remaining three-fourths (3/4th) in equal shares to the Ordinaries of the three dioceses in which I have served, Boston, Worcester and Pittsburgh, for any religious purpose they may choose.

Eleventh:

a. I hereby appoint the Most Reverend Anthony G. Bosco, my sister, Margaret Wright Haverty, and C. Holmes Wolfe, Jr., and Reverend Donald W. Wuerl, if he is still serving as my personal secretary at the time of my death, executors of this will. They are further required, by this Last Will and Testament, to accept recompense for all expenses they shall incur in connection with the travel which may be needed to wind up the affairs of a priest who has residences so far apart and beneficiaries so widely scattered.

b. I direct my said Executors to transfer the items of tangible personal property bequeathed in Articles *First, Second, Third, Fourth, Fifth,* and *Sixth* hereinabove to the legatees thereof at the expense of my personal estate, which will pay such charges as packing, freight, and insurance.

c. I authorize my said Executors, in their discretion and under such terms and conditions as they deem suitable, to appoint one or more individuals, corporations, or other entities to serve as my Literary Executor with respect to such papers, records, and other material as my Executors may make available. In the event such appointment is made, and to the extent permitted by law, my Executors need not account to any court of law with respect to the property so administered by them or with respect to any funds produced thereby. If such funds are produced, they shall be distributed, after payment of all necessary and proper expenses, to the residuary legatees named in Article

475

Tenth hereinabove and in the respective proportions set forth therein.[1]

d. I direct that no bond or other security be required of any fiduciaries administering my estate in any jurisdiction in which any of them may act; or if bond be required, I direct that there shall be no surety on such bond.

e. I give to my said Executors, in addition to the authority conferred by law but subject always to my wishes as hereinabove expressed, the power to sell any or all of my property, real or personal, at public or private sale, at such time and for such price and upon such terms and conditions as they may see fit, or in their discretion to retain the same for distribution in kind, and the power, but not the duty, to invest any cash without being limited to *legal* investments.

Twelfth: If at the time of my death I still retain a power of appointment over the trust committed to me by the late Medora A. Feehan in her will dated June 20, 1952, and since I have at all times attempted to administer this trust in accordance with the letter and spirit of Mrs. Feehan's directions and without benefit to myself or anyone associated with me, as is more fully set forth in the official records relating to said trust, I hereby exercise said appointment in favor of, and direct the payment of the entire principal and any accumulated income, together with any additions that may have been made thereto from any source whatever, to the Roman Catholic Archbishop of Boston, a corporation sole under the laws of Massachusetts, to use for any religious, educational, and charitable purposes which he deems appropriate.

Thirteenth: All estate, inheritance, succession, and other death taxes, imposed or payable by reason of my death, and interest and penalties thereon, with respect to all property comprising my gross estate for death tax purposes, whether or not such property passes under this Will, shall be paid out of the principal of my personal estate, as if such taxes were administration expenses, and without apportionment or right of reimbursement, *Provided,* however, that any such taxes payable with respect to the property over which I was given a power of appointment under the Will of Medora A. Feehan, deceased, shall be paid out of such property prior to the distribution thereof as hereinabove provided. I authorize my Executors to pay all such taxes at such time or times as they deem advisable.

In testimony hereof, I hereunto set my hand and seal and, in the presence of three witnesses, declare this to be my last Will this *3rd* day of *October,* 1978.

John J. Wright (seal)
J. Card. Wright (seal)

Signed, sealed, published and declared by the above-named *John J. Wright,* also known as *John Cardinal Wright,* as and for his Last Will and Testament, in the presence of us, who, at his request, in his presence and in the presence of each other, have hereunto subscribed our names as witnesses.

William M. Helmick
2101 Commonwealth Avenue
Brighton, Mass.

James L. McCune
2101 Commonwealth Avenue
Brighton, Mass.

Mary Madeline McManus
188 Foster Street
Brighton, Mass.

XXXIX

Autobiography: Outline 1909–1978

1. Family and Youthful Background

2. Boston Latin School

3. Boston College:
   with special emphasis on friendships made with members of opposite debating teams who later became good friends: Ed Hanify, Paul C. Reardon.

4. *The Boston Post*

5. Saint John Seminary:
   Ed Murray

6. North American College, Rome:
   characteristics in period 1932–1939 —faculty—friends— choice of dissertation —Father Ed Coffey, S.J. Subsequent interest in nationalism and international peace. Publication and further additional editions of my doctoral dissertation. Scotland —England —France and Corbiac.

7. Saint John Seminary and Saint Clement Shrine

8. League of Catholic Women

9. War Programs:
   France and Italy

10. Secretary to Cardinal O'Connell and Chancery

11. Honorary Degrees

12. Themes of Commencement Talks

13. Relations in the 1940s and 1950s to intellectual movements.

14. The Examiner Club:
    The Club of Odd Volumes
    list of other clubs

15. Leo Rabbette
    Dorothy Wayman

16. Auxiliary Bishop of Boston:
    circumstances
    experiences

17. Community Work

18. *Boston Globe* editorial:
    Frank Buxton

19. Worcester:
    first experiences and impressions—John Gannon—Andy
    Holmstrom—George Booth, *et al.*, —Saint Vincent
    Hospital —Mention two talks that used to infuriate the
    Irish (sad songs and nine young men). —Franco-Ameri-
    cans —*All the World Was Spring* —New Parishes —
    Tornado —Assumption College —Anna Maria Col-
    lege —Governor Herter's Commission for Court Re-
    form. —Stepped up work for unwed mothers —Attitude
    toward Social Service —Lay Retreat Movement in the
    United States —Peace Activity —Public Addresses
    —Hopes for future at that time.

20. Transfer to Pittsburgh:
    significant circumstances of place where confirmation
    of appointment was learned —Father Honan —ethnic
    groups —markedly different religious climate —com-
    munity contacts —Shadyside Presbyterian Church —

479

The Oratory —Roselia —The Latin School, hopes and betrayal —The Kennedy Campaign (reference in Sorensen's book) —Pastoral Council —Father Claude Leetham —The beginning of the change in the younger clergy and signs of oncoming winter —Themes of some interviews or articles at this period —Activities in the National Conference of Bishops.

Appointment to Preparatory Theological Commissions of Vatican Council II —Excerpts from Yzermans' book on American participation in the Council, especially summary of my extra-curricular activities during the Council —Other references from books on the Council —Friendships made at the Council: Bishop Colombo, Bishop Ancel, *et al.*

The Council an opportunity for renewal of contacts with France —Chinon and Saint Joan of Arc —Panegyrics on the latter —Special French ties —Legion of Honor.

21. First Synod of Bishops
    Second Synod of Bishops
    Third Synod of Bishops (one of three presidents)

22. Selection as Cardinal:
    again, strange circumstances of place in all this — Excitement of having temporary office, stationery, etc., of Cardinal in Pittsburgh —Editorial in the *New York Times* —Round of visits in the Diocese —Final Mass at St. Paul Cathedral: Haydn.

23. Titular Church

24. Congregation for the Clergy:
    other Congregations —Catechetical Congress —Congress on the Distribution of Clergy —Problem of First

Confession — Tensions and Changes of the Period —
Quotes from some interviews and speeches of that period.

25. The sudden rise of an unexpected and sometimes painful
opposition:[1]
origin: the Pope's encyclical on *Human Life* — overt
channels: Dan Herr, the *National Catholic Reporter,* odds
and ends of hierarchy, Kenneth Woodward, Xavier
Rynne — Firmer determination than ever to write and
fight for human life — the National Pastoral — Human
Life Foundation.

26. On the more positive and pleasant side:
floods of letters from friends known and unknown
— Quotes from speeches or interviews on the turn of
the tide and the coming spring — Outspoken friends:
priests in England, Cardinal Jean Daniélou, S.J., innumerable laity all over the world.

27. Lourdes trips

28. Visits to Italian dioceses.

XL

Autobiography: Details 1946–1969

1946

1. *Some Important Events:*
   Lunch with French Consul on an urgent matter (May 10 at the Somerset Club, Boston) — Atomic Energy people, two meetings, one with group at League House, Boston, and one with representatives (August).[1]

2. *Lecture and Preaching Tours:*
   Washington, Chicago, Burlington (Vermont) and Portland (Maine).

3. *People:*
   Dana Greeley, Mrs. Bottomley, Cardinal Stepinac, Dr. Vaughan and Dorothy Wayman.

1947

1. *Some Important Events:*
   Episcopal Consecration — named Auxiliary Bishop of Boston (Monday, June 30).

2. *Lecture and Preaching Tours:*
   Portland (Maine), Toledo (Ohio), and Montreal (Canada).

3. *People:*
   Mrs. Feehan, Ed Hanify, French Consul, Mrs. Bottomley, Cardinal Stepinac, Dana Greeley, Dr. Lord, Tom Mahony, Cardinal Tisserant, Italian Consul, Julian Steele, Princess Radziwill, and Jules Verne.

1948

1. *Some Important Events:*
   Retreat to the students of the Matignon High School
   (February 22–24) — De Valera Dinner (March 27) — Medora
   Feehan Day (July 16).

2. *Lecture and Preaching Tours:*
   New York, Baltimore, Washington, Des Moines, Philadel-
   phia — Canada (July 4–12, Shrine of Ste. Anne de Beaupré)
   — Rome and Lourdes (August 13–September 23).

3. *People:*
   Julian Steele, Italian Consul, Elena and Edward Hughes,
   Dorothy Wayman, Mrs. Bottomley, French Consul, Eunice
   Kennedy, Monsignor Furlong, Bill McCarthy, and Arch-
   bishop Yu Pin.

1949

1. *Some Important Events:*
   Red Mass at Washington, D.C. (January 16) — Blessing of
   the Fishing Fleet at Gloucester, Mass. (June 19 and June
   26) — Preacher for the Maryknoll Sisters' Departure Ceremony at Maryknoll, N.Y. (July 3).

2. *Lecture and Preaching Tours:*
   Canada (July 10–16, Shrine of Ste. Anne de Beaupré)
   — Ireland (September 8–October 2).

3. *People:*
   Ed Hanify, Mrs. Bottomley, Princess Radziwill, Joe Sullivan, and Eleanor Roberts Jason.

1950

1. *Some Important Events:*
   Installation as First Bishop of Worcester (Tuesday, March 7).

2. *Lecture and Preaching Tours:*
New York, Buffalo, Detroit, Los Angeles, Portland (Maine),
Washington, Philadelphia. Sail from Montreal, Canada,
on Sunday, July 23 with the Ste. Anne de Beaupré Pilgrimage to Rome.

3. *People:*
Jacques Maritain, Monsignor John Gannon, Jack Deedy,
Mary Melican, Raymond Harold, Dan O'Leary, Father Har-
rington, Father O'Connell, Grace Gummo, Mr. Meagher,
Elena and Edward Hughes, Mrs. Herbert N. Dawes, and
Brother Brassard.

1951

1. *Some Important Events:*
Address the Laymen's Retreat Conference, Pittsburgh, Pa.
(November 6).

2. *Lecture and Preaching Tours:*
New York City, Washington, Raleigh (North Carolina),
Portland (Maine), Philadelphia, Hartford, Albany, Chicago,
and Spain.

3. *People:*
Dorothy Baker, Father Luke O'Connor, S.J., Dorothy
Wayman, Italian Consul, French Consul, and Clare Booth
Luce.

1952

1. *Some Important Events:*
TV Show *Lamp Unto My Feet* — CBS (New York, March
16) — Holy Hour for National Laywomen's Retreat Movement at Old St. Patrick Church, Pittsburgh, Pa. (June
6) — Address on *The Diplomatic Activity of the Holy See*
to the St. Thomas More Society of the Harvard Law

School, Hotel Commander, Cambridge, Mass. (November 16).

2. *Lecture and Preaching Tours:*
   New York City, Philadelphia, Washington, Cincinnati, Columbus, Bridgeport, Detroit, Marquette, Milwaukee, Chicago, Davenport, Seattle, Richmond, and Houlton (Maine).

3. *People:*
   Joe Kennedy, Father Morlion, Congressman Herter, Crotty, Heffernan, Higgins, Maurice Adelman, Hammershaimbs, James Kritzeck, Senator Lodge, and Isabelle Redmond.

1953

1. *Some Important Events:*
   Honorary Degree from Loyola University, Chicago (February 4) — Worcester Tornado (June 9) Honorary Degree from Fordham University (June 10) — Preached at the First Mass of Father Robert F. Drinan, S.J. (St. Ignatius Church, Chestnut Hill, Mass., on July 5) — Inaugurated Days of Recollection and Closed Retreats, Religious of the Cenacle, Bayard Thayer Estate, Lancaster, Mass. (October 31).

2. *Lecture and Preaching Tours:*
   Pilgrimage to the Shrines of Canada (July 27–August 2).

3. *People:*
   The Trappists at Spencer, Gregory Wiggin, Mayor Holmstrom, Father Desautels, A.A., and Governor Herter.

1954

1. *Some Important Events:*
   Honorary Degree from St. John University (March 6) — Television Presentation, *The Madonna in Art,* from the

485

Worcester Art Museum (April 10) — Clergy Retreat at Mundelein, Ill. (April 19–23 and April 26–30) — Clergy Retreat, Raleigh, North Carolina (May 10–14).

2. *Lecture and Preaching Tours:*
   Pilgrimage to Rome and Lourdes (June 23–July 24) — Canadian Pilgrimage for the Marian Year (August 1–7).

3. *People:*
   Father Pelletier, A.A., Judge Meagher, Walter Muir White-hill, and Dr. Gregory Zilboorg.

1955

1. *Some Important Events:*
   Diocesan Retreat at Fort Wayne, Indiana (June 5–10) — Retreat for Clergy, Archdiocese of Denver (July 11–15) — Clergy Retreat, Pueblo, Colorado (July 18–20).

2. *Lecture and Preaching Tours:*
   Pilgrimage to Canada (July 31–August 5).

3. *People:*
   Senator John F. Kennedy and Father Gremillion.

1956

1. *Some Important Events:*
   Retreat for Students, McGill University, Montreal (February 28–March 2) — Sermon for the 400th Anniversary of Saint Ignatius, Saint Ignatius Church, Park Avenue, New York City (March 11) — Communion Breakfast, Newman Club, United States Naval Academy, Annapolis (April 22) — Clergy Retreat, San Francisco Archdiocese (June 18–28).

2. *Lecture and Preaching Tours:*
   Pilgrimage to the Shrines of France and Rome (August 14–September 24).

3. *People:*
   Senator John F. Kennedy, Mayor O'Brien, Father William Chassagne, Father Daniel Rankin, Father Blanchette, and Father H. R. Reinhold.

1957

1. *Some Important Events:*
   Decoration from the Republic of Italy (January 16) — Speaker at the Meeting of the Overseas Press Club, New York City (December 2).

2. *People:*
   Barbara Ward, Father George Tavard, Jane Doherty, Claire Leighton, Joe Benedict, and Alice Curtayne.

1958

1. *Some Important Events:*
   Address to the English Catholic Educational Association, Royal York Hotel, Toronto, Canada (April 8) —Preached at Bishop Hayes' Anniversary Mass, Davenport, Iowa (September 24).

2. *People:*
   Joseph Cunneen, Regine Pernoud, Father Joseph Marique, S.J., and Dr. Joseph Lichten.

1959

1. *Some Important Events:*
   Leave Worcester for Pittsburgh (March 16). —Formal Arrival at St. Paul Cathedral, Pittsburgh, presented documents at the Cathedral Rectory, Press Conference at Newman Hall and in the evening reception of Archbishops and Bishops (March 17). —Installation Mass at St. Paul Cathedral (March 18) —Public Reception at Rockwell

Hall, Duquesne University (March 22) —Honorary Degree from Mount Mercy College (May 12) — Honorary Degree from Georgetown University (June 8).

2. *Lecture and Preaching Tours:*
   New York City (August 5–12), Centenary of the North American College, Rome (October 11th), Milan (October 13th), and Rome (October 18–21).

3. *People:*
   General Ridgway, George Eby, Bishop Elko, Father Mallouk, Ed D'Emilio, Geza Grosschmidt, Gerald Mische (A.I.D.), and Reverend Kincheloe.

1960

1. *Some Important Events:*
   WQED TV, *Meet the People* (February 3) —Lectures at Harvard University (April 29–30) —Mass and Communion Breakfast at Harvard University (December 4) —Easter Blessing of Babies at St. Paul Cathedral.

2. *People:*
   Christopher Dawson and Dr. Litchfield.

1961

Appointment Book Missing

1962

Appointment Book Missing

1963

1. *Some Important Events:*
   Preparatory Meeting for Vatican Council II.

2. *People:*

John-Stephen Gilchrist, Father B. Leeming, S.J., and Archbishop Frane Franic.

1964

1. *Some Important Events:*
   Vatican Council II, Rome (September 12–November 25) —Eucharistic Congress, Bombay, India (November 29–December 12).

2. *People:*
   Bill Ball, Arnold Denys, and Germain Grisez.

1965

1. *Some Important Events:*
   Course on *Ecclesiam Suam* for WDUQ Pittsburgh (April 25) —Dante Sesquicentennial, University of Detroit (May 18) —Daedalus Conference, Boston (October 15).

2. *People:*
   Philip Scharper, Bill Storey, Genevieve Blatt, Homer Jack, and Sister James Regis (Roselia).

1966

1. *Some Important Events:*
   Meeting with U. Thant, United Nations (February 4) —Ordination of Bishop John B. Mc Dowell (September 8) —Meeting with Dr. Martin Luther King, Dallas, Texas (September 25) —Meeting of the Theological Commission, Vatican City (September 26–October 3) —Meeting with the Leaders of the National Council of Churches, New York City (October 24) —Laying of the Cornerstone for the John J. Wright Library at La Roche College (November 23).

2. *Lecture and Preaching Tours:*

489

Scandinavia from November 27 to December 6, 1966. Copenhagen (November 27) visit with the Apostolic Delegate Archbishop Bruno Heim and lecture: *Ecumenism and the Thrust of the Second Vatican Council.* Dinner (November 28) hosted by Archbishop Heim—the American Ambassador present.

3. *People:*
   Bishop Pardue (Episcopalian), Bishop Newell (Methodist), Rabbi Jacob (Rodef Shalom), Rabbi Halperin, and David L. Lawrence.

1967

1. *Some Important Events:*
   Dedication of the Pittsburgh Cenacle (May 30) —Clergy Retreat at Saint Scholastica College, Duluth, Minnesota (June 5–8) —Chaired Symposium on *Creative Arts and Christian Renewal* at Rosary College, Illinois (June 9–10) —Diocesan Pastoral Council, Pittsburgh (June 17–18).

2. *Lecture and Preaching Tours:*
   China—June 26–28 in Taipei and Taiwan. June 29 Mass and Dedication (at the invitation of Archbishop Yu Pin) of the new buildings at the Fu-Jen Catholic University, Taipei. June 30 lecture at Fu-Jen University on *The Mission of Intellectuals in Today's World.* —Seoul, Korea (July 5) —Synod of Bishops (Rome) from September 17 to November 7.

3. *People:*
   Father Moylan, Higgins, Cronin, Lester Hamburg (De Paul Institute), Matt Ahmann, Earl Belle Smith, Herman Will, Rabbi Maurice Eisendrath, and Dr. Ruiz-Giminez.

1968

1. *Some Important Events:*
Work on the Collective Pastoral, *The Church in Our Day* — Ordination of Bishop Appleyard (Episcopal) in Saint Paul Cathedral (February 10) — Diocesan Pastoral Council, Pittsburgh (March 22–23) Inaugural Convocation for Dr. Wesley Posvar as Chancellor of the University of Pittsburgh (March 27) — Attend Funeral Services for Dr. Martin Luther King (at the request of Mrs. Coretta Scott King) at the Ebenezer Baptist Church, Atlanta . . . proceed in 3-mile walk to Morehouse College and participate in the ecumenical service (April 9) — First Anniversary of the Oratory University Parish (April 15) — Funeral for Senator Robert F. Kennedy, Saint Patrick Cathedral, New York City (June 8) — Diocesan Pastoral Council, Pittsburgh (June 14–15) — Dedication of the statue of Saint Benedict the Moor atop Church of Saint Brigid–Saint Benedict, Hill District, Pittsburgh (July 21) — Diocesan Pastoral Council, Pittsburgh (September 14) — Opening of the Diocesan Synod in Saint Paul Cathedral . . . Haydn Mass (December 8).

2. *Lecture and Preaching Tours:*
Rome (August 11–18). Chimbote, Peru (September 18–27).

1969

1. *Some Important Events:*
First General Preparatory Session of the Diocesan Synod (February 9) — Diocesan Pastoral Council, Pittsburgh (March 8) — Mass in Saint Paul Cathedral for Tenth Anniversary in Pittsburgh (March 18) — Announcement by the Apostolic Delegate in Washington that Wright has been named a Cardinal by Paul VI (March 28) — Leave for Rome and the Consistory (April 25) — *"Red Hat"* (April

30) —Mass in Saint Paul Cathedral (May 11) —Civic Reception at the Pittsburgh Hilton (June 2) —Leave Pittsburgh for Rome—via Boston (Televised Mass from Channel 7 Studios, Government Center on June 8), Worcester (Reception at Kimball Hall, Holy Cross College on June 11 and Mass in St. Paul Cathedral on June 12), and New York City (Dinner with the American Hierarchy on June 13) —Sail for Rome on the Raffaello (June 15) —Arrive Naples (June 22).

2. *Lecture and Preaching Tours:*
Rome, on way to Istanbul (February 17), Istanbul for the World Conference on Religion and Peace (February 20).

3. *People:*
Dr. Karl Barth
Father Henri de Lubac, S.J.

XLI

A Conversation with Desmond O'Grady

Cardinal John Wright wryly describes himself as "the most recent Roman ruin". At sixty-nine, he has been sorely tried by cataracts and a rare disease of the leg muscles, which makes him liable to fall without warning.[1]

"I might write a book on famous people who have picked me up", he says, recalling that his first tumble was in a Boston street, "where Yankees stood around to admire me for five minutes before I was taken into a grocery store."

He continues as Prefect of the Vatican Congregation for Clergy, a post he has occupied since 1969. "To be prefect", he has said, "it is more important to be able to think than to be able to walk." His brain is still lucid.

I asked Cardinal Wright if he has been disappointed by the Council's aftermath.

Wright: That's a very delicate question but also a fair one. The things which were uppermost in my mind at the Council have not made out the best. My only major speech at the Council was on the place of laymen in the Church, but I'm not satisfied with their place yet, so far as theology is concerned.

When the cathedral in Boston was built, we had laymen there who devoted enormous talent to fighting for every human and decent cause. I'm thinking of men from the Young Ireland Movement such as John Boyle O'Reilly, who escaped from prison in Australia and reached America: my father used to say they swam from Australia to Boston. O'Reilly

This interview was published in the April 29, 1979, issue of *Our Sunday Visitor.*

and others were far more effective than any laymen I know of today.

It [also] gives me a pip to hear only exaggerated talk about the ecumenical progress deriving from the Council. The seeds for this were planted before the Council.

We Catholics love to claim that we were a ghetto community in the nineteenth-century USA, but we were not. We were an ethnically defined community, but the amount of hostility and difficulties it caused have been exaggerated. There was a period of fear that Catholics would take Protestants' jobs, but nasty incidents are rehashed whereas counter-balancing ones are forgotten.... All that side of Catholic–Protestant relations has been swamped by emphasis on the regrettable *No Catholics Need Apply* memories.

The only framed photo on Henry Cabot Lodge, Jr.'s[2] study wall was of Cardinal O'Connell. He told me O'Connell had encouraged him: "I'm with you all the way, Cabot—just keep your nose clean!"

Cardinal Cushing preached from Protestant and Jewish pulpits before the Council. So did I. We never deviated from the Faith, you can be sure. We were welcome as neighbors.

O'Grady: You make it sound as if we've moved backward rather than forward.

Wright: We grew up—and then got scared. With Dana McLean Greeley, a pastor of the First United Church in Concord, and Maurice N. Eisendrath, a New York rabbi, I established the National Interreligious Conference on Peace, which has held several important ecumenical meetings in Kyoto, Istanbul, New Delhi, and Rome. The seeds for this were planted before the Council. Ecumenism was a reality before

	the Council, with laymen as leaders as they should be.
O'Grady:	You sound disappointed on that aspect of the Council's aftermath.
Wright:	Disappointed is too strong a word. But the Church still has to catch up with the Council, and the world to catch up with the Church. One cramping factor, of course, was that the world's political problems became so acute after the Council that most feel hard-pressed by them.
O'Grady:	Do you think there is anything comparable now to the sense of direction people such as the French Catholic philosopher Jacques Maritain had before the Council?
Wright:	I don't know anyone in the Church today playing a prophetic role as great as Maritain's. He made a devout and decent humanism possible and an increased role for laymen in the Church. I was his confessor when he taught at Harvard and Princeton. I know that Jacques and his wife Raïssa had been through rough times. I feel the key to the difference between him and the New Breed *Thinkers* is that he was capable of suffering. Nowadays, when the shoe pinches, some priests are ready to quit, laymen too ready to evade responsibilities. I recall the sterling work Jacques did when looking after Spanish refugees at L'Eau Vive during the Spanish Civil War and admire him both as a thinker and one who really lived his faith.
	Charles Péguy is another great preconciliar layman who taught a whole generation of Frenchmen that they could love both their country and the Church—despite the fact that his wife was violently anticlerical.
O'Grady:	What authority have priests' councils and pastoral

495

councils particularly in relation to the authority of
bishops?

Wright: The situation ranges from total episcopal absolut-
ism to abdication of responsibility. I have in mind a
United States diocese where a young priest has
been persecuted to death. I write to him each
fortnight. He is now near the Canadian frontier. It's
not the bishop who has ridden him into the ground
but the priests' council.

As a residential bishop, I had difficulty in getting
a priests' council going because some of my priests
wanted assurances that they would still have direct
access to me. Every now and again priests' councils
take dioceses out of the bishop's hands. Another
danger is that they can become self-perpetuating
groups.

I remember one night when Cardinal Cushing
made his regular call to me in Pittsburgh at 11 P.M.
to ask, "How do I get out of this?" I asked how he
had gotten into it. He said he had told the personnel
commission, which was a kind of precursor of the
priests' council, to fill five positions. They made a
complete hash of it, appointing, for instance, a French
priest to a Polish parish. Cardinal Cushing, faced
with a revolt by the five priests, had to sit down
with them and rearrange the assignments.

That shows a danger of priests' councils, but I
think that, on the whole, they've worked well,
provided the bishop attends every meeting to ensure
there are no shenanigans. After all, the priests' council is advisory, not decision-making, and if the bishop
isn't present to hear the advice, what good is it?

Parish pastoral councils have worked less well. I
know of only five that are top class, such as that of
Father Joe Hannon in Pittsburgh. Their greatest

defect is that they can become self-perpetuating instead of involving many parishioners, and sometimes tend to dictate rather than counsel the pastor; think of Arlington.

O'Grady: What impression have you of the morale of the diocesan clergy worldwide? What is their heaviest cross?

Wright: Their morale is spotty. Their heaviest cross is boredom when they engage in nonpastoral work; show me an apostolically busy priest, and I'll show you the happiest man in town.

O'Grady: What positive signs do you see for the future?

Wright: The most active Catholics are in Africa and Asia and in persecuted churches of Europe. I'm always running into United States' bishops on their way to Ireland because there are insufficient vocations in their dioceses. It's not so with the Africans, they made the shift from colonialism smoothly. They're reading the signs of the times infallibly. They're quite happy to let non-Catholics or pagans run the state while they tend to the Church. They're bright: the future belongs to them. Asia too. (Though I read through tears of the possible fate of Taiwan. I came to love it on a visit there.) But think of Korea: the only country converted by laymen, it has plenty of vocations. The future of Catholicism in such places is beyond belief.

O'Grady: What do you think is the Vatican's major misunderstanding of others and others' major misunderstanding of the Vatican?

Wright: Rome, not without reason, takes the position that it's coextensive with civilization. Chesterton has a poem which expresses this—a Roman soldier dying in Suffolk says that he is dying in Rome, "for all the earth is Roman earth". This is a kind of

497

arrogance of which I'm guilty also. Belloc overdid it.

One of the mistakes of non-Catholics with regard to Rome is to consider the Pope as a *semideity.* John Paul II seems to have made it part of his business to clear up that mistake. The other day he married a couple and the girl asked if she could kiss him. "Why not?" was his reply.

Recent popes have shown their humanity increasingly—it's a very interesting development. I never had the idea that the Pope was a *semideity*—and I doubt *they* had. Pius XII had a reputation as being very aloof. I took my parents to him on the fiftieth anniversary of their wedding. He asked my mother what the discs on her bracelet stood for. She explained that they were for her twenty-six children and grandchildren, and he was interested in every detail. Paul VI was tortured by the Council aftermath we spoke about, but he too was very human. Once he asked me what I thought of contemporary preaching. Horrible, was my answer. He asked me what I intended to do about it. I don't know, I replied; because we seem to swing from deadly dullness to the high-flown, above-the-clouds rhetoric of Bossuet. "Don't say that", said Pope Paul, "Bossuet sermons dropped out of my mother's hands as she was dying."

O'Grady: I had in mind also Catholics' misunderstandings about Rome and the Vatican.

Wright: These were largely due, I feel, to the Italianate nature of the Roman Curia. The average intelligent Roman prelate wanted to alter this situation, and it is being altered with Poles, Africans, Australians, Americans, and other non-Italians now playing a big part in the Vatican.[3]

498

O'Grady:	Why do you value the *New Yorker* over many theological reviews?
Wright:	For a darn good reason. It has more to do with existential theology than much speculation. (It is a great achievement for the *New Yorker* people to have put out that magazine without a spot of smut for all these years.) Its cartoons frequently make theological comments. For instance, recently there was a full page cartoon of Moses descending from Mount Sinai with the Tablets of the Law. A Jew greeted him with the words: "It's clear, it's concise, it's good stuff but it won't sell." It must have been a success because the cartoon reappeared with the caption, spoken by a young man, "Could you rewrite that to make it intelligible for my generation?" Half of the column fillers have little theological twists. But remember also that, as well the humor, the *New Yorker* publishes substantial articles such as that on the Dead Sea scrolls.
O'Grady:	What is the greatest sadness in life?
Wright:	Man's inhumanity to man. The stupid reasons for which we go to war. And a bright kid without the money for his education. I was lucky!
O'Grady:	What is your idea of happiness?
Wright:	Good news from home.
O'Grady:	Who is your favorite fictional character?
Wright:	Myles Connolly's *Mr. Blue* in the book of the same name.
O'Grady:	What qualities do you most admire in men?
Wright:	Masculinity.
O'Grady:	And in women?
Wright:	Femininity.
O'Grady:	What is your favorite recreation?
Wright:	Hi-fi.
O'Grady:	Which is your favorite holiday resort?

Wright: When I did take holidays it was on Grand Lake in
             Maine. From everywhere on the lake you could see
             deer.
O'Grady: What is the main trait of your character?
Wright: I like to be liked. And I can sense it when I'm not.
O'Grady: What is your main defect?
Wright: Impatience.
O'Grady: How would you like to die?
Wright: Standing up at the altar.

Conclusion

In 1959, while Bishop of Pittsburgh, Cardinal Wright preached
the sermon at the solemn Mass, held at Saint Patrick Church,
Montreal, Canada, in honor of the beatification of Mother
Marguerite d'Youville. In his sermon, Wright said:

> The life of Mother d'Youville teaches, of course, those lessons
> which are almost commonplace among the truths we learn
> from the lives of all our saints. Her life teaches us how God
> draws good out of evil for those who love Him. It teaches
> how strange, circuitous, are the ways of His providence for
> His saints, those He must chiefly love if only because they so
> greatly love Him. Her life reminds us of how contradiction,
> frustration, heartbreak, and defeat are so often the lot of those
> who strive to be His holy ones and to love Him most. And it
> teaches us, as do the lives of the saints generally, how victory
> is usually hidden in defeat, how the gold of sanctity must be
> tried, as by fire, in adversity.[1]

And so it was a coincidence—Wright would have called it a *holy*
coincidence and *Divine Providence*—that he would spend his last
days in the care of Mother d'Youville's daughters: the Grey
Nuns.

Cardinal Wright died at the Youville Rehabilitation and
Chronic Disease Hospital, Cambridge, Mass., on Friday, August
10, 1979, at 8:15 P.M. The cause of death—after almost two years
in a wheelchair, a series of operations and care at the Tufts-New
England Medical Center—was polymyositis, a degenerative neu-
romuscular disease (diagnosed in him ten years before). At his
death, he was 70 years old.

Wright's body—vested, as per his request, in purple Mass

vestments with a rosary clasped in his hands—was first brought
to the residence of the Cardinal-Archbishop of Boston (where
he had lived while secretary to Cardinals O'Connell and Cushing,
to which he returned frequently throughout the years, and
which he used during the various stages of his final illness) and
was waked, in the Cardinal's residence, on Tuesday, August 14,
from 2 to 9 P.M. On the next day, Wednesday, August 15, his
body was transferred to the Holy Name Church in Boston's
West Roxbury section—which held so many memories of his
Boston roots and early life—and was waked on Wednesday and
Thursday, again, from 2 to 9 P.M.

On Friday, August 17, the funeral Mass was held in the same
church—Boston's cathedral being under repair—at 11 A.M. Cardinal Humberto Medeiros, Archbishop of Boston, was the principal celebrant. Archbishop Jean Jadot, apostolic delegate to the
United States, eleven cardinals, 100 bishops, Father Donald W.
Wuerl (Wright's secretary for 12 years), the Cardinal's nephew
Father John Wright, and hundreds of priests were concelebrants.

Serving as lectors were: former Ambassador to Italy John W.
Volpe (who read from Job 19:1, 23–27); Dr. Annabelle Melville,
a noted church historian, read from Paul's Second Letter to the
Corinthians (2 Cor 5:1, 6–10); and the Gospel (Jn 11:17–27) was
proclaimed by Monsignor Edward G. Murray, Wright's seminary professor, rector, and mentor. Father Donald W. Wuerl led
the 2,000-member congregation in the General Intercessions.

Bishop Vincent M. Leonard, Wright's immediate successor in
the Diocese of Pittsburgh, delivered the following homily:

> "Life is changed, not ended." In this short sentence taken from
> the Preface of the Mass of Christian Burial, the Christian
> teaching as to what occurs at death is expressed as briefly as
> possible. It may appear simplistic and for some persons raise
> more questions than answers. But Paul supports this teaching
> in the second scriptural lesson of this Mass—"For we know
> that when the earthly tent in which we dwell is destroyed we
> have a dwelling place provided for us by God, a dwelling in

the heavens not made by hands but to last forever." For this reason we are full of confidence. We walk by faith, not by sight.

As with Saint Paul, our faith is centered in one who walked this earth as a man, yet was more than a man and proclaimed of Himself to the bereaved Martha, "I am the Resurrection and the life. If anyone believes in me even though he dies, he will live and whoever lives and believes in me will never die." It is faith in the Resurrected Christ and the power of His Resurrection that enables a Christian to bear the finality of things associated with death.

Although comforted and strengthened by our acceptance of Christ's word that death is not the end of life and that we have not here a lasting city, we are still saddened by the event that brings us together this morning.

We are here this morning under the stress of a great sorrow, a sorrow that is not confined to any part of this numerous assemblage but which weighs upon the heart of each one here. For each one of us, as he or she gazes on that casket which stands before the altar, feels that it encloses all that is mortal of one to whom each is indebted in some way or joined to him by some kind deed on his part. Many representatives of the American hierarchy, who revered him as one of the most talented and most learned of their body, are here to bear witness to their fraternal affection. A long career of one of the most distinguished clergymen in the history of the Catholic Church in the United States has closed and its termination leaves all of us the poorer.

It is not my intention this morning to recount in chronological order the events of the life of John Cardinal Wright whose mortal remains lie in that casket nor to catalogue his achievements. Other media are more appropriate for such a presentation.

On June 30, 1947, in the Cathedral of this Archdiocese, Monsignor John Wright was consecrated a Bishop to serve as Auxiliary to the Archbishop of Boston. Last Friday, 32 years later, God called to his rest John Cardinal Wright.

In those 32 years John Cardinal Wright wielded a great

influence not only in the Church of the United States but the Church universal as well. First in Boston, then for 10 years in Worcester as its first Bishop, later in Pittsburgh for 10 years as its eighth Bishop, and finally in Rome for 10 years as Prefect of the Vatican's Congregation for the Clergy, John Wright served and served well his one and only great love—Christ's Holy Church. Once, being interviewed by a reporter of the Pittsburgh Press, he said, "I love the Catholic Church as I love nothing else. I do not think of the Church as an organization—an institution. To me it is the personal presence of Christ in history. I see all truths and all faiths related to the Church and I think the Church has never been more powerful, more influential in the world. The Pope is a symbol of permanence and stability in the midst of chaos." Cardinal Wright invested all the zeal, energy and devotion that most men put into a family or a career of making money into his religion without becoming a fanatic.

From the point of view of the historian, the life of John Wright is a remarkable one. His involvement in social problems and international peace movements, long before it became an acceptable thing to do, his theological expertise in the preparatory work of Vatican Council II and his active role in the Council sessions, his advocacy of a wider place for the laity in the life and mission of the Church, the force of his personality on the pastoral life of three dioceses, the captivating quality of his oratory, the prodigious quantity of his written talks, homilies, retreat conferences, articles and spiritual writings, as well as his ten years as the first American to head a Congregation in the Roman Curia with worldwide responsibilities and his services as a Counselor to three Popes, demand the serious attention of those whose vocation it is—as historians—to study, sort, and codify such accomplishments.

We are not here this morning to weigh these facts, qualities, and accomplishments of John Wright. History will. And with the perspective that only history provides, the life and contribution of John Wright will be proclaimed.

That Cardinal Wright was greatly loved is evident in the prominent place he holds in the hearts of so many in the cities and towns of the dioceses where he served as Bishop, even though his ministry is now a memory, in some cases 10, 20, and even 30 years old.

Someone once remarked of him that as soon as he walked into a room it lit up with his infectious humor, good nature, and love of people. The Dioceses of Boston, Worcester, Pittsburgh, and the Holy City of Rome all recall the radiance of his brilliant personality. One of his constant joys in Rome—as he so often pointed out—was the arrival, usually unannounced, at his office of men and women and children from the States who sought just a moment of his time to recall the day, 15 or 25 years ago, when he confirmed them, married them, or spoke at one of their meetings. He didn't ignore them. They never stopped loving him.

Bishop John Wright was no sectarian shepherd. To spread understanding of the retreat movement among Christian clergymen, Bishop Wright directed a retreat for Protestant ministers at Marydale Retreat House, Erlanger, Kentucky in 1961. It was probably the first retreat directed by a Catholic Bishop for Protestant clergymen. He was the prime mover in the establishment of the Christian Associates of Southwestern Pennsylvania, an ecumenical association that embraces almost all of the Protestant adjudicatories and the Catholic dioceses in that area. While Bishop of Worcester he received the Citizen of the Year award from B'Nai B'Rith. This was one of the first of many honors that was to be given to him by Jewish communities. In Boston and Worcester, as in Pittsburgh, he sponsored and supported projects and programs that alleviated somewhat the burdens of the disadvantaged in these cities. He established and supported two community centers, Ozanam Cultural Center, and Ernest T. Williams Center in totally black neighborhoods in the city of Pittsburgh.

Yet despite all the time that these activities absorbed, he still did not neglect the mission life of the Church. For years, through the generosity of friends, he was able to assist financially a number of missionary Bishops in various parts of the world. Of special interest to him was the city of Chimbote, Peru. Here priests of his diocese who had joined the Saint

James Society carried out their priestly ministry. Four times he visited the city and each time he pledged greater assistance to the people there. He was instrumental in the establishment of a maternity hospital and raised funds to build a high school in the city. To it he gave the Spanish name, "Mundo Mejor" —for a better world. No one ever desired a better world or labored more unstintingly to achieve it for all mankind than John Cardinal Wright. It was he who coined the phrase, "I know of only one race, the human race."

On the day of his episcopal ordination, Bishop Wright took as his motto a line from the ancient Christian writer, Bishop Paulinus of Nola— "Resonare Christum corde romano": To echo Christ with a Roman heart.

In response to this motto, John Wright's life was marked with an intense and untiring effort to preach the word of God—and to do so in the light of the teaching of Christ's Vicar, the Bishop of Rome. The Gospels and the teaching of the Holy Father were the two focal points of his vision. When as a young Bishop he lectured, preached, and wrote, it was very often on the theme of man's brotherhood. His texts mingled freely the words of Christ and the teaching of the Papacy on patriotism, the excesses of nationalism, and the plague of racism.

In his years as a Bishop, he talked, exhorted, and pleaded for social justice and the expanded role of the layman and lay-women in the ongoing work that is conversion to the Kingdom of God. His words ring of Evangelical phrases and papal citations. The admonition of Saint Paul directed to Timothy found a place close to the heart of this Bishop.

"I charge you in the presence of God and of Christ Jesus who is to judge the living and the dead, and by His appearance and His kingdom: preach the word, be urgent in season and out of season, convince, rebuke and exhort, be unfailing in patience and teaching . . . always be steady, endure suffering, do the work of an evangelist, fulfill your ministry" (2 Tim 4:1–5).

When moral problems and dilemmas of a more modern cast challenged the Judeo-Christian tradition of respect for

God's law and man's life, Cardinal Wright stood on the front line, in his diocese, in the Conference of Bishops, in this nation as a gifted, able, and selfless interpreter of Christ's way and the encyclicals that applied it to human life in our day.

In the last ten years of his earthly life John Cardinal Wright was called to serve the Church he so loved—at its very center—Rome. This appointment brought him many joys and also much sorrow. For Cardinal Wright was not a desk man. He could never confine his pastoral instincts and energies to the 9 to 5 schedule. But as he pointed out on the day of his transfer: "A priest receives the call and he goes where he is sent."

Pope Paul VI asked the Cardinal right before his transfer what he would miss most when he left his See in Pittsburgh. He replied: "Holy Father, I think I will miss more than anything else all the opportunities I have there to teach." The Holy Father smiled softly and the audience was over.

When the Cardinal received his red hat there came with it a titular church in Rome—as is the case with every Cardinal. Pope Paul announced that the titular church of Cardinal Wright was to be the newly formed parish, Jesus the Divine Teacher. Within its boundaries is the Roman branch of the Catholic University.

The years of Cardinal Wright's duties in Rome were turbulent ones for the whole Church. The late '60s and early '70s have seen some confusion, agitation and stress within the Mystical Body of Christ. They were not happy times to hold a position of authority or responsibility at any level with the Church or State, let alone one very close to the top. Yet Cardinal Wright faced this new task with the same dedication and vigor that so characterized all his pastoral ministry. He used his Office to speak to an even wider audience—and to speak to them of God. Like an Old Testament prophet, John Wright did not always say things that everyone liked. But he never stopped telling us of God. He implemented Papal directives with a thoroughness that revealed his lifelong respect for the unique place the voice of the Vicar of Christ has within the community of believers—within the Church.

Cardinal Wright's positive, constructive words more often

addressed to troubled laity lent them some solace and perspective at a time when many of the faithful were uncertain as to the direction in which the Church was moving.

His hours far into the night were consumed with much correspondence aimed mainly at calming troubled consciences. His public statements and official activities never left any doubt that his loyalty and allegiance were first and always to the Holy See.

Zeal for the word of God and love for Christ's Church moved this priest and Bishop and Cardinal. He conceived his task to be that of telling all men and women that God loves us, that Jesus who was dead is now alive and that the Church is the way to Christ and His Father. This zeal accounts not only for his travels to all parts of the world—travels which consumed his energies—but also for the streaming pages and pages of talks, sermons, homilies, and articles that poured from his pen, even into his last declining months. This explains the rigorous schedule he insisted on even as it became increasingly clear that his body was wearing out.

Every opportunity to teach he accepted. And when his legs could no longer carry him to the podium, pulpit, or altar—he was satisfied to use a pen and rely on the mails and the printed word. It was enough for him that he could teach.

It is not possible on this occasion to touch upon the many accomplishments of Cardinal Wright which are worthy of public acknowledgment. There comes to mind his contribution not only to the composition and publication of the General Catholic Directory but also the Pastoral Letters of the American Bishops which were substantially affected by his thought and style of expression: his labors in the Diocese of Worcester as its first Bishop and what he helped to accomplish there: and last but by no means least, his personal devotion to Saint Joan of Arc, initiated by him as a young priest and very much a part of his spiritual life to the very end. He has been quoted to the effect that his study of Joan's life made it very clear to him that Bishops also make mistakes.

All this in addition to what I have presented for our reflections makes it perfectly clear that John Cardinal Wright was a great priest in the biblical sense of the word—a devoted shepherd of the flock committed to him in Worcester and Pittsburgh and a loyal and obedient son of Holy Mother Church and that his death is a great loss to Church and Community.

However, the life of the Church goes on. Soon a new Prefect for the Sacred Congregation for the Clergy in Rome will be appointed. Another voice will proclaim the Good News. Other bishops and priests will preach the word.

Our prayers this morning—and our affection—are not for His Eminence, John Cardinal Wright, Church leader and Vatican official. Our hearts and prayers are turned to the man and priest we so long knew and loved—a man who for long years here bore the burden, carried the torch, and never abandoned his place at the foot of the cross. Our prayers are for John Joseph Wright, who for so many of us here and countless others made the faith so real and so beautiful, who made the Church so present and lovable. Our prayers are that God will look on his efforts and bless him, just as he so often in his priestly life raised his arms in benediction over others.

Well may we take to heart these words spoken of him by Pope John Paul II, in his telegram of condolence to the Diocese of Pittsburgh, "May the memory of his diligent and pastoral service to God's people be a constant incentive to charity on the part of all who knew and loved him as a friend and pastor of the flock."

May God grant to John Cardinal Wright eternal rest, light, and peace.

In accord with the directives of his *Last Will and Testament,* the Cardinal's body was brought to Holyhood Cemetery, Brookline, Mass. There, Cardinal Medeiros—assisted by Fathers Wuerl and Wright, in the presence of Dr. Richard Wright, Robert Wright, Alfred Wright, Harriet Wright Gibbons, Margaret Wright Haverty, the other members of the Wright Family, twelve bishops, and about 250 relatives and friends—conducted the graveside prayers. Then Cardinal John Joseph Wright was buried with his parents.[2]

At the graveside, Bishop Carroll T. Dozier, of Memphis, an old friend—perhaps, after Monsignor Murray, the Cardinal's closest friend—"lingered, leaning on his blackthorn cane. . . . 'He was a romantic,' said the bishop. 'He had a terrible press for the last seven or eight years because he stuck to his principles, but he was a romantic and there was a whole lifetime of achievement that cannot be forgotten.' "[3]

Memorial Masses were, of course, held in Worcester and Pittsburgh. And in Rome, on September 22, 1979, Pope John Paul II commemorated the late Cardinal Wright with a solemn papal Mass. In the presence of many cardinals from the Roman Curia, the members of the Congregation for the Clergy, the Diplomatic Corps, clergy, religious, and laity, the Pope said:

> I desired this special concelebration to commemorate, just over a month after his sad decease, the lovable figure of Cardinal John Joseph Wright. He left us silently, and his death, depriving the Sacred College and the Roman Curia of an authoritative member, was and still is a cause of sincere regret for us.
>
> In actual fact who was Cardinal Wright? What are the characteristic features of his personality? We know very well the exterior elements of his biography: born in the United States of America of a family of Irish origin, after a youth marked by exemplary dedication to souls, he was nominated Auxiliary of Boston; then he was appointed Bishop of Worcester and of Pittsburgh, until by the confidence reposed in him by my predecessor Paul VI, of venerated memory, he was called to Rome as Prefect of the Sacred Congregation for the Clergy.
>
> But, beyond these external data, there emerged in him—and it presents itself to us now as the first and fundamental one—an outstanding pastoral quality. Endowed by nature with a rich and warm humanity, he always showed himself to be a Pastor, with all the characteristics that must define the latter according to evangelical teaching, that is, solicitude,

sensitiveness, understanding, the spirit of sacrifice for the sheep of his flock. It was precisely this attitude, matured in his long experience of diocesan life, that caused him to be given, in the post-conciliar period, the task of directing the important Congregation, which is the institution responsible for the guidance and inspiration of the clergy and the Christian people on the pastoral plane.

Wishing, however, to penetrate more deeply into the psychology of the Cardinal, we will find that the secret source that nourished this typical commitment of his was a constant and personal relationship of intimacy with Christ the Lord. He who had chosen as his motto the significant expression "Resonare Christum", made it his concern to keep this contact with him always fresh and alive. He was so convinced of this necessity that he never failed to instil it in priests both by writing and in words.

I am happy to quote, for example, the penetrating preface he wrote for the reprinting of the golden booklet *Manete in Dilectione Mea,* where we read the following sentences: "If you wish, beloved Brothers, to *conservare in aeternum* your priestly identity in this age in which the world is too important for men, try to imitate the Heart of Jesus today more than yesterday." And again: "If you want the Church to be really a sacrament of salvation for modern man, not to lose her own identity and suffer the sharp anguish of spiritual emptiness, direct your whole spiritual life to imitation of the Heart of Jesus."

Here is the focal centre, which explains our Cardinal's dynamism and zeal. Here is the permanently valid indication that he transmits to us, if we do not want—we Bishops and Priests—our ministry to be weakened or nullified. It is, in fact, an indication on which we shall never reflect enough, because it is a natural part of our state, because it calls us urgently to live an intense interior life, centered on Christ "gentle and lowly in heart", nourished by that charity of His, without which, even in the midst of resounding external success—as Saint Paul warns us—one is nothing.

A second lesson comes to us from this outstanding Cardinal:

in the multiform ministry he carried out for brothers, priests and faithful, he kept and showed exemplary attachment to the Magisterium of the Church. He conceived this Magisterium as a living reality, a sacred function, a qualified service for the integrity of faith and in general for the cause of truth, set up within the Church by the Lord's will. One may well think that this fervent adherence and, I would say, devotion to the Church–Teacher, was not unrelated to the uninterrupted tradition of faithfulness of Catholic Ireland.

No text could be better indicated, for this liturgical assembly of ours, than the one of Matthew just proclaimed: after the sublime elevation to the Father ("Confiteor tibi, Pater . . ."), Jesus addresses a persuasive invitation to His disciples to go to Him and accept the easy yoke of His teaching: "*Venite ad me omnes. . . .* " Throughout his whole life, Cardinal Wright endeavored, precisely in that daily contact that I mentioned above, to study Jesus from close at hand, to learn directly from Him the eternal and salutary lessons of meekness and humility of heart. Prior to the *munus docendi,* which was incumbent on him as Bishop and Pastor, he held very dear the *Officium discendi.* We believe, therefore, because of the Lord's formal promise (*et invenietis requiem*), that already on this earth he found relief and peace for his soul; but we also believe, owing to the boundless charity of the same Lord, that he now enjoys these goods, in a full and unchanging form, in the glory of Heaven. Amen.[4]

Abbreviations

AAS   *Acta Apostolicae Sedis* (Rome, 1909–).

ACW   *Ancient Christian Writers: The Works of the Fathers in Translation,* ed. J. Quasten and others (Westminster, Md.: Newman Bookshop, 1946–).

CCL   *Corpus Christianorum,* Series Latina.

CHW   *The Church: Hope of the World—John Cardinal Wright Looks at the Church,* ed. Donald W. Wuerl (Kenosha, Wis.: Prow Books, 1972).

CSEL   *Corpus Scriptorum Ecclesiasticorum Latinorum* (Vienna, 1866–).

PG   *Patrologia Graeca,* ed. J. P. Migne (Paris, 1857–1866).

PL   *Patrologia Latina,* ed. J. P. Migne (Paris, 1844–1864).

RC I   *Resonare Christum, Volume I: 1939–1959 The Boston and the Worcester Years. A Selection from the Sermons, Addresses, Interviews, and Papers of Cardinal John J. Wright.* Prepared and edited by R. Stephen Almagno, O.F.M. (San Francisco: Ignatius Press, 1985).

RC II   *Resonare Christum, Volume II: 1959–1969 The Pittsburgh Years. A Selection from the Sermons, Addresses, Interviews, and Papers of Cardinal John J. Wright.* Prepared and edited by R. Stephen Almagno, O.F.M. (San Francisco: Ignatius Press, 1988).

Saints   *The Saints Always Belong to the Present. A Selection from the Sermons, Addresses, and Papers of Cardinal John J.*

Wright. Prepared and edited by R. Stephen Almagno, O.F.M. (San Francisco: Ignatius Press, 1985).

WIP *Words in Pain.* Cardinal John J. Wright. Prepared and edited by R. Stephen Almagno, O.F.M. (San Francisco: Ignatius Press, 1986).

Notes

Chapter One
Teachers of the Faith

On June 15, 1969, Cardinal Wright left the United States, aboard the SS Raffaello, to assume his duties—as Prefect of the Congregation for the Clergy—at the Vatican. He disembarked at Naples on June 22, the Feast of St. Paulinus of Nola, from whose writings he had taken his episcopal motto: Resonare Christum. See Archbishop Bovone's recollection in *Words in Pain* (*WIP,* 21–22).

In the April 28, 1969, Consistory, Paul VI had named John Wright—together with three other Americans (Carberry, Cooke, and Dearden) and Wright's close friend Jean Daniélou, S.J.,—a cardinal priest, with Gesù Divin Maestro as his titular church.

Together with his duties as Prefect of the Congregation for the Clergy, Wright was appointed to and actively served as a member of the Council for Public Affairs, the Congregations for the Doctrine of the Faith, Bishops, Evangelization, and Catholic Education. He was also a member of the International Theological Commission and part of the Permanent Commissions for the Revision of the Code of Canon Law and for the Sanctuaries of Pompeii and Loreto. And he served on the Commissions for the Interpretation of the Decrees of the Second Vatican Council and that of the Works of Religion (Vatican Bank).

Bishop Donald Wuerl—now Wright's successor as the Bishop of Pittsburgh and for twelve years his secretary in Rome—described Wright's work at the Congregation for the Clergy as a combination of a great deal of desk work and traveling. Those travels, which usually came "under one of three headings: official business . . . visits and talks to gatherings of priests, and pastoral or speaking engagements", are the background for an understanding of the man and his work. See *The Church: Hope of the World—John Cardinal Wright Looks at the Church,* ed. Donald W. Wuerl (Kenosha, Wis.: Prow Books, 1972)

vii. And so, less than two months after his arrival in Rome, we have this first address delivered at Passo della Mendola (Trent, northern Italy) on August 9.

This address was published in *CHW*, 29–41.

[1] Rom 1:11–12.

[2] Rom 1, 2, and 3.

[3] 1 Cor 1:21.

[4] Rom 1:21, 25.

[5] 1 Cor 1:21.

[6] Titus 3:5–7.

[7] 2 Pet 1:4; 1 Jn 3:2.

[8] Rom 10:14.

[9] 1 Tim 2:4; Mt 28:17.

[10] Heb 11:1.

[11] St. Hilary of Poitiers, *Tractatus Super Psalmos, Ps 1:3 (PL* 9, 252).

[12] 2 Cor 2:17.

[13] Mt 5:18.

[14] St. Gregory the Great, *Moralium XXIX, 16 (PL* 76, 503).

[15] Jn 15:5.

[16] St. Augustine, *De Catechizandis Rudibus, C. 4 (PL* 40, 316).

[17] Jn 6:29.

[18] Rom 4:5.

[19] St. Augustine, *In Joannis Evangelium Tractatus 29, 6 (PL* 35, 1630–31).

[20] 1 Th 2:13.

[21] Gal 3:28.

[22] Vatican Council II, *Dogmatic Constitution on the Church,* I:1.

[23] Mrs. Marie Tugendhat (née Littledale) wrote Fr. Almagno as follows:

I first heard his name from my mother, Mrs. Littledale, who had met him in Assisi in the early thirties, 1933 perhaps. She told me he had been like a son to her, accompanying her all over the place and helping her with the language, which she did not speak. She said he was at the time writing his thesis. Young as he was, he was of the greatest comfort to her as she was at the time very worried because I was about to marry a non-Catholic, well disposed but not inclined to be converted. Thanks to him she withdrew her opposition to George Tugendhat, though she remained unhappy about it. He told me himself in later years how well he remembered 'the well-tailored English lady', and that she had meant much to him far as he was from home" (Letter of Tugendhat to Almagno, March 14, 1982).

[24] Dante, *Paradiso:* XXXIII, 145. "L'amor che muove il sole e l'altre stelle".

[25] *A New Catechism* (New York: Seabury Press, 1969). The volume is made up of 502 pages of text with a supplement (pp. 515–74) by E. Dhanis,

S.J., and Jan Visser, C.Ss.R., on behalf of the Commission of Cardinals appointed to examine the text of *A New Catechism.*

[26] St. Augustine, *De Catechizandis Rudibus, C. 2 (PL* 40, 312).

Chapter Two
The Church of Promise

This address was published as follows: "A Church of Promise", *Columbia Magazine* (January 1970): 17–26 and in *CHW,* 1–28.

[1] Mk 2:24.

[2] Samuel Eliot Morison, *Admiral of the Ocean Sea—A Life of Christopher Columbus* (Boston: Little, Brown, 1942), vol. I, 3–6.

[3] Ibid., 6.

[4] *Pastoral Letters of the United States Catholic Bishops, III, 1962–1974 (Washington, D.C.: National Conference of Catholic Bishops, United States Catholic Conference,* 1983*),* 164–94.

[5] John J. Wright, *National Patriotism in Papal Teaching* (Westminster, Md.: Newman Press, 1956).

[6] See "The Pope and the War", *RC* I, 42–53.

[7] See "The Roman Spirit", *RC* I, 295–301.

[8] St. Paulinus of Nola, Carmen XVII (*CSEL* 30, p. 93): " ... per te barbari discunt resonare Christum corde Romano placidamque casti vivere pacem." P. G. Walsh, in his translation of *The Poems of St. Paulinus of Nola (ACW* 40, 112) renders the text as: "In this mute region of the world, the barbarians through your schooling learn to make Christ's name resound from Roman hearts, and to live in purity and tranquil peace."

One time in his student days, Wright came across this text, and it deeply impressed him. He included it in his thesis, and—when ordained bishop—selected it as his motto and included it in his coat of arms.

Cardinal Wright's personal coat of arms is composed of the shield and its charges, the motto beneath the shield, and the external trappings around the shield. Arms: a cauldron in silver resting upon a fire, or rising from the fire, and an eagle of gold between two fleurs-de-lis. The Cardinal's arms are based upon those sometimes attributed to his patron saint, St. John the Evangelist, in allusion to the Roman tradition of St. John before the Latin Gate and the miraculous escape from the cauldron of boiling oil prepared for him under the Emperor Domitian. The fleurs-de-lis are taken from the arms of the Archdiocese of Boston, where Wright was born and served as auxiliary bishop before being named to the See of Worcester and subsequently to the Diocese of Pittsburgh. These fleurs-de-lis also appear frequently on arms associated with the name Wright.

The Cardinal's motto: The words, "Resonare Christum" are from the above-quoted passage in the writings of St. Paulinus of Nola: " . . . per te barbari discunt *resonare Christum* corde Romano, placidamque casti vivere pacem." Wright's translation reads: "Through you the heathens of our world's unheeded parts/ Have learned *to echo Christ* with Roman hearts/ And live a life of chaste and stable peace."

The external ornaments are composed of the scarlet pontifical hat with its fifteen scarlet tassels on each side, arranged in five rows with the episcopal gold cross indicating his Sacred Congregation. These are the presently accepted heraldic trappings of a prelate of the rank of Cardinal-Bishop. Before 1870, the pontifical hat was worn at solemn cavalcades held in conjunction with papal functions. The color of the pontifical hat and the number and color of the tassels are signs of the rank of the prelate. This custom is preserved in ecclesiastical heraldry.

The arms were designed in 1947 after Wright was named an auxiliary to the Archbishop of Boston and titular bishop to the See of Tegea. These arms were designed by Dom William Wilfred Bayne, O.S.B., of the then Portsmouth Priory—now Portsmouth Abbey—in Portsmouth, Rhode Island.

The shield has a tint rose red. The cauldron is, as mentioned, silver, with the eagle and the fleur-de-lis of gold.

This description and explanation of Wright's coat of arms is based—with my additions and corrections—on the text published on p. 12 of the booklet entitled: *The Pontifical Liturgy in Memory of John Cardinal Wright* (Pittsburgh: Saint Paul Cathedral, Aug. 20, 1979). See John J. Wright, *National Patriotism in Papal Teaching* (Westminster, Md.: Newman Press, 1956), xix; also,*Classica et Iberica, A Festschrift in Honor of the Reverend Joseph M.-F. Marique, S.J.,* ed. P. T. Brannan, S.J. (Worcester, Mass.: Institute for Early Christian Iberian Studies, 1975), 417–25.

[9] Jn 19:9.
[10] Col 3:11.
[11] 1 Cor 1:13.

Chapter Three
Pope John and His Secret

This address was published as follows: *L'Osservatore Romano,* Eng. edition (January 22, 1970): 6–7; *The Family* (March, 1970): 32–43 and in *The Church: Hope of the World,* ed. Donald W. Wuerl (Kenosha, Wis.: Prow Books, 1972), 169–80.

[1] Pope John XXIII, *Journal of a Soul,* trans. Dorothy White, rev. ed. (London: G. Chapman, 1980).

[2] Pope John XXIII, encyclical *Mater et Magistra* (May 15, 1961), English translation (Washington, D.C.: National Catholic Welfare Conference, 1961).

[3] Ignatius of Antioch, *Epistola ad Ephesios* (*PG* 5, 686).

[4] Pope John XXIII, encyclical *Pacem in Terris* (April 11, 1963). English translation *Peace on Earth* (New York: America Press, 1963).

[5] Ernesto Balducci, *Papa Giovanni* (Firenze, 1964), 192.

[6] Ibid., 193.

[7] Dante, *Purgatorio,* XXXII: 102. "Di quelle Roma onde Cristo è Romano."

[8] Balducci, *Papa Giovanni,* 194.

[9] Jn 16:33; Mt 28:18–20; 1 Jn 5:4–5.

[10] Balducci, *Papa Giovanni,* 189.

[11] Ibid., 193.

[12] Loris Capovilla, *The Heart and Mind of John XXIII* (London: G. Chapman, 1965), 17–21.

[13] On June 3, 1965, Wright wrote this *Statement on the Death of Good Pope John:*

"The whole world has momentarily been a little chilled, a little darkened by the passing from among us of the warm, luminous presence of this so appealing, so gracious personality. Everyone died a bit when Pope John died.

"And yet the chill is only temporary and the darkening is only for a moment, precisely because of the basic reason which explains the so widespread appeal of this amazing Holy Father whom all the world came to love with such filial affection. That reason is clear: Pope John gave lively and lovable, intimately personal expression, by everything he said, did and was, to universal values, ever ancient, ever new, which decent people instinctively recognized as truly humane and which all believers somehow perceived to be divinely appointed.

"Genial, unaffected, smiling and transparently good, he somehow made the whole world a neighborhood, a friendly community that felt increasingly secure in the very thought that he was around; it is now of one heart in grief at the thought that he is dead.

"It takes great gifts of nature and of grace to be able to make the monumental majesty of St. Peter's seem like everybody's parish church and the marble grandeur of the Vatican seem like the homey rectory of a country priest with whom everyone in the town is at home and at ease. Pope John did just that; he stepped up laughter and friendly love in a world that so often either downgrades or perverts both.

"But now the values he taught, by precept and eloquent amiable example, are the more strong among us just because he lived and died as he did. Their strengthening and clarification constitute his great legacy to all those men of good will to whom he invariably addressed himself. Grateful awareness of that legacy tempers our otherwise tragic feeling of loss. It also adds fervor to the prayers that millions of people all over the world will offer for the repose of the soul of this Good Shepherd who did so much to bring the scattered flock of the Lord closer to one another and to God."

Chapter Four
Priesthood, Humanism, and the Cross

This address, translated into Spanish, was published as a monograph, *Sacerdocio y Humanismo* (Caracas, Centro de Informacion Profesional A.C., 1973), 35 pp. Wright also used this text for two talks to priests: Greensburg, Pa. (1974) and at the Diocesan Clergy Retreat (Dublin, Ireland, 1976).

[1] Heb 13:8.

[2] Terence, *Heauton Timorumenos,* 77.

[3] Wright was elected by the United States' hierarchy as a delegate to the First Synod of Bishops in 1967. See, "The Pope and the Astronauts" in this volume, pp. 262–69.

[4] Terence, *Heauton Timorumenos,* 77.

[5] 1 Cor 3:22–23.

[6] Pascal, *Pensées,* IV (Ed. L. Brunschbicg, 1909), 277.

[7] *Missale Romanum,* "Praefatio de Nativitate Domini".

[8] Jn 10:10.

[9] 1 Cor 3:22–23.

[10] Robert Hugh Benson, *The Friendship of Christ* (Chicago: Thomas More Press, 1984), 73–76.

[11] Lk 8:1.

[12] Wright was a close associate, and confessor, of Jacques Maritain during the period that Maritain spent at Princeton University.

[13] "Protector in te sperantium, Deus, sine quo nihil est validum, nihil sanctum: Multiplica super nos misericordiam tuam; ut, te rectore, te duce, sic transeamus per bona temporalia, ut non amittamus aeterna" (*Breviarium Romanum,* Dominica Tertia Post Pentecostem: Oratio).

[14] Mt 15:32.

[15] *Liturgia Horarum,* In Exaltatione Sanctae Crucis, Ad I Vesperas, Hymnus "Vexilla Regis".

[16] Dorothy Thompson, "The Lesson of Dachau", *Ladies' Home Journal* (1945), taken from *Annals of St. Anthony Shrine* (1953).

Chapter Five
Interview with Alex Kucherov

This interview was published in *U.S. News and World Report* (August 31, 1970): 56–61.

[1] See "The Year of Faith", *RC* II, 436–42.

[2] See "Jesuit Centennial in Boston", *RC* I, 87–89.

[3] James Gollin, *Worldly Goods — The Wealth and Powers of the American Catholic Church, the Vatican, and the Men Who Control the Money* (New York: Random House, 1970), references to Wright on pages 185, 199, 208–9, 391, and 485.

[4] In 1968, Wright — then Bishop of Pittsburgh — contributed a $12,000 grant to the United Movement for Progress (UMP) and a $10,000 salary to its director Willie (Bouie) Haden, a black militant leader. The action produced a wide variety of reactions; from hate mail and phone calls to a reduction in contributions by some parishioners. A few days later, an effigy of Bishop Wright was draped across two trees in front of St. Paul Cathedral, Pittsburgh. It carried a sign reading: "Bouie's Puppet on a String".

Chapter Six
Cardinal Richard J. Cushing, 1895–1970

[1] Rev 21:4–5.

[2] Concerning Wright's relationship to Medeiros, the late Cardinal Humberto Medeiros wrote:

"With the death of His Eminence, John Cardinal Wright, on August 10, 1979, the Catholic Church lost one of its most eloquent spokesmen, one of its most zealous bishops.

"I have many memories of John Wright, the bishop and the cardinal. My knowledge of him goes back to the time I was the Chancellor of the Diocese of Fall River and he was the Bishop of Worcester. He was a man I held in great respect, a man of whom I stood in awe and admiration. It was obvious to me that this young bishop had extraordinary gifts of mind and heart, which he generously put to the service of God and the Church. He initiated and promoted good works of all kinds in Worcester, and later in Pittsburgh, and he did this zealously, with convincing grace, and always with humor. His love for the Church, and his willingness to promote its work and defend its truth and its mission, knew no bounds.

"During the Second Vatican Council—each session of which I attended with Bishop Connolly—and again after I became Bishop of Brownsville and thereby a member of the National Conference of Catholic Bishops—I had the opportunity to observe Bishop Wright at close range. My admiration and esteem for him grew rapidly as I became more deeply impressed by the depth of his intellectual ability, and as I was often moved by his thoroughly cogent and compelling presentation and defense of the faith. If ever a bishop was committed to the active promotion and vigorous defense of the Catholic Church, that man was Cardinal John Wright.

"When His Eminence was elevated to the College of Cardinals and became Prefect of the Sacred Congregation for the Clergy, and when I became Archbishop of Boston soon afterwards, I came to have a closer and more personal relationship with him. As everyone knows, he had a great love for Boston, both as a native Bostonian and as a Catholic whose faith had been nurtured within the Church in the Archdiocese of Boston. He was heard to say on several occasions that his most cherished possessions were his baptismal certificate and his Boston Public Library card!

"He served the Church in Boston faithfully and well, as priest, as seminary professor, as secretary to Cardinal O'Connell and Archbishop Cushing, and as Auxiliary Bishop. The result of his service in Boston was not only an ever deepening love for and commitment to the Church in our Archdiocese, but also a wealth of knowledge and experience which were invaluable to him, and later to me. He never failed to respond to my request for counsel by sharing this knowledge and experience with me. I found him to be unfailingly wise and compassionate whenever I approached him for advice. To his great and everlasting credit, however, he never offered counsel on any matter pertaining to the Archdiocese of Boston unless I first asked for it. He had total and complete respect for my office as Archbishop of Boston, and never tried to influence events to move as he might wish them to move if he had held the office I hold.

"Although I am not a person who easily remembers jokes and funny stories—or even tries—I cannot be faithful to the memory of John Wright without stating that he was never at a loss for humor and laughter. He saw a funny side to nearly everything, and could provoke laughter in nearly every situation. He was a remarkable raconteur of hilarious stories about both the living and the dead, and could easily harken back to some humorous event of the past, or create a humorous situation on a given day of the present. His humor was always present, but it was never lacking in charity. I have no doubt that this genuine humor was also an instrument he used to put people at their ease and relieve tension, thereby advancing the cause to which he was so passionately committed — the building up of the Church in our midst.

"Despite the Cardinal's remarkable achievements as a priest, scholar, writer, Bishop of Worcester, Bishop of Pittsburgh, and finally, as Cardinal Prefect of the Sacred Congregation for the Clergy, and despite enormous admiration and acclaim — not unmixed with criticism at times — it is becoming clearer and clearer to me that his finest moment as a priest and bishop came when he lost his strength, fell victim to illness and had to curtail his activities.

"I was a personal witness to this part of the Cardinal's life, and I was deeply moved by the resignation, born of faith, with which he accepted his disabling sickness and death. He spent much time in the Tufts New England Medical Center in Boston, and he also spent considerable time at the Cardinal's Residence in Boston — especially during the last year of his life.

"I had seen the Cardinal failing in health during his visits to Boston after I became Archbishop in October of 1970, and I had seen his strength declining over the years, either when he visited me in Boston or when I visited him in Rome. I know how frustrated he was by his sickness and by the fact that he could not be in the thick of things, but I also know that he accepted not only the sickness — with its pain and suffering — but also the frustration with a profound spirit of faith and love for the Church, as his portion of the Lord's cross and suffering. He may not have liked it, but he certainly lived it in faith and with great patience.

"During the last year of his life, the Cardinal spent most of his time at Tufts New England Medical Center, the Cardinal's Residence in Boston and the Youville Hospital in Cambridge where he died.

"I consider it a great privilege to have been able to offer him the hospitality of our residence, and I am very happy that we were able to care for him here in Boston for a considerable time. He seemed to be at peace in this house, where he was able to receive the visits of his loving and proud Family, and of the friends from the Boston area with whom he had been associated over the years.

"I was also inspired during this period of the Cardinal's sickness, both in Rome and in Boston, by the completely selfless dedication and service rendered to him by his secretary, Father Donald Wuerl. Suffice it to say that there was nothing that Father Wuerl would not and did not do for His Eminence. I will never be able to forget Father Wuerl's love for and devotion to Cardinal Wright. He became a part of our household while Cardinal Wright was living in my residence or in the hospital, and he gave all of us a remarkable example of dedication and charity.

"In concluding these few recollections of Cardinal Wright let me say first of all that they are by no means complete. I hope, however, that they will help those who read them to understand what a wonderful human being His Eminence was; what a zealous priest and bishop he was for our times; how dedicated he was to God and to the Church, using every gift of nature and grace for the glory of God and the building up of the Church, and finally, how completely he offered himself in loving and true obedience to the will of the Father, making his own the mind of Christ our Lord when faced with suffering—'Father, if You are willing, take this cup away from me. Nevertheless, let Your will be done, not mine' (Lk 22:42–43).

"His Eminence, John Cardinal Wright, lived by faith and he died in the same faith. He was always clear and concise in the proclamation of this faith. He was always militant in its defense and persevering in its practice. We in Boston will always boast of him because of his love for the faith of the Church. May he rejoice in the vision of God in Whom he believed and trusted and Whose love he labored with brilliance and zeal to infuse into the hearts of men and women through the Holy Spirit who was given to him as a successor of the Apostles for the building up of the Church" (Letter of Medeiros to Almagno—February 26, 1982).

[3] In 1939, Cushing was appointed Auxiliary Bishop of Boston, and on the death of Cardinal O'Connell, in 1944, he was appointed Archbishop of Boston, the office he held until his resignation in 1970. See John Cooney, *The American Pope—The Life and Times of Francis Cardinal Spellman* (New York: Times Books, 1984), 268–69. And also James M. O'Toole, *Militant and Triumphant—William H. O'Connell and the Catholic Church in Boston, 1859–1944* (Notre Dame, Ind.: University of Notre Dame Press, 1992).

[4] Job 19:20.

[5] See "Channing and Cheverus", *RC* I, 221–37.

Wright and Walter Muir Whitehill (1905–1978) enjoyed a long and wonderful friendship. Mrs. Whitehill writes as follows:

"Cardinal Wright was far better known to my husband, Walter Muir Whitehill, than to me. They had conversations alone together, as I never did. Walter first met the Cardinal when he was a guest at High Table at Lowell House at Harvard University; at a time when Walter attended these weekly Monday dinners as Allston Burr Senior Tutor at Lowell House. This first meeting was enough, of course, to convince Walter of the Cardinal's extraordinary qualities. One of the friends they proved to have in common was J. Gregory Wiggins, a wood sculptor, not a Roman Catholic, who had done sculptures in the Chapel of Trinity College in Hartford. Walter, a member of the corporation of the Church of the Advent, in Boston, engaged Mr. Wiggins to make the Stations of the Cross for the Church of the Advent, and Walter held an exhibit of Wiggins' work at the Boston Athenaeum" (*The Work of J. Gregory Wiggins Woodcarver Catalogue of an exhibition held in February and March 1951* [Boston: Boston Athenaeum, 1951], *xi–17.* The foreword (v) and catalogue (3–17) are by Walter Muir Whitehill).

"Another exhibit at the Boston Athenaeum that the Cardinal either attended or at least knew about was of work by Boston Catholics, including the first Catholic Bishop, Cheverus" (*A Memorial to Bishop Cheverus with a catalogue of the books given by him to the Boston Athenaeum* [Boston, Boston Athenaeum, 1951], xviii–9.

"Although Wiggins lived in Pomfret, Connecticut, the Cardinal knew and cared for him while John Wright was Bishop of Worcester. He had a radio telephone in his car and knew that Wiggins was very ill, and had a premonition that all was not well. From his radio he learned that Wiggins was dying and went to see him, as he later told Walter.

"The Cardinal was extremely busy, and came rarely, once or twice perhaps, to our house in North Andover. Once was when we were having a dinner party. I do not think we had planned to ask the Cardinal but we learned that he would be free to come. At the dinner he was seated beside Ada Louise Huxtable, the architectural editor of the *New York Times,* a lady who is partly or wholly Jewish. These two had never met before, and had nothing in common except both being cultivated, extremely sophisticated and brilliant conversationalists, with a rare knowledge of the world. They seemed to get on famously. Their talk with each other reinforced observation of the Cardinal's ability not only to tell a good story delightfully, as he often did, but to discourse with intelligence, and frequently with wisdom, on about any subject that came up. On some matters I was sure I should not have agreed with him, but I never heard him speak antagonistically but always tactfully and persuasively, even when his convictions were set.

"He remains in my mind as one of the less than six great men I have been privileged to know" (Letter of Mrs. Whitehill to Almagno—July 4, 1982).

In 1976—two years before Whitehill's death and three years before Wright's— Walter Muir Whitehill took part in the Pittsburgh Bibliophiles Pilgrimage to Italy. In a volume, commemorating the trip, Walter wrote an article—probably his last—on their days in Rome. See, "Roma", in *The Pittsburgh Bibliophiles, Pilgrimage to Italy 1976* (Pittsburgh: The Pittsburgh Bibliophiles, 1978), 9–19. It was also one of the last times that he and Wright were together; and Walter Muir Whitehill wrote enthusiastically about those Roman days and lovingly about his old friend, John Wright.

When Wright received the news of Whitehill's death, he—himself already quite ill and a year before his own death—wrote:

"My health is so-so but I must interrupt my moaning and groaning about myself to issue a call for solidarity in prayer and sympathy with Jane and Walter Whitehill. Margaret called me the other day and said he had had a massive coronary and had been in a coma for just a bit too long. We must surround Jane with our loving support. They are very great people and dear to God but they are in very short supply.

"I suggest that each of us commend him daily to the saints of Spain whom he so dearly loves" (Letter of Wright to Almagno—February 21, 1978).

Some months later, the Cardinal had his copy of *The Pittsburgh Bibliophiles, Pilgrimage to Italy 1976,* and after reading it wrote me:

"I am delighted that you wrote to Walter's wife. You will find her a sound and appreciative friend and she has never forgotten how much you added to her life. Walter was greatly devoted to you and gave you more than a bow in his article. That pleased me very much. It had not occurred to me that the Pittsburgh Bibliophiles, Pilgrimage may well have been the last thing he wrote.

"My letter must be more brief than yours because I am entering the hospital in a couple of weeks for a series of operations and I am forced to husband my energies at the moment. I know you understand. Pray for me like you have never prayed before!" (Wright to Almagno—July 13, 1978).

[6] Walter Muir Whitehill, "Who Rules Here? Random Reflections on the National Origins of those set in Authority over Us", *The New England Quarterly* (September 1970): 448–49.

[7] Job 19:25–27.

[8] Letter from Paul VI to Cardinal Cushing, dated August 20, 1970, was printed in *The Pilot* (September 12, 1970): 1 and 15.

[9] Jn 19:25.

Chapter Seven
Priestly Maturity

This article was published as follows: *Seminarium* (September 1970): 810–30, and in *The Church: Hope of the World,* ed. Donald W. Wuerl (Kenosha, Wis.: Prow Books, 1972), 85–100.

[1] S. Congregatio pro Institutione Catholica, *Ratio Fundamentalis Institutionis Sacerdotalis* (Rome, 1970), 66.

[2] Ibid., 100.

³ Lev 20:26.
⁴ Mt 5:48.
⁵ Eph 4:7–14.
⁶ Eph 4:13.
⁷ 1 Cor 4:1–4.
⁸ Mt 4:19 and Heb 10:7.
⁹ Mt 16:24–25.
¹⁰ Jn 14:1–16 generally.
¹¹ Mt 7:13–14.
¹² Phil 2:6–8.
¹³ Col 1:24.
¹⁴ Rom 12:1.

¹⁵ See Pope Paul VI, "Sacerdoti Autentici di Cristo e della Chiesa", *Insegnamenti*, VI, 1052–53; Pope Paul VI, *Il Sacerdozio* (Milan: Ancora, 1970), 149–50, and Cardinal M. Pellegrino, *Cosa Aspetta la Chiesa Torinese dai Preti di Domani?* (Turin: Elle Di Ci, 1970), 11.

¹⁶ *AAS*, 28 (1936): 44.

¹⁷ Vatican Council II, *Lumen Gentium*, no. 28.

¹⁸ Pope Paul VI, *Il Sacerdozio* (Milan: Ancora, 1970), 344 and S. Congregatio pro Institutione Catholica, *Ratio Fundamentalis Institutionis Sacerdotalia* (Rome: 1970), 66 as well as S. Congregatio pro Clericis, *Litterae Circulares ad Conferentiarum Episcopalium Praesides de Permanenti Cleri, Maxime Iunioris, Institutione et Formatione Secundum Placita Congregationis Plenariae die 18 Octobris Habitae* (Rome: Typis Polyglottis Vaticanis, 1969), 13.

¹⁹ S. Congregatio pro Clericis, *Litterae Circulares*, no. 22 and no. 4. S. Congregatio pro Institutione Catholica, *Ratio Fundamentalis*, nos. 100–101.

²⁰ *Pontificale Romanum*, "De Ordinatione Presbyterorum". See Vatican Council II, *Presbyterorum Ordinis*, no. 19; S. Congregatio pro Clericis, *Litterae Circulares*, no. 5 and S. Congregatio pro Institutione Catholica, *Ratio Fundamentalis*, nos. 100–101. At the end of these citations, Wright added this note: "Sometimes one thinks it would be far more conducive to their maturity if priests spent more time in the reading and meditating of Sacred Scriptures, the Fathers of the Church, the documents of the Magisterium, the works of the established theologians than in being titillated by theological *novelties* (what Maritain called, with slightly excessive impatience, 'theological science fiction') and by a sector of the Catholic press which has appointed itself conscience, teacher, and reformer of the Church."

²¹ Mt 5:48.
²² Vatican Council II, *Presbyterorum Ordinis*, no. 12.
²³ Ibid.
²⁴ Ibid., no. 2.

[25] Gal 2:20.
[26] I Cor 4:1–2.
[27] Eph 4:13.

Chapter Eight
Interview with Jordan Aumann, O.P.

This article was published in *The Priest* (March, 1971): 9–15.

[1] See "Introduction", in *RC* II, 21–22.
[2] See "The Formal Call of the Synod", in *RC* II, 484–93.

Chapter Nine
Defense of Man

This address was printed by Sullivan Brothers of Lowell, Mass., and published as a pamphlet: *Defense of Man by John Cardinal Wright— Conference at Anna Maria College—May 2, 1971.* It was also translated into Spanish as: "La Humanae Vitae—Una Defensa Profetica del Hombre", in *Iglesia de la Exaltacion de la Santa Cruz* (May, 1977): 94–102.

[1] I Cor 3:23.
[2] David Knowles, *Peter Has Spoken: The Encyclical without Ambiguity* (London: Catholic Truth Society, Document 413, 1968).

Chapter Ten
Contemporary Humanism

This article was published as follows: *The Sign* (June, 1971): 43–47 and in *Catholic Position Papers—Seido Foundation for the Advancement of Education,* Japanese edition (November, 1976), 5 pp.

[1] Terence, *Heauton Timorumenos,* 77.
[2] Ronald A. Knox, *Reunion All Round* (London: Society of SS. Peter and Paul, 1914), and "The New Sin" in *Essays in Satire* (London: Sheed and Ward, 1954), 77ff.

Chapter Eleven
The New Catechetical Directory

This article was published in *Homiletic and Pastoral Review* (December 1971): 7–24. It was also translated into Italian as: "Il Nuovo Direttorio Catechetico e l'Iniziazione ai Sacramenti della Penitenza e dell'Eucaristia", *Palestro del Clero* 23 (December 1, 1971): 1394–1418.

¹ S. Congregation for the Clergy, *General Catechetical Directory* (Washington, DC: USCC, 1971).

² For more information on the relationship between Wright and Hugo, see: John Hugo, *Your Ways Are Not My Ways* (Pittsburgh, Pa.: Encounters with Silence, 1986), 2 vols.

³ Mt 10:28.

⁴ John Henry Newman, *Parochial and Plain Sermons* vol. IV (London: Rivingtons, 1870), p. 39; (San Francisco: Ignatius Press, 1987), 750–52.

⁵ Ibid.

⁶ Ibid., p. 40; Ignatius Press ed., pp. 751–52.

⁷ Ibid., pp. 40–41; Ignatius Press ed., p. 752.

⁸ St. Augustine, *In Epist. Joann. Tractatus* VII, 8.

Chapter Twelve
Maritain's Two Most Recent Books

¹ William Wordsworth, *The French Revolution, As It Appeared to Enthusiasts* (1809), and *The Prelude*, bk. II, 1.108.

² Jacques Maritain, *The Peasant of the Garonne: An Old Layman Questions Himself about the Present Time,* trans. M. Cuddihy and E. Hughes (New York: Holt, Rinehart and Winston, 1968).

³ Jacques Maritain, *On the Church of Christ* (Notre Dame, Ind.: University of Notre Dame Press, 1973).

⁴ William Clancy, "Jacques Maritain's Yes—But No!" in *Commonweal* (April 12, 1968): 107–10.

⁵ Maritain, *On the Church of Christ,* 240.

⁶ Wright was a close associate, and confessor, of Jacques Maritain during the period that Maritain spent at Princeton.

⁷ Maritain, *The Peasant of the Garonne,* 91.

⁸ Ps 85:11.

⁹ Maritain, *The Peasant of the Garonne,* 154.

[10] Ibid., 51.

[11] Ibid., 233.

[12] Ps 46:10.

[13] Maritain, *The Peasant of the Garonne,* 116–26 and 264–69.

In 1962, the then Holy Office—now the Congregation for the Doctrine of the Faith—while in no way impugning Fr. Teilhard's spiritual integrity, issued a *Monitum* against an uncritical acceptance of his ideas. See *AAS* 54 (1962): 526.

Due to the influence of Frank J. Sheed and the genuine friendship as well as enormous respect that Wright had for the Jesuit scholar-cardinals Henri de Lubac and Jean Daniélou, Wright—while accepting the Monitum—changed his ideas about many aspects of Teilhard's thought. See Frank J. Sheed, *The Church and I* (London: Sheed and Ward, 1974), 152, 223, 276–78, and "La Porpora nella Compagnia di Gesù", *Gesuiti—Annuario della Compagnia di Gesù* (1969–1970): 125–26.

Sometime in 1976, Cardinal Wright told me that when he came to write his autobiography, he definitely wanted to include an item—concerning Teilhard de Chardin and himself—that was completely unknown. The Cardinal mentioned, briefly in that 1976 conversation and at a time when he was already ill, that in 1951 or 1952 Cardinal Spellman had sent him to St. Ignatius Jesuit Residence, Park Avenue, to speak with Fr. Teilhard. Alas, as with so many other interesting and important vignettes from a life that was so rich, the details of Wright's meeting and conversation with Teilhard de Chardin will never be known.

[14] Rudyard Kipling, *The Return.*

[15] Maritain, *On the Church of Christ,* 258–59.

[16] From the early days of the St. Benedict Center—the Newman Chaplaincy at Harvard University—Wright was a close friend and penitent of Leonard Fenney, S.J. (1897–1978). When the Jesuit poet and essayist's theological views were censured by the Church (the August 8, 1949, *Letter from the Holy Office,* dismissal from the Society of Jesus in 1949, and excommunication in 1954), Wright was auxiliary bishop in Boston and later bishop in nearby Worcester. In 1958, some of Feeney's followers moved with him to a farm at Still River, Mass., in the Diocese of Worcester. In 1972—while Wright was Prefect of the Congregation for the Clergy—he, together with Bishop Bernard Flanagan of Worcester and Cardinal Humberto Medeiros of Boston, was successful in having all censures against Fr. Feeney removed. See "The Rise of Bishop Wright—The Feeney Case", in Joseph Dever, *Cushing of Boston* (Boston: Bruce, Humphries, 1965), 137–47, and, Jeffrey Wills, ed., *The Catholics of Harvard Square* (Petersham, Mass.: St. Bede's Publications, 1993).

[17] *Boulter's Monument* (1745), 1.377.

Chapter Thirteen
Teaching the Faith

[1] Hilaire Belloc, *Europe and the Faith* (New York: Paulist Press, 1920).
[2] Eph 4:5.

Chapter Fourteen
Worcester

[1] Wright was installed as the first bishop of Worcester, Mass., on March 7, 1950, and served there until March 18, 1959, when he was installed as the eighth bishop of Pittsburgh, Pa.

Here follows the complete text of his homily at the Installation Mass:

"Let our first words in this proud Cathedral be words of gratitude to Almighty God for the graces of this day, of submission to His Holy Will for the years that are to come, of petition through His Incarnate Son, our Sole High Priest, for guidance and strength and every needed blessing in the work to which we this day dedicate our minds and hearts, our every faculty and source.

"Let our next words be the renewal of the prayers already chanted before the altar this morning . . . above all to the patrons of the Roman Church, the holy Apostles Peter and Paul, the one the source of our jurisdiction, the other patron of the cathedral and the protector of its throne. May they and all the saints second our earnest petition to God that the faith may prosper in these parts, nor ever fail; that His Holy Spirit diffused in the hearts of priests and people alike may be the bond of our unity in every word and work of this diocese.

"I am proud in speaking for the first time as head of this diocese to make my first official pronouncement an expression of the gratitude of the Church in Worcester, blended with my personal indebtedness to our Holy Father, the Pope, for his paternal and provident establishment of the See so long desired by the faithful in these parts and so cordially welcomed, not merely by the Catholic, but by all those who, loving this County and City of Worcester, seek its spiritual advantage; to His Excellency, the Apostolic Delegate in the United States, for his official personal graciousness to this See and its first bishop; to my archbishop, metropolitan of New England, for the historic part that he has played in this day's unfolding of God's plan for His Church, for his incomparable goodness to me; for his fatherly generosity to the infant Church of Worcester and the dynamic inspiration which his presence here this morning will give the newest of his suffragan sees, but surely the one with the most reasons to render his abiding love and unqualified loyalty.

"We in Worcester gratefully appreciate the benevolence of the archbishops, bishops and the priests who have come here this morning to show us their friendship and pledge to us their prayers.

"We promise them the prayers of our diocese and its bishop that God may prosper them and all their works. We are particularly anxious to express our gratitude to the bishop-elect of our mother see of Springfield for his presence here this morning, when he has so many plans and preparations to preoccupy him. We ask God particularly to bless Bishop Weldon and the priests and people of the special household to which our Church must always look as to its ancestral home.

"We are grateful to his excellency, the governor of the Commonwealth; to their honors the mayors of Boston and Worcester and the other cities of this county; to the honorable Senator from Massachusetts, Mr. Lodge; to the President's Secretary of Labor, Mr. Tobin; to the members of Congress; the representatives of the Massachusetts Great and General Courts; officials of the executive, legislative and judicial levels of the civil community, for their presence here this morning. Busy members all and particularly burdened in this moment of history, they have nonetheless taken time to bear witness this morning to the sincere regard of America's several authorities for the things of spirit, the legitimate concerns of religion and prosperous functioning of the Church in our American community.

"I promise our grateful prayers for them and I pledge our loyal deference to this authority, truly divine in its origin and sacred in its nature.

"We are grateful to all those who have sacrificed time and personal convenience to be with us this morning as the Diocese of Worcester begins its history, and to those tens of thousands more, those of the house of faith and others to let us know their love, to strengthen us by their friendly encouragement and to do us so many generous, kindly courtesies. Surely we could not possibly begin the life of this diocese with more good will and more spontaneous goodness of every kind than has been manifested to the Diocese of Worcester and its first bishop by the press, radio, by public officials, by individuals and groups inside and outside Worcester and the Church. We are humbly grateful.

"Finally I cannot forget in the happiness of this day those who, under God, really made it possible; the saintly bishops, priests and people of Worcester, England of old, who must this day be gratified, even in Heaven, that a see, bearing the name they love and made glorious, is again inscribed among the militant units which do battle for Christ in communion with Rome. Certainly their prayers must be with us in a special way as we begin our diocese in the Heart of the Commonwealth, which is the ecclesiastical heart of New England.

"Neither can we forget, as we rejoice this morning, the blessed dead who gave so much and so gladly of themselves and their poor possessions and rich prayers that the church might take root and prosper and come to fullness here. I think back with pious gratitude to the Irish, who came here just a century ago to seek here freedom for themselves and their faith; freedom they have used well in the service of their faith, of the neighbors who shared a like freedom and the nation which respected their faith.

"I think of the valiant French-speaking people who have brought to this part of America so much that is best and most holy in the genius of France and who have made more beautiful our region with the names of their French saints and the traditions of their Catholic ancestors.

"So too we think of the others, more recent in their coming but equal in fidelity and merit—industrious Italians, Polish, Lithuanian, Syrian and Nordic people, out of whose prayers and work this diocese was born.

"For all of them, we return grateful thanks to God. Wherever they may be in Church triumphant or suffering, we are prayerfully conscious of our debt to them and we pray God to make us worthy in some degree of their loyalty and His Love."

[2] Horace, *Odes* IV, ix. 25. See "Channing and Cheverus", *RC* I, 221–37.

[3] Jack Frost and John G. Deedy, *The Church in Worcester, New England—A Modern Diocese with an Ancient Name* (Worcester, Mass.: Hawthorne Press, 1956). Carroll T. Dozier, "The Bishop and the Community of the Local Church", *Worship* (January, 1983): 4–14.

Chapter Fifteen
The Pope and the Astronauts

This article was published in *World* (June 18, 1972): 35–37.

[1] 1 Cor 2:9.
[2] Gen 1:28.
[3] Ps 8.

Chapter Sixteen
Joseph E. Sullivan 1895–1972

[1] Sir 45:1.
[2] Ps 1.
[3] Col 3:17, 23–24.
[4] Sir 45:1.
[5] *Order of Christian Funerals.*

Chapter Seventeen
What Was the Real Mind of Pope John?

This article was published in *Homiletic and Pastoral Review* (November 1972): 10–24. It was also translated into Maltese as: *Papa Gwanni XXIII* (Gozo: Orphans Press, 1973).

[1] See "Bibliography and Sources" in Peter Hebblethwaite, *Pope John XXIII* (Garden City, N.Y.: Doubleday, 1985), 505–22.

[2] *Discorsi, Messagi, Colloqui del Santo Padre Giovanni XXIII, 1958–1963* (Vatican City: Typis Polyglottis Vaticanis, 1960–1967), 5 vols. and index.

[3] Pope John XXIII, *Journal of a Soul,* trans. Dorothy White (London: G. Chapman, rev. ed., 1980), 334–37.

[4] Ibid., 287.

Chapter Eighteen
Our Tainted Nature's Solitary Boast

[1] Heb 5:1–4.
[2] Mt 11:28–30.

Chapter Nineteen
Things Old and New

This interview was first published in *Catholic Position Papers,* series A, no. 6 (December, 1972) by the Seido Foundation of Japan. In 1975,

Scepter Publishers reprinted it, as a pamphlet, with the title: *Things Old and New.*

¹ S. Congregation for the Clergy, *General Catechetical Directory* (Washington, D.C.: USCC, 1971). The Second International Catechetical Congress was held, from September 20–25, 1971, at the Pontifical University of the Lateran, Rome. See, "The Point of Contemporary Catechetics". Opening Address to the International Catechetical Congress, in *CHW,* 50–68.

² *Atti Secondo Congresso Catechistico* (Rome: Editrice Studium, 1971).

³ Jn 1:14.

⁴ The Nicene Creed.

⁵ Mt 22:36–40.

⁶ Mt 13:52.

Chapter Twenty
Contemporary Preaching

This interview was first published in *CRIS* (*Centro Romano di Incontri Sacerdotali,* 1974, documenti 13). Later, it was translated into English and published as "Contemporary Preaching—An Interview by Joaquin Alonso", *The Priest* (March, 1974): 18–21; and as a pamphlet, with the same title, by the Daughters of St. Paul.

¹ Paul VI appointed Wright to the 1974 Synod on Evangelization.

² *Liturgia Horarum,* In Exaltatione Sanctae Crucis, Ad I Vesperas, Hymnus "Vexilla Regis"; Heb 13:8 and Mt 28:20.

³ The Nicene Creed.

⁴ Cicero, *Epist. ad Atticum* Lib. 7, Ep. 11, par. 2.

Chapter Twenty-One
Crisis in the Priesthood

This interview was published in *Crossroads* (February 1974): 4–8.

¹ Jn 6:66.

² Msgr. Edward G. Murray (1906–1986), who was a close friend of the Wright Family—and the Cardinal's seminary professor, rector, mentor, lifelong friend and confidant—described Mr. and Mrs. John Wright as "the salt

of the earth" and noted that Mrs. Harriet Wright (1882–1969) "had a dynamism which the Cardinal inherited". See, *RC* I, p. 17.

Eleanor Roberts, a staff writer for the *Boston Herald American,* wrote: "Whenever anyone asked Cardinal John Wright's mother the obvious question: 'Aren't you proud of your son?' she had but one answer: 'Which son?'

" 'We were all equal in her eyes,' the Cardinal told me in Rome last May. 'That's what made her such a wonderful mother. She loved each child for himself.'

"The Cardinal's favorite story about his mother goes back to the time of her audience with Pope Pius XII when he said to her, 'You must be very proud of your son.'

" 'She held out her charm bracelet to him — each medallion on it inscribed with the names of her children and grandchildren — and told him in detail about each one starting with 'My son, the doctor',' the Cardinal said. The Cardinal has three brothers, Robert H., of Cleveland, Dr. Richard Wright of Milton and Alfred of Dedham.

"The Cardinal, in personality, is very much like his mother, forceful and dynamic.

"Known as 'Hattie' to most of her friends, Mrs. Wright was the kind of mother who expected the most of her children — and got it.

"She was the soul of orderliness. Once this writer invoked her wrath when she mentioned in a feature story on her son John's elevation to Bishop of Pittsburgh that his desk was 'cluttered.'

" 'You're in the doghouse with my mother,' the Cardinal reported the following morning. 'She wanted to know how you'd dare to say such a thing when she brought up all her children to be orderly and neat,' he chuckled.

"No generation gap ever existed in the Wright home. 'We related very well. Mother was very purposeful and she communicated this to us,' the Cardinal said.

"She always knew what interested each of us. She always had time to listen and to make a point of trying to understand even when my brother Dick came home from medical school and discussed technical things with her.'

"Although it was a source of pain to each of her children to see their dynamic mother lie so seriously ill at Marian Manor in South Boston for the past 1 and 1/2 years, they were all grateful she was fully aware that her son, John, had been elevated to the cardinalate.

" 'I told my mother, and I knew I got through to her,' the Cardinal said on the flight to Rome. 'We were gathered at her bedside and she looked up and said, 'You're all going to Rome.'

" 'We are all so grateful for the wonderful care my mother received from the Carmelite nuns at Marian Manor,' his brother, Alfred, said last night. 'Sister Veronica, who took care of Mother, was so dedicated—everything she did was special.'

"Now the boy who took those long walks with his mother and was so devoted to her will celebrate her funeral Mass on Wednesday morning" ("Mrs. Wright Dead at 87", *The Boston Herald Traveler* [December 29, 1969]: 1 and 8).

Besides her three sons, Mrs. Wright had two daughters, Mrs. Harriet Gibbons of Milton and Mrs. Margaret Haverty of Brighton, twenty grandchildren and two great-grandchildren.

See also *WIP,* pp. 28–29.

Chapter Twenty-Two
The Invisible Cloud of Witnesses

[1] "Those boughs which shake against the cold, Bare ruined choirs, where late the sweet birds sang" (Shakespeare, *Sonnet* 73).

[2] Paul Claudel, *Coronal* (New York: Pantheon Books, 1943), 226–27.

[3] Heb 11:1–39.

[4] Heb 13:8.

[5] Jn 19:37–38 and 16:27.

[6] "Behold Your Mother: Woman of Faith", in *The Pastoral Letters of the United States Catholic Bishops,* vol. III (Washington, DC: NCCB/USCC, 1983), 429.

Chapter Twenty-Three
Witness of the Laity

This address was published in *Columbia* (December 1974): 9–15. It was translated into Italian by R. Stephen Almagno, O.F.M., and published as "La Testimonianza dei Laici", *Palestra del Clero* (January 1975): 3–18.

[1] See *RC* II, 165–73, "The Place of the Laity in the Church", and 541–42.

[2] Eph 4:5.

[3] Vatican Council II, *Dei Verbum,* no. 10.

[4] St. Jerome, *Dialogus contra Luciferianos,* 19 (*PL* 23, 172).

[5] Vatican Council II, *Lumen Gentium,* no. 12.

Chapter Twenty-Four
The Sacred Heart of Jesus: Persuasive Symbol for Our Times

This address was in *L'Osservatore Romano,* Eng. ed. (October 24, 1974): 14.

Chapter Twenty-Five
Dear Worcester: A Love Letter

This letter was published in the *Catholic Free Press* (April 16, 1975): 1 and 3.

[1] Dr. Joanne Mongeon, one of Wright's teenagers, wrote: "He was the Bishop of Worcester and I was a 13-year-old high school freshman.

"It was the day of the finals for the diocesan oratorical contest, and I was nervous. As I looked out into the audience in the Little Theatre of the Worcester Auditorium, I felt sick to my stomach and wished I could somehow get off that stage.

"Then my eyes met those of the bishop, and he winked. I grinned, and winked back. When it came time for me to speak, and I began to give Robert Benchley's *Romance of Digestion,* I gave Benchley's comical description of the tongue, stared intensely at Bishop Wright, and said, 'Don't look at your tongue!'

"Bishop Wright began to roar laughing and our friendship had begun. When he gave me the trophy which was half as tall as I was, he congratulated me and asked me where I came from. When I told him that I came from St. Augustine's in Millville, but was representing St. Mary's of Milford, he asked if Francis Parnell was my brother. I said 'yes,' and Bishop Wright was delighted. Francis had been one of the first diocesan CYO officers, and the bishop said he was glad to meet another member of the family.

"Then, in the spring, I returned to the Worcester Auditorium as part of a cheerleading squad from St. Augustine's for the annual tournament. Since Millville is a town of 1,500 people, and we were in competition with groups from Worcester and all over the diocese, we believed we were wasting our time. But Fr. Jim Kelly, our assistant pastor, had helped our coach, Miss Margaret Carroll, to form us into a well-trained unit. To our intense, crying pleasure, we were announced as the winners of first prize.

"Encircling Bishop Wright, we cried with delight, as he laughed. Someone snapped a picture, and that picture became the shot that went around the world. For months, Bishop Wright received copies of newspapers from as far away as Japan, all containing our picture. Finally, the picture was blown into a wall-sized print which adorned the game room at Newman House, then the home of the CYC. Everyone who walked into the room was greeted by that very graphic representation of the extent to which the bishop enjoyed being with his young people.

"In October, Bishop Wright came for Confirmation. As we knelt waiting for him to confirm each of us individually, I looked at the communion railing, for fear that I would laugh if I looked at him. Now he was in front of me. He tapped me on the cheek, as was customary then, and then chucked me on the chin—as was not customary. As I looked up, he began to laugh with joy, and I laughed, too. Bishop Wright made me realize that my Christian life had to be one of joy if it were to be consistent with the rest of my life.

"I've never forgotten the realization Bishop Wright gave me that day. After he had become Cardinal Wright, I wrote to him, and told him that he, and Msgr. Martin, the CYC director, and Frs. Jim Clifford and Jim Kelly, associate pastors while I was a teenager in Millville, had all helped me to see the Christian life as one of a joyful acceptance of Jesus and His message. Cardinal Wright sent me a letter of appreciation, as well as a copy of the magazine *Crossroads,* which contained an interview with Cardinal Wright on the lay apostolate. Several times over the years, I met Cardinal Wright briefly—in Worcester or at Anna Maria, my alma mater. Always he would greet me affectionately, and tease my husband about having to put up with my enthusiasm.

"When I read of Cardinal Wright's death, I felt the absence of his presence, even though I am well aware that spiritually he is alive and well and living among us. He left a tremendous donation to the world: the giving of himself to so many cost him a great deal. For many, he seemed at the end to be very conservative—insisting on priestly celibacy, supporting *Humanae Vitae,* urging a return to the early reception of First Penance.

"And yet, when I think of Cardinal Wright, I picture him standing in Mt. Carmel Recreation Centre, his cape flowing, his arms open to welcome as we would arrive for some CYC function or other. 'Here comes Millville!' he would laugh. He gave us a sense of self-worth, of belonging to a Universal Church that extended beyond our imagination. Whether he was urging us to attend Eastern Rite liturgies, or celebrating with solemnity a liturgy for Pius XII, he gave us a realization that belief in Jesus is *joyfully possible* and absolutely essential.

"I praise God for Bishop Wright, as he will always be in my prayers. For he was a shepherd who made me feel I belonged to a Christian family which, despite its internal frictions, can be a tremendous source of love and peace, and great, great joy. Thank you, Lord, for the presence in my life of John Cardinal Wright, Bishop of Worcester and Pittsburgh, and our ambassador to Rome" (Joanne Mongeon, "The Teenager and the Bishop", *The Providence Visitor* [August 23, 1979]: 3).

[2] See also Jack Frost and John G. Deedy, *The Church in Worcester New England—A Modern Diocese with an Ancient Name* (Worcester, Mass.: Hawthorne Press, 1956); Robert L. Reynolds, "Worcester: A New Diocese on the New England Scene", *Jubilee* (February, 1956): 6–16; *The Catholic Free Press* (August 17, 1979): 1, 4, 6–9; Carroll T. Dozier, "The Bishop and the Community of the Local Church", *Worship* (January, 1983): 4–14; Robert L. Reynolds, "Bishop Who?", *Catholic Free Press* (March 1, 1985): 6.

Chapter Twenty-Six
Brothers Helping Brothers

[1] Prov 18:19.
[2] Cf. Heb 11:1.

Chapter Twenty-Seven
Stat Crux

This sermon was published in *The Boston Globe* (April 21, 1975): 1 and 12.

[1] Heb 13:8.
[2] Jean Cheverus (1808–1823), Benedict J. Fenwick (1825–1846), John B. Fitzpatrick (1844–1866), John J. Williams (1866–1907), William H. O'Connell (1906–1944), Richard J. Cushing (1944–1970), Humberto Medeiros (1970–1983), and Bernard Law (1984–   ).

Chapter Twenty-Eight
Crisis in Vocations: Causes and Solutions

This article was published in *L'Osservatore Romano,* Eng. ed. (June 12, 1975): 4.

Chapter Twenty-Nine
Saint Elizabeth Ann Seton

This article was published in *L'Osservatore Romano,* Eng. ed. (October 2, 1975): 9–10.

[1] See *Saints,* 93–99.

[2] In 1982, Ambassador Volpe wrote:

"I first met Cardinal Wright when he was secretary to Cardinal Cushing. He struck me as a young man of real promise and intelligence. He impressed me with his wonderful speaking voice.

"As the years passed I got to know him better and better—even after he left Boston and became bishop of the new Diocese of Worcester. There he showed not only his priestly qualities but also his administrative abilities in setting up a new diocese. The people of Worcester took to him—Catholics, Protestants and Jews—and took to him very quickly.

"I remember one evening, in particular, when he was present at a dinner when I was being honored as Man of the Year by the Worcester Chapter of the UNICO National—an organization of professional persons who were Italo-Americans. Now, one of our Democratic state senators had quipped something about me, in a joking way, but it could have been taken negatively. When it came time for Bishop Wright to speak, he told the audience—after his opening remarks—that he was sure they all knew that Rome wasn't built in a day. Then he said: 'I'm sure, however, that you do not know why. It was because John Volpe didn't have the contract.'

"In Pittsburgh, I had the good fortune to visit him three or four times. While there I attended Mass in his chapel and had breakfast with him. I also talked with various persons in the Diocese; and was impressed with how warmly he was received by everyone.

"When he went to Rome, I saw him from time to time. And when I served as Ambassador to Italy (1973–1977) we saw a great deal of each other—an average, I would say, of at least every five or six weeks, either at the villa for lunch or dinner, or at his apartment, or at some function he was attending and had asked me to go along with him.

"I can think of many occasions when we were together. To name two— one was in connection with a visit we made to Livorno for the blessing of the cornerstone of the first church in Italy named after Mother Seton. He gave a wonderful address and, as usual, started off with something humorous. He was, indeed, a witty man; but it was wit with a purpose. This was his way of getting the audience's attention. He had a great gift for oratory—a gift that few really possess.

"When Mother Seton was canonized, we had a Mass and the Cardinal was the principal celebrant and delivered the sermon. It was all extremely inspiring and he captivated the hearts and minds of all present.

"Here in Boston he was admired by all—even though he had left Boston many years before.

"I feel that there is no question that he helped me in my own life with his example and with the many talks we had. He was truly a worker for God and for the souls of men and women" (Letter of Volpe to Almagno, December 29, 1981).

Chapter Thirty
Pope Pius XII: A Personal Reminiscense

This article was published in *L'Osservatore Romano*, Eng. ed. (March 11, 1976): 3.

[1] See *RC* I, 42–53.

Chapter Thirty-One
Jean Daniélou, S.J. 1905–1974

This article was published in *Bulletin des Amis du Cardinal Daniélou* 2 (June 1976): 86–90. It was translated into French by R. Stephen Almagno, O.F.M., and published as "Le Cardinal Daniélou devant la souffrance".

[1] From August 2–7, 1973, the Centro Volontari della Sofferenza held an International Congress at Mariazell, Austria. See *Sviluppo Integrale della Persona dell'Ammalato* (Rome: Edizioni Centro Volontari della Sofferenza, 1974); and the July–August, 1973, issue of the periodical *L'Ancora*, which devoted the entire issue to the congress.

[2] *Jean Daniélou 1905–1974 (Paris: Axes-Le Cerf, 1975).*

[3] "Necessità Ontologica per la Chiesa che Quotidianamente si Completi La Passione di Nostro Signore Gesù Cristo", in *Sviluppo Integrale della Persona dell'Ammalato*, 25–35.

[4] See, Henri de Lubac, S.J., "Cardinal Daniélou: An Evangelical Man", *L'Osservatore Romano*, Eng. ed. (August 8, 1974): 7.

[5] *L'Ancora*, 6–7.

[6] Wright was a close friend of Daniélou long before they were, together, made cardinals by Paul VI in 1969. Saddened by his friend's death, Wright

was especially disturbed that—despite the documentation by the Jesuit Provincial of France and Henri Marrou of the French Academy—the circumstances of Cardinal Daniélou's death continued to give rise to insinuations and accusations in first the French and then the international press. This article was one of Wright's attempts to honor his friend. See André Costes, S.J., and Henri-Irénée Marrou, "Sur la mort du Cardinal Daniélou", translated and presented as "Cardinal Daniélou—A Vindication", *The Tablet* (May 17, 1975): 468. And also two other important texts: "Cardinal Daniélou: A Self-Portrait" (a summary of his autobiography: *Et qui est mon prochain?*), published in *L'Osservatore Romano*, Eng. ed. (August 7, 1975): 7–8, and Ambroise-M. Carré, O.P., "Jean Daniélou", *The Tablet* (April 17/24, 1976): 398–99.

Chapter Thirty-Two
From Gallitzin to Weakland

¹ Sir 44:1–2.
² Sir 44:1–2.

Chapter Thirty-Three
My Two Most Cherished Documents

¹ Wright had a lifelong devotion to St. Joan. See R. Stephen Almagno, O.F.M., "Entrevue avec le Cardinal John J. Wright relative au don de sa collection johannique à la Bibliothèque publique de Boston", *Bulletin de la Société des Amis du Vieux Chinon* (1977): 17–22; R. Stephen Almagno, O.F.M., *Cardinal John Wright the Bibliophile* (Pittsburgh: Pittsburgh Bibliophiles, 1980); and Edward J. Ward, "Joan of Arc Collection Graces BPL's Cheverus Room", *Pilot* (Dec. 7, 1979): 5.

Chapter Thirty-Four
The Hunger for the Spirit and the Sense of Vocation

This sermon was published in *L'Osservatore Romano,* Eng. ed. (August 12, 1976): 6 and as "A Paralysis in the Sense of Vocation", *Origins* (August 26, 1976): 162–64.

[1] Is 6:8.

[2] Vatican Council II, *Perfectae Caritatis,* no. 8.

Chapter Thirty-Five
In the Old North Church:
Reflections for the Bicentennial Year 1976

[1] Lk 18:8.

[2] See "Introduction", *RC* I, 16.

[3] Ps 73:26.

Chapter Thirty-Six
A Gift to the Boston Public Library

This article was dictated to Almagno by Wright in 1976. It was then translated by Fr. Almagno into French and published as "Entrevue avec le Cardinal John J. Wright relative au don de sa collection johannique à la Bibliothèque publique de Boston", *Bulletin de la Société des Amis du Vieux Chinon* (1977): 17–22. In 1980, Almagno published it as a monograph, *Cardinal John Wright the Bibliophile* (Pittsburgh: Pittsburgh Bibliophiles, 1980).

[1] "Joan of Arc, They Are Calling You!" Words by Alfred Bryan and Willie Weston. Music by Jack Wells. (New York: Waterson, Berlin and Snyder Co., 1917).

[2] "According to Philip J. Mc Niff, Director of the Library, Cardinal Wright made only one condition to the gift: that the room selected to house the collection never be named for him but bear the name Cheverus in honor of the first bishop of Boston, Jean Louis Lefebvre de Cheverus. . . . It was his desire to underplay himself and his lifelong admiration for Bishop Cheverus that led the late Cardinal to insist that the room be named in honor of the

first bishop of Boston" (Edward J. Ward, "Joan of Arc Collection Graces BPL's Cheverus Room", *Pilot* [Dec. 7, 1979]: 5).

3 See n. 5 on pp. 524–26 of this volume.

4 See "Introduction", *RC* I, 15.

5 See "Jeanne d'Arc", *The Saints,* 120–32.

6 "In accordance with an exchange of letters between myself and the Trustees of the Boston Public Library I hereby ratify and confirm my gift of books, objects of art, medals, medallions, stained glass pieces or other items pertaining to the life, work and memory of Saint Joan of Arc, wherever located (including the altarpiece reredos and the original sculpture of Saint Joan of Arc given by me to St. Paul Cathedral, Pittsburgh, Pennsylvania, if at any time and for whatever reason these are no longer used in the Saint Joan Chapel therein), to the Boston Public Library of Boston, Massachusetts, to be kept in the Bishop Cheverus Room as a reminder of the French first Bishop of Boston and the French missionaries of Catholicism in New England, as well as the French influence, thanks to Catholics and Protestants, in the city of my birth. I further give to the said Trustees, to be kept in the said Room all articles relating to Saint Joan of Arc, Chinon or related items located in my residence in Rome" (Cardinal John J. Wright, *Last Will and Testament*).

The Joan of Arc statue, in St. Paul Cathedral, Pittsburgh, is the work of Frederick C. Shrady (1908–1990). A convert to Catholicism, Shrady's work is represented in the collections of the Metropolitan Museum of Art and the Vatican Museum, among others. Among his works are Peter, Fisher of Men, in the plaza of Fordham University's Lincoln Center Campus (1969), the Mother Seton statue in St. Patrick Cathedral, New York (1975), and the Fatima statue in the Vatican Gardens (1982). See "Frederick C. Shrady" by Wolfgang Saxon, in *The New York Times* (Jan. 22, 1990): C10.

Chapter Thirty-Seven
Confirmation: The Layperson's Ordination

This article was published in *L'Osservatore Romano,* Eng. ed. (June 1, 1978): 9–10.

Chapter Thirty-Eight
Last Will and Testament

[1] Cardinal Wright's executors appointed R. Stephen Almagno, O.F.M., professor at the University of Pittsburgh, to serve as literary executor. Ignatius Press, San Francisco, published six volumes—as selected and edited by Almagno from the cardinal's papers: *Mary Our Hope* (1984), *The Saints* (1985), *Words in Pain* (1986), *Resonare Christum, I (1939–1959): The Boston and Worcester Years* (1985); *Resonare Christum, II (1959–1969): The Pittsburgh Years* (1988); and *Resonare Christum, III (1969–1979): The Rome Years* (1995).

Chapter Thirty-Nine
Autobiography: Outline (1909–1978)

[1] In 1972, Desmond O'Grady published "Cardinal John Wright—An American with a Roman Connection" in the August 4, 1972, issue of the *National Catholic Reporter*.

In that same issue, the following editorial appeared: "The insightful interview with Cardinal Wright by *N.C.R.'s* correspondent Desmond O'Grady in this issue presents both a problem and a challenge.

"The cardinal comes through the interview as a charming gentleman, a loyal churchman, delightful raconteur, master of the bon mot and a sophisticated citizen of the world—all of which he is. But in our opinion this is one-dimensional, for he is also, we believe, a man whose beliefs are dangerous in the long run for the very church he loves so deeply.

"Among other things, we believe Cardinal Wright's actions and words demonstrate a harmful bias in favor of the institutional church against the freedom, growth and development of the individual Christian. (Some of his recent addresses have been summarized in a recently published book edited by his secretary Father Donald W. Wuerl, *The Church: Hope of the World*, published by Prow Books, Kenosha, Wis.).

"This characteristic of the cardinal explains a question asked so often by the liberals: What made the liberal internationalist Bishop Wright of the 1950s become the conservative Cardinal Wright of the present, more Roman than the Romans, according to his critics?

"The answer, of course, is that Cardinal Wright really never was a liberal. He was and is, first and foremost, a *Roman* Catholic, a papalist of the first magnitude. Those of us familiar with him in the 50s well remember his championing of Pius XII's advanced social teachings, and especially of his firm position on papal authority, even extending, in his opinion, to relatively informal statements and addresses of the pontiff.

"It should therefore have come as no surprise when John Wright threw his weight completely and apparently uncritically behind Pope Paul's unfortunate *Humanae Vitae*. He was the author of *Human Life in Our Day*, the American hierarchy's statement of support for Paul's ill-timed encyclical that accelerated polarization within the church.

"It is this defense of the institution against the cries of the multitudes for freedom and liberation that we find so anachronistic and ultimately detrimental to the credibility and reality of the Christian community. Had the cardinal lived in an earlier, more inquisitional age, we might speculate that as he turned the thumbscrew for the faith he would genuinely be pained at your pain—but he would nevertheless, still turn the screw.

"This complexity of Cardinal Wright (and each of us to some degree) is symbolic of the problems facing the contemporary intrachurch dialogue. The church is not divided into good and bad guys, white and black hats. Most of our problems and most Christians are in the broad gray area of humanity in which the majority of us find ourselves. At the very least we owe each other charity, candor and consideration. Pejorative labels, ill-advised reading of our enemies out of the church and the hardline methods of another era are all out of place.

"The challenge is for all of us, each loyal to the church in his own way, to live and fight for our principles in a bloodless, nonviolent and Christian manner. We shall all have won something if observers from the sidelines are moved to exclaim: See how those Catholics (including Cardinal Wright and N.C.R.) love one another" ("NCR Editorials: Wright the Enigma", *National Catholic Reporter* [Aug. 4, 1972]: 4).

Many articles, and several books, took the same position; and Wright was hurt. Msgr. John Tracy Ellis, Fr. William Clancy, and John Deedy—among others—have all given their opinion on "Wright the Enigma". Wright's biographer will have to unravel the mystery and say the final word.

Chapter Forty
Autobiography: Details (1946–1969)

The reader—and Wright's biographer—will find precious material in: William Clancy, "John Cardinal Wright Sacerdos et Pontifex", *Commonweal* (Aug. 31, 1979): 453–54; Christopher Derrick, "Cardinal Wright: Some

Personal Reminiscences", *The Wanderer* (Sept. 6, 1979): 4; John Tracy Ellis, *Catholic Bishops—A Memoir* (Wilmington, Del.: Michael Glazier, 1983), 76, 115, 122–28, and 155; Dan Herr, "Listening for the Echo", *The Sign* (Nov. 1962): 37–38, 78–79, and "Ecclesiastics I Have Known—Part II", *The Critic* (Winter 1987): 97–100; Rawley Myers, "An Able Leader: John Cardinal Wright", *Pastoral Life* (Sept. 1977): 39–42, and "A New Newman", *Homiletic and Pastoral Review* (June 1977): 55–59; Vincent T. Mallon, "Resonare Christum", *Homiletic and Pastoral Review* (Feb. 1982): 64–68; Desmond O'Grady, "Cardinal John Wright—An American with a Roman Connection", *National Catholic Reporter* (Aug. 4, 1972): 1, 6, and 15; A. E. P. Wall, "John Wright 1909–1979", *The Chicago Catholic* (Aug. 17, 1979): 6; Joan Wright, "Niece Remembers 'Uncle John' For His Wit, Love of Family", *Pilot* (Sept. 28, 1984): 8; Donald W. Wuerl, "Cardinal John Wright—An Appreciation", *L'Osservatore Romano*, Eng. ed. (Sept. 24, 1979): 9; Patricia Bartos, "Prayers for Dear Friend", *Pittsburgh Catholic* (Aug. 24, 1979): 7 and 9 (Bartos quotes Wuerl's sermon at the Mass, celebrated in St. Paul Cathedral, Pittsburgh, on the tenth anniversary of Wright's death); Donald W. Wuerl, "Cardinal John Wright—Teacher of the Faith", *Pittsburgh Catholic* (Aug. 4, 1989): 6; and in many of the bibliographical citations presented in the six volumes published from Wright's papers.

Wright's future biographer would also do well to follow the suggestions, and heed the warning, given by John Deedy, founding editor of the *Catholic Free Press* under Wright and then editor of the *Pittsburgh Catholic* from 1959 to 1967 when he left to become the managing editor of *Commonweal*.

On August 17, 1979—a week after Wright's death—Deedy wrote as follows in the *Worcester Telegram* (where he was a staff writer until 1951 when he became editor of the *Catholic Free Press*):

"The obituary writers are generous, as obituary writers inevitably are. But the historians are often in the wings and I fear that on the basis of the press Cardinal John J. Wright received during the last fifteen years of his life, they are going to give him a hard time.

"For, of course, it is not the obituary writers, nor is it the eulogist who gives shape to history. In our day of opinion journalism, it is more the day-to-day news writers and the analysts. And the liberals among them had long since ceased to be kind. They turned on Cardinal Wright, a one-time favorite, in the 1960s—during the Vatican Council II years, to be precise—primarily because he did not perform at the council as they would have had him perform.

"It was a bad rap, for the liberal media had made the man into their image. They took Cardinal Wright's liberalism of the 1950s and projected it to council issues without taking into account that the grounds of contention had shifted, and that theology was involved now, not just socio-political questions such as nationalism, international government, disarmament, and matters of the common secular good.

"On all those topics, Cardinal Wright got a *guaranteed pure* rating from the press. His liberalism was sure and predictable, and the news writers and analysts made the presumption that it would be in Rome as it had been in Boston, Worcester and Pittsburgh. It wasn't and it couldn't have been, not if Cardinal Wright was to be consistent with his past. The media should have known that. It just hadn't listened very carefully to his theological pronouncements.

"Cardinal Wright belonged to that special and not unusual breed in Roman Catholicism distinguished by progressive sociology and conservative theology. But whereas the liberal media could make allowances for this dichotomy in others, they didn't in the instance of Cardinal Wright. Instead, as one writer would word it, Wright was an opportunist, busy building a power base before hoisting his flag. The flag was termed *the flag of black reaction.*

"It was all so unfair, if only because Cardinal Wright was the center of perhaps the greatest liberal victory of Vatican II, the passage of the Declaration on Religious Freedom. The document not only erased Catholicism's traditional understanding of exclusive religion authenticity. It also set afoot, for better and occasionally for worse, the freedom movement within theology itself. For by asserting the theological meaning of religious freedom in the world, the council document paved the way for the assertion of Christian freedom within the church on moral questions such as birth control, divorce and second marriages, and on disciplinary questions, such as whether priests and nuns were to remain virtually serfs of bishops and superiors. It wasn't what the bishops had in mind when they voted the document, nor the pope when he signed it and made it official. But it is what happened, and we have a different church because of it. A better church, too.

"All the credit for the Declaration on Religious Freedom is given to Father John Courtney Murray, the eminent American Jesuit theologian, whose life was consumed with questions relating to religious freedom, particularly in a church-state context. Murray suffered for his interest and in 1958 was silenced and forbidden to preach or write on the subject. He was eventually rehabilitated, and brought to the council as a peritus—a theological expert—by Cardinal Spellman. However, it was then Bishop Wright, a member of the crucial Theological Commission, who proved to be the instrument for Father Murray's impact.

"I was in Rome in those heady days, and I remember the incident well. The day was November 11, 1963, and the Theological Commission was meeting under the presidency of Cardinal Alfredo Ottaviani, a reactionary and for years an intense foe of Father Murray, to review the secret text on religious freedom. Father Murray probably had been invited to the meeting by Bishop Wright—the point is in dispute—and without Cardinal Ottaviani's knowledge. Whoever got him there, it was Bishop Wright who called for his recognition, a courageous move considering Cardinal Ottaviani's enormous power.

"Cardinal Ottaviani, recently deceased, and then almost totally blind, did not recognize the distinguished and tall figure of Father Murray, and he leaned to his neighbor, Cardinal Leger of Montreal, to inquire who was speaking. Cardinal Leger, a council liberal, replied bluntly, "peritus quidam" or "one of the experts." Father Murray continued with his presentation and, to Cardinal Ottaviani's consternation, he carried the day. Next day the commission voted 18–5 to release the religious freedom text, and the rest is history. The council eventually voted the declaration of religious freedom that at last caught Roman theology up with the rest of the enlightened world.

"I was with Bishop Wright that night, and in fifteen years of close association as editor of his diocesan papers in Worcester and Pittsburgh, I never knew him to be in a more exuberant mood. So much contributed to that mood: the success of the Theological Commission on a point of prime concern; the rousing reception given him after the meeting by his brother American bishops; the enormous personal satisfaction of having successfully sponsored Father John Courtney Murray in the midst of some of his bitterest enemies. There was also the satisfaction of seeing triumph a principle ever close to Cardinal Wright's heart, the right of every person to worship in freedom and according to the dictates of his or her conscience. I know he was depressed by many aspects of the chain reaction that the Religious Freedom Declaration set off within theological circles, but he never had any doubts that in the long view of history that declaration was vital to the church.

"He and I were very close in those days, but less so after I went to *Commonweal* in 1967 as managing editor. *Commonweal*'s sudden interest in theology and its decided theological liberalism annoyed him, the more so since over the years he had been a quiet financial supporter of the magazine and a frequent contributor of articles. It was like being confronted with an ingrate kid. Though he sponsored the theology studies of at least three lay persons, I am convinced that he regarded theology as the proper preserve of clerics, one rather within boundaries laid out by Rome. *Commonweal* was better off sticking with social comment, political and cultural matters.

"Of course, as the post-conciliar period unfolded, his distress with

Commonweal was nothing compared with his upset with maverick theologians and assertive priests and nuns. He was outspoken in their regard, and this only fueled the tension between him and his critics in the press. Some treated him unmercifully, and got personal about it. Gary MacEoin, for instance, in his book, *The Inner Elite: Dossiers of Papal Candidates,* disparaged Cardinal Wright for his "princely" ways (which wasn't entirely malicious) and added that he was a "connoisseur of whiskey", as if to say that Cardinal Wright was a drinker of some measure. He enjoyed a relaxing drink. However, he was anything but what MacEoin's phrase suggested. Many were the late nights that I was with him when he was unwinding in the study of his house on High Ridge Road in Worcester after a long, busy day. He'd hand me a can of beer. He'd open a Coke for himself (or Moxie when it could be had) and nibble at a box of Ritz crackers. This was hardly the fare of a connoisseur of any kind.

"I hope Cardinal Wright gets a good biographer—not a hagiographer, but a solid, fair biographer. There's so much of the record to be straightened out. What I fear is that because of financial considerations none of the large commercial publishing houses will underwrite a biography of him, and that it will be left to some graduate student somewhere to produce a doctoral dissertation which an indiscriminating publishing house will rush into print in order to have the only Wright biography on the market. Agreed, such a biography could be fair and outstanding. But given attitudes in some graduate schools that I know, I wouldn't want to bet on it. Cardinal Wright's positions on the ordination of women, married clergy, birth control and a number of other topics rendered him extremely unpopular among many graduate-school faculty members, and they are the ones who direct dissertations. It would be just Cardinal Wright's luck to end up the victim of an *unfriendly* biographer. His vulnerability is quickened by his failure to write his memoirs, which would have put his side of controversy on the public record. That's much to be regretted.

"On the other hand, the world is full of honest scholars, to say nothing of his countless friends and admirers, among whom I count myself. I'm sure these people will not stand by and let Cardinal Wright's memory be denigrated.

"What he deserves and his life demands are sophisticated interpreters who will see him for what he was: an honest man who was predictable only in terms of his life for God, the church and all humanity. Interpreters, in a word, who will see him much as did Israel Shenker, then of *Time* magazine, when he was composing his "all-star squad" of Vatican II liberals and conservatives. He listed Cardinal Wright at center—on both teams. Shenker was being whimsical, but he clued to the complexity of the man, and his value on both ideological sides of things.

"Cardinal Wright wasn't perfect. No one is. But he was a good man. That's the best that can be said about anyone" (John Deedy, "Doing the Wright Biography Will Require Some Subtlety", *Worcester Telegram* [Aug. 17, 1979]: 6).

Chapter Forty-One
A Conversation with Desmond O'Grady

This article was published as "A Conversation in Rome with Cardinal John Wright", *Our Sunday Visitor* (April 29, 1979): 6–7. The text was prefaced with these words: "Cardinal John Wright, prefect Congregation for the Clergy, was interviewed in Rome recently by our Vatican correspondent, Desmond O'Grady. Shortly thereafter Cardinal Wright returned to the United States for surgery."

[1] Wright had contracted polymyositis, "a slowly progressive and eventually severely disabling muscle" disease. "As the disease progresses patients typically have difficulty walking and may eventually need a wheelchair. In some cases", as was true for the Cardinal, "it is even fatal" (Jane E. Brody, "Personal Health", *New York Times* [Mar. 30, 1989]: 16).

[2] In 1981, Henry Cabot Lodge wrote his impressions of Cardinal Wright:

"Cardinal Wright had an exceptional talent enabling him to grasp a large number of topics at the same time; he also had an encyclopedic knowledge and memory—and with all this went a formidable sense of humor. He appeared frequently to be overwhelmed with laughter by the things which his observant eye detected. Anybody who knew him felt his enormous generosity of heart and his love for his fellow man.

"After I had had the privilege of really getting to know him better, I realized that he did not labor under the burdens which afflict most of us: his grasp was so broad and his knowledge was so extensive that he could easily fall into thinking about many things all at once. Out of this intellectual activity came a torrent of all sorts of brilliant ideas.

"When the Cardinal became Bishop of Pittsburgh, Chairman Nikita Khruschev, while visiting the United States at President Eisenhower's invitation, created apprehension as to how he would be received. Pittsburgh's large population was understandably filled with grief and anger since many of their relations had endured much at the hands of Moscow.

"Bishop Wright, however, did not evade the issue. He wrote a persuasive statement to the media in which he said that Americans would, of course, recognize that Chairman Khrushchev was in Pittsburgh as a chief of state, that he was a guest of the country and that he should be treated with all due courtesy. As a result, the visit of Chairman Khrushchev was accomplished without incident.

"Perhaps this example of Cardinal Wright's remarkable capacity to influence men and women will explain how he managed during his life to make so many friends, how it was that he knew so much—and taught so much—and how it was that he lived a life so rich in service to his fellow man. Lucky indeed were those who came to know him.

"It was my privilege to know Cardinal Wright for a long time—in Massachusetts, in Pittsburgh and in Rome. Wherever he was, his talents shone—always trying to work for peace and ease the lot of humanity" (Letter of Henry Cabot Lodge to Almagno, December 14, 1981. See "Khrushchev in Pittsburgh", *RC* II, 45–46).

[3] See, Desmond O'Grady, "Cardinal John Wright: An American with a Roman Connection", *National Catholic Reporter* (Aug. 4, 1972): 1, 6, and 15.

Conclusion

[1] See "Marguerite d'Youville", in *Saints Always Belong to the Present,* 84.

[2] "If acceptable to the Holy See, and notwithstanding any and all understandings made in or with appropriate authorities of the Diocese of Worcester or that of Pittsburgh, I desire to be buried with my father and mother in Holyhood Cemetery, Brookline, Massachusetts. I ask that, in addition to the inscription of my name consistent with the inscription of theirs, there be carved on the stone marking our graves my motto, under my name, but enlarged to include two further words from the poem by Paulinus of Nola from which the motto is taken so as to read: 'Resonare Christum corde Romano' " (Cardinal John J. Wright, *Last Will and Testament*).

Not a few persons were surprised—even disappointed—that Wright had decided to be buried in Boston. Some of this—as hinted in his *Last Will and Testament:* "If acceptable to the Holy See, and notwithstanding any and all understandings made in or with appropriate authorities of the Diocese of Worcester or that of Pittsburgh . . . "—was of his own doing.

Fr. Richard D. Mc Grail—while accepting the obvious reason, namely, that Wright wanted to be buried with his parents—offered further insights as to the appropriateness of the Cardinal's choice:

"Why Brookline and its Holyhood Cemetery as the burial site of Cardinal Wright?

"That's a question of the minds of many. The answer to it may be quite simple: also buried there are his father and mother, parents familiar with and to Worcesterites for nine years when their son was spiritual overseer of the welfare of Worcester County.

"There are further reasons, also fitting, for the cardinal's choice, diplomatic and historical reasons. Like Boston's third and fourth bishops, John Fitzpatrick (a Boston Latin School graduate, like the Cardinal) and John Williams (the last Boston bishop to have jurisdiction of Worcester County before the establishment of the Springfield Diocese in 1870), he could have opted for interment in Holy Cross Cathedral in Boston where he was auxiliary bishop; or in St. Paul's in Worcester where he was the first bishop; or in St. Paul's in Pittsburgh where he was the eighth bishop. In choosing none of the three, he offended none.

"Knowing the Cardinal's love for and devotion to St. Joan of Arc presents the possibility of his having decided on France, as his burial plot, as did Boston's first bishop, Jean Cardinal Cheverus in the cathedral of Bordeaux. Or in Rome, in his titular church, where he served under Paul VI, John Paul I, and Pope John Paul II.

"If not inside a cathedral, why not burial on the grounds of that foremost church, as other clergy had elected, founders of churches here in Worcester County? Frs. Ryan at Blessed Sacrament in Worcester, O'Reilly at St. Paul's in Blackstone, Hanrahan at Sacred Heart in West Fitchburg, Power in the Cemetery in front of St. Anne's in Shrewsbury.

"His committal might have been among his fellow clergy. Such plots exist in all three dioceses where the Cardinal ministered. Some of such sites in the Diocese of Worcester are in Milford, noteworthy for its Irish round tower, casting its shadow over the graves of several priests including Rev. Patrick Cuddihy, owner of the town's granite quarry which gave so much employment to so many men who worshipped at the church he erected, St. Mary's. Or as at St. John's in Clinton in the circular plot which covers the remains of St. John's first two pastors, Frs. O'Keefe and Patterson. Several other priests are buried there, among whom is Cardinal Wright's dear friend, the gentle and brilliant chaplain at Lancaster's Cenacle Retreat House, the English convert Fr. William J. C. Evers. And what about St. John's Cemetery in Worcester, where among others Rev. John Boyce, the Irish-born pastor of St. John's on Temple Street, the noted writer and eloquent speaker (Paul Peppergrass), is buried?

"Cardinal Wright, thought of as the second founder of Assumption College (devastated by the tornado of 1953, and rebuilt and relocated with his aid) and Anna Maria College (having moved from Marlboro, outside the Worcester Diocese, to Paxton within, during his term as bishop and at his urging) would not have unexpectedly chosen either place or some Boston or

Pittsburgh collegiate setting for interment. After all, Boston's second bishop, Benedict Joseph Fenwick, founder of Holy Cross College, is buried there in the Jesuit cemetery in back of Fenwick Hall. And one of Bishop Fenwick's successors, Boston's fifth bishop, William Cardinal O'Connell, whom young Fr. John Wright served as secretary on returning from studies in Rome, is buried on the grounds of another educational institution, St. John's Seminary in Brighton, where Msgr. John Wright taught for several years before his consecration as auxiliary bishop to Archbishop Richard Cushing.

"It would not seem strange if the Cardinal preferred to be buried on the grounds of some institution serving the needy, whether in Boston or Pittsburgh or Worcester, like Our Lady of Mercy School for Exceptional Children. During his nine years of leadership here, aid to such handicapped individuals was one of his priorities. This was also true of Boston's sixth bishop, Richard Cardinal Cushing, who to the surprise of no one and delight to all, chose to be buried at St. Coletta School in Braintree, like Worcester's, a school for exceptional children.

"Yet in deciding to be buried at Holyhood, the history-conscious cardinal does not break with tradition, but rather extends it. Among the neighbors of the former newspaperman (while a college student) will be John Boyle O'Reilly. For 20 years he was editor of America's oldest Catholic newspaper, the *Pilot,* and for 18 years he was, with Archbishop Williams, co-owner of that paper. His statue graces the Boston Fenway in Holyhood. Down the street on Boston's Commonwealth avenue, the statue of Mayor Patrick Collins stands, while he himself is buried close by O'Reilly. The eloquent lawyer had much in common with the Cardinal, ever active in the speaking arena since his days as a debater at Boston College. Governor and later Secretary of Labor Maurice Tobin (who was among those at Bishop Wright's installation here in 1950), who is memorialized in the massive bridge that spans the Mystic River is also buried at Holyhood. Governor Tobin was a man after the Cardinal's heart, running for politics on a reform platform, bringing integrity to public office.

"John F. Kennedy's father, Ambassador Joseph Kennedy, is buried near the Wright's plot. The Cardinal was close to the Kennedys, and was an advisor to the presidential candidate, particularly when he helped on the touchy issue: can a Catholic in the White House be simultaneously true to both country and conscience?

"One final association with the past is the bell at Holyhood's chapel. It once hung in the belfry of the original Cathedral of the Holy Cross in downtown Boston. The building was sold and demolished when the new cathedral on Washington street in the South End—now being restored—was erected. The bell was preserved, though silent now at Holyhood. But if one listens hard enough, its voice can again be heard as it once was heard by America's first bishop, John Carroll, who in 1803 dedicated and blessed the church that housed it and the congregation it summoned to worship.

"It was heard by John Cheverus, Boston's first bishop, as well as by its second, third and fourth bishops: Fenwick, Fitzpatrick and Williams, and the generations of Catholics their reigns spanned.

"Also breaking silence is the voice of the poet John Boyle O'Reilly, whose lines from the poem *Living* apply to John Joseph Wright as he is remembered in Boston, Worcester, Pittsburgh, Rome:

> " 'Who waits and sympathizes with
>   the prettiest life,
> And loves all things, and reaches up
>   to God
> With thanks and blessing—He
>   alone is living.' "

Richard D. Mc Grail, "Why Holyhood as Cardinal Wright's Resting Place?", *The Catholic Free Press* (Aug. 17, 1979): 9.

[3] James T. Franklin, "Home for the Last Time", *The Boston Globe* (Aug. 18, 1979): 2.

[4] *L'Osservatore Romano*, Eng. ed. (Oct. 1, 1979): 7.

Index

birth control (*Continued*)
society's position on,
170–73
See also contraception
bisexuality, 169, 170
Blake, Eugene Carson, 63
Bombay, 62–63
Boorstin, Daniel, 376–77
Booth, George, 260, 379
Bordeaux, Henri, 165
Borghese Palace (Italy), 96
Bosco, Anthony G., 475
Bossuet, Jacques-Bénigne,
327
Boston Athenaeum, 134,
459–60, 525n. 5
Boston Case, 234–35, 411–12
Boston College, 474
Boston Common, 42
Boston Herald American, 536n.
2
Boston Herald Traveler, 537n.
2
Boston Heresy, 234–35,
411–12
Boston Latin School, 453–54,
460–61, 474, 554n. 2
Boston Public Library, 431,
453–62, 473
Bovone, Archbishop Alberto,
515
Bramante, Donato, 243–44
Brassard, Brother, 376, 380
Brigitte (Bridget) of Sweden,
Saint, 435

Britain, 163, 216
See also England
Bulfinch, Charles, 390
Burke, Thomas, 393
business and economics,
120–22, 133, 285–87

Cambrensis, Giraldus, 232
Canada, 130, 162, 163, 207–8,
210–11
canonizations by Church,
130, 405–6, 453–54,
458, 541–42n. 2
Capovilla, Loris,
*The Heart and Mind
of John XXIII,* 75–
76
CARA (Center for Applied
Research in the
Apostolate), 53
Carberry, John, 515
*Cardinal John Wright the
Bibliophile* (Almagno),
543n. 1, 544
Carnegie Institute, 72
Carré, Ambroise-M.,
"Jean Daniélou", 542–43n.
6
Carroll, Bishop John, 404–5,
422–23, 556n. 2
Carroll, Margaret, 538n. 1
Cartesian philosophy. *See*
Descartes, René
catechetics, 25–37, 155
content of, 33–37

Congregation for the Clergy,
90, 118, 472
functions of, 155–56,
311–12
approval of catechisms,
311–12
education of priests, 98,
149–50
and objectives, 49–50
*General Catechetical
Directory,* 187, 194–211
Litterae Circulares, 527n. 20
resistance against doctrinal
attacks, 311–12
Wright as Prefect of, 17,
22, 49–50, 90, 155–56,
332, 334, 480–81, 493,
510–11, 515, 522–23n. 2,
530n. 16
See also *General Catechetical Directory*
Congregation of the Council,
188–89
Congregation for the
Doctrine of the Faith,
155–56, 399, 515, 530n.
13
Congregation for
Evangelization, 515
Congregation for the
Liturgy, 155–56
Congregation for Religious,
155
Congregation of the
Seminaries, 98

Congregation for Studies,
292
conjugal act. *See* human
sexuality
Connolly, Bishop, 522n. 2
Connolly, Miles,
Mr. Blue, 499
conscience and age of
discretion, 189–90,
198–201
conservatism, 123–24, 212–13
and John XXIII's views,
277, 285, 287, 291
and Maritain's views,
212–19, 228–29
of Paul VI, 60
and Wright's views, 50,
412, 546–52n. 1
Considine, Robert, 185
Consortium Perfectae
Caritatis, 341–49
Constantinople (Turkey), 278
Constitution on the Church
(Hugo), 201, 202
contraception, 55, 59, 106,
122
and government, 172–73,
184
Humanae Vitae on, 166,
167–68, 170–71, 173
Lambeth Conference on,
169
and social evolution,
170–73
See also birth control

Eucharist (*Continued*)
Pius X (*Quam Singular*)
on, 187–94, 196, 199,
207
role of, 189–91, 194–95, 463
Europe, 123, 130, 243–44
problems of priests in, 117,
161–62
and solicitude for the
Church, 40, 42–43
See also specific countries
euthanasia, 165
evangelization,
and Congregation for the
Clergy, 49–50
defined, 323
as means for saving
mankind, 25–27, 29
power of, 194–95
and priests,
function of, 88, 322–23
as ministers of the
gospel, 301–6
as witnesses, 326–28
and secular humanism,
94–95
styles of, 326–28
and teachers, 25–37
themes for, 33–37, 323–31
See also education
Evers, William J. C., 554n. 2
exceptional children. *See*
children, exceptional
existentialism, 27, 79
exploration, 27, 42–44

Eye of Enoch (Shirlaeus), 264
family, 240
birth control vs. family
planning, 106–9
as first school, 257, 330–31,
364
in modern society, 330–31,
400–401
Fatima, 62–63
Faulhaber, Cardinal, 439
Feehan, Medora A., 476–77
Feeney, Leonard, 234–35,
530n. 16
Fenwick, Bishop Benedict
Joseph, 555n. 2, 556n. 2
Fisher, John, Saint, 185,
361–62, 435, 464
Fitzpatrick, Bishop John,
389–92, 396, 554n. 2,
556n. 2
Flanagan, Bishop Bernard,
376, 378, 382, 530n. 16
Florence, Council of (1438),
234, 237, 238
Fogazzaro, Antonio, 248
Fontana, Francesco, 264, 265
Ford, Lauren, 456
Fordham University (Bronx,
New York), 545n. 6
Foreign Mission Association,
284
France, 39, 130, 163, 216
and liberal arts, 104
modernism, 248–49
politics in, 47–48, 123

Francis of Assisi, Saint, 97, 322–23
Francis de Sales, Saint, 98, 327
Frost, Jack,
    The Church in Worcester New England—A Modern Diocese with an Ancient Name, 540n. 2
Furlong, Msgr. Walter, 378

Gabriel, Saint, 288–89
Galileo, 232, 234, 247–48, 265
Gallitzin, Demetrious Augustin, 422–29
Gannon, Msgr. John, 381–82
General Catechetical Directory (Congregation for the Clergy),
    binding parts, 253–54
    completeness of, 316–19
    congress for, 253–57
    effect on teaching of Christian doctrine, 307–9
    emphases and repetition in, 309–10, 319
    on initiation to penance and Eucharist, 187, 194–211
    and methodology, 313–14, 319
    and other catechisms, 312–13, 317–21
    and other publications, 310–12

and teaching authority of the Church, 315–16
    themes in, 324
genetics experimentation, 169–70
Geneva, Switzerland, 62–63, 278
Germany, 39, 41, 104, 130, 248–49
Ghana, Africa, 255–56
Gibbons, Harriet Wright (sister), 471–72, 509–10, 537n. 2
Gnosticism, 252
"God is dead" theology, 70, 80, 243, 384, 440
government, 97, 100
    contraception in social programs, 172–73
    morality in, 56–59
    support for parochial schools from, 121–22
    See also specific country or continent
Grant, Ulysses S., 395
Grata Recordatio (John XXIII), 283
Greeley, Dana McLean, 494
Gregory I (the Great), Saint, 30–31, 443
Gregory XIII, 266
Gregory XVI, 45–46
Grienberger, 266
Grimaldi, Francesco Maria, 265

Guano, Bishop, 407
Guitton, Jean, 449–50

Haddad, Ed, 381–82
Haden, Willie (Bouie), 521n. 4
Hannon, Joe, 496
Hanrahan, Father, 554n. 2
Harpers' Weekly, 396
Harrington, Msgr., 381
Haverty, Margaret Wright
    (sister), 471–72, 474,
    509–10, 537n. 2
Heart and Mind of John XXIII,
    The (Capovilla), 75–76
Hebblethwaite, Peter,
    Pope John XXIII, 534n. 1
Helmick, William M., 477
Henry VIII (king of
    England), 361, 464
Herr, Dan,
    "Listening for the Echo",
    547–48n. 1
Herzfeld, Charles,
    Science and the Church, 182
Hevelius, 265, 266
Higgins, Mrs. Aldus, 374
Hilary of Poitiers, Saint, 28
Holland, 42, 117, 118
Holmstrom, Andy, 260
Holy Cross Cathedral
    (Boston, Mass.),
    386–97
holy orders, sacrament of, 89,
    322, 338

compared to other
    sacraments, 122, 151,
    463–69
explanation of, 147, 153,
    463, 464
Holy Spirit, 59, 433–40, 466
Homer, 82
Homiletic and Pastoral Review,
    "A New Newman",
    547–48n. 1
    "Resonare Christum"
    (Mallon), 547–48n. 1
homosexuality, 169, 170
hope and discouragement,
    342–49, 441–42, 447
Hugo, John, 201–4
    Children and the Sacrament
    of Penance, 202
    Constitution on the Church,
    201, 202
    Your Ways Are Not My
    Ways, 529n. 2
Humanae Vitae (Paul VI),
    as prophetic, 173–75
    significance of, 169–73
    subjects and positions of,
    64, 108–9, 166–73
    traditions of, 165–66
    Wright support of, 539n.
    1, 547n. 1
humanism, 95, 96
    Christian humanism,
    86–88, 179–86
    in classical sense, 176–77,
    178

International Catechetical
Congress, 311, 535n. 1
International Commission for
Religion and Peace, 20
International Eucharistic
Congress, 430, 432,
433–40
International Priests'
Congress, 368, 370
International Theological
Commission, 359, 515,
549–50n. 1
Ireland, 130, 497
Ireland, Archbishop John,
461
Iron Curtain countries, 117,
163
Isenberg, Arnold, 460–61
Istanbul, Turkey, 62–63
Iswolsky, Helene, 457
Italy, 39, 163, 248–49

Jadot, Jean, 502
James, Saint, 131
James, Bruno Scott, 97
Jansenism, 189, 193
Jeanne d'Arc (asteroid), 263
Jerome, Saint, 80, 361
Jerusalem, 62–63
Jesus Christ, 34, 204, 318, 342
    as distinct but not sepa-
    rate from mankind, 84,
    86–87, 96, 163
    and men as ministers of
    the gospel, 301–6

priest as perfect like,
140–41
Sacred Heart as symbol
of modern society,
368–72
on self-discipline, 144–45
and the truth, 83, 214, 348
Jews, 234
Joan of Arc, Saint, 434
canonization of, 453–54,
458
items pertaining to,
431–32
gift to Boston Public
Library, 453–62,
545n. 6
as part of history, 176, 185,
234, 263
Wright's devotion to, 232,
376, 431–32, 453–62,
543n. 1, 554n. 2
Joan of Arc (Twain), 454
John XXIII, 59, 68–69, 471
apostolic letters,
Apostolorum Choro, 289
Causa Praeclara, 289
Oecumenicum Concilium,
289
Sanctitatis Altrix, 288–89
call for Vatican II by, 103,
104–5, 124, 277, 289–90
and children, love of, 68,
295
comparisons,
Moses, 278

John XXIII (*Continued*)
Paul VI, 63, 68, 73–74,
76, 165–66, 278
death of, 519–20n. 13
*Discorsi, Messaggi, Colloqui
del Santo Padre Giovanni
XXIII*, 281
encyclicals,
Ad Petri Cathedram,
281–82
Grata Recordatio, 283
Mater et Magistra, 67,
285–87, 291
Pacem in Terris, 67–68,
287–88
Paenitentiam Agere, 288
Princeps Pastorum,
283–85
*Sacredotii Nostri
Primordia*, 282–83
exhortations,
Sacrae Laudis, 290
Veterum Sapientia,
290–92
humor of, 71, 73, 74, 280
Journal of a Soul, 66–67,
281, 295
joy of, 69–70, 519–20n. 13
as liberal or conservative,
277, 285, 287, 291
motto of, 67, 279
on papacy, 73–76
personality and spirit of,
60, 66–77, 277–80,
285–86, 288, 291–94

persons as important to,
70–75
publications of, 280–95
relationship with,
Cushing, 136
Wright, 71–74, 519–20n.
13
and vocations, 66, 76–77
John the Apostle, Saint, 34,
70, 295
John the Baptist, Saint, 83,
288, 316, 327
John the Evangelist, Saint,
517n. 8
John Paul I, 22
John Paul II, 10, 22, 498, 509,
510–12
Johnson, Samuel,
*Dictionary of the English
Language*, 238
Joseph, Saint, 289
Journal of a Soul (John XXIII),
66–67, 281, 295
Journet, Cardinal, 230–31
joy, 271–72, 416
humanistic priest as man
of, 99–100
of John XXIII, 69–70,
519–20n. 13
as missing in modern
society, 257–58
and solicitude for the
Church, 37, 38, 39
of Wright, 539–40n. 1
See also humor

573

577

O'Reilly, John
Boyle (*Continued*)
Living, 556n. 2
O'Rourke, George, 378
Orthodox Church, 62–63,
113, 126, 236, 278
Orthodoxy (Chesterton), 238
O'Toole, James M.,
*Militant and Triumphant—
William H. O'Connell
and the Catholic Church
in Boston,* 524n. 3
Ottaviani, Alfredo Cardinal,
549–50n. 1
overpopulation. *See*
population growth
Ozanam, Frederic, 434

Pacem in Terris (John XXIII),
67, 287–88
Paenitentiam Agere (John
XXIII), 288
Pandosium phaericum
(Argolus), 264
papacy, 42, 262, 326, 497–98
authority of, 166, 355
Bordeaux on, 165
infallibility of, 60, 364, 366
John XXIII on, 73–76
Knights of Columbus
loyalty to, 61–62, 64
opinions on recent popes,
Maritain, 59, 60, 124,
413–14
Wright, 59–65, 124–26
Pius XI on, 165

resistance to, 46, 47, 59–60,
394–96
and Vatican support for
parochial schools,
121–22
parents, 59, 357
and age of discretion,
187–88, 193
first infancy, 197–98
second infancy, 197–
201
as first teachers of Faith,
257, 308, 330–31, 364
*General Catechetical Direc-
tory* use by, 307–8
Humanae Vitae on, 166
rights and duties of, 193,
203–4, 311–12
See also children; family
parish councils. *See* pastoral
councils
Parochial and Plain Sermons
(Newman), 204
Pasteur, Louis, 241
pastoral councils, 155–56,
157–58, 495–97
*Pastoral Directory of the
Congregation of Bishops,*
369
Pastoral Life,
"An Able Leader: John
Cardinal Wright"
(Myers), 547–48n. 1
patriotism, regional, 374–75,
429, 441
Patterson, Father, 554n. 2

581

preaching (*Continued*)
See also evangelization
Presbyterorum Ordinis (Vatican
Council II), 151–52,
527n. 20
press. *See* media
priesthood, 138, 338–39
crisis in, 79–81, 332–40,
399
future of, 163–64, 333–36
historical background,
74–75, 79–80
holy orders as sacrament,
89, 122, 147, 151, 153,
322, 338
John XXIII's encyclical
on, 282–83
laity as sharing in, 353,
354
Latin as language of studies for, 290–92
Maritain on confusion of
term *Church,* 229–39
priests as unfit for, 111–12,
114–15, 139, 149, 333
priests, 66, 399–400
charismatic, 81, 328
in concentration camps,
100–102
in crisis of self-identity,
100, 162–63, 277, 332–40
as distinct but not separate
from mankind, 304–6
expectations of laity for,
74, 449–50

function of, 339–40
direction from Vatican
II, 156–58
evangelization, 301–6,
322–23
as witnesses, 81–83,
112–13, 326–28
humanistic,
characteristics of, 83–
102
compassion of, 97–98
examples of, 87–88
function of, 86–88,
97–98
as men of love, 92–93,
100
image of, 334–36
laicization of, 94, 336–37
and Maritain on term
Church, 229–39
maturity of, 90–92, 100
formation in seminaries,
139–54
in modern society,
141–42, 145, 163–64,
207–8
and perfection, 140–41,
151
and Scripture, 140–41,
149
and self-discipline,
144–53
and self-giving, 146–53
and self-knowledge,
141–53, 335

remarriage of divorced
Catholics. *See* divorce,
and remarriage
Renaissance, 41–42, 125,
243–44
Rerum Novarum (Leo XIII),
285
Resonare Christum I (Wright),
546n. 1
Resonare Christum II
(Wright), 546n. 1
Resonare Christum III
(Wright), 546n. 1
Retz, Gilles de, 458
Reunion All Round (Knox),
178
Reynolds, Richard, 365
Reynolds, Robert L.,
"Bishop Who?", 540n. 2
"Worcester: A New
Diocese on the New
England Scene", 540n.
2
rhythm method. *See* family,
birth control vs. family
planning
Ricci, Matteo, 266
Riccioli, John Baptist,
265–66
The Almagest, 265
Ricquet, Father, 101
Robbins, Wallace, 380
Roberts, Eleanor, 536n. 2
Roche, James Jeffrey, 392–
93
Roman College, 266, 296

Roman Empire, 125
Roosevelt, Franklin D., 403
Rosary, 283, 289, 331
Rosenblum, Victor G.,
170–71
Ryan, Father, 554n. 2

Sacco, Nicola, 176
sacraments. *See specific*
sacraments
Sacred College of Cardinals,
292
Sacred Heart of Jesus,
as symbol of modern
society, 368–72, 511
Sacredotii Nostri Primordia
(John XXIII), 282–83
Sacred and Profane Love
(painting), 96
sacrifice. *See* self-giving
Saint and the Devil, The
(Winwar), 458
Saint Joan's Chapel (Saint
Paul's Cathedral), 461
Saint Joan (Shaw), 454
Saint John's Cemetery
(Worcester, Mass.),
259–60
Saint John's Seminary, 441
Saint Leonard's Church
(Boston, Mass.), 441
Saint Patrick's Cathedral (New
York), 545n. 6
Saint Paul's Cathedral
(Pittsburgh, Pa.), 461,
473, 545n. 6

Serra, Junípero, 74
Seton, Elizabeth Ann, Saint,
    402–9, 541–42n. 2
Seton, William, 404
sexuality. *See* human
    sexuality
Shakespeare, William, 43, 85
Shaw, George Bernard,
    Saint Joan, 454
Sheed, Frank J.,
    The Church and I, 530n. 13
Shenker, Israel, 551
Shirlaeus, Anthony Mary,
    Elias, 264
    Eye of Enoch, 264
Shrady, Frederick C., 458,
    545n. 6
sick, sacrament of the, 463
Siger of Brabant, 227
Sign,
    "Listening for the Echo"
    (Herr), 547–48n. 1
Sisters of Charity, 402–3, 408
Sistine Chapel (Rome, Italy),
    84–85
Soames, Mary Churchill, 456
social justice, 20, 53, 213
    Cushing's pilgrimages for,
        129–31, 134–35
    and government programs,
        386–87
    and morality in tech-
        nology, 57–59
Society of Jesus, 264–67
society, modern, 119–20,
    341–42, 364

and age of discretion, 191,
    194
conscience and sacraments
    in, 189–90
and crisis in,
    Christianity, 103–5, 116,
        125–26
    culture, 80–81, 242–43,
        245–58
    vocations, 336, 399,
        400–401, 433–35
evangelization in, 328–31,
    438
humanism in, 176–86
Maritain on Church in,
    221–26
priesthood in, 79–102
    and maturity, 141, 145,
        163–64, 207–8
problems in,
    confusion, 219–20, 399,
        447–49
    contradictions, 382–84
    depersonalization, 446
    immaturity, 153, 163–64,
        208, 218
    instability, 100
    joy as missing, 257–58
    loss of sense of sin, 210,
        329
    moral order, 167
    permissiveness, 288
    pessimism, 44–45
    population growth and
        resources, 105–8
    preoccupation, 324, 325

Wright, John J.
  Cardinal (*Continued*)
    in Commission for the
      Revision of the Code
      of Canon Law, 515
    in Commission for the
      Sanctuaries of Pompeii
      and Loreto, 515
    in Commission for the
      Works of Religion, 515
    in Congregation for
      Bishops, 515
    in Congregation for
      Catholic Education,
      515
    as Congregation for the
      Clergy Prefect, 17, 22,
      49–50, 90, 155–56, 332,
      334, 480–81, 493, 510–11,
      515, 522–23n. 2, 530n. 16
    in Congregation for the
      Doctrine of the Faith,
      515
    in Congregation for
      Evangelization, 515
    in Council for Public
      Affairs, 515
    death of, 17, 501, 523n. 2,
      525–26n. 5, 539n. 1,
      548n. 1
    burial, 18, 470, 509–10,
      553–56n. 2
    funeral Mass, 18, 502–9
    illness, 501–2, 523–24n.
      2, 525–26n. 5, 552n. 1
    Last Will and

      Testament, 431,
      470–77, 509, 545n. 6,
      553n. 2
    memorial Masses,
      510–12
    education of,
      as adult, 160, 478–79
      as youth, 30, 119, 431,
      453–54, 460–61, 478
    external ornaments of,
      518n. 8
    family of, 535–37n. 2
    historical support of
      papacy, 60–61
    human and spiritual quali-
      ties of, 17–23, 523n. 2
    humor of, 19, 413, 505,
      522–23n. 2, 539–40n. 1,
      541n. 2
    in International Commis-
      sion for Religion and
      Peace, 20
    in International Theologi-
      cal Commission, 359,
      515, 549–50n. 1
    interviews with,
      Alonso, 322–31
      Aumann, 155–64
      Kucherov, 103–26
      O'Grady, 493–500
      Schweinberg, 332–40
      Seido Foundation,
      307–21
    and Joan of Arc, devotion
      to, 232, 376, 431–32,
      453–62, 543n. 1, 554n. 2

Wright, John J.
Cardinal (*Continued*)
as Knight of Columbus,
60, 350
as liberal or conservative,
50, 412, 546–52n. 1
most cherished documents,
430–32, 522n. 2
motto of, 61, 470, 506, 511,
515, 517–18n. 8
opposition to, 481,
546–47n. 1
publications,
*The Church: Hope of the
World,* 546n. 1
in *Human Life in Our
Day,* 57, 546–47n. 1
Mary Our Hope, 546n.
1
*National Patriotism in
Papal Teaching,* 518n.
8
The Pope and the War,
410
Resonare Christum I,
546n. 1
Resonare Christum II,
546n. 1
Resonare Christum III,
546n. 1
*The Saints Always
Belong to the Present,*
546n. 1, 553n. 1
*Statement on the Death
of Good Pope John,*
519–20n. 13

Words in Pain, 546n. 1
relationship with,
Bell, 446–48
Cushing, 127–38, 496,
501–2, 541–42n. 2
Daniélou, 542–43n. 6
Feeney, 530n. 16
Hugo, 529n. 2
John XXIII, 71–74,
519–20n. 13
John Paul I, 22
John Paul II, 10, 22, 509,
510–12
Kennedy family, 555n. 2
Maritain, 234–35, 520n.
12, 529n. 6
Medeiros, 502, 509–10,
521–24n. 2, 530n.
16
Mongeon, 538–40n. 1
Murray, E. G., 535–36n.
2
Paul VI, 17, 22, 507,
542–43n. 6
Pius XII, 263, 410–14,
546–47n. 1
Teilhard de Chardin,
530n. 13
Volpe, 541–42n. 2
Whitehill, 524–26n. 5
role in Vatican II, 22,
547–50n. 1
in Synod of Bishops, 480,
520n. 3
at Synod on Evangeli-
zation, 535n. 1

597

Wright, John J.
Cardinal (*Continued*)
of Title of Christ the
Divine Teacher, 17, 22,
441, 470, 507
travels and preaching by,
17–18, 19–20, 22, 35,
482–92, 515
in United States Catholic
Conference, 53
vision of Church by, 18,
20–21
Wright, Richard (brother),
471–72, 509–10, 536n. 2
Wright, Robert H. (brother),
471–72, 509–10, 536n. 2
Wuerl, Donald W., 515
"Cardinal John Wright
—An Appreciation",
547–48n. 1

"Cardinal John Wright—
Teacher of the Faith",
547–48n. 1
relationship with Wright,
475, 502, 509–10,
523–24n. 2

Xavier, Francis, Saint, 266

Young Ireland Movement,
493
Your Ways Are Not My Ways
(Hugo), 529n. 2
Youville, Marguerite d', 501
Youville Hospital (Cam-
bridge, Mass.), 501,
523n. 2
Yugoslavia, 117, 118

Zola, Emile, 91